ANNUAL EDITIONS

World Politics 12/13

Thirty-Third Edition

EDITOR

Robert Weiner

University of Massachusetts—Boston

Dr. Robert Weiner received his PhD in international relations from New York University. He is the Graduate Program Director of International Relations at the University of Massachusetts/Boston, a Center Associate at the Davis Center for Russian and Eurasian Studies at Harvard University, and a Fellow at the Center for Peace, Democracy, and Development at the University of Massachusetts/Boston. His research interests cover theories and concepts of international relations, Eastern Europe, comparative foreign policy, diplomacy and war, genocide, and the European Union and the emerging democracies. He is the author of *Romanian Foreign Policy at the United Nations* (Praeger, 1984) and *Change in Eastern Europe* (Praeger, 1994). He also is the author of a number of book chapters, and his articles have been published in such journals as *Orbis, Problems of Postcommunism, The International and Comparative Law Quarterly, Sudost Europa, Demokratizatsiya,* and *The International Studies Encyclopedia.*

Connect
Learn
Succeed™

ANNUAL EDITIONS: WORLD POLITICS, THIRTY-THIRD EDITION

Published by McGraw-Hill, a business unit of The McGraw-Hill Companies, Inc., 1221 Avenue of the Americas, New York, NY 10020. Copyright © 2013 by The McGraw-Hill Companies, Inc. All rights reserved. Printed in the United States of America. Previous editions © 2012, 2011, and 2009. No part of this publication may be reproduced or distributed in any form or by any means, or stored in a database or retrieval system, without the prior written consent of The McGraw-Hill Companies, Inc., including, but not limited to, in any network or other electronic storage or transmission, or broadcast for distance learning.

Some ancillaries, including electronic and print components, may not be available to customers outside the United States.

This book is printed on acid-free paper.

Annual Editions® is a registered trademark of The McGraw-Hill Companies, Inc.
Annual Editions is published by the **Contemporary Learning Series** group within the McGraw-Hill Higher Education division.

2 3 4 5 6 7 8 9 0 QDB/QDB 1 0 9 8 7 6 5 4 3 2

ISBN: 978–0–07–8051258
MHID: 0–07–8051258
ISSN: 1098–0300 (print)
ISSN: 2159–0990 (online)

Managing Editor: *Larry Loeppke*
Developmental Editor: *Debra A. Henricks*
Senior Permissions Coordinator: *Shirley Lanners*
Senior Marketing Communications Specialist: *Mary Klein*
Senior Project Manager: *Joyce Watters*
Design Coordinator: *Margarite Reynolds*
Cover Graphics: *Studio Montage, St. Louis, Missouri*
Buyer: *Susan K. Culbertson*
Media Project Manager: *Sridevi Palani*

Compositor: Laserwords Private Limited
Cover Image Credits: Protests near UNAMA Office in Mazar-i-Sharif, Afghanistan; United Nations Photos #468800 (inset) and #468799 (background)

Editors/Academic Advisory Board

Members of the Academic Advisory Board are instrumental in the final selection of articles for each edition of ANNUAL EDITIONS. Their review of articles for content, level, and appropriateness provides critical direction to the editors and staff. We think that you will find their careful consideration well reflected in this volume.

ANNUAL EDITIONS: World Politics 12/13
33rd Edition

EDITOR

Robert Weiner
University of Massachusetts—Boston

ACADEMIC ADVISORY BOARD MEMBERS

Preface

In publishing ANNUAL EDITIONS we recognize the enormous role played by the magazines, newspapers, and journals of the public press in providing current, first-rate educational information in a broad spectrum of interest areas. Many of these articles are appropriate for students, researchers, and professionals seeking accurate, current material to help bridge the gap between principles and theories and the real world. These articles, however, become more useful for study when those of lasting value are carefully collected, organized, indexed, and reproduced in a low-cost format, which provides easy and permanent access when the material is needed. That is the role played by ANNUAL EDITIONS.

Every day, seemingly random events, situations, and incidents occur around the globe as states interact with one another, as well as non-state actors such as transnational terrorist organizations, international organizations, nongovernmental organizations, and multinational corporations. September 11 underscored the unpredictability of world politics as the hope for perpetual peace, marked by the end of the Cold War, seemed to be destroyed forever. Global instability in the international system seems to be endemic, whether in the form of the collapse of the international financial architecture, revolutions, military coups, political assassinations, ethnic cleansing, and genocide. *Annual Editions: World Politics 12/13* and its collection of articles is designed to help the beginning student of international relations make some sense out of this complex mosaic of seemingly unrelated events that appear to unfold in a somewhat chaotic fashion. Is there any sense of order at all to the thousands of international interactions and events that take place in the world arena? With the end of the Cold War, and after 9/11, the world seemed to be even more anarchic than before. Instead of a world society enjoying a peace dividend, the international system in the post-Cold War era, has turned out to be a far more disorderly and dangerous place than anyone ever would have imagined it would be, as Americans were shocked into realizing how vulnerable they were after the events of 9/11. One of the effects of 9/11 on the international system was that the traditional realist concept of the defensive borders of the country as a hard shell protecting its citizens from attack was shattered.

However, as a matter of fact, the condition or state of the international system may not be quite as disorderly as a superficial impression of it would lead us to believe. The international system may not be quite as chaotic or anarchic as it seems to be at first glance, even following the horrific events of 9/11. It could be said, that the international system, such as it is, may exist in a state of semi-anarchy, rather than total chaos, even if it lacks a strong world government. The logic of semi-anarchy in turn, has an effect on the behavior of states in the international system.

In a further effort to introduce some sense of order into the study of international relations, political scientists use the notion of international systems. Of course, the idea of an international system is a logical construction, which has been invented by political scientists. However, we can then say that the international system has a structure, which as mentioned earlier, consists of different types of actors, with many more non-state actors than state actors. In spite of the phenomenon of globalization, which is supposed to be eroding the traditional notion of state sovereignty, many political scientists still believe that the state is the primary actor in the international system.

The collection of articles in this book provides the student with information and analysis about some of the most recent, important developments in the international system. They provide the student with the best available analysis of the most important developments that occurred in the international system in 2011, ranging from the continuing evolution of the international system towards multipolarity with the rise of China and the BRICs; the relationship between the Arab Spring and the overall process of global democratization; the grand strategy of the Obama administration as well as the implications of the killing of Osama bin Laden; U.S. efforts to implement an exit strategy from the wars in Iraq and Afghanistan; the efforts of the international community to deal with international war criminals; the financial problems in the Eurozone, which jeopardize global recovery from the 2008 recession; and global environmental issues, which threaten human security.

I would like to express my thanks to the editorial team at McGraw-Hill, especially Managing Editor Larry Loeppke, and Development Editor Debra Henricks for their assistance in working on this book. I also appreciate the comments and feedback of the members of the Advisory Board. I would also like to express my thanks to my graduate students, Kyle Vale, Jeremy Lowe, and Chikere Uchegbu, who helped me in locating and collecting the articles for this volume.

Robert Weiner
Editor

The Annual Editions Series

VOLUMES AVAILABLE

Adolescent Psychology

Aging

American Foreign Policy

American Government

Anthropology

Archaeology

Assessment and Evaluation

Business Ethics

Child Growth and Development

Comparative Politics

Criminal Justice

Developing World

Drugs, Society, and Behavior

Dying, Death, and Bereavement

Early Childhood Education

Economics

Educating Children with Exceptionalities

Education

Educational Psychology

Entrepreneurship

Environment

The Family

Gender

Geography

Global Issues

Health

Homeland Security

Human Development

Human Resources

Human Sexualities

International Business

Management

Marketing

Mass Media

Microbiology

Multicultural Education

Nursing

Nutrition

Physical Anthropology

Psychology

Race and Ethnic Relations

Social Problems

Sociology

State and Local Government

Sustainability

Technologies, Social Media, and Society

United States History, Volume 1

United States History, Volume 2

Urban Society

Violence and Terrorism

Western Civilization, Volume 1

World History, Volume 1

World History, Volume 2

World Politics

Contents

UNIT 1
The Multipolar International System

Unit Overview   xviii

The concepts in bold italics are developed in the article. For further expansion, please refer to the Topic Guide.

UNIT 2
Democratization

The concepts in bold italics are developed in the article. For further expansion, please refer to the Topic Guide.

UNIT 3
Foreign Policy and Terrorism

UNIT 4
War, Arms Control, and Disarmament

The concepts in bold italics are developed in the article. For further expansion, please refer to the Topic Guide.

UNIT 5
International Organization, International Law, and Human Security

The concepts in bold italics are developed in the article. For further expansion, please refer to the Topic Guide.

UNIT 6
International Political Economy

UNIT 7
Global Environmental Issues

The concepts in bold italics are developed in the article. For further expansion, please refer to the Topic Guide.

The concepts in bold italics are developed in the article. For further expansion, please refer to the Topic Guide.

Correlation Guide

The *Annual Editions* series provides students with convenient, inexpensive access to current, carefully selected articles from the public press. **Annual Editions: World Politics 12/13** is an easy-to-use reader that presents articles on important topics such as *democratization, human rights, political economy,* and many more. For more information on *Annual Editions* and other *McGraw-Hill Contemporary Learning Series* titles, visit www.mhhe.com/cls.

This convenient guide matches the units in **Annual Editions: World Politics 12/13** with the corresponding chapters in one of our best-selling McGraw-Hill Political Science textbooks by Rourke/Boyer.

Annual Editions: World Politics 12/13	**International Politics on the World Stage, Brief, 8/e by Rourke/Boyer**
Unit 1: The Multipolar International System	**Chapter 2:** The Evolution of World Politics **Chapter 5:** Globalization: The Alternative Orientation
Unit 2: Democratization	**Chapter 6:** Power, Statecraft, and the National State: The Traditional Structure
Unit 3: Foreign Policy and Terrorism	**Chapter 3:** Levels of Analysis and Foreign Policy **Chapter 9:** Pursuing Security
Unit 4: War, Arms Control, and Disarmament	**Chapter 9:** Pursuing Security
Unit 5: International Organization, International Law, and Human Security	**Chapter 6:** Power, Statecraft, and the National States: The Traditional Structure **Chapter 7:** Intergovernmental Organizations: Alternative Governance **Chapter 8:** International Law and Human Rights **Chapter 9:** Pursuing Security
Unit 6: International Political Economy	**Chapter 5:** Globalization: The Alternative Orientation **Chapter 10:** National Economic Competition: The Traditional Road **Chapter 11:** International Economics: The Alternative Road
Unit 7: Global Environmental Issues	**Chapter 12:** Preserving and Enhancing the Biosphere

Topic Guide

This topic guide suggests how the selections in this book relate to the subjects covered in your course. You may want to use the topics listed on these pages to search the Web more easily.

On the following pages a number of websites have been gathered specifically for this book. They are arranged to reflect the units of this Annual Editions reader. You can link to these sites by going to www.mhhe.com/cls.

All the articles that relate to each topic are listed below the bold-faced term.

xiv

Internet References

The following Internet sites have been selected to support the articles found in this reader. These sites were available at the time of publication. However, because websites often change their structure and content, the information listed may no longer be available. We invite you to visit www.mhhe.com/cls for easy access to these sites.

Annual Editions: World Politics 12/13

General Sources

Avalon Project at Yale Law School
http://avalon.law.yale.edu/default.asp

A vast source of data about international relations, especially important historical documents, ranging from ancient documents to the twenty-first century.

British International Studies Association
www.bisa.ac.uk

An academic organization designed to promote the study of international relations in the United Kingdom and beyond. Organizes conferences and workshops on such themes as U.S. foreign policy and terrorism. It also provides links to the work of the English school of International relations.

Carnegie Endowment for International Peace
www.ceip.org

One of the goals of this organization is to stimulate discussion and learning among experts and the public on a wide range of international relations issues.

Central Intelligence Agency
www.cia.gov

Use this official home page to learn about many facets of the CIA and get connections to other sites and resources such as the CIA World Factbook, which provides extensive statistical information about every country in the world.

Chatham House
www.chathamhouse.org

A British-based organization that provides access to papers dealing with such themes as "Libya: Policy Options for Transition" and various conferences such as the Economics of the Arab Spring. Mainly focuses on research dealing with energy, environment and resource governance, and international economics and regional security issues. It publishes the journal *International Affairs* and the monthly magazine *The World Today*.

(CIAO) Columbia International Affairs Online
www.ciaonet.org

Contains a wide variety of information, including articles and journals, excerpts from books, working papers, and conference proceedings.

Fletcher-Ginn Multilaterals Project
http://fletcher.tufts.edu/multilaterals

It makes available the texts of major international multilateral conventions and other instruments, mostly after 1945, but also includes the Treaty of Westphalia and the Covenant of the League of Nations.

International Political Science Association
www.ipsa.org

This is the major international professional political science organization, which sponsors world conferences, including the 2012 world congress meeting in Madrid, focusing on the theme of "Reshaping Power, Shifting Boundaries." The IPSA has a major portal that provides links to the top 300 websites for political science. The aim of the portal is to "foster online research," and states that it is specially concerned with making online access available to scholars from developing countries.

International Relations Security Networks
www.isn.ethz.ch

This site is maintained by the Swiss government and is a clearing house for extensive information about international relations and security policy.

The International Studies Association
www.isanet.org

This a United States-based organization for professionals in the field. It provides information about conferences, jobs, journals, grants, and publishing opportunities. It is also a major portal to a variety of sources in international relations.

World Wide Virtual Library: International Affairs Resources
www.etown.edu/vl

Surf this site and learn about specific countries and regions, research think tanks and organizations, and study such vital topics as international law, development, the international economy, human rights, and peacekeeping.

UNIT 1: The Multipolar International System

African Union
www.africa-union.org

The official website for the African Union, accessible in multiple languages, including Arabic, English, and French.

Central Europe Online
www.centraleurope.com

This site contains daily updated information under headings such as news on the web today, economics, trade, and the economy.

The Foreign Ministry of China
www.mfa.gov.cn/eng

Contains the Chinese position on such issues as the development of multipolarization in the international system, where China states that the "trend towards world multipolarization has not changed." Contains links to activities, speeches, and communiqués.

The French Foreign Ministry
www.diplomatie.gouv.fr/en

Contains information on foreign policy priorities, development and humanitarian action, disarmament and arms control, environmental and sustainable development, and the global economy. In 2011, emphasis as being placed on the famine in the Horn of Africa.

Japan's Ministry of Foreign Policy
www.mofa.go.jp

The official site for Japan's foreign policy statements and press releases, archives, and discussions of regional and global relations.

Internet References

Ministry of Foreign Affairs of the Russian Federation
www.mid.ru/brp_4.nsf/main_eng

Contains links to documents on foreign policy, such as the foreign policy concept of the Russian Federation. Also contains links to statements, speeches, and press releases on a wide variety of international relations topics.

UNIT 2: Democratization

Al Jazeera
http://english.aljazeera.net

A major source of information about the revolutions in the Middle East, but also provides a Middle Eastern perspective on global news.

Arab Net
www.arab.net

An online resource for the Arab world in the Middle East and North Africa, presents links to 22 Arab countries. Each country page classifies information using a standardized system.

The Economist Intelligence Unit's Index of Democracy 2010
www.ciaonet.org/wps/eiu/0020841/index.html

Contains an analysis of the state of democracy in 165 countries, and categorizes countries according to whether they are "full democracies, flawed democracies, hybrid regimes, and authoritarian regimes."

Freedom House
www.freedomhouse.org

Provides an index ranking all states as to whether they are free, partly free, and not free. Uses charts and maps to indicate the status of democratization in countries and regions around the world. Contains reports on the progress of democratization in the Middle East.

Fund for Peace
www.fundforpeace.org/global

Compiled a failed state index for 2011. Ranked 177 countries using 12 social, economic, and political indicators dealing with economic, social, and political pressure on states. Somalia is ranked number one at the top of the list of failed states.

International Foundation for Election Systems
www.ifes.org

This is an "applied" research center that operates in over 100 countries around the world, which applies technical assistance to promote democracy. Contains surveys on democratic change and an extensive collection of data on national elections, political parties, and research on the status of women in the Middle East and North Africa.

Middle East Online
www.middle-east-online.com/english

An extensive source of critical information about developments in the Middle East.

UNIT 3: Foreign Policy and Terrorism

The National Security Archive
www.gwu.edu/~nsarchiv

This is not a government-owned archive, but is operated privately by George Washington University and is an invaluable source of declassified documents.

Office of the Coordinator for Counterterrorism
www.state.gov/s/ct

This site provides links to country reports on terrorism, a list of state sponsors of terrorism, and lists of foreign terrorists organizations.

U.S. State Department
www.state.gov

This site provides information organized by categories, as well as background notes on specific countries. Also contains videos of statements and press conferences by officials.

UNIT 4: War, Arms Control, and Disarmament

The Bulletin of the Atomic Scientists
www.thebulletin.org

This site allows you to read more about the Doomsday clock and other issues, as well as topics related to nuclear weaponry, arms control, and disarmament.

The Correlates of War Project
www.correlatesofwar.org

This site provides you with access to an enormous amount of data dealing with the quantitative variables of war.

International Crisis Group
www.crisisgroup.org

The International Crisis Group is an organization "committed to strengthening the capacity of the international community to anticipate, understand, and act to prevent and contain conflict." Go to this site to view the latest reports and research concerning conflicts around the world.

International Security Assistance Force
www.nato.int/ISAF

This is the web page of the NATO force that is operating in Afghanistan.

National Defense University
www.ndu.edu

This site contains information on current studies. This site also provides a look at the school where many senior marine and naval officers and senior civilians attend prior to assuming top level positions.

Peace Research Institute at Oslo
www.prio.no

The purpose of the Institute is "to conduct research on the conditions for peaceful relations between states, groups, and people." It provides data on armed conflicts and wars from around the world.

Stockholm International Peace Research Institute
www.sipri.org

This Institute conducts research on conflict, arms control, and disarmament. It publishes a yearbook, and provides important data dealing with military expenditures and arms transfers.

UNIT 5: International Organization, International Law, and Human Security

Amnesty International
www.amnesty.org

A nongovernmental organization that is working to promote human rights and individual liberties worldwide.

Internet References

Genocide Watch Home Page
www.genocidewatch.org

Website for a nongovernmental international campaign to end genocide.

Human Security Gateway
www.humansecuritygateway.com

The HSRP's Human Security Gateway contains over 30,000 entries that are free of charge on a broad range of global security issues accessible by region, country, or topic. Other linked but separately maintained web pages are the Afghanistan Conflict Monitor and Pakistan Conflict Monitor.

International Court of Justice (ICJ)
www.icj-cij.org

The International Court of Justice is the primary judicial organ of the United Nations. The ICJ acts to resolve matters of international law disputed by specific nations.

The International Criminal Court
www.icc-cpi.int/Menus/icc

The ICC is a permanent tribunal to prosecute individuals for genocide, war crimes, and crimes against humanity.

International Criminal Tribunal for the Former Yugoslavia
www.icty.org

Established by the UN Security Council in 1993 and as of 2011 was conducting the genocide trials of top Bosnian Serb leaders Radovan Karadzic and Mladic Ratko.

International Criminal Tribunal for Rwanda
www.unictr.org

Established by the UN Security Council in 1994 and has convicted a number of Rwandan officials for committing genocide.

United Nations Home Page
www.un.org

Here is the gateway to information about the United Nations.

UNIT 6: International Political Economy

Eurobarometer
http://ec.europa.eu/public_opinion/index_en.htm

Monitors European public opinion in connection with the various issues dealing with European integration.

Europa
http://europa.eu.int

Europa is the major site of the European Union (EU), and will lead you to the history of the EU, the EU treaties, the EU's position on various issues and relations with member states and candidates for membership.

International Monetary Fund
www.imf.org

This link brings you to the homepage of the International Monetary fund.

World Bank
www.worldbank.org

Links to press releases, statements, projects, and details of relations with member states.

UNIT 7: Global Environmental Issues

Arctic Map
http://geology.com/world/arctic-ocean-map.shtml

Map shows the Arctic Ocean and bordering countries and also contains an international Bathymetric chart of the Arctic Ocean.

Food and Agricultural Organization
www.fao.org

The major UN affiliated organization dealing with food and agriculture. Contains links to the global food price monitor, which contains extensive graphs and data, and the Rome Emergency Meeting in July 2011 on emergency aid to the Horn of Africa. Contains a Hunger Portal with links to information dealing with various aspects of hunger.

The International Atomic Energy Agency (IAEA)
www.iaea.org

The major international organization dealing with the peaceful uses of nuclear energy and the proliferation of nuclear weapons, established in 1957. Contains links to a Fukushima nuclear safety update, links to a nuclear energy safety conference, which took place at the IAEA's headquarters on June 24, 2011, and a video of a fact-finding IAEA team visiting the Fukushima site. Also contains links to a report on a "World Free of Nuclear Weapons."

RealClimate
www.realclimate.org

This site contains reports of climate scientists on recent events related to global warming and information about recent severe climate events.

World Food Program
www.wfp.org

Major organization dealing with emergency food aid to stricken areas of the world. Contains links to activities dealing with the famine in the Horn of Africa in 2011 and a hunger map that shows where hunger and malnutrition are hitting the hardest.

UNIT 1

The Multipolar International System

Unit Selections

Learning Outcomes

After reading this Unit, you will be able to:

- Define "liberal international order."

- Explain why the emerging powers will continue to work within the current liberal international order.

- Discuss the significance of some of the territorial issues between India and China.

- Define hegemony.

- Describe the hegemonic characteristics of China.

- Explain what the role of China will be in a more pluralistic international system.

- Identify some of the major problems that NATO faces in adjusting to new threats.

- Explain why the BRIC countries should be viewed as a bloc.

Student Website

www.mhhe.com/cls

Internet References

African Union
www.africa-union.org
Central Europe Online
www.centraleurope.com
The Foreign Ministry of China
www.mfa.gov.cn/eng
The French Foreign Ministry
www.diplomatie.gouv.fr/en
Japan's Ministry of Foreign Policy
www.mofa.go.jp
Ministry of Foreign Affairs of the Russian Federation
www.mid.ru/brp_4.nsf/main_eng

The main change that has occurred recently in the international system is the realization that the United States is no longer a global hegemony, and that the concentration of power in the world cannot be described as unipolar. There may have been a unipolar moment and a period of triumphalism in Washington in 1990–1991, in the immediate aftermath of the Cold War and the defeat of Saddam Hussein. But that unipolar moment is gone and it is necessary to realize that the current international system is multipolar in terms of the distribution of power. The decline of the United States, which had served as the center of the global financial system, was evidenced in 2011 by the crisis that took place over raising the ceiling of the national debt. The difficulties that the Republicans and the Democrats experienced in reaching an agreement on the national debt resulted in the downsizing of the United States' credit rating by Standard and Poor from AAA to AA+, while Fitch Ratings and Moody's decided to keep the rating at AAA. There seems to be a general consensus among international relations specialists that a multipolar system exists, or if it has not yet solidified, it is in the process of emerging with perhaps at least six or seven centers of power. International systems don't stay the same, but change when the overall distribution of power in the system changes. The concept of the international system itself is a logical construct, which consists of a structure and units that interact with each other. The most important units of the international system are states, in spite of the rise of a wide variety of non-state actors. Realists and neorealists, as opposed to liberal internationalists, believe that states are the most important units in the international system, and that power relationships are relative and not absolute. The international system was bipolar during the Cold War, in which power was concentrated around the two superpowers, but the bipolar system has been followed by an emerging multipolar system. In the emerging multipolar system, the structure of power is marked by the resurgence of Russia, and the growing importance of other emerging centers of power, such as China, Brazil, India, and South Africa.

G. John Ikenberry argues that "although the United States' position in the global system is changing, the liberal international order is alive and well" and "China and other emerging great powers do not want to contest the basic rules and principles of the liberal international order" because they have prospered from it, since it is "a mutual aid society." According to Ikenberry, China, India, and Brazil have benefitted from a liberal international order that is based on the Westphalian concept of state sovereignty, decentralization, balance of power, and a system of open trade and free markets. The rise of China is a critical factor in shaping the multipolar system, and Aaron Friedberg points out in his article, "Hegemony with Chinese Characteristics," that "Seen from Beijing, Washington is a dangerous, crusading, liberal . . . power that will not rest until it imposes its views on the entire planet" and that "the United States and the People's Republic of China are locked in a quiet but increasingly intense struggle for power and influence, not only in Asia, but around the world." Stephen Szabo also takes a less optimistic view of the impact of China's rise on the international system when he predicts the development

© Department of Defense photo by Tech. Sgt. Cherie A. Thurlby, U.S. Air Force

of "A more pluralistic, less structured security system that [will incorporate] a decline in America's power [and] a rapid increase in China's relative power, but without an accompanying willingness to take on global responsibilities." Moreover, the rise of China and India in the international system has been marked by a continuation of differences between the two emerging powers over territories and boundaries, as Jeff Smith writes that "[China and India] share a long and more importantly, contested border, and a close proximity that can magnify grievances, encourage friction, and perpetuate a zero-sum mentality" the author observes that "China's and India's primary disputes may be on land and sea, but their parrying stretches beyond geographic boundaries, into cyberspace, the media, and international diplomacy." The multipolar nature of the international system has also been characterized by the rise of the so-called BRIC [Brazil, Russia, India, China] states. Timothy Shaw, in "Can the BRICs Become a Bloc?" stresses that "the importance of the BRICs has increased in recent years but questions remain as to how cohesive is this new 'global middle'?" The BRIC states may not be as a cohesive force as they might seem to be, given the differences that exist in their bilateral relations with the United States, the different political systems that each one possesses, and also the vast geographical distances that separate them from each other. Nevertheless, Shaw concludes that the BRICs contribute to the new multilateralism as an embryonic bloc "especially given the decline of United States unilateralism." However, the Great Powers are still the primary actors in the international system, despite the phenomenon of globalization and the increasing salience of non-state actors such as international organizations like NATO, nongovernmental organizations, multinational corporations, and terrorist groups. NATO, which was originally created in 1949 as a collective defense organization to defend western Europe against a Soviet attack, continued into the post-Cold War world with a new global strategy that resulted in a projection of its power out of area into such countries as Kosovo, and later Afghanistan. In 2011, NATO was engaged in a military intervention in Libya, which has resulted in increased stresses and strains within the alliance, and which has also drawn attention to the decline in defense spending among the European members of NATO in comparison to the United States and some of the emerging powers. Commenting on this, NATO Secretary-General Anders Fogh Rasmussen writes that there has been "a relative decline of European defense spending compared to that of the emerging powers or the United States." The Secretary-General stresses that the NATO operation in Libya has underscored the unpredictability of threats that Europe faces and the need for smart defense in a time of financial austerity.

The Future of the Liberal World Order
Internationalism after America

G. John Ikenberry

There is no longer any question: wealth and power are moving from the North and the West to the East and the South, and the old order dominated by the United States and Europe is giving way to one increasingly shared with non-Western rising states. But if the great wheel of power is turning, what kind of global political order will emerge in the aftermath?

Some anxious observers argue that the world will not just look less American—it will also look less liberal. Not only is the United States' preeminence passing away, they say, but so, too, is the open and rule-based international order that the country has championed since the 1940s. In this view, newly powerful states are beginning to advance their own ideas and agendas for global order, and a weakened United States will find it harder to defend the old system. The hallmarks of liberal internationalism—openness and rule-based relations enshrined in institutions such as the United Nations and norms such as multilateralism—could give way to a more contested and fragmented system of blocs, spheres of influence, mercantilist networks, and regional rivalries.

The fact that today's rising states are mostly large non-Western developing countries gives force to this narrative. The old liberal international order was designed and built in the West. Brazil, China, India, and other fast-emerging states have a different set of cultural, political, and economic experiences, and they see the world through their anti-imperial and anticolonial pasts. Still grappling with basic problems of development, they do not share the concerns of the advanced capitalist societies. The recent global economic slowdown has also bolstered this narrative of liberal international decline. Beginning in the United States, the crisis has tarnished the American model of liberal capitalism and raised new doubts about the ability of the United States to act as the global economic leader.

For all these reasons, many observers have concluded that world politics is experiencing not just a changing of the guard but also a transition in the ideas and principles that underlie the global order. The journalist Gideon Rachman, for example, says that a cluster of liberal internationalist ideas—such as faith in democratization, confidence in free markets, and the acceptability of U.S. military power—are all being called into question. According to this worldview, the future of international order will be shaped above all by China, which will use its growing power and wealth to push world politics in an illiberal direction. Pointing out that China and other non-Western states have weathered the recent financial crisis better than their Western counterparts, pessimists argue that an authoritarian capitalist alternative to Western neoliberal ideas has already emerged. According to the scholar Stefan Halper, emerging-market states "are learning to combine market economics with traditional autocratic or semiautocratic politics in a process that signals an intellectual rejection of the Western economic model."

But this panicked narrative misses a deeper reality: although the United States' position in the global system is changing, the liberal international order is alive and well. The struggle over international order today is not about fundamental principles. China and other emerging great powers do not want to contest the basic rules and principles of the liberal international order; they wish to gain more authority and leadership within it.

Indeed, today's power transition represents not the defeat of the liberal order but its ultimate ascendance. Brazil, China, and India have all become more prosperous and capable by operating inside the existing international order—benefiting from its rules, practices, and institutions, including the World Trade Organization (WTO) and the newly organized G-20. Their economic success and growing influence are tied to the liberal internationalist organization of world politics, and they have deep interests in preserving that system.

In the meantime, alternatives to an open and rule-based order have yet to crystallize. Even though the last decade has brought remarkable upheavals in the global system—the emergence of new powers, bitter disputes among Western allies over the United States' unipolar ambitions, and a global financial crisis and recession—the liberal international order has no competitors. On the contrary, the rise of non-Western powers and the growth of economic and security interdependence are creating new constituencies for it.

To be sure, as wealth and power become less concentrated in the United States' hands, the country will be less able to shape world politics. But the underlying foundations of the liberal international order will survive and thrive. Indeed, now may be the best time for the United States and its democratic partners to update the liberal order for a new era, ensuring that it continues to provide the benefits of security and prosperity that it has provided since the middle of the twentieth century.

The Liberal Ascendancy

China and the other emerging powers do not face simply an American-led order or a Western system. They face a broader international order that is the product of centuries of struggle and innovation. It is highly developed, expansive, integrated, institutionalized, and deeply rooted in the societies and economies of both advanced capitalist states and developing states. And over the last half century, this order has been unusually capable of assimilating rising powers and reconciling political and cultural diversity.

Today's international order is the product of two order-building projects that began centuries ago. One is the creation and expansion of the modern state system, a project dating back to the Peace of Westphalia in 1648. In the years since then, the project has promulgated rules and principles associated with state sovereignty and norms of great-power conduct. The other project is the construction of the liberal order, which over the last two centuries was led by the United Kingdom and the United States and which in the twentieth century was aided by the rise of liberal democratic states. The two projects have worked together. The Westphalian project has focused on solving the "realist" problems of creating stable and cooperative interstate relations under conditions of anarchy, and the liberal-order-building project has been possible only when relations between the great powers have been stabilized. The "problems of Hobbes," that is, anarchy and power insecurities, have had to be solved in order to take advantage of the "opportunities of Locke," that is, the construction of open and rule-based relations.

At the heart of the Westphalian project is the notion of state sovereignty and great-power relations. The original principles of the Westphalian system—sovereignty, territorial integrity, and nonintervention—reflected an emerging consensus that states were the rightful political units for the establishment of legitimate rule. Founded in western Europe, the Westphalian system has expanded outward to encompass the entire globe. New norms and principles—such as self-determination and mutual recognition among sovereign states—have evolved within it, further reinforcing the primacy of states and state authority. Under the banners

of sovereignty and self-determination, political movements for decolonization and independence were set in motion in the non-Western developing world, coming to fruition in the decades after World War II. Westphalian norms have been violated and ignored, but they have, nonetheless, been the most salient and agreed-on parts of the international order.

A succession of postwar settlements—Vienna in 1815, Versailles in 1919, Yalta and Potsdam in 1945, and the U.S., Soviet, and European negotiations that ended the Cold War and reunified Germany in the early 1990s—allowed the great powers to update the principles and practices of their relations. Through war and settlement, the great powers learned how to operate within a multipolar balance-of-power system. Over time, the order has remained a decentralized system in which major states compete and balance against one another. But it has also evolved. The great powers have developed principles and practices of restraint and accommodation that have served their interests. The Congress of Vienna in 1815, where post-Napoleonic France was returned to the great-power club and a congress system was established to manage conflicts, and the UN Security Council today, which has provided a site for great-power consultations, are emblematic of these efforts to create rules and mechanisms that reinforce restraint and accommodation.

The project of constructing a liberal order built on this evolving system of Westphalian relations. In the nineteenth century, liberal internationalism was manifest in the United Kingdom's championing of free trade and the freedom of the seas, but it was limited and coexisted with imperialism and colonialism. In the twentieth century, the United States advanced the liberal order in several phases. After World War I, President Woodrow Wilson and other liberals pushed for an international order organized around a global collective-security body, the League of Nations, in which states would act together to uphold a system of territorial peace. Open trade, national self-determination, and a belief in progressive global change also undergirded the Wilsonian worldview—a "one world" vision of nation-states that would trade and interact in a multilateral system of laws. But in the interwar period of closed economic systems and imperial blocs, this experiment in liberal order collapsed.

After World War II, President Franklin Roosevelt's administration tried to construct a liberal order again, embracing a vision of an open trading system and a global organization in which the great powers would cooperate to keep the peace— the United Nations. Drawing lessons from Wilson's failure and incorporating ideas from the New Deal, American architects of the postwar order also advanced more ambitious ideas about economic and political cooperation, which were embodied in the Bretton Woods institutions. This vision was originally global in spirit and scope, but it evolved into a more American-led and Western-centered system as a result of the weakness of postwar Europe and rising tensions with the Soviet Union. As the Cold War unfolded, the United

States took command of the system, adopting new commitments and functional roles in both security and economics. Its own economic and political system became, in effect, the central component of the larger liberal hegemonic order.

Another development of liberal internationalism was quietly launched after World War II, although it took root more slowly and competed with aspects of the Westphalian system. This was the elaboration of the universal rights of man, enshrined in the UN and its Universal Declaration of Human Rights. A steady stream of conventions and treaties followed that together constitute an extraordinary vision of rights, individuals, sovereignty, and global order. In the decades since the end of the Cold War, notions of "the responsibility to protect" have given the international community legal rights and obligations to intervene in the affairs of sovereign states.

Seen in this light, the modern international order is not really American or Western—even if, for historical reasons, it initially appeared that way. It is something much wider. In the decades after World War II, the United States stepped forward as the hegemonic leader, taking on the privileges and responsibilities of organizing and running the system. It presided over a far-flung international order organized around multilateral institutions, alliances, special relationships, and client states—a hierarchical order with liberal characteristics.

Today's international order is not really American or Western—even if it initially appeared that way.

But now, as this hegemonic organization of the liberal international order starts to change, the hierarchical aspects are fading while the liberal aspects persist. So even as China and other rising states try to contest U.S. leadership—and there is indeed a struggle over the rights, privileges, and responsibilities of the leading states within the system—the deeper international order remains intact. Rising powers are finding incentives and opportunities to engage and integrate into this order, doing so to advance their own interests. For these states, the road to modernity runs through—not away from—the existing international order.

Joining the Club

The liberal international order is not just a collection of liberal democratic states but an international mutual-aid society—a sort of global political club that provides members with tools for economic and political advancement. Participants in the order gain trading opportunities, dispute-resolution mechanisms, frameworks for collective action, regulatory agreements, allied security guarantees, and resources in times of crisis. And just as there are a variety of reasons why rising states will embrace the liberal international order, there are powerful obstacles to opponents who would seek to overturn it.

To begin with, rising states have deep interests in an open and rule-based system. Openness gives them access to other societies—for trade, investment, and knowledge sharing. Without the unrestricted investment from the United States and Europe of the past several decades, for instance, China and the other rising states would be on a much slower developmental path. As these countries grow, they will encounter protectionist and discriminatory reactions from slower-growing countries threatened with the loss of jobs and markets. As a result, the rising states will find the rules and institutions that uphold nondiscrimination and equal access to be critical. The World Trade Organization—the most formal and developed institution of the liberal international order—enshrines these rules and norms, and rising states have been eager to join the WTO and gain the rights and protections it affords. China is already deeply enmeshed in the global trading system, with a remarkable 40 percent of its GNP composed of exports—25 percent of which go to the United States.

China could be drawn further into the liberal order through its desire to have the yuan become an international currency rivaling the U.S. dollar. Aside from conferring prestige, this feat could also stabilize China's exchange rate and grant Chinese leaders autonomy in setting macroeconomic policy. But if China wants to make the yuan a global currency, it will need to loosen its currency controls and strengthen its domestic financial rules and institutions. As Barry Eichengreen and other economic historians have noted, the U.S. dollar assumed its international role after World War II not only because the U.S. economy was large but also because the United States had highly developed financial markets and domestic institutions—economic and political—that were stable, open, and grounded in the rule of law. China will feel pressures to establish these same institutional preconditions if it wants the benefits of a global currency.

Internationalist-oriented elites in Brazil, China, India, and elsewhere are growing in influence within their societies, creating an expanding global constituency for an open and rule-based international order. These elites were not party to the grand bargains that lay behind the founding of the liberal order in the early postwar decades, and they are seeking to renegotiate their countries' positions within the system. But they are nonetheless embracing the rules and institutions of the old order. They want the protections and rights that come from the international order's Westphalian defense of sovereignty. They care about great-power authority. They want the protections and rights relating to trade and investment. And they want to use the rules and institutions of liberal internationalism as platforms to project their influence and acquire legitimacy at home and abroad. The UN

Security Council, the G-20, the governing bodies of the Bretton Woods institutions—these are all stages on which rising non-Western states can acquire great-power authority and exercise global leadership.

No Other Order

Meanwhile, there is no competing global organizing logic to liberal internationalism. An alternative, illiberal order—a "Beijing model"—would presumably be organized around exclusive blocs, spheres of influence, and mercantilist networks. It would be less open and rule-based, and it would be dominated by an array of state-to-state ties. But on a global scale, such a system would not advance the interests of any of the major states, including China. The Beijing model only works when one or a few states opportunistically exploit an open system of markets. But if everyone does, it is no longer an open system but a fragmented, mercantilist, and protectionist complex—and everyone suffers.

It is possible that China could nonetheless move in this direction. This is a future in which China is not a full-blown illiberal hegemon that reorganizes the global rules and institutions. It is simply a spoiler. It attempts to operate both inside and outside the liberal international order. In this case, China would be successful enough with its authoritarian model of development to resist the pressures to liberalize and democratize. But if the rest of the world does not gravitate toward this model, China will find itself subjected to pressure to play by the rules. This dynamic was on display in February 2011, when Brazilian President Dilma Rousseff joined U.S. Treasury Secretary Timothy Geithner in expressing concern over China's currency policy. China can free-ride on the liberal international order, but it will pay the costs of doing so—and it will still not be able to impose its illiberal vision on the world.

Democracy and the rule of law are still the hallmarks of modernity and the global standard for legitimate governance.

In the background, meanwhile, democracy and the rule of law are still the hallmarks of modernity and the global standard for legitimate governance. Although it is true that the spread of democracy has stalled in recent years and that authoritarian China has performed well in the recent economic crisis, there is little evidence that authoritarian states can become truly advanced societies without moving in a liberal democratic direction. The legitimacy of one-party rule within China rests more on the state's ability to deliver economic growth and full employment than on authoritarian—let alone communist—political principles. Kishore Mahbubani, a Singaporean intellectual who has championed China's rise, admits that "China cannot succeed in its goal of becoming a modern developed society until it can take the leap and allow the Chinese people to choose their own rulers." No one knows how far or fast democratic reforms will unfold in China, but a growing middle class, business elites, and human rights groups will exert pressure for them. The Chinese government certainly appears to worry about the long-term preservation of one-party rule, and in the wake of the ongoing revolts against Arab authoritarian regimes, it has tried harder to prevent student gatherings and control foreign journalists.

Outside China, democracy has become a near-universal ideal. As the economist Amartya Sen has noted, "While democracy is not yet universally practiced, nor indeed universally accepted, in the general climate of world opinion democratic governance has achieved the status of being taken to be generally right." All the leading institutions of the global system enshrine democracy as the proper and just form of governance—and no competing political ideals even lurk on the sidelines.

The recent global economic downturn was the first great postwar economic upheaval that emerged from the United States, raising doubts about an American-led world economy and Washington's particular brand of economics. The doctrines of neoliberalism and market fundamentalism have been discredited, particularly among the emerging economies. But liberal internationalism is not the same as neoliberalism or market fundamentalism. The liberal internationalism that the United States articulated in the 1940s entailed a more holistic set of ideas about markets, openness, and social stability. It was an attempt to construct an open world economy and reconcile it with social welfare and employment stability. Sustained domestic support for openness, postwar leaders knew, would be possible only if countries also established social protections and regulations that safeguarded economic stability.

Indeed, the notions of national security and economic security emerged together in the 1940s, reflecting New Deal and World War II thinking about how liberal democracies would be rendered safe and stable. The Atlantic Charter, announced by Roosevelt and Winston Churchill in 1941, and the Bretton Woods agreements of 1944 were early efforts to articulate a vision of economic openness and social stability. The United States would do well to try to reach back and rearticulate this view. The world is not rejecting openness and markets; it is asking for a more expansive notion of stability and economic security.

Reason for Reassurance

Rising powers will discover another reason to embrace the existing global rules and institutions: doing so will reassure their neighbors as they grow more powerful. A stronger China will make neighboring states potentially less secure, especially if it acts aggressively and exhibits revisionist ambitions. Since this will trigger a balancing backlash,

Beijing has incentives to signal restraint. It will find ways to do so by participating in various regional and global institutions. If China hopes to convince its neighbors that it has embarked on a "peaceful rise," it will need to become more integrated into the international order.

China has already experienced a taste of such a backlash. Last year, its military made a series of provocative moves—including naval exercises—in the South China Sea, actions taken to support the government's claims to sovereign rights over contested islands and waters. Many of the countries disputing China's claims joined with the United States at the Regional Forum of the Association of Southeast Asian Nations (ASEAN) in July to reject Chinese bullying and reaffirm open access to Asia's waters and respect for international law. In September, a Chinese fishing trawler operating near islands administered by Japan in the East China Sea rammed into two Japanese coast guard ships. After Japanese authorities detained the trawler's crew, China responded with what one Japanese journalist described as a "diplomatic 'shock and awe' campaign," suspending ministerial-level contacts, demanding an apology, detaining several Japanese workers in China, and instituting a de facto ban on exports of rare-earth minerals to Japan. These actions—seen as manifestations of a more bellicose and aggressive foreign policy—pushed ASEAN, Japan, and South Korea perceptibly closer to the United States.

As China's economic and military power grow, its neighbors will only become more worried about Chinese aggressiveness, and so Beijing will have reason to allay their fears. Of course, it might be that some elites in China are not interested in practicing restraint. But to the extent that China is interested in doing so, it will find itself needing to signal peaceful intentions—redoubling its participation in existing institutions, such as the ASEAN Regional Forum and the East Asia Summit, or working with the other great powers in the region to build new ones. This is, of course, precisely what the United States did in the decades after World War II. The country operated within layers of regional and global economic, political, and security institutions and constructed new ones—thereby making itself more predictable and approachable and reducing the incentives for other states to undermine it by building countervailing coalitions.

More generally, given the emerging problems of the twenty-first century, there will be growing incentives among all the great powers to embrace an open, rule-based international system. In a world of rising economic and security interdependence, the costs of not following multilateral rules and not forging cooperative ties go up. As the global economic system becomes more interdependent, all states—even large, powerful ones—will find it harder to ensure prosperity on their own.

Growing interdependence in the realm of security is also creating a demand for multilateral rules and institutions. Both the established and the rising great powers are threatened less by mass armies marching across borders than by transnational dangers, such as terrorism, climate change, and pandemic disease. What goes on in one country—radicalism, carbon emissions, or public health failures—can increasingly harm another country.

Intensifying economic and security interdependence are giving the United States and other powerful countries reason to seek new and more extensive forms of multilateral cooperation. Even now, as the United States engages China and other rising states, the agenda includes expanded cooperation in areas such as clean energy, environmental protection, nonproliferation, and global economic governance. The old and rising powers may disagree on how exactly this cooperation should proceed, but they all have reasons to avoid a breakdown in the multilateral order itself. So they will increasingly experiment with new and more extensive forms of liberal internationalism.

Time for Renewal

Pronouncements of American decline miss the real transformation under way today. What is occurring is not American decline but a dynamic process in which other states are catching up and growing more connected. In an open and rule-based international order, this is what happens. If the architects of the postwar liberal order were alive to see today's system, they would think that their vision had succeeded beyond their wildest dreams. Markets and democracy have spread. Societies outside the West are trading and growing. The United States has more alliance partners today than it did during the Cold War. Rival hegemonic states with revisionist and illiberal agendas have been pushed off the global stage. It is difficult to read these world-historical developments as a story of American decline and liberal unraveling.

Paradoxically, the challenges facing the liberal world order now are artifacts of its success.

In a way, however, the liberal international order has sown the seeds of its own discontent, since, paradoxically, the challenges facing it now—the rise of non-Western states and new transnational threats—are artifacts of its success. But the solutions to these problems—integrating rising powers and tackling problems cooperatively—will lead the order's old guardians and new stakeholders to an agenda of renewal. The coming divide in world politics will not be between the United States (and the West) and the non-Western rising states. Rather, the struggle will be between those who want to renew and expand today's system of multilateral governance arrangements and those who want to move to a less cooperative order built on spheres of influence. These fault lines do not map onto geography, nor do they split the

West and the non-West. There are passionate champions of the UN, the WTO, and a rule-based international order in Asia, and there are isolationist, protectionist, and anti-internationalist factions in the West.

The liberal international order has succeeded over the decades because its rules and institutions have not just enshrined open trade and free markets but also provided tools for governments to manage economic and security interdependence. The agenda for the renewal of the liberal international order should be driven by this same imperative: to reinforce the capacities of national governments to govern and achieve their economic and security goals.

As the hegemonic organization of the liberal international order slowly gives way, more states will have authority and status. But this will still be a world that the United States wants to inhabit. A wider array of states will share the burdens of global economic and political governance, and with its worldwide system of alliances, the United States will remain at the center of the global system. Rising states do not just grow more powerful on the global stage; they grow more powerful within their regions, and this creates its own set of worries and insecurities—which is why states will continue to look to Washington for security and partnership. In this new age of international order, the United States will not be able to rule. But it can still lead.

Critical Thinking

1. What is the struggle over international order all about?
2. What is the significance of the Westphalian system?
3. How can China be drawn into the liberal international order?

G. JOHN IKENBERRY is Albert G. Milbank Professor of Politics and International Affairs at Princeton University and the author of *Liberal Leviathan: The Origins, Crisis, and Transformation of the American World Order* (Princeton University Press, 2011), from which this essay is adapted.

NATO after Libya
The Atlantic Alliance in Austere Times

Anders Fogh Rasmussen

NATO's sea and air mission in Libya is the first major military engagement undertaken since the global financial crisis. With European NATO allies drastically reducing their defense spending, there were legitimate fears as to whether they could still afford to respond to such complex crises. Reports early on that the operation lacked sufficient strike capabilities reinforced these fears. But the unprecedented speed, scale, and sustained pace of execution of Operation Unified Protector tell a different story. As of early May, the pace of air sorties had remained high since the beginning of the operation, and strikes had accounted for just under half of those sorties. When requirements changed as Muammar al-Qaddafi's forces altered their tactics, NATO allies provided more of the high-precision strike capabilities that the commanders needed. Meanwhile, more than a dozen ships have been patrolling the Mediterranean Sea and enforcing the UN arms embargo.

The mission in Libya has revealed three important truths about military intervention today. First, to those who claimed that Afghanistan was to be NATO's last out-of-area mission, it has shown that unpredictability is the very essence of security. Second, it has proved that in addition to frontline capabilities, such as fighter-bombers and warships, so-called enablers, such as surveillance and refueling aircraft, as well as drones, are critical parts of any modern operation. And third, it has revealed that NATO allies do not lack military capabilities. Any shortfalls have been primarily due to political, rather than military, constraints. In other words, Libya is a reminder of how important it is for NATO to be ready, capable, and willing to act.

Although defense is and must remain the prerogative of sovereign nations, an alliance that brings Europe and North America together requires an equitable sharing of the burden in order to be efficient. Downward trends in European defense budgets raise some legitimate concerns. At the current pace of cuts, it is hard to see how Europe could maintain enough military capabilities to sustain similar operations in the future. And this touches on a fundamental challenge facing Europe and the alliance as a whole: how to avoid having the economic crisis degenerate into a security crisis. The way Europe responds to this challenge could determine its place in the global order and the future of security.

NATO allies should concentrate on taking fresh steps on three fronts: strengthening European defense, enhancing the transatlantic relationship, and engaging with emerging powers on common challenges. But before turning to prescriptions, it is important to look at the facts: what happened in Libya and whether the financial crisis has affected the global distribution of military power.

The Spending Gap

Operation Unified Protector has shown that European countries, even though they spend less on their militaries than the United States or Asian powers, can still play a central role in a complex military operation. Indeed, after the United States, Europe still holds the world's most advanced military capabilities. The question, however, is whether Europe will be able to maintain this edge in five or ten years.

This is particularly worrying when one considers the ongoing redistribution of global military power, a shift embodied in the relative decline of European defense spending compared to that of emerging powers or the United States. As European countries have become richer, they have spent less on defense. Since the end of the Cold War, defense spending by the European NATO countries has fallen by almost 20 percent. Over the same period, their combined GDP grew by around 55 percent. The picture is somewhat different in Asia. According to the Stockholm International Peace Research Institute, between 2000 and 2009, India's defense spending grew by 59 percent, and China's tripled. This led to a double leap forward: a transformation of these countries' armed forces and their acquisition of new weapons systems.

If one compares Europe's defense spending with that of the United States, the contrast is also large. By the end of the Cold War, in 1991, defense expenditures in European countries represented almost 34 percent of NATO's total, with the United States and Canada covering the remaining 66 percent. Since then, the share of NATO's security burden shouldered by European countries has fallen to 21 percent.

Many observers, including some in government circles on both sides of the Atlantic, argue that the biggest security challenge facing the West is rising debt levels in Europe and the United States. They have a fair point; after all, there can be no military might without money. Others even argue that there is little need to worry if European nations invest less in defense, since this reflects a Europe that is whole, free, and at peace. But these arguments fail to consider three important facts.

First, military might still matters in twenty-first-century geopolitics. The security challenges facing Europe include conflicts in its neighborhood, such as in Libya; terrorism from failed states further away; and emerging threats such as the proliferation of weapons of mass destruction and cyberwarfare. What defines these threats is both their diversity and their unpredictability. Investing in homeland security and retrenching will not be enough to counter them.

Nor will it be enough to rely only on soft power. Nobody is advocating a return to nineteenth-century gunboat diplomacy, but in an unpredictable environment, hard power can enable peace. Just as the presence of a police officer may deter a burglar, the projection of military power can help prevent and, in extreme cases, diminish threats, as well as ultimately open the way for political solutions. Events in Libya have underlined that although a military approach cannot solve a conflict on its own, it is a necessary tool in a wider political effort. Europe needs to build a strong continuum of hard and soft power so that it can respond to the full spectrum of crises and threats.

Second, new economic and military powers, such as Brazil, China, and India, are entering the field. It would be wrong to see their presence simply as a challenge to the West or to assume that they pose a military threat to NATO. After all, lifting hundreds of millions of people out of poverty benefits everyone. Those countries have little interest in overthrowing the global system on which their prosperity was built. Instead, Europe should welcome what these nations can offer to international security in terms of military capabilities.

If Europe is creating a security gap, then these powers could, in theory, reduce this gap. Yet this is unlikely to happen because the interests of these powers and the interests of Western ones may not coincide, and it is not certain that emerging powers have the same approach to addressing security challenges. In the case of Libya, for instance, although Brazil, China, India, and Russia consciously stepped aside to allow the UN Security Council to act, they did not put their military might at the disposal of the coalition that emerged. (China did dispatch a military vessel and planes to the region, but only to help evacuate its citizens.) The episode serves as a reminder that emerging powers' interests will not necessarily coincide with Europe's. The paradox, then, is that the global order enjoys more stakeholders than ever before and yet it has very few guarantors. Europe is still one of them, but for how long?

Third, the transatlantic partnership remains the main engine of global security. The partnership has been successful in sharing common goals and values, while boasting interoperable and rapidly deployable forces. But the United States is facing its own budgetary challenges, and as Libya has shown, Washington will not always take the lead when it comes to power projection. The United States will demand with an even stronger voice that Europeans assume their responsibilities in preserving order, especially in Europe's periphery. But if European defense spending cuts continue, Europe's ability to be a stabilizing force even in its neighborhood will rapidly disappear. This, in turn, risks turning the United States away from Europe.

Smarter Defense

The obvious solution to all these problems would be for Europe to spend more on defense. In light of the unfolding events in the Middle East, a debate on whether to reverse the decline in defense spending has begun in several European capitals. But given the economic environment in Europe, it is highly unlikely that governments there will make any significant changes. Thus, the way forward lies not in spending more but in spending better—by pursuing multinational approaches, making the transatlantic compact more strategically oriented, and working with emerging powers to manage the effects of the globalization of security.

First of all, Europe should pursue a "smart defense" approach. Smart defense is about building security for less money by working together and being more flexible. This requires identifying those areas in which NATO allies need to keep investing. The operation in Libya has underlined the unpredictability of threats and the need to maintain a wide spectrum of military capabilities, both frontline and enabling ones. Keeping a deployable army, a powerful navy, and a strong air force costs money, however, and not all European countries can afford to have a bit of everything. So they should set their priorities on the basis of threats, cost-effectiveness, and performance—not budgetary considerations or prestige alone.

Smart defense also means encouraging multinational cooperation. As the price of military equipment continues to rise, European states acting alone may struggle to afford high-tech weapons systems such as the ones used in Libya. European nations should work in small clusters to combine their resources and build capabilities that can benefit the alliance as a whole. Here, NATO can act as a matchmaker, bringing nations together to identify what they can do jointly at a lower cost, more efficiently, and with less risk.

Second, European countries can help bridge the gap with the United States by increasing their contribution of two ingredients, deployable and sustainable capabilities, as well as mustering the political resolve to use them. To pair both ingredients, Europe and North America should strengthen their connections through an open and truly strategic dialogue, with both sides sitting around the same table to discuss issues of common concern. Promoting this dialogue has been one of my main priorities within NATO since the adoption of the alliance's "strategic concept" at the Lisbon summit last November. But there is room for improvement. Particular efforts must be made to ensure that the two major Euro-Atlantic security providers, NATO and the EU, cooperate more closely. This will be essential, as both will have a role in helping states transitioning to more democratic systems. For instance, in the Middle East, both NATO and the EU could assist in reforming the security sectors of nascent and fragile democracies.

Third, Europe and the United States should work more closely with emerging powers. This is not going to be easy, so building confidence will be essential. The process can begin by fostering a mutually assured dialogue with these countries, which would help defuse crises, overcome disagreements, and clear up misperceptions. Working together could eventually lead to a common understanding of how to build twenty-first-century global security, which entails a sense of shared responsibility. This way, what too often seems like a zero-sum scenario can be turned into a win-win one.

NATO can make a major contribution to this new global security understanding. The alliance can build on the already extensive partnership network it has established and consult key emerging powers. It can continue to address common security challenges that transcend national borders. Of course, the UN Security Council must remain the overall source of legitimacy for international peace and stability. A more inclusive dialogue among the main security stakeholders, however, would help it prevent and manage crises.

The economic challenges that European nations face are immense, but that must not prevent them from seeing the wider strategic picture. Uncoordinated defense cuts could jeopardize the continent's future security. Libya can act as a wake-up call, but this mission needs to be followed by deeds. Making European defense more coherent, strengthening transatlantic ties, and enhancing NATO's connections with other global actors is the way to prevent the economic crisis from becoming a security crisis.

Critical Thinking

1. What have been the effects of the military intervention in Libya on NATO?
2. What new threats does NATO face?
3. How can NATO make a major contribution to a new global security understanding?

ANDERS FOGH RASMUSSEN is Secretary-General of NATO.

Sino-Indian Relations

A Troubled History, An Uncertain Future

JEFF M. SMITH

Few now dispute that the magnificent rise of China and India has fundamentally transformed the geopolitical landscape of the 21st century. In the United States, their emergence has prompted interest in the two Asian giants, home to more than a third of the world's population, with a focus on how their geopolitical influence will affect the United States. The Washington foreign policy community has framed China as a challenge and a competitor, while India is increasingly portrayed as an opportunity and an ally. Yet while the heightened focus on Sino-US and Indo-US relations is welcome, few US analysts have bothered to examine the third, and perhaps most volatile, leg of this equation: the Sino-Indian relationship.

History is littered with examples of rising powers upending the status quo and challenging the established order. Strategic thinkers in the United States have mulled the potential of conflict with China since the moment the Soviet Union collapsed. However, it is at least as likely that if superpower conflict does emerge in the 21st century, it will be between China and India. This scenario is by no means guaranteed, and perhaps not even probable. Formal relations are cordial. However, unlike the United States and China, the two do not have the luxury of a vast ocean to separate them. Rather, they share a long and, more importantly, contested border and a close proximity that can magnify grievances, encourage friction, and perpetuate a zero-sum mentality. It is therefore incumbent upon the United States to seek a greater understanding of Sino-Indian relations, particularly of the issues that divide them and the historical context that underpins their interactions.

> **[China and India] share a long and, more importantly, contested border, and a close proximity that can magnify grievances, encourage friction, and perpetuate a zero-sum mentality.**

A Relationship That Starts with War

A convenient starting point for analyzing contemporary Sino-Indian relations is their birth as modern nations only two years apart: India, when it gained independence from Britain in 1947, and Communist China, when Mao Zedong and his Red Guards declared victory in the Chinese civil war in 1949. Drawn together by anti-imperialist sentiment and Asian fraternity, the two nations enjoyed something of a Golden Age throughout their first decade as independent countries, a period often characterized by a popular phrase of the time: "Hindi-Chini bhai-bhai," or "Indians and Chinese are brothers." In 1954, the two signed the "Five Principles of Peaceful Coexistence," or Panchsheel, which codified the principles of mutual non-aggression and non-interference.

However, the era of Sino-Indian harmony would last only a few short years. China's invasion and annexation of Tibet in 1950 had already made more than a few Indians uncomfortable, but at the time, India's leaders quieted voices of protest in the interest of bilateral comity. However, when the Dalai Lama led a failed uprising against Chinese rule in 1959, India was intimately drawn into what China considered an internal conflict. With his rebellion crushed, the Dalai Lama and his beleaguered followers fled into northern India seeking safe haven, and New Delhi, to the great frustration of Beijing, granted it.

Adding fuel to the fire, as the Dalai Lama episode was unfolding, both India and China began a dangerous game of brinksmanship along their poorly demarcated 2,100 mile-long border. In 1958, India discovered that Chinese workers had built a strategically placed road through territory claimed by both sides along India's northwestern border with China. The precise border in Aksai Chin, as this 15,000 square mile portion of desolate Tibetan plateau is called, had become a matter of contention between British-ruled India and China since the late 19th century. In India's northeast, there was a major controversy as well. There, India claimed its border with China extended to the McMahon line, a boundary drawn by India's British overlords in 1914, whereas China laid claim to 32,000 square miles of territory south of that line, which the Chinese refer to as South Tibet. The British rulers of India had reached agreement on the McMahon line with the leadership of Tibet (which was autonomous at the time) at a conference in Simla in 1914. China, which stormed out of the Simla talks, refused to recognize the legitimacy of the McMahon line and insisted Tibet lacked the authority to redraw its boundaries.

Particularly after India discovered the Chinese road in Aksai Chin, both countries began sending patrols and establishing border posts deeper and deeper into the barren edges of the disputed territory. Historians have placed particular blame upon Indian Prime Minister Jawaharlal Nehru, who underestimated China's willingness to use force—and failed to heed the warnings of his military advisors—when he implemented an assertive "Forward Policy" with India's border posts. But while India's policy may have aggravated the situation, it was China that, after a year of minor skirmishes, launched a coordinated offensive on both the eastern and western fronts on October 20, 1962. India fast earned the sympathy and support of the international community (including, ironically, both the United States and Soviet Union); however, it was dealt a humiliating military defeat in a war that lasted just one month, the sting of which lingers to this day.

The result of that short war was that China quickly seized Aksai Chin, which today remains under its administration. However, in the northeast, after advancing several miles into Indian territory, China instituted a unilateral ceasefire on November 20 and recalled its troops behind the McMahon line. The resulting status quo—with China in control of Aksai Chin and India in control of all of the territory up to the McMahon line (roughly contiguous with the present day state of Arunachal Pradesh)—has held to this day.

The Border, Round Two

Fast forward 35 years, and developments along those same sections of the disputed border have partially soured Sino-Indian relations again. This was not supposed to be the case. Sino-Indian relations did continue to deteriorate throughout the 1960s and 1970s. Though officially a leader of the Non-Aligned Movement (NAM), India was drawn firmly into the Soviet bloc during this period, particularly after the Indo-Soviet Treaty of Friendship and Cooperation in 1971. At the same time, Beijing, now estranged from its Communist comrades in Moscow, deepened its ties to the United States and began supplying military and nuclear technology to India's archrival, Pakistan.

However, with the exception of a few minor border skirmishes, by the 1980s the two neighboring countries were enjoying a broad thaw in relations, initiating a series of border negotiations in 1981 that have spanned the past three decades and well over a dozen rounds. A major breakthrough in 1988 saw Indian Prime Minister Rajiv Gandhi visit Beijing, and in the 1990s high-level exchanges occurred with regularity. Consulates were reopened, cultural exchanges initiated, and trade at the border encouraged.

In fact, as late as 2005, the two seemed on the verge of a major breakthrough on the border issue. That year, China had dropped its longstanding challenge to Indian sovereignty over the tiny Himalayan enclave of Sikkim, which officially became an Indian state in 1975. The concession was part of a quid pro quo, for New Delhi had recognized Chinese sovereignty over Tibet in 2003. Also in 2005, India and China outlined "guiding principles and political parameters" for a final settlement of the border dispute.

There were further reasons to be optimistic. Beginning in the 1990s, China began making encouraging moves—including substantial concessions—to resolve land border disputes with its other neighbors. Final border resolutions were concluded with Kyrgyzstan (1996), Kazakhstan (1998), Russia (2008), Vietnam (2008), and, most recently, Tajikistan (2011).

Yet the direction of Sino-Indian relations took a turn for the worse in 2006—ironically the "India-China friendship year"—with the disputed border taking center stage. On November 14, on the eve of a four-day visit to New Delhi by Chinese President Hu Jintao, China's Ambassador to India, Sun Yuxi, inflammatorily revived China's claim to the territory south of the McMahon line. Although China's External Affairs Ministry played down the remarks of the ambassador, who was recalled the following year, the episode marked the beginning of a period of escalating tensions.

India, for its part, had announced just a few months earlier that it intended to upgrade its infrastructure in Arunachal Pradesh (AP) by building seven "strategic roads." The announcement was a reversal of a longstanding strategy which sought to ensure a lack of infrastructure along the Indian side of its border with China. By this counterintuitive logic, roads and bridges would only serve to facilitate the advance of an invading army. However, it left India utterly incapable of moving troops and supplies into defensive positions. This deficiency was exacerbated by China's feverish development of infrastructure on its own side of the border. In a reflection of this deficit, in January 2010, the *Hindustan Times* reported that the Chinese forces could cover 250 miles a day along the border, while Indian forces could move at only half that speed. Meanwhile, India has only one actionable airfield positioned near the border in Assam, whereby China has five airfields in Tibet and Chinese warplanes can reach New Delhi within 20 minutes from their forward base in Demchok.

From 2006 onward, points of friction along the border continued to grow. Indian officials and media outlets began reporting on frequent incursions by Chinese patrols across the border in the eastern and western sectors. Brahma Chellaney, a prominent Indian strategic affairs analyst, noted in 2009 that cross-border "forays" by Chinese troops had doubled from 2006 to 2008, from 140 to 270 annually. In May of 2007, an Indian Administrative Service officer from Arunachal Pradesh was denied a visa to China on the grounds that it was already a part of China. Beijing began implementing a policy of stapling visas to separate pieces of paper for citizens of Arunachal Pradesh (AP), while denying visas altogether for AP officials (in 2009, China began implementing the same policy for Kashmir, which in diplomatic terms equates to a challenge of Indian sovereignty over those territories). All the while, China was raising angry protests every time a high-ranking Indian official or the Dalai Lama visited or announced plans to visit Arunachal Pradesh.

India Buckles Down

In September 2007, it was India's turn to raise the stakes. New Delhi announced that it would base squadrons of its most potent fighter aircraft, the Sukhoi-30MKI, in Tezpur, Assam,

13

which is neighbor to Arunachal Pradesh. A year later, India made public plans to raise two new mountain divisions trained in high altitude combat to be sent to the northeast, bringing its total troop strength in the region to over 100,000. And in 2009, Indian officials announced they would upgrade airfields and install special mountain and lightweight radars in the northwest, near Aksai Chin.

The military plans reflected a fundamental and still evolving shift in strategic thinking in New Delhi about the potential threat China poses and the flaws of India's own national security strategy. This change was most visibly demonstrated in New Delhi's announcement of a change in its strategic defense doctrine in December 2009. Indian strategic planning had always centered on potential conflicts with Pakistan, with which it had fought three major wars and a lower intensity conflict since independence. However, in 2009, India announced that it was revising its Pakistan-centric "Cold Start" doctrine in favor of a "Two-Front War" doctrine, by which both Pakistan and China would receive equal attention. According to Indian Army Chief General Deepak Kapoor, there is now a proportionate focus given to the western and northeastern fronts. Indeed, in recent years Indian government officials and to a greater degree, military officers, have become more candid about their concerns over their eastern neighbor. In 2009, Indian Air Force Chief Marshal Fali Homi Major bluntly admitted that China is an entirely different "ball-game" compared to Pakistan, with China undoubtedly posing the greater threat.

> In 2009, Indian Air Force Chief Marshal Fali Homi Major bluntly admitted, 'China is a totally different ballgame compared to Pakistan . . . they are certainly the greater threat.'

The doctrinal shift has taken tangible form in India's 10-year, US$100 billion military modernization program. New Delhi has a massive tender pending for 126 Medium Multi-Role Aircraft and a long-term, US$10 billion contract with Russia to develop and field at least 300 fifth generation fighters. It recently bought over a dozen C-17s and C-130J heavy lift aircraft and is working intensively on indigenous missile technology, upgrading its Brahmos cruise missiles, and extending the range of its Agni-class ballistic missiles, the newest versions of which can allegedly reach deep into China.

Most importantly, though, India is investing heavily in naval capabilities designed to project force—and protect its interests—in the Indian Ocean. It is currently building two indigenous aircraft carriers (to be completed in 2015 and 2020) to complement the refitted carrier it recently bought from Russia for US$2.3 billion, the Admiral Gorshkov, and the aging Soviet era carrier it currently operates. New Delhi is also upgrading its present-day fleet of 16 submarines by constructing six French-designed Scorpene subs and building three indigenous, nuclear-powered, ballistic missile submarines, in addition to the nuclear-powered Kilo-class submarine it leased from Russia last year. Finally, last year India commissioned the first of what will [. . .] eventually be a fleet of 10 stealth frigates and has now completed three in an eventual fleet of seven Kolkata-class stealth destroyers.

The New Arena

India is focusing heavily on naval capabilities because friction in the Sino-Indian relationship is not restricted to their disputed border. Indeed, the most contentious arena for China and India may not be their land border at all, but the Indian Ocean. A growing number of strategic commentators, not least Robert Kaplan in his new book on the Indian Ocean region, *Monsoon*, have acknowledged the nearly limitless strategic significance of the ocean, home to the globe's principal oil shipping lanes. Indeed, nearly 70 percent of the global traffic of petroleum products traverses the Indian Ocean, so there are few countries on earth for whom the Indian Ocean does not have some significance.

Over the past decade or so, China has made a concerted effort to boost its profile in the Indian Ocean region, a policy designed to compensate for what Beijing sees as perhaps its greatest strategic weakness: the security of its energy imports. 85 percent of the oil bound for China will pass through the Indian Ocean over the next decade, including through one of the "main navigational choke points of world commerce," the Strait of Malacca. China has always feared that this narrow, 500-mile stretch of water between Indonesia and Malaysia could be used by a potential adversary to choke off its energy supply and starve its economy into submission—and China's leaders have watched closely as India boosts its military profile in the Andaman and Nicobar islands, Union Territories of India that sit near the mouth of the Strait of Malacca.

China has attempted to address this strategic liability and raise its profile in the Indian Ocean with its now famous "string of pearls," an elaborate network of investments in port facilities, listening posts, and infrastructure projects along the Indian Ocean rim in countries like Burma, Sri Lanka, Pakistan, and Bangladesh. The strategy serves a dual purpose. Most obviously, it gives China a more vibrant presence in the Indian Ocean from which to monitor developments and ship movements. It is also likely to earn Chinese civilian and military ships privileged access at various port facilities—access that would be critical in any conflict in the Indian Ocean. Additionally, however, the string of pearls is designed to provide China with alternative, overland energy access routes that can bypass the naval chokepoints—hence the construction of deep water ports, gas pipelines, and inland infrastructure projects, such as roads and rail links in South and Central Asia.

Needless to say, for India, the historic overlord of the Indian Ocean littoral region, China's growing profile is seen as an encroachment on its "strategic space." China indeed has been currying favor in capitals traditionally within India's geopolitical orbit. In Nepal, China has cultivated ties to the major parties, particularly the ascendant Maoists. In Sri Lanka, China stepped in as a patron and supplier of arms when India cut off military supplies to the government in Colombo over human rights abuses during its war with the Tamil Tigers. In Burma, China has won energy contracts and investment opportunities by warmly embracing the repressive military junta, while India, struggling with the moral dilemma of engaging an odious regime, has lost influence. In whichever direction India looks, it appears China's influence is on the rise.

Beyond Borders

China and India's primary disputes may be on land and at sea, but their parrying stretches beyond geographic boundaries, into cyberspace, the media, and international diplomacy. In 2010, an investigation by Canadian researchers found that a Chinese "Shadow Network" had breached Indian embassies around the world, stolen sensitive information on major Indian missile and armament systems, and penetrated the Dalai Lama's organization. The chairman of India's Cyber Law and IT Act Committee, Pavan Duggal, recently warned that China had raised a cyber army of roughly 300,000 people whose only job is to intrude upon the secured networks of other states. In the international arena, the two have sparred at the Asian Development Bank (ADB), where China tried to block a US$2.9 billion loan to India that would have funded a flood management project in Arunachal Pradesh, and at the Nuclear Suppliers Group, where China nearly torpedoed the US-India nuclear deal in 2008. China remains the only veto-wielding member of the Security Council not to endorse India's bid for a permanent seat on the Council. Further irritants include Chinese plans to build dams on Himalayan rivers that flow downstream into India and an announcement in 2010 that China would build two new nuclear reactors in Pakistan (in violation of nuclear nonproliferation commitments).

China and India's primary disputes may be on land and at sea, but their parrying stretches beyond geographic boundaries, into cyberspace, the media, and international diplomacy.

A final dimension is the role of the media in exacerbating Sino-Indian tensions. Chinese leaders at the highest levels have vocally complained—with some justification—about the role India's leading English language dailies have played in sensationalizing every Sino-Indian disagreement and obsessing over the "China threat." Chinese Prime Minister Wen Jiabao has raised the issue with Indian leaders. Furthermore, China's ambassador to India this year suggested New Delhi should guide the public toward avoiding a verbal war. India's Foreign Secretary was forced to remind her Chinese counterparts that a free media was part of a "vibrant" and "noisy" democracy.

While China's tightly controlled, state-run media is generally more reserved, at the height of Sino-Indian tensions in 2009, the Communist Party mouthpiece, the *Global Times,* printed an unusually bellicose article ("India's unwise military moves"), shining a rare light on China's more hawkish views

toward India. In response to news that India was moving new troops to its northeastern border, the piece warned that India's moves could only lead toward a rivalry and asked India to consider the consequences of a potential confrontation with China.

In a passage that has since been removed from the article on the *Global Times'* website, the piece added that China would not make any compromises in its border disputes with India.

Concluding Analysis

The effects of this game of brinksmanship being played by China, and to a lesser degree India, have so far been constrained by prudent and cautious political leaders in both capitals. However, the longer the aura of confrontation perpetuates, the more it generates a momentum of its own. Hawkish comments by officials and newspaper editors are easily dismissed; however, shifts in military doctrines and public opinion are much harder to reverse.

Nevertheless, it is critically important not to overstate the degree of animosity in Sino-Indian relations. The two countries enjoy booming economic ties, including US$60 billion in annual bilateral trade, projected to surge to US$100 billion by 2015. High-level governmental exchanges are frequent, and the official discourse often diplomatic and complimentary. Many on the Indian left, and within its powerful government bureaucracy, see China more as friend than foe. China, as it does with all its neighbors, frequently stresses the need for peaceful coexistence, mutual respect, and non-interference in each others' affairs. Leaders in both capitals have committed to resolving their border disputes through peaceful means and diplomatic negotiations. However, actions speak louder than words, and while the potential for conflict remains low in the short term, many Sino-Indian divisions are widening rather than narrowing.

It is hard not to view the rise in tensions over the past five years as a story of Chinese provocations against India. This perception is buttressed by several factors. One is that China's provocations have been tangible, documentable policies, while Beijing's complaints about India are more abstract. For instance, Beijing clearly harbors animosity toward India for hosting the Dalai Lama, who, it argues rather unconvincingly, is trying to incite unrest in Tibet. Thus, to many Chinese, India is a willing accomplice. China also appears uncomfortable with the budding Indo-US alliance, which Beijing sees as part of a larger design by the United States to encircle it with an anti-China coalition. It is perhaps not a coincidence that the spike in Sino-Indian tensions, beginning in 2006, came shortly after the United States and India signed the landmark US-India nuclear deal and entrenched their strategic alliance. Finally, as China works to curry influence in South Asia, India is itself pursuing a "Look East" policy, signing free trade deals and boosting military cooperation with countries in China's "orbit," like Vietnam, Malaysia, Japan, and South Korea.

Another explanation is that China has simply been more provocative. Of course, provocative need not be illegitimate. China is within its right to pursue greater influence in South

Asia and modernize its military, and India is within its rights to be concerned by these moves. But it is hard to view other policies—border incursions, challenges to India's sovereignty over Kashmir, confrontation at international institutions, cyber-attacks—as benign and not specifically designed to provoke India.

So why is China stirring trouble with India at a time when Beijing is at great pains to stress the concept of its "peaceful rise" and settling land border disputes with other neighbors? The unapologetically opaque nature of the Communist regime in Beijing poses formidable challenges to deducing China's intent. However, the most convincing argument yet articulated is that China's hawks—who have grown increasingly synonymous with the People's Liberation Army—want to keep India "bogged down" in domestic problems, focused on Pakistan, and generally distracted as China expands its influence and snaps up resources in South and Central Asia. Indian Prime Minister Manmohan Singh alluded to as much in a private interview with Indian newspapers in 2010. At the time, Singh said that China wanted to keep India at a "low-level equilibrium" and was tempted to use Kashmir to accomplish that end.

If this is indeed Beijing's aim, its efforts are misguided and counterproductive. China's policies have simply heightened concern in New Delhi about China's rise and drawn India's attention away from Pakistan, towards focusing on any Chinese move that carries a hint of aggression. If Beijing has complaints about Indians hyping the "China threat," it has only itself to blame.

Critical Thinking

1. Why does India consider China to be a threat to its national security?
2. What are the geopolitical factors involved in Sino-Indian tensions?
3. What has been the role of the media in exacerbating Sino-Indian tensions?

JEFF M. SMITH is the Kraemer Strategy Fellow at the American Foreign Policy Council. Smith has given briefings at the Pentagon and to the Senate Select Committee on Intelligence and guest lectured on national security issues.

From *Harvard International Review,* Spring 2011, pp. 107–113. Copyright © 2011 by the President of Harvard College. Reprinted by permission via Sheridan Reprints

Hegemony with Chinese Characteristics

AARON L. FRIEDBERG

The United States and the People's Republic of China are locked in a quiet but increasingly intense struggle for power and influence, not only in Asia, but around the world. And in spite of what many earnest and well-intentioned commentators seem to believe, the nascent Sino-American rivalry is not merely the result of misperceptions or mistaken policies; it is driven instead by forces that are deeply rooted in the shifting structure of the international system and in the very different domestic political regimes of the two Pacific powers.

The United States and the People's Republic of China are locked in a quiet but increasingly intense struggle for power and influence, not only in Asia, but around the world.

Throughout history, relations between dominant and rising states have been uneasy—and often violent. Established powers tend to regard themselves as the defenders of an international order that they helped to create and from which they continue to benefit; rising powers feel constrained, even cheated, by the status quo and struggle against it to take what they think is rightfully theirs. Indeed, this story line, with its Shakespearean overtones of youth and age, vigor and decline, is among the oldest in recorded history. As far back as the fifth century BC the great Greek historian Thucydides began his study of the Peloponnesian War with the deceptively simple observation that the war's deepest, truest cause was "the growth of Athenian power and the fear which this caused in Sparta."

The fact that the U.S.-China relationship is competitive, then, is simply no surprise. But these countries are not just any two great powers: Since the end of the Cold War the United States has been the richest and most powerful nation in the world; China is, by contrast, the state whose capabilities have been growing most rapidly. America is still "number one," but China is fast gaining ground. The stakes are about as high as they can get, and the potential for conflict particularly fraught.

At least insofar as the dominant powers are concerned, rising states tend to be troublemakers. As a nation's capabilities grow, its leaders generally define their interests more expansively and seek a greater degree of influence over what is going on around them. This means that those in ascendance typically attempt not only to secure their borders but also to reach out beyond them, taking steps to ensure access to markets, materials and transportation routes; to protect their citizens far from home; to defend their foreign friends and allies; to promulgate their religious or ideological beliefs; and, in general, to have what they consider to be their rightful say in the affairs of their region and of the wider world.

As they begin to assert themselves, ascendant states typically feel impelled to challenge territorial boundaries, international institutions and hierarchies of prestige that were put in place when they were still relatively weak. Like Japan in the late nineteenth century, or Germany at the turn of the twentieth, rising powers want their place in the sun. This, of course, is what brings them into conflict with the established great powers—the so-called status quo states—who are the architects, principal beneficiaries and main defenders of any existing international system.

The resulting clash of interests between the two sides has seldom been resolved peacefully. Recognizing the growing threat to their position, dominant powers (or a coalition of status quo states) have occasionally tried to attack and destroy a competitor before it can grow strong enough to become a threat. Others—hoping to avoid war—have taken the opposite approach: attempting to appease potential challengers, they look for ways to satisfy their demands and ambitions and seek to incorporate them peacefully into the existing international order.

But however sincere, these efforts have almost always ended in failure. Sometimes the reason clearly lies in the demands of the rising state. As was true of Adolf Hitler's Germany, an aggressor may have ambitions that are so extensive as to be impossible for the status quo powers to satisfy without effectively consigning themselves to servitude or committing national suicide. Even when the demands being made of them are less onerous, the dominant states are often either reluctant to make concessions, thereby fueling the frustrations and resentments of the rising power, or too eager to do so, feeding its ambitions and triggering a spiral of escalating demands. Successful policies of appeasement are conceivable in theory but in practice have proven devilishly difficult to implement. This is why periods of transition, when a new, ascending power begins to overtake the previously dominant state, have so often been marked by war.

While they are careful not to say so directly, China's current rulers seem intent on establishing their country as the preponderant power in East Asia, and perhaps in Asia writ large. The goal is to make China the strongest and most influential nation in its neighborhood: a country capable of deterring attacks and threats; resolving disputes over territory and resources according to its preferences; coercing or persuading others to accede to its wishes on issues ranging from trade and investment to alliance and third-party basing arrangements to the treatment of ethnic Chinese populations; and, at least in some cases, affecting the character and composition of their governments. Beijing may not seek conquest or direct physical control over its surroundings, but, despite repeated claims to the contrary, it does seek a form of regional hegemony.

Such ambitions hardly make China unique. Throughout history, there has been a strong correlation between the rapid growth of a state's wealth and potential power, the geographic scope of its interests, the intensity and variety of the perceived threats to those interests, and the desire to expand military capabilities and exert greater influence in order to defend them. Growth tends to encourage expansion, which leads to insecurity, which feeds the desire for more power. This pattern is well established in the modern age. Looking back over the nineteenth and twentieth centuries, Samuel Huntington finds that

> every other major power, Britain and France, Germany and Japan, the United States and the Soviet Union, has engaged in outward expansion, assertion, and imperialism coincidental with or immediately following the years in which it went through rapid industrialization and economic growth.

As for China, Huntington concludes, "no reason exists to think that the acquisition of economic and military power will not have comparable effects" on its policies.

Of course the past behavior of other states is suggestive, but it is hardly a definitive guide to the future. Just because other powers have acted in certain ways does not necessarily mean that China will do the same. Perhaps, in a world of global markets and nuclear weapons, the fears and ambitions that motivated previous rising powers are no longer as potent. Perhaps China's leaders have learned from history that overly assertive rising powers typically stir resentment and opposition.

But China is not just any rising power, and its history provides an additional reason for believing that it will seek some form of regional preponderance. It is a nation with a long and proud past as the leading center of East Asian civilization and a more recent and less glorious experience of domination and humiliation at the hands of foreign invaders. As a number of historians have recently pointed out, China is not so much "rising" as it is *returning* to the position of regional preeminence that it once held and which its leaders and many of its people still regard as natural and appropriate. The desire to reestablish a Sino-centric system would be consistent with what journalist Martin Jacques describes as

> an overwhelming assumption on the part of the Chinese that their natural position lies at the epicentre of East

Asia, that their civilization has no equals in the region, and that their rightful position, as bestowed by history, will at some point be restored in the future.

Conservative scholar Yan Xuetong puts the matter succinctly: the Chinese people are proud of their country's glorious past and believe its fall from preeminence to be "a historical mistake which they should correct." If anything, the "century of humiliation" during which China was weak and vulnerable adds urgency to its pursuit of power. For a nation with China's history, regaining a position of unchallengeable strength is not seen as simply a matter of pride but rather as an essential precondition for continued growth, security and, quite possibly, survival.

Deep-seated patterns of power politics are thus driving the United States and China toward mistrust and competition, if not necessarily toward open conflict. But this is not all there is to the story. In contrast to what some realists claim, ideology matters at least as much as power in determining the course of relations among nations. The fact that America is a liberal democracy while China remains under authoritarian rule is a significant additional impetus for rivalry, an obstacle to stable, cooperative relations, and a source of mutual hostility and mistrust in its own right.

Relations between democracies and nondemocracies are always conducted in what political theorist Michael Doyle describes as an "atmosphere of suspicion," in part because of "the perception by liberal states that nonliberal states are in a permanent state of aggression against their own people." Democracies, in short, regard nondemocracies as less than legitimate because they do not enjoy the freely given consent of their own people. In their heart of hearts, most self-governing citizens simply do not believe that all states are created equal or that they are entitled to the same degree of respect regardless of how they are ruled.

Seen in this light, disputes between the United States and China over such issues as censorship and religious freedom are not just superficial irritants that can be dissolved or wished away. They are instead symptomatic of much deeper difficulties. To most Americans, China's human-rights violations are not only intrinsically wrong, they are also powerful indicators of the morally distasteful nature of the Beijing regime. While the United States may be able to do business with such a government on at least some issues, the possibility of a warm, trusting and stable relationship is remote to say the least.

Democracies also tend to regard nondemocracies as inherently untrustworthy and dangerously prone to external aggression. Because of the secrecy in which their operations are cloaked, the intentions, and often the full extent of the military capabilities of nondemocratic states, are difficult to discern. In recent years, U.S. officials have pressed their Chinese counterparts to be more "transparent" about defense programs, but there is little expectation that these pleas will be answered in any meaningful way. And even if Beijing were to suddenly unleash a flood of facts and figures, American analysts would regard them with profound skepticism, scrutinizing the data for signs of deception and disinformation. And they would be right to do so; the centralized, tightly controlled Chinese government is far better situated to carry off such schemes than its open, divided and leaky American counterpart.

Their capacity for secrecy also makes it easier for nondemocracies to use force without warning. Since 1949, China's rulers have shown a particular penchant for deception and surprise attacks. (Think of Beijing's entry into the Korean War in December 1950, or its attack on India in October 1962.) This tendency may have deep roots in Chinese strategic culture extending back to Sun Tzu, but it is also entirely consistent with the character of its current domestic regime. Indeed, for most American analysts, the authoritarian nature of China's government is a far greater concern than its culture. If China were a democracy, the deep social and cultural foundations of its strategic and political behavior might be little changed, but American military planners would be much less worried that it might someday attempt a lightning strike on U.S. forces and bases in the western Pacific.

Such fears of aggression are heightened by an awareness that anxiety over a lack of legitimacy at home can cause nondemocratic governments to try to deflect popular frustration and discontent toward external enemies. Some Western observers worry, for example, that if China's economy falters its rulers will try to blame foreigners and even manufacture crises with Taiwan, Japan or the United States in order to rally their people and redirect the population's anger. Whatever Beijing's intent, such confrontations could easily spiral out of control. Democratic leaders are hardly immune to the temptation of foreign adventures. However, because the stakes for them are so much lower (being voted out of office rather than being overthrown and imprisoned, or worse), they are less likely to take extreme risks to retain their hold on power.

But the mistrust between Washington and Beijing is not a one-way street—and with good reason. China's current rulers do not see themselves as they once did, as the leaders of a global revolutionary movement, yet they do believe that they are engaged in an ideological struggle, albeit one in which, until very recently, they have been almost entirely on the defensive. While they regard Washington's professions of concern for human rights and individual liberties as cynical and opportunistic, China's leaders do not doubt that the United States is motivated by genuine ideological fervor. As seen from Beijing, Washington is a dangerous, crusading, liberal, quasi-imperialist power that will not rest until it imposes its views and its way of life on the entire planet. Anyone who does not grasp this need only read the speeches of U.S. officials, with their promises to enlarge the sphere of democracy and rid the world of tyranny.

Seen from Beijing, Washington is a dangerous, crusading, liberal, quasi-imperialist power that will not rest until it imposes its views on the entire planet.

In fact, because ideology inclines the United States to be more suspicious and hostile toward China than it would be for strategic reasons alone, it also tends to reinforce Washington's willingness to help other democracies that feel threatened by Chinese power, even if this is not what a pure realpolitik calculation of its interests might seem to demand. Thus the persistence—indeed the deepening—of American support for Taiwan during the 1990s cannot be explained without reference to the fact that the island was evolving from an authoritarian bastion of anti-Communism to a liberal democracy. Severing the last U.S. ties to Taipei would remove a major source of friction with China and a potential cause of war. Such a move might even be conceivable if Taiwan still appeared to many Americans as it did in the 1970s, as an oppressive, corrupt dictatorship. But the fact that Taiwan is now seen as a genuine (if flawed) democracy will make it extremely difficult for Washington to ever willingly cut it adrift.

Having watched America topple the Soviet Union through a combination of confrontation and subversion, since the end of the Cold War China's strategists have feared that Washington intends to do the same to them. This belief colors Beijing's perceptions of virtually every aspect of U.S. policy toward it, from enthusiasm for economic engagement to efforts to encourage the development of China's legal system. It also shapes the leadership's assessments of America's activities across Asia, which Beijing believes are aimed at encircling it with pro-U.S. democracies, and informs China's own policies to counter that influence.

As China emerges onto the world stage it is becoming a source of inspiration and material support for embattled authoritarians in the Middle East, Africa and Latin America as well as Asia—antidemocratic holdouts who looked to be headed for the garbage heap of history after the collapse of the Soviet Union. Americans may have long believed that growth requires freedom of choice in the economic realm (which is presumed to lead ineluctably to the expansion of political liberties), but, at least for now, the mainland has successfully blended authoritarian rule with market-driven economics. If it comes to be seen as offering an alternative model for development, China's continued growth under authoritarian rule could complicate and slow America's long-standing efforts to promote the spread of liberal political institutions around the world.

Fear that the United States has regime change on the brain is also playing an increasing role in the crafting of China's policies toward countries in other parts of the world. If the United States can pressure and perhaps depose the current leaders of Venezuela, Zimbabwe and Iran, it may be emboldened in its efforts to do something similar to China. By helping those regimes survive, Beijing wins friends and allies for future struggles, weakens the perception that democracy is on the march and deflects some of America's prodigious energies away from itself. Washington's efforts to isolate, coerce and possibly undermine dictatorial "rogue" states (such as Iran and North Korea) have already been complicated, if not defeated, by Beijing's willingness to engage with them. At the same time, of course, China's actions also heighten concern in Washington about its motivations and intentions, thereby adding more fuel to the competitive fire.

It may well be that any rising power in Beijing's geopolitical position would seek substantial influence in its own immediate neighborhood. It may also be true that, in light of its history, and regardless of how it is ruled, China will be especially concerned with asserting itself and being acknowledged by its neighbors as the first among equals. But it is the character of the nation's domestic political system that will ultimately be decisive in determining precisely how it defines its external objectives and how it goes about pursuing them.

As Ross Terrill of Harvard's Fairbank Center points out, when we speak of "China's" intentions or strategy, we are really talking about the aims and plans of today's top leaders or, as he describes them, "the nine male engineers who make up the Standing Committee of the Politburo of the Chinese Communist Party." Everything we know of these men suggests that they are motivated above all else by their belief in the necessity of preserving CCP rule. This is, in one sense, a matter of unadulterated self-interest. Today's leaders and their families enjoy privileges and opportunities that are denied others in Chinese society and which flow directly from their proximity to the sources of political power. The end of the Communist Party's decades-long reign would have immediate, painful and perhaps even fatal consequences for those at the top of the system. Rising stars who hope one day to occupy these positions and even junior officials with more modest ambitions will presumably make similar calculations. This convergence of personal interests and a sense of shared destiny give the party-state a cohesion that it would otherwise lack. Party members know that if they do not hang together they may very well hang separately—and this knowledge informs their thinking on every issue they face.

But the motivation to continue CCP rule is not rooted solely in self-interest. The leadership is deeply sincere in its belief in the party's past achievements and future indispensability. It was the CCP, after all, that rescued China from foreign invaders, delivered it from a century of oppression and humiliation, and lifted it back into the ranks of the world's great powers. In the eyes of its leaders, and some portion of the Chinese people, these accomplishments in themselves give the CCP unique moral authority and legitimize its rule.

Looking forward, party officials believe that they are all that stands between continued stability, prosperity, progress and an unstoppable ascent to greatness on the one hand and a return to chaos and weakness on the other. An analysis of the leaked secret personnel files of the current "fourth generation" of Chinese leaders (with Mao Tse-tung, Deng Xiaoping and Jiang Zemin leading the first three) by Sinologists Andrew Nathan and Bruce Gilley concludes that, on this question, there is no evidence of dissension or doubt. President Hu Jintao, his colleagues and their likely successors are aware of the numerous internal and external challenges they face, but they are confident that they, and they alone, can find the solutions that will be needed to keep their country moving forward and enable it to achieve its destiny. Indeed, they believe that it is precisely the magnitude and complexity of the problems confronting China that makes their continued rule essential.

The party's desire to retain power shapes every aspect of national policy. When it comes to external affairs, it means that Beijing's ultimate aim is to "make the world safe for authoritarianism," or at least for continued one-party rule in China. Over the last several decades this focus on regime security has led, first of all, to an emphasis on preserving the international conditions necessary for continued economic growth. The party's ability to orchestrate rapid improvements in incomes and personal welfare is its most tangible accomplishment of the past thirty years and the source of its strongest claim to the gratitude and loyalty of the Chinese people. Economic growth, my Princeton colleague Thomas Christensen argues, "provides satisfaction and distraction to the population, and, therefore garners domestic support for the Party (or at least reduces active opposition to the Party)." Growth also generates revenues that the regime can use to "buy off opposition and to channel funds to poorer regions and ethnic minority areas to try to prevent violent uprisings."

As China has grown richer and stronger, the regime's pursuit of security has also led it to seek an increasing measure of control over the world outside its borders. This outward push has both offensive and defensive motivations. As the steward of national greatness, the party has the responsibility of returning China to its rightful place at the center of Asia. The visible deference of others will provide evidence of the regime's success in this regard and will help to reinforce its legitimacy at home. Especially if economic growth should falter, "standing up" to traditional enemies and resolving the Taiwan issue and other disputes on Beijing's terms are likely to become increasingly important parts of the CCP's strategy for retaining its hold on power. China's leaders believe that the stronger their country appears abroad, the stronger their regime will be at home.

Conversely, the appearance of weakness or the widespread perception that the nation has been defeated or humiliated could be extremely dangerous to the party's prospects for continued rule. Underlying concerns about its legitimacy make the regime more sensitive to slights and setbacks, and even more determined to deter challenges and to avoid defeat, than it might otherwise be. The best insurance against such risks is for China to accumulate an overwhelming preponderance of power in its neighborhood.

Moreover, the CCP's hypersensitivity to what it sees as "separatism" is a direct result of its belief that it must retain tight central control in all places and at all times. Pleas for greater autonomy from Tibet or Xinjiang are thus seen as deadly threats to national unity and hence to continued Communist Party rule. The regime believes that if it loosens its grip, even a little, the entire country will spring apart. China's leaders see the need to develop sufficient strength to deter its neighbors from providing aid and comfort to separatist groups and will build the capabilities to intervene directly to stop them, should that become necessary.

Even as it grows stronger and, in certain respects, more self-confident, the CCP continues to dread ideological contamination. Pliant, like-minded states along its borders are far more likely to help Beijing deal with this danger than flourishing liberal democracies with strong ties to the West. The desire to forestall "peaceful evolution" at home gives the regime another compelling reason to want to shape the political development of its neighbors.

To sum up: China's current rulers do not seek preponderance solely because they are the leaders of a rising great power or simply because they are Chinese. Their desire for dominance and control is in large measure a by-product of the type of political system over which they preside. A strong liberal-democratic China would certainly seek a leading role in its region and perhaps an effective veto over developments that it saw as inimical to its interests. But it would also be less fearful of internal instability, less threatened by the presence of democratic neighbors, and less prone to seek validation at home through the domination and subordination of others.

Though not everyone is convinced, it is likely that a more democratic China would ultimately create a more peaceful, less war-prone environment in Asia. In the view of some realists, domestic reforms will only make Beijing richer, stronger and hence a more potent competitor without deflecting it from its desire to dominate East Asia and settle scores with some of its neighbors. It is undoubtedly true that even if, in the long run, China becomes a stable, peaceful democracy, its passage will prove rocky. The opening of the nation's political system to dissent and debate is likely to introduce an element of instability into its foreign policy as new voices are heard and aspiring leaders vie for popular support. As one observer, economist David Hale, ruefully points out: "An authoritarian China has been highly predictable. A more open and democratic China could produce new uncertainties about both domestic policy and international relations."

Nationalism, perhaps in its most virulent and aggressive form, is one factor likely to play a prominent role in shaping the foreign policy of a liberalizing Middle Kingdom. Thanks to the spread of the Internet and the relaxation of restraints on at least some forms of "patriotic" political expression, the current regime already finds itself subject to criticism whenever it takes what some "netizens" regard as an overly accommodating stance toward Japan, Taiwan or the United States. Beijing has sought at times to stir up patriotic sentiment, but, fearful that anger at foreigners could all too easily be turned against the party, the regime has also gone to great lengths to keep popular passions in check. A democratically elected government might be far less inhibited. U.S.-based political scientist Fei-Ling Wang argues that a post-Communist regime would actually be more forceful in asserting its sovereignty over Taiwan, Tibet and the South China Sea. As he explains:

A "democratic" regime in Beijing, free from the debilitating concerns for its own survival but likely driven by popular emotions, could make the rising Chinese power a much more assertive, impatient, belligerent, even aggressive force, at least during the unstable period of fast ascendance to the ranks of a world-class power.

The last proviso is key. Even those who are most confident of the long-term pacifying effects of democratization recognize the possibility of a turbulent transition. In his book *China's Democratic Future,* Bruce Gilley acknowledges that democratic revolutions in other countries have often led to bursts of external aggression and he notes that, since the start of the twentieth century, pro-democracy movements in China have also been highly nationalistic. Despite these precedents, Gilley predicts that, after an interval of perhaps a decade, a transformed nation will settle into more stable and cooperative relationships with the United States as well as with its democratic neighbors.

Such an outcome is by no means certain, of course, and would be contingent upon events and interactions that are difficult to anticipate and even harder to control. If initial frictions between a fledgling democracy and its better established counterparts are mishandled, resulting in actual armed conflict, history could spin off in very different and far less promising directions than if they are successfully resolved. Assuming the transition can be navigated without disaster, however, there are good reasons to believe that relations will improve with the passage of time. One Chinese advocate of political reform, Liu Junning, summarizes the prospects well. Whereas a "nationalistic and authoritarian China will be an emerging threat," a liberal, democratic China will ultimately prove "a constructive partner."

This expectation is rooted in more than mere wishful thinking. As the values and institutions of liberal democracy become more firmly entrenched, there will begin to be open and politically meaningful debate and real competition over national goals and the allocation of national resources. Aspiring leaders and opinion makers preoccupied with prestige, honor, power and score settling will have to compete with others who emphasize the virtues of international stability, cooperation, reconciliation and the promotion of social welfare. The demands of the military and its industrial allies will be counterbalanced, at least to some degree, by groups who favor spending more on education, health care and the elderly. The assertive, hypernationalist version of China's history and its grievances will be challenged by accounts that acknowledge the culpability of the Communist regime in repressing minorities and refusing to seek compromise on questions of sovereignty. A leadership obsessed with its own survival and with countering perceived threats from foreign powers will be replaced by a government secure in its legitimacy and with no cause to fear that the world's democracies are seeking to encircle and overthrow it.

A democratic China would find it easier to get along with Japan, India and South Korea, among others. The trust and mutual respect that eventually grows up between democracies, and the diminished fear that one will use force against another, should increase the odds of attaining negotiated settlements of outstanding disputes over borders, offshore islands and resources. A democratic government in Beijing would also stand a better chance of achieving a mutually acceptable resolution to its sixty-year standoff with Taiwan. In contrast to today's CCP rulers, a popularly elected mainland regime would have less to gain from keeping this conflict alive, it would be more likely to show respect for the preferences of another democratic government, and it would be more attractive to the Taiwanese people as a partner in some kind of federated arrangement that would satisfy the desires and ease the fears of both sides.

For as long as China continues to be governed as it is today, its growing strength will pose a deepening challenge to American interests. If they want to deter aggression, discourage coercion and preserve a plural, open order, Washington and its friends and allies are going to have to work harder, and to cooperate more closely, in order to maintain a favorable balance of regional power. In the long run, the United States can learn to live with a democratic China as the dominant power in East Asia, much as Great Britain came to accept America as the preponderant power in the Western Hemisphere. Until that day, Washington and Beijing are going to remain locked in an increasingly intense struggle for mastery in Asia.

Critical Thinking

1. Are China's current rulers intent on establishing their country as the preponderant power in Asia?
2. Why should China be considered different from other rising powers?
3. What are the factors that contribute to tension between China and the United States?

AARON L. FRIEDBERG is a professor of politics and international affairs at the Woodrow Wilson School at Princeton University. His book, *A Contest for Supremacy: China, America, and the Struggle for Mastery in Asia,* will be published in August by W. W. Norton & Company.

From *The National Interest,* July/August 2011, pp. 18–27. Copyright © 2011 by National Interest. Reprinted by permission.

Welcome to the Post-Western World

"A more pluralistic, less structured security system [will incorporate] a decline in America's power [and] a rapid increase in China's relative power, but without an accompanying willingness or ability to take on global responsibilities. . . ."

STEPHEN F. SZABO

Security Global Trends, 2011

In the wake of the recent global financial crisis, doubts have challenged once-prevalent assumptions about the international security order that globalization has fostered. Optimists formerly argued that globalization, because it promotes economic interdependence as well as open markets and the unfettered exchange of people and ideas, would assure an increasingly benign international order. Prosperity would trump nationalism and war. Besides, backing up these positive trends was the power of a benign hegemon, the United States.

Today we increasingly witness the down-sides of globalization. Examples include the resurgence or continued rise of nondemocratic capitalist or semi-capitalist states like Russia and China, the end of the latest wave of democratization with the freezing of the "color" revolutions in Georgia and Ukraine, and the rise of right-wing populism and of counter-globalization movements in Europe and, more importantly, the United States. Continuing economic difficulties, combined with war fatigue resulting from the conflicts in Iraq and Afghanistan, have left America inward-looking, self-preoccupied, and politically polarized.

At the same time, security threats, rather than being subsumed by consumerism and global cosmopolitanism, have begun to shake the international order. Some of these threats are associated with the interdependence and openness spread by globalization: namely, the rise of non-state actors in the form of transnational terrorists and criminal organizations; the use of the internet and information technologies for crime, terrorism, and cyber warfare; and a ballooning of human trafficking and illegal migration.

Globalization has also revived geopolitical security competition for the natural resources needed to feed rapidly growing emerging economies, especially China and India. It has revived, too, the use of minerals, energy supplies, water, and food for traditional mercantilist ends. This in turn has increased disputes over territory from the high Arctic to the South China Sea, while aggravating transnational environmental challenges.

The proliferation of weapons of mass destruction is another downside of globalization, with the exchange of scientific knowledge, technology, and hardware made more sinister by the combination of disaffected states, failed states, and nongovernmental actors. And now security competition is spreading to space, with antisatellite systems poised to blind intelligence, command and control, and global positioning systems.

Will economic and financial interdependence really prevent war and neutralize some of these less benign sides of globalization? Many argued before World War I that interdependence had made war obsolete. Yet the interdependence evident in the world today is qualitatively different. Today the production chains of most multinational corporations are so dispersed that a war would paralyze industry, along with postindustrial sectors such as finance, services, and information technologies. Even a limited war on the Korean peninsula would result in a financial meltdown, coming as it would in a region in which two of the world's three largest economies are located. A war with Iran would cause major energy shortages and disruptions in energy markets.

For terrorists who seek to wreak great damage at minimal cost, however, such economic disruptions are a major incentive, as the attacks of September 11, 2001, showed. Providing additional motivation for terrorists is the sharp contrast between life prospects in the networked world of countries closely tied into the global system, and prospects in the ghettos of failed states and closed authoritarian societies.

The emerging security order is also one in which rising or reemerging powers in Asia, especially China, are displacing the Western powers that have dominated international politics for at least two centuries. In the past, such shifts of power in the international system have been accompanied by major wars. Will this transition be more benign?

We can certainly expect that a more pluralistic, less structured security system will evolve over the coming decades. The key elements of this new system will include a decline in America's power and ability to exercise world leadership; a rapid increase in China's relative power, but without an accompanying willingness or ability to take on global responsibilities; a decline in the international importance of Europe, including Russia; the growing autonomy of regional actors and of regional security dynamics; and the danger that non-state actors pose to the security of large urban centers.

The United States, which since World War II has served as the global rule maker and enforcer, will remain the world's leading military power for at least the next decade. But this power will be reduced, and hard strategic choices will have to be made. America's political gridlock will hamper US leadership both at home and abroad. Fiscal and domestic constraints will not allow America's continued role as the guarantor of global security.

Fiscal and domestic constraints will not allow America's continued role as the guarantor of global security.

Indeed, the United States now represents a classic case of overstretch: The country's international and domestic commitments and ambitions far exceed its capabilities and reach. This will have important implications for at least three key regions: Europe, Asia, and the Middle East.

Europe to the Side

The United States has been in the process of shifting its security focus away from Europe since the end of the cold war. This is not surprising. Europe was the fulcrum of the cold war; with the end of the threat posed by the Soviet Union, it was to be expected that Europe would figure less in America's security calculations.

The Old Continent, after a period that saw dynamic expansion of the European Union and NATO, has now encountered difficult times. Both the EU and NATO have overexpanded and are facing the consequences. The widening of both institutions has been far easier than their deepening, and this now threatens their cohesion. Within NATO there is little appetite for further enlargement after the 2008 Russo-Georgian war and recent political developments in Ukraine, which have pulled that country further from the West.

The EU is facing a crisis as well. The euro is not guaranteed to survive the economic imbalances that divide the euro zone's troubled south (plus Ireland) from the more stable and dynamic north. Germany is far less willing than before to serve as Europe's paymaster.

The Old Continent also faces formidable challenges, both to its economic future and to its social and political cohesion, in the form of demographic decline—and not just on account of aging populations. Most European societies' inability to integrate their significant Muslim minorities, coupled with the threat of terrorism carried out by Muslim-linked groups, means that the nature of the security challenges facing Europe will be more internal than interstate.

There is no real prospect of a return to national rivalries on the scale that Europe witnessed before World War II. And no hegemonic power threatens Europe. Russia is in serious decline. Its demographic future is even less promising than Europe's: The Russian population is projected to shrink to 111 million by 2050 (down from today's 143 million). With its brittle and corrupt financial and political systems, heavy dependence on the export of raw materials, and collapsing infrastructure in its energy sector, Russia has the economic profile of a third world country rather than that of a dynamic emerging power. Russia's military is in bad shape. Only its substantial nuclear arsenal and its permanent seat on the United Nations Security Council keep Moscow from being an even more marginal player.

While Russia can play a spoiler role, both in its region and regarding Iran, its most likely and profitable strategy is a European one that ties its economy and modernization to the West. Moscow, therefore, poses no real threat to European stability and has incentives to play a cooperative role on the continent. The only other potential hegemon in the region, Germany, remains as the former US secretary of state Henry Kissinger once described it: too large for Europe to contain, yet too small to provide a stable order.

All the European states are rapidly demilitarizing. An element of nuclear deterrence will remain, with the British and French retaining nuclear forces, and the EU will still resolve national disputes within its web of interconnections and its elaborate system of binding security. Emerging security challenges regarding counterterrorism and homeland security will continue to be met with transatlantic cooperation, but this will not require a major investment of US resources or attention.

The idea of a global NATO, and a strong security partnership between the United States and Europe outside the region, is highly unlikely to materialize in light of substantial defense budget cuts in Europe and disillusionment with NATO after the Afghanistan war. Even America's most valuable European military ally, the United Kingdom, will be incapable of maintaining a substantial capability to operate outside Europe, considering its recent defense review and substantial budget cuts to come. If the United States is to have a special relationship in the future, it is more likely to be with Australia than Britain.

Europe, in short, is likely to remain a partner with the United States on a number of global issues, but is unlikely to play much of a military role outside its region or to be a real partner in security in the Middle East or Asia. The diminishment of US involvement in Europe will pressure the Europeans to deal more on their own with the security issues that they still confront in their region, including instability on their periphery in the western Balkans, the southern Mediterranean, and the lands between the EU and Russia.

Will the EU use the Lisbon Treaty's constitutional revisions to create an effective common foreign policy? Or will a concert of powers led by Germany and France shape European responses to security threats? With the United States no longer playing its old role as a European power, Europeans will not be able to avoid such questions anymore. Necessity may forge the virtues of greater independence.

The Global Backwater

While the Middle East will continue to command international attention, it is unlikely to pose a major challenge to American strategic interests. This is a region that chronically underperforms both politically and economically. It is a backwater of stagnant authoritarian and failed states whose leading exports, besides oil, seem to be terrorism and instability. It remains divided along religious and ethnic lines and is held back by cultures that seem immune to serious modernization or dynamism. The main security challenges revolve around Iran, terrorism, and the Palestinian-Israeli conflict.

The very real threat posed by Iran could lead to American involvement in a war. If this were to occur, it would have major consequences for the region and for the US role in the world. But what is more likely to develop is a containment policy orchestrated by the United States and joined by regional players that are eager to isolate Iran in its attempt to act as regional hegemon. Most of the states in the Middle East have Sunni Muslim majorities, in contrast to Shiite Muslim Iran. Turkey will also wish to balance Iran. The removal of Iraq as a check on Iran's designs has created a vacuum that other states will need to fill.

For at least the next decade, America will need to provide a deterrent to a nuclear Iran, and will need to maintain some sort of military presence in the region—but not to the extent that it has in Iraq and Afghanistan. The withdrawal or substantial draw-down of US forces from Iraq and Afghanistan will allow the local and regional balancing forces freer rein. Thus, a US military presence may still be required, but it will be far smaller than it is today and more "over the horizon" than "boots on the ground."

Whether this will be enough to reassure Iran's neighbors and prevent further nuclear proliferation will be a key question. The major danger posed by Iran is the threat that it presents to an already shaky international nonproliferation regime. On the other hand, if the United States can develop a good working relationship with Vietnam, what is to prevent an eventual accommodation with Iran—particularly given the strong civil society in that country, which affords hope for positive changes in the future?

Terrorism will continue to be a major problem in the Middle East, given the authoritarian nature of many of the states there and the existence of failed or failing states unable to control their own territory. However, the experience of the past decade teaches us that a successful strategy cannot employ the military as a major component. If another major terrorist attack is launched against American population centers and it proves more devastating than the attacks of 9/11, it will be crucial that the US response be more limited and focused than the one that followed the earlier attacks. The United States must pursue the criminal groups involved, but not launch another global war on terrorism.

Terrorist attacks hold the potential for turning the United States further inward, for provoking a "Fortress America" response. This is clearly the big wild card and game changer in the security future, and it is disturbing to think that decisions to limit civil liberties and withdraw from foreign commitments may lay in the hands more of terrorists than of states.

Oil and access to it will remain a vital interest for industrial and postindustrial states for at least the medium term. Israel's future is also a key variable for security prospects in the region. If current trends continue, the most important threat to the future of the Jewish state will come from within, through a growing Arab and Palestinian population. Expansion of settlements and the failure to secure a two-state solution will confront Israel with the prospect of a Jewish minority in an Arab sea. However, this is the type of long-term security threat that the United States and other outside parties cannot do much about.

If, on the other hand, a settlement can be reached, some sort of outside force will be needed to provide for the security that neither the Israelis nor the Palestinians can provide on their own. Here the United States may have to furnish some forces within a larger multilateral context, but this would be a small price to pay for a stable resolution of this long-standing dispute.

Although the Middle East is likely to remain an unstable area, it will not be the region of central strategic interest to America or to the larger international system. Provided the US-Saudi relationship remains stable, and given the oil-producing states' need to maintain both their income streams and independence from Iran, access to oil should not be a major factor in security policy. What America does at home regarding energy policy will be at least as important as its military strategy.

Although the Middle East is likely to remain an unstable area, it will not be the region of central strategic interest.

In general, the United States has misplaced its security focus, overvaluing its strategic stake in this region while undervaluing the importance of its security interests in Asia. The Middle East, in contrast with Asia's dynamism, will continue to be a global backwater, and its demand for US and international attention will fade accordingly.

China's Shadow

The rise of Asia is the key factor in the emerging security system. American strategic interests will inexorably shift to multiple challenges associated with the rise of China and the region around it. Asia lacks the sort of multilateral institutions that Europe has in the EU and NATO. What Asia does have, unlike both Europe and the Middle East, is a hegemonic power. The shadow of China is extending quickly over a region unsettled by Beijing's new assertiveness. With more power come a new psychology, a new strategic culture, and new strategic doctrines.

Asia has some important middle-sized powers in South Korea and Japan, and another potential great power in India, but none of these has the strategic weight to balance Chinese power alone, nor do they have such weight together. India is located in an especially bad and unstable neighborhood, and it remains to be seen whether its astonishing diversity proves a strength or a fatal flaw.

The United States, consequently, will have to be the centerpiece and pivot for any alliance balancing China. The other powers in the region face the choice of either accommodating Beijing via bandwagoning and acceding to its wishes, or balancing China through alliances. For most countries the former approach is the more likely, given the region's growing dependence on the Chinese economy, and given the advantage in geographic proximity that China enjoys over the United States. Perceptions in the region about the strategy each country should pursue will also be influenced by the decline of American power.

The United States will be more preoccupied with this region in the coming decades. In fact, US defense planning is already starting to shift from the Atlantic Ocean and the Mediterranean Sea to the western Pacific and the Indian Ocean. It is unclear if Washington will be able to help facilitate a peaceful rise for China or if the two countries will end up in a destabilizing rivalry.

China's mercantilist policy is aimed at feeding economic growth, which in turn allows the Communist Party elite to maintain its hold on power. This implies a continued expansion of the search for natural resources outside the country, in order to fuel the Chinese engine, and a growing geopolitical competition for these resources. It also implies the expanded use of Chinese financial power to influence the policies of other states and to undermine resistance to Chinese policies and interests. This strategy of influence extends beyond Asia to all the world's regions, including Europe and the United States.

While the Chinese military is already expanding its vision and doctrine outside its immediate neighborhood, the use of Chinese economic power is likely to be more influential and more difficult for the United States to counter. China is not the Soviet Union. The USSR was a one-dimensional power, entirely reliant on its military. China, in contrast, boasts a successful form of market economy in which the United States and the West have a substantial stake, and it has growing economic power to which America and the West are vulnerable.

This context precludes any type of cold war–like containment strategy based heavily on military means. The strategic situation today is more fluid, and what the Soviets called "the correlation of forces" is much more in China's favor than it ever was for the Soviet Union.

The United States is still a key player on the Korean peninsula and will continue to be the guarantor of security against a dangerous and unpredictable North Korea. Japan is also likely to want to keep the US military presence close by, along with its extended nuclear umbrella, as a hedge against Chinese intimidation and as an alternative to an independent Japanese nuclear deterrent. Nevertheless, the wide geographical scope and cultural diversity of Asia preclude the types of multilateral balancing arrangements that thrived in Europe. As yet there is no prospect for an Asian NATO.

New Priorities

The key questions facing the new international security order will center on what type of system will replace the one dominated since the end of World War II by American power. US hegemony was the pillar of the postwar system of multilateral institutions like the International Monetary Fund, the World Bank, and the UN. The dollar has been the world's reserve currency, and the American military has maintained a global balance. Western Europe was a key partner in this system and has benefited from it.

Now it is clear that the Western-centric order is coming to a rapid end. The dollar continues to decline as the major reserve currency; eventually it will be supplanted by a combination of currencies, including the Chinese renminbi. The Group of 20 has already replaced the Group of 7 industrial nations as the world's primary managing body. The question is: Will the basic postwar template for global governance be modified, yet continued, with new powers in the mix? Or will it be eroded or more forcibly replaced by the powers that have emerged as a consequence of globalization?

The emerging powers, particularly China, Brazil, India, Turkey, and South Africa, are unlikely to want to preserve an international system that they see as serving Western interests and dominance. They will be jealous of their sovereignty and economic development goals and, while desiring a greater weight in global decision making, will not have a global vision to go with that weight. They are more likely to become veto and regional powers rather than global ones. China may be the sole but very important exception to this, given the global scope of its economy.

This all implies a system of shifting coalitions. China will not rule the world, simply because the world is too diverse and because the global awakening that has put such significant limits on US power will also limit the power of China and other emerging markets. How this kind of non-system will cope with the common challenges of a globalized order will be the central issue of the twenty-first century.

The implication for Washington is that it must develop clear strategic priorities and link them to diminished capabilities. The defense budget, in particular, will not be immune to substantial cuts as the United States comes to grips with decades of profligacy and overextension.

Asia must be America's top security priority. And US strategy must be truly multidimensional: It should rely far less on the military and far more on smart power that utilizes partnerships with key regional actors and floating coalitions. Demands on the United States as a security provider remain great and in some regions are even growing. Yet America's ability to meet these demands is shrinking quickly and is unlikely to rebound.

Critical Thinking

1. What is the downside of globalization?
2. Why won't the Middle East be the region of central strategic interest to the United States?
3. Why are US security interests in Asia more important than its security interests in the Middle East?

STEPHEN F. SZABO is executive director of the Transatlantic Academy.

Can the BRICs Become a Bloc?

> ... equity market performance is just one manifestation of the staggering rise in BRICs' importance to the global economy ... Our 'BRICs dream' that these countries together could overtake the combined GDP of the G7 by 2035—first articulated in our 2003 *Global Economics Paper* "Dreaming with BRICs: the path to 2050"—remains a worthy 'dream' (Goldman Sachs 2007: 5).

TIMOTHY M. SHAW

A mid-2010 OECD (2010) study confirms that the balance in the world economy is shifting from North to South with, by 2020, the emerging and developing economies matching those of the OECD. Within another two decades—by 2030—the OECD expects the South to account for 60% of world GDP. In response, the OECD is encouraging a handful of countries to join the 30-member group. At the core of these emerging economies is a burgeoning proportion of multinational corporations (MNCs) from the Global South, including 'new' icons like Cemex, Embraer, Infosys, Lenovo, Tata, Vale (BCG 2009, Goldstein 2007, van Agtamel 2007). In addition, most Sovereign Wealth Funds (SWFs) are located in the South, especially in the Middle East and Asia (e.g. Brunei, Malaysia, Singapore and Taiwan). But it is the corporations and markets of the so-termed BRICs (Brazil, Russia, India and China) that are leading the global economic reversal (Xu & Bahgat 2010).

Together the BRICs are central features of the profound, current shifts in 'global governance.' Their emerging respectability, if not centrality, was recognised mid-decade through the Heiligendamm Process, which formalised the presence and participation of the 'Outreach Five' (O5)—which includes the BRICs, Mexico and South Africa—at the annual G8 summits. This, arguably facilitated the turn-of-the-decade emergence of the G20 (Shaw, Cooper and Antkiewicz 2007). With the latter advancing from only a meeting of finance ministers and central bankers to include government leaders, the incumbent 8 + 5 formula of the G8 summits has since become somewhat redundant.

The BRICs may lie at the core of a new 'global middle,' but how cohesive are they as emerging economies/markets/powers and societies? Further, whose interests

do they represent in the evolving multilateral forums and alliances of the day?

Aside from distinctive histories, geographies and ecologies, the BRICs divide along several salient dimensions: two are federal democracies with established capitalist economic structures and ubiquitous civil societies; the other pair are at best semi-capitalist democracies. The new multilateralism increasingly involves a trend from inter-governmental to non-governmental relations and coalitions, and from club to network diplomacy (Heine 2006) involving new actors and technologies. Brazil and India, with relatively developed private companies and civil society organisations (such as think tanks) can practise and exploit 'public diplomacy'; the more statist regimes of China and Russia cannot. Conversely, Brazil and Russia are major exporters of raw materials whereas China and India are major importers. And three out of four are nuclear powers, with just Brazil being the exception in the nuclear-free southern part of the western hemisphere. Such differences have become more pronounced around the current global economic crisis.

Finally, there are profound and exponential societal imbalances in some of the BRICs, especially China (124 male births to 100 female) and India (108 to 100), with long-term implications for human and regional developments and security (*The Economist*, 2010).

The BRICs and the Evolving International System

The BRICs are large, complicated, federal political economies so their interests may be multiple. Thus, no one direction may be apparent: some communities, including diasporas, corporations, regions or cities head in one direction, others in another.

Such tensions are apparent in the BRIC Summits which are coming to cover a broad canvas, reflective of a diversity of interests and institutions. Conversely, aside from subgroupings, the BRICs have deepened their collaboration by developing a range of inter-governmental networks, spanning finance ministers and central bank governors, cooperatives, development banks, judicial and statistical officials, along with business forums and think tanks.

In addition, the BRICs are of growing importance not just for industrial production but increasingly for agriculture too, especially Brazil. While agricultural output is set to stagnate in the North, it will expand by over 25% in the trio of BRICs other than Brazil, where it is anticipated to rise by 40% after 2020. This explains the rising centrality of agricultural production for energy rather than food (UN-FAO 2010). Such trends inform the BRICs' policy on, say, the BASIC environmental alliance (which includes Brazil, India and China and South Africa) or the G20 Cairns Group. To some extent the BASIC alliance reflects common interests around climate change and constitutes the BRICs' response to diplomatic pressure on the matter arising from the Copenhagen Summit of end-2009.

Finally, the impact of the BRICs, especially China, on those 'fragile states' which have a concentration of energy and minerals has been profound. In Africa, support for state leaders from Equatorial Guinea, Sao Tome, Angola and the Sudan has come from Chinese and other state energy and mining companies, leaving little competitive space for local civil society or even the private sector (Cheru & Obi 2010, Shaw, Cooper & Antkiewicz 2007). Thus the continent is increasingly divided into state regimes heavily supported by China and those with relatively developed and autonomous NGOs and MNCs with fewer linkages with the Asian power.

But China's readiness to overlook others' criteria or conditionalities, such as prevailing environmental, governance and human rights norms, means it can exert its own leverage. Whether this amounts to a 'Beijing Consensus' coming to succeed that of Washington remains contentious.

In all, as emerging powers the BRICs can contribute to new multilateralism, especially given the decline of United States unilateralism. Yet, although they constitute an embryonic bloc, they are unlikely to become much more cohesive or unanimous given historical and structural differences, distinctive societal values and norms, and economic and diplomatic competitiveness.

References

BCG (2009). 'The 2009 BCG 100 New Global Challengers' (Boston, January).

Cheru, Fantu & Cyril Obi (eds) (2010). *The Rise of China & India in Africa* (London: Zed for NAI).

Goldman Sachs (2007). *BRICs & Beyond* (New York, November).

Goldstein, Andrea (2007). *Multinational Companies from Emerging Economies: composition, conceptualization & direction in the global economy* (London: Palgrave Macmillan).

Heine, Jorge (2006). 'On the Manner of Practising the New Diplomacy' (Waterloo: CIGI, October. Working Paper #11).

OECD (2010). 'Perspectives on Global Development: shifting wealth' (Paris, June).

Shaw, Timothy M, Andrew F Cooper & Agata Antkiewicz (2007). 'Global and/or Regional Development at the Start of the 21st Century? China, India & (South) Africa' *Third World Quarterly* 28(7): 1255–1270.

The Economist (2010). 'Gendercide' Vol 394, No 8672, March 6: 13 & 77–80.

UN-FAO (2010). 'Agricultural Outlook 2010–19' (Paris, June).

van Agtmael, Antoine (2007). *The Emerging Markets Century: how a new breed of world class companies is overtaking the world* (New York: Free Press).

Xu, Yi-chong & Gawdat Bahgat (eds) (2010). *The Political Economy of Sovereign Wealth Funds* (London: Palgrave Macmillan, forthcoming).

Critical Thinking

1. Identify the BRIC member countries and make a list of their common international interests.

2. Identify two important international policy areas where BRIC countries disagree on what should be done in the future.

3. After compiling the list of common international interests of the BRIC countries, explain why you feel these interests will or will not be enough to allow these nation-states to operate as a bloc on at least a few international issues.

TIMOTHY M. SHAW is Professor Emeritus & Director of the Institute for International Relations at the University of the West Indies, St. Augustine Campus, Trinidad and Tobago.

This article first appeared in *The China Monitor*, June 2010, pp. 4–6, published by the Centre for Chinese Studies, Stellenbosch University, South Africa. Copyright © 2010 by Timothy M. Shaw. Reprinted by permission of Timothy M. Shaw and CCS at Stellenbosch University.

UNIT 2
Democratization

Unit Selections

Learning Outcomes

After reading this Unit, you will be able to:

- Explain what is meant by the process of democratization.
- Describe some of the problems associated with the transition to and the consolidation of democracy.
- List the major factors that led to the downfall of Mubarak's regime.
- Explain why the Egyptian revolution has not resulted in a complete change.
- Determine the effect of the rise of Islamist groups on the popular Arab revolutions.
- Define "failed state."
- Describe some of the problems which Bangladesh has experienced in making the transition to democracy.
- Discuss the trends that have characterized the process of global democratization recently.
- Determine the effect of the Arab revolutions on Moscow and Beijing.

Student Website

www.mhhe.com/cls

Internet References

Al Jazeera
http://english.aljazeera.net

Arab Net
www.arab.net

The Economist Intelligence Unit's Index of Democracy 2010
www.ciaonet.org/wps/eiu/0020841/index.html

Freedom House
www.freedomhouse.org

Fund for Peace
www.fundforpeace.org/global

International Foundation for Election Systems
www.ifes.org

Middle East Online
www.middle-east-online.com/english

Global democratization generally has proceeded in waves. From an historical point of view, the most recent wave of democratization occurred in Eastern Europe and the former Soviet Union from 1989 to 1991, with the collapse of the communist system. The Arab Spring, in which long-standing dictatorial regimes were overthrown in the Middle East, by uprisings based on popular revolutions, could be viewed as the latest example of global democratization. The first revolution occurred in Tunisia. Jeffrey Goldberg in "Danger: Falling Tyrants," engages in a case study of the revolution in Tunisia, but also raises the question that "as dictatorships crumble across the Middle East, what happens if Arab democracy means the rise of radical Islamism?" The collapse of regimes in the Middle East certainly caught the Obama administration by surprise, since the initial reaction of the United States was to view the revolution in Egypt cautiously, and not to immediately support the idea that Mubarak should step down until it was clear that the revolution was succeeding. Early statements by Secretary of State Hillary Clinton seemed to indicate this rather conservative approach, since for decades Mubarak had functioned as a strategic ally of the United States and was viewed by Washington as a force for stability in the Middle East. The Egyptian revolution was stimulated by what happened in Tunisia at the beginning of 2011. The process of democratization in Egypt has yet to be completed to satisfy the rising expectations of the Egyptian people. The military, which had remained neutral in the Egyptian uprising, subsequently put pressure on Mubarak to resign as President, and is in control of the process of democratization there. Dina Shehata, in "The Fall of the Pharoah" writes that "... Mubarak's downfall was the result of three factors: increasing corruption and economic exclusion, the alienation of the youth, and the 2010 elections and divisions among the Egyptian elite over questions of succession." However, Shehata, observes that the revolution has not resulted in complete change, leaving the military and state bureaucracy in control.

The revolutions in three Middle Eastern states—Syria, Libya, and Yemen—turned into protracted civil conflicts. The Syrian regime, under Bashar Assad, has cracked down brutally and ruthlessly on the demonstrators. The regime in Damascus has become increasingly more isolated as neighboring countries such as Turkey and Saudi Arabia called on Assad to stop the repression. The United States, after waiting for some time, also urged president Assad to step down. However, unlike the situation in Libya, where a significant amount of oil is involved, the United States had no plans to engage in a military intervention in Syria. In Libya, a fractious coalition of rebels, working together in the National Transitional Council, had been fighting since February 15/16, and seemed to be on the verge of victory at the end of August as their forces overran Gadaffi's stronghold in Tripoli. Even though Gadaffi would not surrender and at the time had eluded capture. Given the importance of Libya as an oil producer, a great deal of concern was expressed in the West as to what would happen next in filling the power vacuum that had been created by the fall of Gadaffi's regime. As Dirk Vandewalle stresses, Gaddafi "has hollowed out the Libyan state, eviscerated all opposition in Libyan society, and in effect created a

© Copyright Thomas Hartwell/2003

political tabula rasa on which a new free people will now have to scratch out a future." It also could be argued that the victory of the revolutionaries in Libya would not have been possible without the intervention of NATO, which provided tactical military support to the revolutionaries, by bombing the loyalist forces and attacking the presidential compound in Tripoli a number of times. The decision for NATO military intervention in Libya, which was authorized by the UN Security Council on March 17, 2011, was extremely controversial. For example, Russia and China did not vote for the Security Council resolution that authorized the intervention. One could interpret the mandate of the Security Council resolution as enabling NATO warplanes to protect civilians, but not to attack military targets. There was also some concern expressed among NATO members that the intervention in Libya was diverting resources and effort away from the war in Afghanistan. Efforts at regime change in Yemen also resulted in armed conflict there.

President Saleh of Yemen, who had been in power for 33 years, had been pursuing a pro-Western policy, by supporting the United States in the Global War against Terror. The attempt at regime change in Yemen degenerated into a bitter civil conflict. Although the country had already been wracked by years of conflict between the government and jihadist rebel forces, President Saleh was seriously wounded in June 2011 in an attack on his palace and fled to Saudi Arabia where he remained to receive medical treatment. Elsewhere in the region, the Gulf sheikdom of Bahrain, which faced an uprising by the Shia, was of great strategic importance to the United States because it served as a base for the U.S. Sixth Fleet. Saudi Arabia, with the backing of the Gulf Cooperation Council, intervened militarily in Bahrain to maintain the regime in power.

It remains to be seen what will follow the democratization of the regimes in the Middle East. As Shadi Hamid points out, the democratic governments formed after the popular revolutions in the Middle East will "include significant representation of mainstream Islamic groups" and the United States may discover "more convergence of interest than it expects." The process of democratization in the Middle East, however, did not spread to other parts of the world. China, for example, took preemptive action to make sure that there would be no contagion effect from what was happening in the Middle East. Graeme Robertson points out that ruthless dictatorships are one of the most enduring political archetypes that have persisted into the twenty-first century, but believes that the "Arab revolutions have clearly been a matter of great concern for the rulers in Russia and China."

As has also been seen in the efforts at democratization in Russia over the past 20 years, the process of democratization may depend on such factors as the method of exit from the previous regime, the political culture of the society that is undergoing the transition to democracy, and the legacy of the past. It is not that easy to graft the model of liberal democracy—a model which developed over the course of several hundred years in the United States and the United Kingdom—onto a political culture that differs from the western cultural concept of democracy. An example of some of the difficulties associated with going through the process of the consolidation of democracy is highlighted by Jalal Alamgir in "Bangladesh's Quest for Political Justice." Alamgir writes that "Bangladesh's foremost political achievement has been the institutionalization of free and fair elections. But two basic ingredients of democratic consolidation have been missing: commitment to human rights and equality before the law."

Furthermore, as Joshua Kurlantzick points out, the impression gained from the Arab Spring that democracy is continuing to spread, is belied by the fact that there has been some regression in some cases. Analyses by Freedom House, and other think tanks such as the Bertelsmann Foundation, show that there actually has been a freeze in the empirical spread of democracy and a qualitative decline in democracy as well. Kurlantzick states that "the truth is that the Arab Spring is somewhat of a smokescreen . . . for democratic meltdowns, not democratic revolutions, . . . are now the norm." Kurlantzick observes that the number of electoral democracies worldwide has declined to the lowest point since 1995. Furthermore, the Obama administration has downgraded democracy promotion. The widespread number of failed states, stand as a testimony to the failure of democracy, as illustrated by Somalia, Chad, and Sudan, which are ranked at the top of the Fund for Peace's Failed State's Index. The Fund for Peace uses a variety of variables, as well 100 subvariables, to rank 177 countries, based on the economic, social, and political pressures that may contribute to the transformation of a state into a failed state. In 2011, Somalia continued to be ranked number one on the list, due to such factors as the lack of a stable government, continued rebellions, terrorism, and the pervasiveness of such criminal behavior as piracy.

The Fall of the Pharaoh

How Hosni Mubarak's Reign Came to an End

Dina Shehata

For almost 60 years, Egyptians have celebrated Revolution Day on July 23, to commemorate the day in 1952 when Gamal Abdel Nasser and the Free Officers overthrew the monarchy to establish a republic. Next year, the country will celebrate Revolution Day on January 25—the first day of the mass protests that forced Hosni Mubarak, the country's president for 30 years, from power.

For the 18 days from January 25 to February 11, when Mubarak finally stepped down, millions of Egyptians demonstrated in the streets to demand, as many chanted, "*isqat al-nizam,*" "the fall of the regime." The Mubarak government first met these protests with violence, but its vast security apparatus soon crumbled in the face of an overwhelming numbers of protesters. Then, the state attempted to use propaganda and fear-mongering to scare the population back into its embrace, but this, too, failed. Finally, the Mubarak regime resorted to making concessions. However, these were too limited, and the death toll from the protests had already grown too high. Fearing that more violence would hurt the military's legitimacy and influence, the army broke with Mubarak and forced him to leave office.

The immediate trigger for the outbreak of protests in Egypt was the Jasmine Revolution in Tunisia in mid-January, which demonstrated that sustained and broad-based popular mobilization can lead to political change, even in a police state such as Tunisia. But other factors had long been at work in Egyptian politics and society. In particular, Mubarak's downfall was the result of three factors: increasing corruption and economic exclusion, the alienation of the youth, and the 2010 elections and divisions among the Egyptian elite over questions of succession. When these currents came together, they inspired a broad cross section of Egyptian society to achieve the unthinkable: removing Mubarak from power.

But the revolution did not lead to full regime change. Instead, it has achieved partial change: the military and the state bureaucracy remain in control and are likely to dictate the terms of the country's political transition over the coming months. What follows this transition will depend on whether the forces that staged the revolution can remain united and organized or whether some groups, such as the Muslim Brotherhood, strike a separate deal with the military. If this were to happen, the secular and youth movements that were the driving force behind the January 25 revolution would be effectively marginalized.

Nasser's Bargain

In the 1950s and 1960s, the Nasser regime, which was at once authoritarian and populist, forged a ruling bargain with labor and the middle class. All political parties were banned and all civil-society organizations, including trade unions, came under the direct control of the regime. In return, the state provided social and welfare services in the form of government employment; subsidies for food, energy, housing, and transportation; and free education and health care.

In the early 1990s, a looming economic crisis caused by unsustainable levels of external debt forced Mubarak's government to sign an agreement on economic reform with the World Bank. Over the next two decades, the Egyptian government undertook a series of structural adjustments to the economy that reduced spending on social programs; liberalized trade, commodity prices, and interest rates; suspended the longtime guarantee of government employment for university graduates; privatized a number of public-sector companies; and suspended subsidies for many commodities. As state expenditures declined, public spending on social services—including education, health care, transportation, and housing—stagnated, and the quality of these services deteriorated.

Factory workers, landless peasants, government employees, and those who produce goods for the local market (as opposed to for export) suffered most. They depended on government services and subsidies, as well as on market protections, and many saw their fortunes fall as a result of the economic liberalization. At the same time, a new Egyptian business elite emerged: some people exploited the period of economic reform and openness to turn their contacts with the regime and international markets into vast fortunes. Just below this newly minted business aristocracy, a well-off middle class also began to develop. Thus, there soon emerged a two-tiered society: the majority of the Egyptian population was increasingly marginalized, while a small minority prospered like never before. Moreover, economic reform and liberalization led to the emergence of an unholy alliance between the ruling elite and the business elite. A select few—those closely aligned with the ruling National Democratic Party (NDP)—found themselves with special privileges to buy up public lands and public companies or put on a fast track to obtain state licenses and contracts.

Over the past five years, many workers—both blue-collar laborers and educated professionals—took to organizing strikes and other protests to show their anger at their economic disenfranchisement. These protests took place outside the control or leadership of the country's labor unions and professional syndicates, which were constrained by laws that limited their freedom to strike or carry out any protest. In 2008, property-tax collectors established Egypt's first independent trade union since 1959, the year that all such unions were brought under the control of the state. In 2010 alone, there were around 700 strikes and protest actions organized by workers across the country. However, these protests tended to focus exclusively on labor-specific demands and to shy away from political issues.

Young Man's Burden

Egypt, like much of the Middle East, is in the middle of a dramatic and growing youth bulge. Today, more than half the total population of the Arab countries is under the age of 30; in Egypt, more than one-third of the population is between 15 and 29.

This demographic group faces a particularly frustrating paradox: according to the World Bank, the Middle East has both the fastest-rising levels of schooling and the highest level of youth unemployment in the world (25 percent, compared to a global average of 14.4 percent). Youth unemployment is highest among those with more education: in Egypt in 2006, young people with a secondary education or more represented 95 percent of the unemployed in their age group. Those who do find jobs often work for low pay and in poor conditions. This combination of high unemployment and low pay has kept many young Egyptian men from marrying and forming families. Approximately half of all Egyptian men between the ages of 25 and 29 are not married.

As a result of constraints on political life and civil society, youth in Egypt have been denied outlets for political and civic participation. Most cannot remember a time before the country's emergency law was last imposed, in 1981, which allowed the regime to freely persecute its challengers. Less than five percent of young people in Egypt belong to political parties, and less than 45 percent have ever participated in elections.

Partly because of such limitations, religious groups such as the Muslim Brotherhood were able to capitalize on widespread social grievances to recruit and mobilize young people in large numbers during the 1980s and 1990s. But after the state's harsh persecution of Islamists in the 1990s, youth activists began to express their grievances through a new generation of protest movements open to members of all ideological backgrounds and to those without any particular ideology at all.

One such movement is Kefaya, which has attracted legions of previously apolitical youth. In 2004 and 2005, it organized a series of high-profile protests calling for the end of Mubarak's presidency and the country's emergency law. In 2008, youth activists from Kefaya formed the April 6 Movement in solidarity with textile workers who were planning a strike for that date. The movement attracted 70,000 members on Facebook, making it the largest youth movement in Egypt at the time. Members of both the April 6 Movement and Kefaya were behind the creation of another popular Facebook group, one supporting Mohamed ElBaradei, the former head of the International Atomic Energy Agency, who returned to Egypt in February 2010.

Perhaps the most important Facebook group would arise some months later when, in June 2010, activists associated with the ElBaradei campaign created a Facebook page called "We are all Khaled Said" in memory of a young man who was beaten to death by police officers in Alexandria. Their page attracted more than one million supporters and became the focal point for a number of large protests against state abuses in the summer of 2010. By the end of 2010, Egypt's youth activists had succeeded in bypassing many of the long-standing constraints on political and civic life in the country. Although they may not have fully realized it at the time, all they needed to see their mission to the end was a final, triggering event—and that was gathering momentum some 1,300 miles away, in Tunisia.

The Edifice Cracks

As labor and youth unrest grew, another struggle was taking shape between Egypt's old guard, representing the military and the bureaucracy, and the new guard, representing Mubarak's son Gamal and his supporters in the business community and the ruling party.

Beginning in the mid-1970s, in an attempt to bolster his legitimacy both at home and abroad, then Egyptian President Anwar al-Sadat began to liberalize the political system. He allowed opposition parties and movements to gain some representation in the country's elected assemblies. As long as the ruling NDP maintained its two-thirds majority and its control over the real levers of power, the Egyptian opposition could contest elections and maintain a limited presence in parliament and in civil society. When Mubarak came to power, he continued to follow this same formula with few adjustments.

However, over the last five years, the Mubarak regime began to violate this implicit agreement, by imposing renewed constraints on the ability of political parties and movements to organize and to contest elections. Moreover, the state heavily manipulated the 2010 parliamentary elections in favor of the NDP, effectively denying all opposition groups any representation in parliament. (With opposition groups represented on the ballot but prevented from winning any races, the NDP won 97 percent of the seats.) For some in the opposition, the fraudulent elections of 2010 marked a departure from the limited political pluralism instituted by Sadat. The New Wafd party and the Muslim Brotherhood, among others, began to reconsider the utility of participating in elections under such conditions.

The regime's tactics in the 2010 elections were part of a broader plan to ensure a smooth succession from Mubarak to his son Gamal during the upcoming presidential election in 2011. This plan was the pet project of a group of business-men closely associated with Gamal—such as Ahmed Ezz, a steel tycoon and a leading figure in the NDP—who had come to assume greater influence over the ruling party and the government in recent years. Not only did the country's opposition strongly oppose the succession plan, but many important factions within the state bureaucracy and the military were also skeptical. As 2010 came to a close, the country's ruling edifice was beginning to crack.

These underlying forces in turn spurred on the groups that participated in the mass protests in January and February: youth movements, labor groups, and the political parties that were excluded from joining parliament in 2010, including the Muslim Brotherhood. Youth activists agreed to hold protests against state brutality on Police Day, January 25. This demonstration begat others, and as the size and momentum of the protests grew, these activists formed the Coalition of January 25 Youth to present a series of demands to the regime: the resignation of Mubarak, the lifting of the state of emergency, the release of all political prisoners, the dissolution of parliament, the appointment of a government of independent technocrats, the drafting of a new constitution, and the punishment of those responsible for violence against the protesters. Egypt's youth activists refused to negotiate with Omar Suleiman, a Mubarak confidant who was appointed vice president on January 29 as a means of appeasing the protesters.

At the outset, Egypt's opposition was divided over whether to participate in the demonstrations. Some groups, such as Kefaya, the National Association for Change, the Democratic Front Party, the Tomorrow Party, and the New Wafd Party, endorsed and joined the January 25 protests, whereas other groups, such as the Muslim Brotherhood and the leftist Tagammu Party, did not officially join the protests until January 28 (although many of their younger members participated on January 25).

Many of the political groups taking part in the uprising disagreed over their demands and over how best to achieve them. Groups such as Kefaya, the National Association for Change, and the Democratic Front Party and individual leaders such as ElBaradei and Ayman Nour endorsed the demands of the youth coalition and refused to negotiate with the regime until after Mubarak stepped down. Others, however—the Muslim Brotherhood, the New Wafd Party, the Tagammu Party, and a number of independent public figures—agreed to enter into negotiations with Suleiman. These talks turned out to be short-lived: the regime refused to make any real concessions, and the protests on the street continued to escalate.

For its part, the Muslim Brotherhood threw its full weight behind the protests but purposefully kept a low profile. Its young members were an integral part of the coalition that had organized the protests, and according to some of the organizers, Brotherhood supporters constituted about one-third of the crowd occupying Tahrir Square. Muslim Brothers made up a large share of the protesters in those cities where the group has long had a large following, such as Alexandria and El Mansura. However, throughout the protests, the Brotherhood was careful not to use religious slogans or to overshadow the secular, pro-democracy activists who were driving the demonstrations.

During the first two weeks of the revolution, labor movements and professional groups did not play a visible role, partly because the regime had shut down all economic activity during this time. However, during the final week, as economic activity resumed, workers and professionals began to organize strikes. In the two days preceding Mubarak's resignation, the country was approaching a state of total civil disobedience, with workers striking en masse in the transportation, communications, and industrial sectors. Judges, doctors, university professors, lawyers, journalists, and artists also organized protests. According to Shady El Ghazaly Harb, a leading Egyptian youth activist, it was this development that finally convinced the military to oust Mubarak and assume control.

Last Days of the Pharaoh

During the three weeks of protests in January and February, groups that had previously competed with one another—Islamists and secularists, liberals and leftists—joined forces against the regime. There were fears that the opposition would fragment and that some factions would strike a separate deal with the regime, but such a turn of events never happened—although this had more to do with the Mubarak government's refusal to make any concessions and its apparent willingness to use violence. In the end, it was the unity of the opposition and broad-based popular mobilization that forced the military to oust Mubarak.

Unlike the opposition, the regime suffered from multiple divisions during the crisis. In the first week, the state tried to defuse the protests by sacking Gamal Mubarak as assistant secretary-general of the NDP and purging the businessmen closely associated with him from the ruling party and the cabinet. This effectively aborted the much-despised succession scenario and removed the new business elite from its privileged economic and political position.

Mubarak hoped that by removing Gamal and his business cronies, the protests would begin to lose steam. Indeed, these measures seemed to satisfy the majority of Egyptians; many observers in the media and even some opposition figures predicted that the revolution would come to a halt. However, the next day, after Mubarak announced that he would step down in September, security forces and hired vigilantes violently cracked down on the protesters—11 were shot and killed in Tahrir Square alone—turning the momentum back against the regime. Demands for Mubarak's immediate resignation intensified, and at that point, many new groups, mainly workers and professionals, joined the protests in large numbers.

The military, which until then had backed Mubarak while refraining from using force against the protesters, began to show signs of sedition. Throughout the crisis, the protesters had welcomed the presence of the military on the streets and urged it to side with them against Mubarak, as the military had done in Tunisia just weeks earlier. But until the last days of the crisis, the military seemed to back Mubarak's plan to remain in power until September and oversee an orderly transition to democracy. It took new groups joining the protests and the rising prospect of a confrontation between the protesters and the presidential guard for the military to finally break with Mubarak. On February 10, a spokesperson for the High Council of the Armed Forces delivered a communiqué that stated that the council supported the legitimate demands of the people. Mubarak was expected to resign that same night, but he did not. The next day, the military ousted him. The High Council of the Armed Forces assumed control of the country, and one week later, it announced the suspension of the constitution and the dissolution of both houses of parliament.

Democracy's Unfinished Business

The revolution that pushed Mubarak from office has resulted in only a partial dissolution of his regime. The primary victims of this turn of events have been Mubarak's family, the business elites closely associated with it, leading figures in the state bureaucracy and the NDP, and members of the much-despised state security apparatus. The regime's basic structure remains largely intact, however: the military and the state bureaucracy are still in firm control of the country and in a position to dictate the course of the transition in the coming months. As of this writing, the High Council of the Armed Forces rules Egypt. The state bureaucracy, which comprises some six million people, remains in place, with state ministries and agencies largely unchanged and still responsible for managing day-to-day affairs.

Two scenarios seem possible. The first scenario involves speedy elections held over the summer, both parliamentary and presidential. This option appears to be favored by the military and the Muslim Brotherhood, but it is rejected by most of the groups that took part in the revolution. Such a schedule would benefit only those individuals and groups that are already positioned to achieve electoral success in the near future—namely, those associated with the NDP and the Muslim Brotherhood, the only two political organizations in Egypt with long-standing networks and bases of support that could be mobilized on short notice. Were such elections held, the outcome would probably be a power-sharing arrangement between the regime (or some new incarnation of it) and the Muslim Brotherhood, leaving little representation for the secular and youth groups that drove the revolution.

The second scenario would see the appointment of a three-member presidential council made up of two civilians and a military figure and the formation of a new cabinet composed of technocrats not affiliated with any one party. This option has been put forward by ElBaradei and is the apparent preference of the country's secular political parties and youth movements. The next step would be to hold presidential elections, followed by direct elections for an assembly that would then draft a new constitution. Until these elections were held, the presidential council would lift all constraints on political parties, the media, and civil-society organizations, which would allow secular forces the chance to organize themselves and attract voters. Parliamentary elections would follow the new constitution and the creation of new political parties, likely within one or two years. Such an arrangement would level the playing field and would allow secular parties and movements to compete more effectively with the NDP and the Muslim Brotherhood.

There are fears that if the first scenario prevails, the democratic revolution will be aborted and the old regime—under the guise of NDP loyalists in an alliance with the Muslim Brotherhood—will reassert itself. A new parliament, dominated by former NDP members and the Muslim Brotherhood would guide the drafting of the new constitution and would set the parameters of a new political system. Some important liberalization measures might be adopted to quell popular discontent, but full democratization would be unlikely.

If, however, Islamists and secularists remain united, the street stays mobilized, and international pressure is applied to the military, the second scenario may prevail. In this case, the various groups that drove the revolution would have the time to organize themselves into viable political parties—and only that can produce genuine democratic change.

Critical Thinking

1. Why did the United States support the Mubarak regime for more than three decades?

2. What are the implications of the Egyptian revolution for relations with Israel?

3. Which scenario do you think is most likely in Egypt? The first or the second? Why?

Dina Shehata is Senior Researcher at the Al-Ahram Center for Political and Strategic Studies, in Cairo.

The Rise of the Islamists

How Islamists Will Change Politics, and Vice Versa

Shadi Hamid

For decades, U.S. policy toward the Middle East has been paralyzed by "the Islamist dilemma"—how can the United States promote democracy in the region without risking bringing Islamists to power? Now, it seems, the United States no longer has a choice. Popular revolutions have swept U.S.-backed authoritarian regimes from power in Tunisia and Egypt and put Libya's on notice. If truly democratic governments form in their wake, they are likely to include significant representation of mainstream Islamist groups. Like it or not, the United States will have to learn to live with political Islam.

Washington tends to question whether Islamists' religious commitments can coexist with respect for democracy, pluralism, and women's rights. But what the United States really fears are the kinds of foreign policies such groups might pursue. Unlike the Middle East's pro-Western autocracies, Islamists have a distinctive, albeit vague, conception of an Arab world that is confident, independent, and willing to project influence beyond its borders.

There is no question that democracy will make the region more unpredictable and some governments there less amenable to U.S. security interests. At their core, however, mainstream Islamist organizations, such as the Muslim Brotherhood in Egypt and Jordan and al Nahda in Tunisia, have strong pragmatic tendencies. When their survival has required it, they have proved willing to compromise their ideology and make difficult choices.

To guide the new, rapidly evolving Middle East in a favorable direction, the United States should play to these instincts by entering into a strategic dialogue with the region's Islamist groups and parties. Through engagement, the United States can encourage these Islamists to respect key Western interests, including advancing the Arab-Israeli peace process, countering Iran, and combating terrorism. It will be better to develop such ties with opposition groups now, while the United States still has leverage, rather than later, after they are already in power.

Smart Politics

The Middle East's mainstream Islamist movements, most of which are branches or descendants of the Egyptian Muslim Brotherhood, began as single-issue parties, preoccupied with proselytizing and instituting sharia law. Beginning in the 1990s, however, for various reasons in each case, they increasingly focused on democratic reform, publicly committing themselves to the alternation of power, popular sovereignty, and judicial independence. That said, Islamists are not, and will not become, liberals. They remain staunch social conservatives and invariably hold views that most Americans would find distasteful, including that women's rights should be limited and the sexes segregated. Given the chance, they will certainly try to pursue socially conservative legislation.

Yet to the consternation of their own conservative bases, the region's mainstream Islamist groups have also shown considerable flexibility on core ideological concerns. Despite popular support in the Arab world for the implementation of sharia, for example, many Islamist groups, including the Egyptian Muslim Brotherhood, have gradually stripped their political platforms of explicitly Islamist content. In the past few years, instead of calling for an "Islamic state," for example, the Muslim Brotherhood began calling for a "civil, democratic state with an Islamic reference," suggesting a newfound commitment to the separation of mosque and state (although not of religion and politics). This move seems to have been deliberately aimed, at least in part, at alleviating international fears; with the goal of improving its image, moreover, the group launched an internal initiative in 2005 called Reintroducing the Brotherhood to the West.

When it comes to foreign policy, mainstream Islamists have rhetorically retained much of the Muslim Brotherhood's original Arab nationalism and anti-Israel politics. Today's Egyptian and Libyan Muslim Brotherhoods and Tunisia's al Nahda refuse to recognize Israel's right to exist and call for the liberation of all of historic Palestine. They also view Hamas not as a terrorist group but as a legitimate force of resistance.

Still, Islamist groups did not create the anti-Israel sentiment that exists in Arab societies; they simply reflect and amplify it. In a 2005 Pew Global Attitudes poll, 100 percent of Jordanians polled were found to hold unfavorable views of Jews. In Morocco, home to the Arab world's largest Jewish community, the figure was 88 percent. The Middle East provides such fertile ground for public posturing against Israel that many groups—not only Islamists but also leftists and nationalists—seek to outdo one another in demonstrating their dislike for Israel.

A country's physical proximity to the Israeli-Palestinian conflict informs how aggressive such posturing is. It is no accident that Jordan's Islamic Action Front—the political arm of the Jordanian Muslim Brotherhood—is one of the more vehemently anti-Israel Islamist groups in the Arab world, given that a majority of the Jordanian population is of Palestinian origin. Unlike many of its counterparts, the IAF still uses religious language to frame the conflict; in its 2007 electoral platform, the party affirmed that the conflict between the Israelis and the Palestinians is "theological and civilizational," and not one of borders or territories, as many groups now frame it. The IAF's so-called hawks, who tend to be of Palestinian origin, advocate even closer ties with Hamas. In Algeria and Tunisia, by contrast, Palestine ranks much lower as a priority for local Islamists.

From Shadow to Stage

Although most Islamist groups share a broadly similar ideology, their expression of it has differed depending on their unique domestic and regional constraints and whether the group happens to be included in government. When a group is not included in government, and the ruling elite is unpopular and generally pro-Western, Islamists are more likely to define themselves in opposition to the government's policies to garner support.

Taking a hard line against Israel, for example, has been an effective way for Islamists in opposition to criticize regimes that they see as beholden to Western interests and antidemocratic. For example, before Jordan's 2007 parliamentary elections, the IAF released a statement arguing that freedoms in Jordan had diminished after Amman signed a peace treaty with Israel in 1994. Their attempt to connect pro-Israel policy with a loss of freedom was convincing, because it happened to be true. In 1989, before the treaty, Jordan had held free elections for the first time in decades, and Islamists and nationalists won a majority of the seats. But with peace with Israel on the horizon in the early 1990s, the king grew increasingly more autocratic, dismissing the parliament and enacting a new electoral law designed to limit Islamists' power at the polls.

As political systems across the Middle East open up, Islamist groups such as the Egyptian Muslim Brotherhood and al Nahda will likely try to move from the opposition into coalition or unity governments. During the euphoria of the democratic transition, new political parties—perhaps including Salafi groups that are more hard-line than the older Islamist organizations—will proliferate. As the parties compete for votes, the incentives for Islamists to indulge in anti-American posturing to win the votes of the faithful may be greater.

Once actually in government, however, a new set of constraints and incentives will prevail. Rather than ruling, Islamists will likely be partners in coalition or national unity governments. Indeed, none of the Islamist groups in question even plans to run a full electoral slate; the Egyptian Muslim Brotherhood, for example, has explicitly stated that it will not seek a parliamentary majority. Islamists will be satisfied with dominating narrower parts of the government. They are likely to try to gain influence in ministries such as health and justice, while avoiding more sensitive portfolios, such as defense and foreign affairs.

Notably, the Middle East's generally secular security establishments have been hesitant in the past to hand over control of defense and foreign affairs to Islamists. Consider, for example, Necmettin Erbakan, the former leader of Turkey's Welfare Party, who was elected prime minister in 1996, making him the first-ever democratically elected Islamist head of government anywhere. Before coming to power, Erbakan had routinely denounced Israel and pledged to revisit existing military arrangements with the Jewish state. Yet once in office and faced with a powerful secular military and judicial establishment, he reversed course. During his one year in office, Erbakan presided over a deepening of relations with Israel and signed military agreements that allowed Israeli pilots to train in Turkish airspace. His government also set up joint naval drills with Israel in the Mediterranean.

Moreover, mainstream Islamist groups are surprisingly sensitive to international opinion. They remember the outcry that followed Islamist electoral victories in Algeria in 1991 and the Palestinian territories in 2006 and know that a great deal is at stake—hundreds of millions of dollars of Western assistance, loans from international financial institutions, and trade and investment. Islamists are well aware that getting tied up in controversial foreign policy efforts would cause the international community to withdraw support from the new democracies, thus undermining the prospects for a successful transition.

That is why, for example, in 2003, although Turkey's staunchly secular Republican People's Party overwhelmingly voted against supporting the U.S.-led war in Iraq, most of the ruling Islamist-leaning Justice and Development Party voted for it: the Bush administration exerted heavy pressure and offered billions of dollars in aid. And even Hamas—still regarded as the most radical of the mainstream Islamist groups—tempered its policies toward Israel after its 2006 electoral victory, saying it would accept the 1967 borders between Israel and the Palestinian territories.

For similar reasons, even before coming to power, some officials in the Egyptian and Jordanian Muslim Brotherhoods have explicitly stated that they would respect their countries' peace treaties with Israel (although others have threatened to leave the organization if it ever recognizes Israel). Despite the recent alarm, if Islamists join a coalition government in Egypt, moderation will likely prevail, and the country's 1979 Camp David peace agreement with Israel will be accepted, however reluctantly, as a fact of life.

Accidentally Aligned

Islamist and U.S. interests can come together almost incidentally as well. The Syrian Muslim Brotherhood—brutally repressed by President Hafez al-Assad in the 1980s—has long shared U.S. fears of a powerful Iranian-Syrian-Hezbollah axis.

Its opposition to the Syrian regime is well documented; the government made mere membership in the Brotherhood punishable by death. Like the United States, the group has often criticized Iran as a dangerous sectarian regime intent on projecting Shiite influence across the Arab world. Defying public opinion, Syrian Muslim Brotherhood figures even criticized Hezbollah for provoking Israel to attack Lebanon in 2006.

Similarly, the Lebanese Muslim Brotherhood, known as al-Gama'a al-Islamiyya, has opposed Syria and Hezbollah's role in Lebanon and allied itself with the pro-U.S. March 14 alliance. Elsewhere, mainstream Sunni Islamists, while applauding Iran's support of Palestinian resistance, have been careful to maintain their distance from the Shiite clerical regime, which they see as a deviation from traditional Islamic governance.

This is not to say that the United States has nothing to be concerned about. Democratic governments reflect popular sentiment, and in the Middle East, this sentiment is firmly against Israel and U.S. hegemony in the region. If the Arab-Israeli conflict persists or, worse, war breaks out, Middle Eastern governments—Islamist or not—will come under pressure to take a strong stand in support of Palestinian rights.

In mature and young democracies alike, such pressure can be difficult to resist. The case of Jordan in the early 1990s is worth considering. In 1991, the Muslim Brotherhood, which had won a plurality of the vote in the 1989 elections, gained control of five ministries, including education, health, justice, religious affairs, and social development, as part of a short-lived coalition government. (This marked the first time—and one of the only times—the Brotherhood has held executive power anywhere in the world.) When, in late 1990, the United States began preparing to take military action against Saddam Hussein in response to his invasion of Kuwait, Jordan's parliament condemned the Western aggression and intensified its pressure on King Hussein to oppose the U.S. intervention—which he did, despite the obvious international consequences. For its part, the Muslim Brotherhood—a staunch opponent of Saddam's secular regime—at first spoke out against the Iraqi aggression and expressed full support for Kuwait. But as Jordanians took to the streets to protest the war, the Brotherhood reversed course, riding the wave of anti-Americanism to even greater popularity.

The Islamist Experiment

So what does all of this mean for Tunisia, Egypt, and other countries facing popular upheaval? Like many others, Muslim Brotherhood activists in Egypt's Tahrir Square broke into applause when, on February 1, U.S. President Barack Obama called for a meaningful and immediate transition to genuine democracy in Egypt. Numerous Muslim Brotherhood members even said they wished the Obama administration would more forcefully push for Hosni Mubarak's ouster. Meanwhile, Sobhi Saleh, the only Brotherhood member on the country's newly established constitutional committee, told *The Wall Street Journal* that his organization was "much closer to the Turkish example," suggesting that the Brotherhood would evolve in a more pragmatic, moderate direction.

For their part, the Western media have tended to idealize the revolutions sweeping the Middle East. Tahrir Square was portrayed as a postideological utopia and Egyptians as pro-American liberals in the making. True, Egyptians (and Tunisians and Libyans) have wanted democracy for decades and showed during their revolution a knack for protest, peaceful expression, and self-governance.

But for all the changes of the past months, the United States remains a status quo power in a region undergoing radical change. Arabs across the region have been protesting an authoritarian order that the United States was, in their view, central in propagating. At their core, the revolutions sweeping the Middle East are about dignity and self-determination. For the protesters, dignity will mean playing a more active and independent role in the region. The moment of apparent convergence between Islamists and the United States during the revolutions does not mean that they will—or should—agree on all foreign policy questions in the future.

During the uprisings, the protesters have sensed that U.S. pressure on the autocratic regimes would prove critical to their success. Like any political group, Islamists are more cautious when they are vulnerable. But once Islamist groups solidify their position, they will have less patience for U.S. hectoring on Israel or the peace process. Already, they have started speaking more openly about their regional ambitions. On February 17, Mohammed Badie, the Egyptian Muslim Brotherhood's "general guide," stated that the revolution "must be a starting point for Egypt to take up its place in the world again, through recognizing the importance of our responsibilities toward our nations and defending them and their legitimate demands." Meanwhile, Hammam Said, the hard-line leader of the Jordanian Muslim Brotherhood put it more bluntly: "America must think seriously about changing its policy in the region, for people will no longer remain submissive to its dictates."

It will take a while for the new governments in Tunisia and Egypt to form cogent foreign policies, but Washington should start thinking ahead to mitigate the long-term risks. In the transition phase, the introduction of constitutional and institutional reforms to devolve power will be critical. Proportional electoral systems that encourage the formation of coalition governments may be better than majoritarian systems because they would make foreign policy formulation a process of negotiation among many parties, necessarily moderating the result. Already, most mainstream Islamists have significant overlapping interests with the United States, such as seeing al Qaeda dismantled, policing terrorism, improving living standards and economic conditions across the Arab world, and consolidating democratic governance.

By initiating regular, substantive dialogue with Islamist groups to work on areas of agreement and discuss key foreign policy concerns, the United States might discover more convergence of interests than it expects. Indeed, one of the few low-level dialogues the United States has had with an Islamist group—that with Morocco's Justice and Development Party—has been successful, leading the party to be relatively restrained in its criticism of the United States. At any rate, the revolutions have made the shortsightedness of current U.S.

policy—studiously avoiding formal contacts with the Muslim Brotherhood and like-minded groups—clear. The West knows much less about Egypt's most powerful opposition force than it should, and could.

The United States can take precautions—and it should—but this does not alter an unavoidable reality. Anti-Israel public opinion will remain a feature of Middle Eastern politics until a final and equitable peace treaty is struck. Whether that happens anytime soon will depend in part on Hamas. If Hamas finally joins a national unity government in the Palestinian territories that then negotiates an accommodation with Israel, this will effectively resolve other Islamist groups' Israel problem. Emboldened by the revolutions, however, Hamas is unlikely to be so cooperative.

For decades, Islamists postponed the difficult question of what they would do in power for a simple reason: the prospect of power seemed so remote. But the democratic wave sweeping the region has brought Islamists to the fore. What comes next may be the Arab world's first sustained experiment in Islamist

integration. Fortunately, for all their anti-Americanism, mainstream Islamists have a strong pragmatic streak. If they have not already, they will need to come to terms with regional realities. And, for its part, the United States—and the rest of the international community—will need to finally come to terms with Islamists.

Critical Thinking

1. How can the United States learn to live with political Islam?
2. How will the rise of the Islamists affect the Arab-Israeli peace process?
3. How will mainstream Islamists come to terms with regional realities?

SHADI HAMID is Director of Research at the Brookings Doha Center and a Fellow at the Saban Center for Middle East Policy at the Brookings Institution.

Arab Autocrats May Be Tottering, but the World's Tyrants Aren't All Quaking in Their Steel-Toed Boots

GRAEME ROBERTSON

Dictatorships Are All about the Dictator

Rarely, If Ever

In the first months after the Arab revolutions began, the world's televisions were filled with instantly iconic images of a crumbling old order: the Ben Ali clan's seaside villa on fire in Tunisia, Hosni Mubarak's stilted pre-resignation speeches in Egypt, Muammar al-Qaddafi's rambling, defiant diatribes from a bombed-out house in Libya. They were a reminder that one of the most enduring political archetypes of the 20th century, the ruthless dictator, had persisted into the 21st.

How persistent are they? The U.S. NGO Freedom House this year listed 47 countries as "not free"—and ruled over by a range of authoritarian dictators. Their numbers have certainly fallen from the last century, which brought us quite a list: Stalin, Hitler, Pol Pot, Pinochet, Khomeini, and a host of others now synonymous with murderous, repressive government. But invoking such tyrants, while a useful shorthand in international politics, unfortunately reinforces a troublesome myth: that dictatorships are really only about dictators.

The image of a single omnipotent leader ensconced in a mystery-shrouded Kremlin or a garishly ornate presidential palace took hold during the Cold War. But dictatorships don't just run themselves. Performing the basic tasks expected of even a despotic government—establishing order, levying taxes, controlling borders, and overseeing the economy—requires the cooperation of a whole range of players: businessmen, bureaucrats, leaders of labor unions and political parties, and, of course, specialists in coercion like the military and security forces. And keeping them all happy and working together isn't any easier for a dictator than it is for a democrat.

Different dictatorships have different tools for keeping things running. The communist regimes of the 20th century relied on mass-membership political parties to maintain discipline, as did some non-communist autocracies. The authoritarian system that ruled Mexico for 70 years—what Peruvian novelist and Nobel Prize winner Mario Vargas Llosa once called "the perfect dictatorship"—was orchestrated by the nationalist Institutional Revolutionary Party, a massive organization whose influence extended from the president's compound in Los Pinos to the local seats of government in every tiny village. Egypt's recently departed Hosni Mubarak was similarly buttressed for three decades by his National Democratic Party.

Then there's the junta option: a military-run dictatorship. These have advantages—discipline and order, and the capacity to repress opponents, among them—but also drawbacks, most notably a small natural constituency that doesn't extend far beyond the epaulet-wearing classes. The generals who ruled Brazil from 1964 to 1985 solved this problem by offering controlled access to a parliament in which economic elites and other powerful interests could voice their demands and participate in governance. However, this proved to be a difficult balancing act for a military that found it hard to manage elections and the pressures of a public increasingly dissatisfied with its record on the economy and human rights, and the generals ultimately headed back to their barracks.

At the extreme, some authoritarian governments do approximate the dictator-centric regimes of the popular imagination. Mobutu Sese Seko, who ruled Zaire (now the Democratic Republic of the Congo) for more than 30 years, and the Duvalier dynasty in Haiti are classic examples. Here, order is maintained largely by distributing patronage through personal or other networks: clans, ethnic groups, and the like. But paradoxically, these are the most unstable dictatorships. Keeping a government operating smoothly is difficult in the absence of a broad organizational or institutional base, and the whole system rises and falls with the fate of one man.

The Power of the Masses Can Topple Autocrats

Not by Itself

In 1989, people power swept across Eastern Europe. Mass strikes in Poland brought the country's communist rulers to the table to negotiate their way out of power. After hundreds of thousands of people gathered in Prague's Wenceslas Square, one of Eastern Europe's most brutal communist regimes crumbled and handed over power in Czechoslovakia to a motley crew of playwrights, priests, academics, and friends of Frank Zappa. In East Germany, teeming crowds simply walked out of communism's westernmost showpiece to seek asylum in, and then reunification with, the West. And people power, as Ferdinand Marcos found to his dismay in the Philippines in 1986, was not limited to communism or Eastern Europe.

But there was far more to the collapse of communism in Eastern Europe and autocratic regimes elsewhere than the impressive moral authority of crowds. As the Chinese showed in Tiananmen Square in 1989, capitulating to pro-democracy activists in the streets is hardly the only option. There have been plenty of other places where people power has failed disastrously in the face of a well-organized military response. In Hungary, the popular uprising of 1956 was brutally crushed by Red Army tanks. Burma's 2007 Saffron Revolution produced little more than life sentences for the country's dissident Buddhist monks; Iran's 2009 Green Revolution fell to the batons of the Basij two years later.

What distinguishes people power's successes from its failures? Size, of course, matters, but autocrats tend to fall to crowds only when they have first lost the support of key allies at home or abroad. The Egyptian military's decision to abandon Mubarak and protect the protesters gathered in Cairo's Tahrir Square, for instance, was crucial to the president's downfall this February.

How can demonstrators persuade regime stalwarts to jump ship? In Eastern Europe, the geopolitical sea change engineered by Soviet leader Mikhail Gorbachev and his allies obviously helped—but you can't exactly bring down the Iron Curtain again. Regimes with professionalized militaries separate from civilian authorities might be more vulnerable to defections; regimes based on highly ideological political parties are less likely to see their members break ranks. The credible threat of ending up at the war crimes tribunal in The Hague or having your Swiss bank accounts frozen can work wonders as well. But unfortunately for protesters, predicting authoritarian reactions to uprisings is far from an exact science—which is little consolation when your head is being cracked by a riot cop.

The More Brutal the Dictator, the Harder to Oust
Unfortunately, True

Reflecting on the French Revolution, Alexis de Tocqueville observed that the "most dangerous moment for a bad government is when it begins to reform." What was correct in the 18th century is, sadly, still true in the 21st. It is probably not a coincidence that the list of authoritarians removed by street protest in recent years is largely populated by rulers whose regimes allowed at least a modicum of political opposition. Tyrants like Serbia's Slobodan Milosevic, Georgia's Eduard Shevardnadze, Kyrgyzstan's Kurmanbek Bakiyev, and Egypt's Hosni Mubarak

may have been horrible in many ways, but their regimes were undoubtedly more permissive than those of many who have held onto power to this day.

De Tocqueville was right: The most dangerous moment for a bad government is when it begins to reform.

If this is true, why do any dictators allow opposition in the first place? And why don't they simply go the full Tiananmen at the first sign of protest? Because running a truly ghastly dictatorship is tougher today than it used to be.

Running a truly ghastly dictatorship is tougher today than it used to be.

The interconnections of 21st-century civilization make it harder to control information and far more difficult and costly to isolate a country from the outside world than it was in the 20th. The death of communism, meanwhile, has robbed leftists and right-wing strongmen alike of a cover story for their anti-democratic practices. In the past decade, rulers of countries such as Uzbekistan and Yemen have used the West's newfound fear of militant Islam—and the logistical necessities of the United States' post-9/11 wars—to similar ends, but they number far fewer than the ideological tyrants who divvied up whole continents under Cold War pretexts a generation ago.

The result is that in more and more places, rulers are compelled to justify their practices by adding a touch of "democracy." Vladimir Putin chose to stand down—though not far down—in 2008 rather than break Russia's constitutional ban against a third consecutive presidential term, and even the Chinese Communist Party allows some competitive elections at the town and village levels. There are exceptions to this trend, of course: Turkmenistan, North Korea, and Burma spring to mind. But such regimes feel increasingly like remnants of the late, unlamented 20th century, rather than harbingers of things to come.

Personality Cults Are Crazy
Crazy Like a Fox

Do North Koreans really believe that Kim Jong Il can change the weather based on his mood? Do Libyans think Qaddafi's Green Book is a brilliant work of political philosophy? Do Turkmen really think that the Ruhnama, the religious text authored by their late post-Soviet dictator—and self-styled spiritual leader—Saparmurat Niyazov, is a sacred scripture on par with the Quran and the Bible?

Probably not, but for the dictators' purposes, they don't have to. As political scientist Xavier Márquez has argued, personality cults are as strategic as they are narcissistic. Part of the problem that dictators' would-be opponents face is figuring out who else opposes the leader; compelling the populace to publicly embrace preposterous myths makes that harder still. Official mythmaking is also a means of enforcing discipline within the regime. Stalin—the progenitor of the modern dictator personality cult—understood well that his self-mythologizing would be too much for some of his old comrades to swallow; Lenin, after all, had specifically warned against it. But those who might have objected were swiftly dispatched. For the apparatchiks who remained, submitting to the cult was humiliating—and humiliation is a powerful tool for controlling potential rivals.

But personality cults, like most authoritarian technologies, have their drawbacks. The bigger the cult, the bigger the challenge of succession. Heirs to the throne really have just two options: dismantle the cult or go one better. The former is perilous; in the Soviet Union, Nikita Khrushchev's famous 1956 secret speech—the posthumous critique of Stalin that gave us the term "personality cult"—was, after all, secret, deemed too explosive for the Soviet public. Today, North Korea's ruling Kim family illustrates the hazards of the alternative: Now that the official newspapers have already reported that the current Dear Leader, Kim Jong Il, has mastered teleportation, what's his son and newly designated heir, Kim Jong Un, supposed to do for an encore?

Sometimes It Takes a Dictator to Get the Job Done
Actually, It Doesn't

The past two years have not done much to advertise the abilities of the Western democratic model of government to take large and painful but necessary actions. Frustrated over everything from a failure to balance budgets to an apparent inability to face up to the challenges of climate change, more than a few Westerners have turned their gaze wistfully toward the heavy-handed rule of the Communist Party in China. "One-party autocracy certainly has its drawbacks," the *New York Times'* Thomas Friedman wrote in a 2009 column. "But when it is led by a reasonably enlightened group of people, as China is today, it can also have great advantages." This March, Martin Wolf wrote in the *Financial Times* about how "China has achieved greatness."

This romanticizing of authoritarianism is not new; Augusto Pinochet's murderous regime in 1970s Chile was once cheered by many in Washington as an ugly but necessary instrument of economic reform. Yearning for a strong hand, however, is rooted in several fallacies. First, it conflates the failings of one form of democracy—in Friedman's case, the gridlocked American version—with an entire category of governance. Second, it assumes that dictators are more able than democrats to undertake unpopular but essential reforms. But unpopular decisions don't simply become popular because an autocrat is making them—just remember the late North Korean finance chief Pak Nam Gi, who ended up in front of a firing squad following the public backlash against the confiscatory currency reform the

Kim regime pushed through in 2009. In fact, authoritarians, lacking the legitimacy of popular election, may be even more fearful of upsetting the apple cart than democrats are. In Putin's Russia, for instance, leaders are unable to dial back the massive military expenditures that keep key constituencies quiet but that even their own ministers recognize to be unsustainable.

Besides, suggesting that dictators can force better policies upon their people assumes that a dictator is likely to know what those better policies are. The idea that there are technocratic solutions to most economic, social, and environmental problems might be comforting, but it is usually wrong. Such questions rarely have purely technical, apolitical answers—and only in a democracy can they be aired and answered in a way that, if not entirely fair, is at least broadly acceptable.

Digital Revolutions Are Bad News for Autocrats
Not Necessarily

New technologies—from the fax machine to the Internet to Facebook—have invariably been heralded as forces for upending dictatorial regimes. And of course, if cell phones and Twitter made no difference at all, then pro-democracy activists wouldn't use them. But the real test of technology is its ability to shift the balance of power between dictators and those trying to unseat them—to make revolutions more frequent, faster, or more successful. And though it's too early to know for sure, the arc of revolutions in 2011 doesn't look that different so far from the lower-tech upheavals of 1989, or, for that matter, 1848.

What makes a difference is how quickly authoritarians can work out how to counter a new innovation, or use it themselves. Sometimes this happens quickly: The barricades invented in Paris that made the revolutions of 1848 possible were briefly useful, but militaries soon figured out how to use cannons against them. Similarly, today's authoritarians are already learning how to use cell phones and Facebook to identify and track their opponents. In Iran, for instance, Facebook posts, tweets, and emails were used as evidence against protesters in the wake of the failed Green Revolution.

As it happens, some of the most enduring innovations have been the least technological. Mass protests, petitions, and general strikes, though now ubiquitous tactics, were at first ideas as novel as Twitter, and they have continued to play a crucial role in spreading democracy and civil rights around the world. It's a useful reminder that not all the new tools that matter come in a box or over a Wi-Fi connection.

Dictatorship Is on the Way Out
Not in Our Lifetime

The recent upheavals in the Middle East, though inspiring, have happened against a gloomy backdrop. Freedom House reported that in 2010, for the fifth year in a row, countries with improving political and civil rights were outnumbered by ones where they were getting worse—the longest such run since the organization started collecting data in 1972. Two decades after the Soviet Union's collapse, democracy may be robust in formerly communist Central Europe, Latin America, and even the Balkans, but most former Soviet states remain quite authoritarian. And though a few Arab countries are newly freed of their tyrants, they are still very much in transition. Being poor or corrupt, as Egypt and Tunisia are, does not rule out being democratic—think of India—but it does make it harder to build a stable democratic system.

Nevertheless, the Arab revolutions have offered a spark of hope, one that has clearly worried dictators in places as far off as Moscow and Beijing. The question is what the world's liberal democracies should do, or not do, to push things along. Survey the United States' long history of democracy-promotion successes and failures, and the inescapable lesson, even setting aside recent adventures in Iraq and Afghanistan, is that less is usually more. Providing aid—as the United States did to the opposition in places like Serbia, Ukraine, and Georgia—or simply setting an example are better means of toppling a dictator than actually doing the toppling.

But in either case, it's important to remember that powerful Western friends aren't everything. After all, the lesson of Tunisia and Egypt is that dictators sometimes fall despite, not because of, American help.

Critical Thinking

1. Why is the most dangerous moment for a very bad government when it begins to reform?

2. What is the relationship of personality cults to autocratic rule?

3. How can liberal democracies help to promote democracy around the world?

Reprinted in entirety by McGraw-Hill with permission from *Foreign Policy,* May/June 2011, pp. 36–39. www.foreignpolicy.com. © 2011 Washingtonpost.Newsweek Interactive, LLC.

After Gaddafi

How Does a Country Recover from 40 Years of Destruction by an Unchallenged Tyrant?

Dirk Vandewalle

Libya was on the brink of tectonic change as *News-week* went to press, with the regime of Muammar Gaddafi in a state of dramatic fulmination and ruin. As we watch that country become a patchwork of liberated zones and violently defended redoubts of the regime, we should be concerned about what a post-Gaddafi transition will mean, given the fact that the man has hollowed out the Libyan state, eviscerated all opposition in Libyan society, and, in effect, created a political tabula rasa on which a newly free people will now have to scratch out a future.

Libya will begin afresh after Gaddafi, in a comprehensive reconstruction of everything civic, political, legal, and moral that makes up a society and its government. But it remains dauntingly unclear where new leadership will come from. Perhaps some of the tribal chieftains will unite behind one of their own; perhaps some of the regime's overseas opposition figures will return, not so much as saviors but as masons who might lay a new foundation over the rubble. Or perhaps some younger Libyans, with overseas degrees under their belt, or young entrepreneurs, will rise to the occasion. There are even rumors that the heir to the country's monarchy may want to throw his hat in the ring.

Events in the eastern city of Benghazi, where the local population has spontaneously started to clean up the debris left by recent battles, give one hope that this traumatized country can still pull together while avoiding worse bloodshed. Getting Libya back on its feet will be an unwieldy, and probably fractious, process in which many scores are settled against those who once supported the Gaddafi regime. But the problem is, of course, that much like in the former Soviet satellites in Eastern Europe, virtually everyone at one point or another had to deal with the regime to survive. Unless political authority can be restored quickly, the sorting out of claims will undoubtedly be a bloody affair in light

of the pent-up frustration that is now being released. Libya has no fireproof options, and comparisons with Tunisia and Egypt—whose uprisings so energized the Libyan people—offer no road map to a Libyan civic reconstruction. Libya is truly a case apart. But how did Libya get to this state? How did its people come to be so shorn of political structure and experience? All answers, it would seem, begin and end with Gaddafi.

There was, for all the usual showmanship, something touching about Gaddafi's last visit to Italy a few months ago. Dressed in his singular combination of Arab cloak and Western-style white business suit, he had pinned a grainy black-and-white picture to his lapel—which Prime Minister Silvio Berlusconi studiously avoided looking at. The picture was of a shackled Omar al-Mukhtar, a Cyrenaican tribal leader and Libya's national hero, who was taken prisoner in 1931 after resisting the Italian colonial invasion for several years. He was hanged by the Italians before an assembly of Libyan prisoners—his cloak and glasses remain a central exhibit in Libya's national museum on Green Square in Tripoli.

It was Gaddafi's way of paying homage to a man he believed represents the ideal of a true Libyan: a tribal warrior, brave, uncompromising, willing to take on insurmountable odds. Gaddafi wanted to remind Berlusconi of the horrors of the Italian occupation—during which as much as half the population of Cyrenaica, Libya's eastern province, may have died. It was no surprise that Gaddafi, in his first speech after the uprising against him spread across Libya, invoked these same qualities to explain that he would fight to the end and was willing to die as a (self proclaimed) martyr.

History, particularly the disastrous Italian legacy in Libya, has been a constant element in Gaddafi's speeches since he took power in a bloodless coup in 1969. He was barely 27 years old at the time, inspired by Gamal Abdel

Nasser, neighboring Egypt's president, whose ideas of Arab nationalism and of the possibility of restoring glory to the Arab world, would fuel the first decade of Gaddafi's revolution. And while it was also clear from the start that he was unimpressed with the niceties of international diplomacy, no one could have predicted in 1969 how confrontational his path would be, both to his own citizens and to the world.

With a zeal that bordered on obsession, Gaddafi set about reforming Libya, trying to confect a tribal community writ large in a country that had been ruled since its independence in 1951 by a lackluster monarchy with close ties to the West. What Gaddafi wanted to institute was what he called a *Jamahiriya,* a political system that is run directly by tribesmen without the intermediation of state institutions—a sort of grand conclave akin, on a national scale, to the Afghan *loya jirga.* When it turned out that Libya, which was still a decentralized society in 1969, had little appetite for his centralizing political vision and remained largely indifferent to his proposals, the young idealist quickly turned activist.

In the Green Book, a set of slim volumes published in the mid-1970s that contain Gaddafi's political philosophy, a blueprint is offered for a dramatic restructuring of Libya's economy, politics, and society. In principle, Libya would become an experiment in democracy. In reality, it became a police state where every move of its citizens was carefully watched by a growing number of security apparatuses and revolutionary committees that owed loyalty directly to Gaddafi. And a darker element now started to appear in his speeches, harking back once more to the colonial period: the notion that a group of Libyan traitors inside Cyrenaica had made the capture of Omar al-Mukhtar and the defeat of the Libyan mujahedin possible. This notion of a fifth column that would allow Libya's enemies—the United States, Islamic radicals, and, conveniently, internal opposition—to infiltrate the *Jamahiriya* became a justification to destroy anyone who stood in Gaddafi's path. Even those who had left Libya and gone into exile were not safe, pursued by hit squads tasked to shoot down what Gaddafi called "stray dogs." In an ugly echo, those fighting in the streets against his revolution were also labeled dogs (and cockroaches)—fit only, Gaddafi thundered, for obliteration.

The impact on Libya of the Green Book's directives was calamitous. Having crushed all opposition by the mid-1970s, the regime systematically snuffed out any group that could potentially oppose it—any activity that could be construed as political opposition was punishable by death, which is one reason why a post Gaddafi Libya, unlike a post-Mubarak Egypt, can have no ready-made opposition in a position to fill the vacuum. Nowhere was

Gaddafi's inclination to root out opposition more tested than in his dance with the country's tribes. The tribes—the Warfalla, the Awlad Busayf, the Magharha, the Zuwaya, the Barasa, and the smallest of them all, the Gadafa, to which he belonged—offered a natural form of political affiliation, a tribal ethos that could be tapped into for support. And perhaps, in the aftermath of Gaddafi, they could serve as a nucleus around which to build a new political system.

For this quality—this institutional potential—Gaddafi feared they might coalesce into groups opposing his rule. So, during the first two decades after the 1969 coup, he tried to erase their influence, arguing that they were an archaic element in a modern society. But as their power proved enduring, and as the challenges to his rule grew in the 1980s and '90s, he gradually and willy-nilly brought them back into his fold. In a brilliant move that co-opted tribal elders, many of whom were also military commanders, he created the Social Leadership People's Committee, through which he could simultaneously control the tribes and segments of the country's military.

The late 1970s and '80s were the period of Gaddafi's rule imprinted most vividly in people's minds: the terrorist incidents; the confrontation with President Reagan, who bombed Libya in April 1986; and the growing isolation of Libya as international sanctions were imposed. Lockerbie was the logical endpoint for a regime that had lost all international legitimacy. In the aftermath of the bombing, Gaddafi attempted to rally Libyans into massive demonstrations, but they had become largely apathetic—neutered by their own predicament—and none rose to the call for another wave of political activism. The revolution was dying rapidly, and the Libyan ruler, surrounded, as all dictators are, by sycophants who ward off any contrary advice, simply went on as if nothing had changed.

But the sanctions bit fiercely, and while the regime still had the coercive power to put down any uprisings that took place in the 1990s, it became clear to Gaddafi's closest advisers that the potential for unrest had reached unprecedented levels. The way out was to come to an agreement with the West that would end (he sanctions, allow Libya to refurbish an aging oil infrastructure, and provide a safety valve by permitting Libyans to travel abroad once more.

When Libya announced its intent to renounce weapons of mass destruction in December 2003—after a long process of behind-the-scenes diplomacy initially spearheaded by Britain—Libyans hoped that it would mark the reintegration of their country with a world from which they had so long been shut out. Their hope came, in part, to be focused on Saif al-lslam, one of Gaddafi's sons who, as a self-styled reformer, pontificated on the need to open up Libya's political system. Always impeccably dressed in Western suits (in contrast to his father's outlandish wrap-arounds), Saif—with a shaved head and coruscating smile—embodied the new Libya everyone wanted to see.

Saif also became, almost overnight, the darling of the Western press, enthralled by the spectacle of a young modernist with a Ph.D. from the London School of Economics bringing reform to his father's foul dictatorship. It was seemingly lost on the pundits that this apostle of reform possessed no real credentials beyond being the son of Gaddafi and the author of a couple of execrable books on economic development. The pundits, crucially, also failed to detect the potential severity of the opposition to him inside Libya.

Libya's love affair with Saif al-Islam and his reformist ideas ended very abruptly after the uprising against the Gaddafi regime, when he went on Libyan national television in a last-ditch attempt to assuage the demonstrators. Under his father, Libyans had become inured to rambling, incoherent speeches that made Fidel Castro seem like Cicero. But even by those standards, the son's speech was surreal and Orwellian: surreal because Saif, much like his father, seemed unable to grasp what the revolt in Benghazi and Cyrenaica meant for the regime; also surreal because the suggestion he made to start a national dialogue in the wake of the extensive killing and violence was no longer even remotely realistic; and Orwellian because the once likely heir apparent to the Libyan regime used precisely the kind of apocalyptic language his father had used for 40 years to justify his rule.

Muammar Gaddafi never envisioned that his rule would come to an end. "The Revolution Everlasting" was one of the enduring slogans of his Libya, inscribed everywhere from bridges to water bottles. But the uprising in Benghazi was fueled with enough political energy and uncorked fury to spread across the eastern part of the country— a spontaneous defiance of a regime that had, for four decades, mismanaged the country's economy and humiliated its citizens. Within a few days the country was split in half, with eastern Cyrenaica and its main city Benghazi effectively independent—a demonstration of the kind of people's power Gaddafi had always advocated. Reality, in effect, outgrew the caricature. Undoubtedly the irony was lost on Gaddafi and his supporters, who fought on with rabid ferocity and utter disregard for life in Tripolitania, the northwestern part of the country.

As the confrontation between Gaddafi's old revolution and the new, popular one intensified, a question that had hovered over the country in recent years assumed great urgency: what would a post-Gaddafi Libya look like? For all those long years of his rule, Gaddafi had ruthlessly used a set of divide-and-rule policies that not only kept his opponents sundered from each other, but had also completely enfeebled any social or political institution in the country.

Beyond Gaddafi, there exists only a great political emptiness, a void that Libya somehow will need to fill. What will now be required of Libya will be something Gaddafi deliberately avoided for 42 years: the creation of a modem state where Libyans become true citizens, with all the rights and duties this entails. The obstacles will be formidable. After systematically destroying local society, after using the tribes to cancel each other out, after aborting methodically the emergence of a younger generation that could take over Libya's political life—all compounded by the general incoherence of the country's administrative and bureaucratic institutions—Gaddafi will have left a new Libya with severe and longstanding challenges. It is not yet clear where new leadership will come from, and how institutions can rapidly be built to prevent groups from pursuing their self-interest at the expense of what will remain a very weak state for a considerable amount of time.

A characteristic of many oil exporters is that since their revenues flow straight into state coffers, where they can be used without accountability by those in power, they produce regimes that pay scant attention to issues of political representation. Regimes can use oil revenues strategically to provide patronage that effectively keeps them in power. Nowhere has this been orchestrated better than in Libya under Gaddafi. After him, Libya's new rulers will need to find ways to bring together a large number of groups throughout society that until now have shared very little except the oil riches of the country and whose interests were deliberately played off against each other by the divide-and-rule tactics of the regime. Unfortunately, there are very few models for Libya to follow, except perhaps those outside the region. The likelihood of a number of disparate groups demanding greater accountability and representation as the country finds its way suggests the Balkans rather than neighboring Egypt or Tunisia as likely precursors for state building in Libya. And as with the Balkans, the international community could have a large and positive role to play by providing expertise and, temporarily, security forces.

For all his buffoonery, if Gaddafi understood one thing clearly about Libya, it was that its history could be a powerful force, and could be harnessed—as he did in his invocations of Omar al-Mukhtar and the resistance against colonialism—for a remorseless political project. That project, in fact, devastated Libya at every level. Whoever Libya's new rulers turn out to be, their challenge will be to learn from the lessons of its recent sad history, and then to move resolutely forward with compromise and wisdom—qualities that the Gaddafi regime came to lack so abjectly.

Critical Thinking

1. What was the impact of Gaddafi's Green Book on Libya?
2. Why did NATO intervene in Libya?
3. What was the relationship between the Italian occupation of Libya and Gaddafi's power?

Danger: Falling Tyrants

As dictatorships crumble across the Middle East, what happens if Arab democracy means the rise of radical Islamism? Does promoting American values while protecting American interests—most notably, containing Iran and preserving our access to oil—require the Obama administration to call for more democracy in one country while propping up the monarch next door? In a word, yes.

JEFFREY GOLDBERG

The Librairie al Kitab is a crowded bookstore on Avenue Habib Bourguiba, the main boulevard of Tunis, the once-drowsy capital of the previously lethargic North African republic of Tunisia. Today, of course, Tunisia is known as the cockpit of the Great Arab Revolt of 2011. During the reign of the now-deposed president, the debauched kleptocrat Zine el-Abidine Ben Ali—whose capitulation in January in the face of furious street protests triggered uprisings across the Arab world—the employees of the Librairie al Kitab kept a weather eye on the secret police. As luck would have it, the secret police kept their headquarters just across the street, in a whitewashed building housing the Interior Ministry. If the Librairie al Kitab had dared to carry a book containing even an insinuation of Ben Ali's perfidy, it would have been "goodbye to the bookstore," Kamel Hmaïdi, one of the employees, told me when I visited in late March. "We would go to jail," he said, pointing out the window toward the looming ministry building. "Just there."

Today, though, the display window of Librairie al Kitab is a shrine to the glories of free speech, given over in large part to works excoriating Ben Ali's regime and his family. The titles include *Le silence tunisien; La Tunisie de Ben Ali: La société contre le régime;* and *Ben Ali: Le ripou,* which translates to "Ben Ali: The Rotten One." Also: a number of books illuminating the transgressions of various other Arab dictators, and two books on the pitiable life and ghastly death of the Tunisian fruit-and-vegetable seller Mohamed Bouazizi, whose self-immolation, provoked by unending privation and the intolerable humiliation of a policewoman's face-slapping assault, set off the revolution. The store had sold several hundred copies of *Le ripou* since January, Hmaïdi said.

Some time earlier, in Damascus, I had visited a bookstore in search of a reasonably non-hagiographic biography of Syria's hereditary dictator, Bashar al-Assad. I could not find a single one, only book-length condemnations of Western treachery, and copies, in three languages, of *The Protocols of the Elders of Zion.* It was a suffocating little shop. The Librairie al Kitab, by contrast, is a joyous place: little else in the world could give a visitor from a free nation as much happiness as the sight of a bookstore in a once-totalitarian state selling, finally, the books it wants to sell, without fear of imprisonment and ruin.

It is true that Ben Ali, for all his now well-cataloged sins, was not a top-tier Middle Eastern tyrant. His secret police operated with a degree of refinement, at least in comparison with the thuggish practices of Hosni Mubarak's secret agents; and his cult of personality was underdeveloped, certainly when compared with that of his neighbor to the east, Muammar Qaddafi. But Ben Ali was a virtuoso thief, a ravenous looter of the state treasury. The new head of the Central Bank of Tunisia, Mustapha Kamel Nabli, brought back from self-imposed exile to help right his country's broken economy, described his work so far as an adventure in forensic accounting. "Anything they could steal, they stole," he told me. "I think it will take years for us to understand the extent of the corruption. The family of Ben Ali treated Tunisia as their personal property."

Ben Ali's wife, Leïla Trabelsi, an arriviste hairdresser who would dispatch government airplanes to Saint-Tropez for shopping trips, carried herself as if she were the uncrowned queen of Carthage. Her daughter and son-in-law maintained a mansion of extraordinary size and tackiness on the Mediterranean, whose grounds included a very Uday Hussein-esque enclosure for a pet tiger named Pasha. On at least one occasion they sent a government aircraft to Europe to fetch their favorite frozen yogurt. Before they fled to Saudi Arabia, Ben Ali and his wife reportedly looted the Central Bank, taking as much as a ton and a half of gold bullion. All told, the family may have stolen billions of dollars from the treasury. Thirty percent of young people in Tunisia are unemployed.

A former American ambassador to Tunisia, Robert Godec, told me recently that the family's brazenness infuriated ordinary Tunisians. (His acerbic observations about Ben Ali's family, made in cables later exposed by Wikileaks, are believed by many Tunisians to have provided a crucial spark to the anti-Ben Ali movement.) "My sense was that there was profound anger at Ben Ali, his wife, and many of their family members," Godec said. "When the family wanted a piece of land, the local municipality would tell the owner there was a problem with the title. Then the title would be suddenly transferred to an entity controlled by someone in the family. You can understand how people could become quite angered by this."

Godec, like other American officials, warned Ben Ali about his sinking reputation, but the president, he said, had no patience for reproachful Americans. And of course, American diplomats understood that there was utility for the United States in maintaining close relations with Ben Ali. Like Mubarak (and even the late-stage Qaddafi, who enjoyed a several-year period of détente with the U.S.), Ben Ali was a foe of Islamic radicalism, and his intelligence services provided not-inconsequential help in the American campaign against al-Qaeda. "Whenever we raised issues of political freedom or corruption, the answers were always the stock answers: 'We're threatened by the Islamist party, we're facing extremists, you Americans don't understand that we're your only true friends.'"

Of course, various American administrations, embracing the "realist" notion that stability in Middle East countries brought about through repression could be maintained in perpetuity, accepted Ben Ali's self-interested analysis of his centrality to the struggle against terrorism, even though Tunisia has the most secular of North Africa's populations, and one of the most highly educated.

It is this history of sometimes full-throated American support for Ben Ali's leadership that accounts for the brisk sales of many anti-American books, some of them screedish, in the Librairie al Kitab. "Those books are popular," Kamel Hmaïdi said. "The books about Ben Ali are more popular."

I cut short my shopping when I heard a commotion outside the store. Demonstrators were marching in the direction of the Interior Ministry. The only thing more thrilling to an American heart than the sight of a once-censored bookstore selling what it wants to sell is the sight of young citizens of a formerly authoritarian country gathering to demand their rights.

The Interior Ministry building was surrounded by coils of concertina wire; armored personnel carriers and Humvees were parked inside the wire, and soldiers patrolled the perimeter, though it was unclear whether the soldiers were meant to protect the ministry from the protesters, or the protesters from the remnants of the secret police. The demonstrators, marching up from the Casbah, which was the scene of much of the violence of the January revolution, were mainly young people in their teens or 20s, and they were vociferous, even volatile. I joined the crowd. Hundreds of these demonstrators pressed right up to the concertina wire. One of the signs, interestingly, carried the *Shahada,* the Muslim profession of faith. Another read in English, Our Freedom Can't Wait—Malcolm X.

I asked the demonstrators around me, "What are we protesting today?" A university student named Latifa said, "The Interior Ministry refuses to let women be photographed for their identity cards wearing the hijab," the traditional head covering religious Muslim women wear—and in some countries, are compelled by law to wear. "They force women to remove the hijab," she continued. "This is an insult to Islam. We are demanding that the ministry allow us to wear the hijab at all times."

Oh.

Just then I noticed that a number of the young men in the crowd were bearded, and that many, though certainly not all, of the women kept their hair covered. These protesters did not conform to the stereotype of the typical secular Tunisian, yet here they were, in numbers. "Our leaders will understand that Tunisia is a Muslim country," one of the demonstrators, an unemployed college graduate named Ezzedine Brahim, told me. Brahim described himself as a "youth supporter" of the main Tunisian Islamist party, Ennahda, which was recently made legal after a 20-year ban. He said he was convinced that Islamist-led parties would come to dominate Tunisian politics. My expression must have betrayed me, because he continued: "Yes, everyone says that Tunisia is a secular state, but what they don't understand is that underneath everything, we are Muslims. The power of Islam has been released." I asked him a bellwether question: Do you believe women should be made to wear the hijab in public? He answered, "We are striving for a society in which women understand that they are expected to be modest."

Would you compel them to wear the hijab, if you gained power? "There is no compulsion necessary," he said. "In a just society, men and women would understand the roles they are supposed to play."

Suddenly there was another commotion; a group of protesters had split off and seemed to be harassing a middle-aged man in a dark suit. "You are an enemy of Islam!" one of the protesters yelled, as the man scurried away. I did not know it yet, but this man was my next appointment. He was Abdelhamid Largueche, a well-known academic and proponent of secularism, as well as a member of the recently created Committee for the Protection of the Revolution, a body of 71 Tunisians meant to advise the government. When we met later at a nearby hotel, he said, "If those people take over this country, I'm finished."

"Will they take over?" I asked.

"This is hard to imagine. There is a silent majority of Tunisians who don't want these Islamists near them. Religion is a private affair here, more than most any other Arab nation," he said. "Our revolution is an exceptional revolution. It calls for modernity. But as we know from history, they do not need the support of the majority to get their way."

I asked Largueche whether he thought the demonstrators would get their way on the hijab. "Let us hope that this is not representative of the future," he said.

Later that day, I was on the phone with a Tunisian acquaintance who mentioned the creation of a local Salafist party. This surprised me. Salafists are ascetic medievalists—they are considerably more immoderate than the Muslim Brothers, who are themselves not archetypes of moderation. (The Saudi Arabian Wahhabi clerical elite are Salafists, for example.) Meeting a Salafist in ostensibly secular Tunis is like finding a Tea Party member on the Berkeley City Council. But these sorts of disorienting moments are becoming common in the Middle East.

In these early days of the Arab revolt, President Obama and his administration, already busy with other wars, are struggling for clarity. At a time when policy makers are wrestling with what might be called, in a nod to the president, the fierce incoherence of now, the administration has to bring about the marginalization of anti-modern, anti-Western, Islamist-oriented political parties, while not seeming to be working toward that goal. It has to continually decide which governments of the Middle East deserve the support of the United States and which deserve abandonment. This question points up a core contradiction of the moment: at the same time America is working for permanent and dramatic democratic change in certain republics of the Middle East, it has, 235 years after freeing itself from the rule of a despotic king, gone into the monarchy-maintenance business, propping up kings, emirs, and sheikhs who, though they may be as venal as Ben Ali, Qaddafi, and Mubarak, have oil the West needs, and who serve as a counterbalance to the greatest threat facing the U.S. in the Middle East, the Islamic Republic of Iran.

Creating an overarching doctrine suitable for the moment is an almost impossible task, particularly during a crisis that demands from American policy makers analytical humility, doctrinal plasticity, and a tolerance for contradiction. Analytical humility is called for because the trajectories of the Middle East's revolutions are still difficult to discern, and because it is not yet clear that tyranny is, in fact, in permanent eclipse. Doctrinal plasticity, which in a less value-neutral way could be called hypocrisy, is a necessity because, while it is true that President Obama, to the surprise of many, has shown himself to be more of a liberal interventionist than a cold-eyed realist, it is also true that America retains fixed, and vital, interests across the Middle East, interests that have already forced America to side with monarchs over the masses they rule. And a tolerance for contradiction is vital not only because America's democratically elected government is scrambling to keep monarchs on their thrones, but because people across the Middle East are embracing American ideals—freedom of speech, financial transparency, leaders who are chosen by the people and are accountable to them—while at the same time distancing themselves from America itself, and rejecting American assumptions about what freedom is meant to look like.

As it happened, the day before the pro-hijab demonstration, Hillary Clinton had made a flash visit to Tunis, in order to praise the revolution, meet with the leaders it had brought to power, and listen to rank-and-file citizens, including and especially women, whose place in the world is a main preoccupation of her tenure as secretary of state. Her most public event on this visit took place at a television studio outside Tunis, before an audience of mainly young people, few of whom, judging by appearance, seemed to be traditional Muslims. "One of the reasons I'm so optimistic about Tunisia is because women in Tunisia have played a role in the professional, public, economic life—every aspect of life in Tunisia—since independence," Clinton told the crowd, which, in the main, greeted her warmly. (Tunisia achieved independence from France in 1956.) "I have met with, by now, I would imagine, many, many hundreds of leaders everywhere. And it is so rare when a leader raises with me the pride he has in the women of his country. I often raise it with them. I'll say, 'You can't really be fully developed if you don't use the potential of 50 percent of your population.' The president, the prime minister, and the foreign minister all raised

it on their own. And they said, 'There will be no going back in the democratic revolution of Tunisia for our women; they will be full participants.' "

Clinton's campaign for women's enfranchisement is, of course, well known across the world, and even an inadequately briefed prime minister of a small nation (particularly one seeking an increase in American financial aid) would know to preempt Clinton's exhortations by touting his own deeply felt feminism. But it's also empirically true that Tunisia is an outlier in the Arab world on matters related to women. In Cairo, a woman's uncovered head has become something of an unusual sight, but in Tunisia it's the norm. Which is why the pro-hijab demonstration in Tunis gave me whiplash, and which is why I raised it with Clinton when I saw her at her State Department office a few weeks ago. She discussed the issue of hijab-wearing, and all that it signifies, in a measured way. Her main worry, she said, is legislation that would mandate the wearing of the hijab.

"What I want to see is the freedom to choose," Clinton said. "My model would be our own country. Women are able to dress as they choose in accordance with their own personal desires, and I would like to see this available for women everywhere, so that there is no compulsion." The Obama administration has maintained a flexible, even positive, attitude about the hijab (unlike the French government, which sees covered women, and particularly fully veiled women, as a threat to the country's national security, and to its cultural identity). In a speech delivered in Cairo in 2009, President Obama, in the course of attempting to reset America's relations with the Muslim world, even boasted of America's tolerance for the hijab:

Freedom in America is indivisible from the freedom to practice one's religion. That is why there is a mosque in every state of our union . . . That is why the U.S. government has gone to court to protect the right of women and girls to wear the hijab, and to punish those who would deny it.

This particular assertion in the Cairo speech was not met with joy by some Middle Eastern women's-rights activists I spoke with at the time, women who believed that the U.S. should do nothing to celebrate the hijab—something that many Muslim women hope to shed when they come to America.

When Clinton talked to me about the hijab, however, she made clear that an attempt to pressure women in any way to cover themselves—anything on "the continuum of compulsion"— would represent a red line for her. "When people start to say that there are certain things that women should not be permitted to do, and the only way we can stop them is pass laws, like you can't drive in Saudi Arabia, or you can't vote . . . that's a red line, and that infringes on the rights of women. Therefore I am against it. Any society in the 21st century that is looking toward modernization, and certainly [any society] claiming to be democratic, needs to protect the right to make these choices."

This was a blunt message, delivered, quite obviously, in the direction of conservative religious forces; the secretary of state, correctly, sees the forced imposition of the hijab as a proxy for the ascendance of fundamentalist Islamism. So I asked her about the rise of the Muslim Brotherhood, and of parties espousing ideologies similar to that of the Brotherhood.

As winter turned to spring, it was becoming clear in Egypt that the Brotherhood, whose strength was downplayed by most Western commentators during the early days of the revolt in Egypt, was emerging as a power broker of surpassing importance.

The Muslim Brotherhood is a global organization with autonomous branches, some more radical than others (the terrorist group Hamas, in Gaza, is a Muslim Brotherhood offshoot, for instance). There is a diversity of opinion, but those who affiliate with the Brotherhood believe, generally, in the primacy of Muslim law; in the supremacy of Islam; and in the idea that women and men should play their traditional roles in society. They also tend to believe that the West (and Israel, the country they consider a Western outpost in the Middle East) seeks, through conspiracy, to undermine their way of life. American analysts are spending a great deal of time studying the Brotherhood in Egypt and elsewhere (the Brotherhood's Jordan branch, the Islamic Action Front, is that country's most potent opposition political force), and there is some debate, in and out of administration circles, about the true views of the organization, especially in Egypt. Since the Arab revolution began, the Muslim Brotherhood has shown signs of fracturing along ideological lines, but its leaders have proved somewhat adept at playing politics, particularly that aspect of politics in which hard questions are ducked. I recently had a conversation with Mohamed Morsy, one of the Brotherhood's senior leaders, in which he refused, to an almost comical degree, to grapple with two simple questions: Could the Brotherhood support a Christian for the Egyptian presidency? Could it support a woman? (The Brotherhood's 2007 draft party platform, from which the organization is now trying to distance itself, makes clear that a Christian could not serve as president of Egypt.)

"Which Christian?" Morsy responded when I first asked.

I explained: not a particular Christian, but any Christian.

"There are no Christians running for president," he said.

Yes, I know. It's a theoretical question.

"This is a nonsense question," he said. So I asked him if the Brotherhood had ideological objections to a woman's running for president.

"Which woman?" he asked.

It is worth remembering, particularly at a time when the Muslim Brotherhood is attempting to soften its image, that the group's essential platform remains unchanged. The Muslim Brotherhood's avowed creed is "Allah is our objective. The Prophet is our leader. Quran is our law. Jihad is our way. Dying in the way of Allah is our highest hope."

I asked Clinton whether she worried about the rise of the Muslim Brotherhood's ideology, particularly as it related to the future of women in the Arab Middle East. "Well, I think we don't know enough yet to understand exactly what they're morphing into. For me, the jury is out," she said. "There are some Islamist elements that are coming to the surface in Egypt that I think, on just the face of it—they're coming out of jails, coming out of the shadows—are inimical to a democracy, to the kind of freedom of expression, freedom of assembly, freedom of conscience that was the aspiration of Tahrir Square."

This was, if anything, an even more measured answer than one expects from Clinton. But in this fluid period, when there is a reasonable chance—not a large one, but still a reasonable one—that the Muslim Brotherhood might splinter, or perhaps even find itself in vigorous competition with more-secular-minded parties, Clinton and Obama recognize that the Brotherhood could turn harsh American criticism into a campaign advantage, particularly among more rural, poorly educated, and traditionalist voters.

Over the past several months, Obama administration officials have spoken more about the establishment of universal red lines (parties espousing violence, for instance, will meet with Obama's disapproval), and about aiding all parties in their attempts to master the democratic process, than they have about the ideological dangers posed by the rise of Islamist-oriented parties. "Our interest in these transitions is to ensure that a broad, diverse set of parties are capable of organizing and mounting competent campaigns," Benjamin J. Rhodes, a deputy national-security adviser, told me, adding that the Obama administration does not want anxiety about the rise of Muslim parties to unduly influence its policies. "The president's view is that we can't let ourselves be driven by fear of change, particularly because change is coming." He went on, "This is not fatalism. You have to take a step back and acknowledge that it is a good thing when people are demanding the same rights that we ourselves believe in. Indigenous democratic movements are what the U.S. wants, even if they create short-term challenges and complexities." Another administration official, speaking on condition of anonymity, put it more bluntly: "Do you really think that if we announced ourselves as the enemy of the Muslim Brotherhood that this is going to do anything except help the Muslim Brotherhood?"

En route to Tunis, I had stopped off in Jordan, where I paid a visit to the royal palace. Senators John McCain and Joseph Lieberman had passed through a few weeks earlier, to see King Abdullah II. Their visit, I quickly learned, was simultaneously a source of bemusement and irritation for the Jordanian government. The two senators, of course, advocate an assertive foreign policy, and both are associated with neoconservative striving for robust and quick democratization of the Middle East. "They came in and said that Jordan should open up its political space for more parties, and be more aggressive about democratization within the parameters of a constitutional monarchy," a senior Jordanian official told me. "And then they said, 'But whatever you do, don't allow the Muslim Brotherhood to gain more power.' So they want us to be open and closed at the same time."

King Abdullah is in a tough spot these days. His popularity is lower than at any other point in his 12-year reign, as discontent—mainly generated by allegations of corruption in his government—takes hold. Jordan, like most Middle East countries, has been a *mukhabarat,* or secret-police, state, but it has always created some space for politics and dissent. The sort of dissent I heard in Jordan on this last trip was unlike anything I had heard before. One Friday morning, I visited Zarqa, a city not far from the capital, Amman. It is a rough, poor place; its most famous son is the arch-terrorist Abu Musab al-Zarqawi.

The Islamic Action Front, the Muslim Brotherhood's local political party, was holding a rally after prayers. One of its leaders, Zaki Bani Rsheid, stood on the back of a flatbed truck parked on a narrow street as hundreds of men gathered to listen. All along the rooftops stood men from Jordanian intelligence, the Mukhabarat, ostentatiously filming the proceedings. "It is not your job to protect the corruption of the regime!," Bani Rsheid said, looking to the roofs. "Remember, what is acceptable today will not be acceptable later! Today we are asking for the reform of the regime. Tomorrow we will be asking you for something else!" A threat like that, made aloud, in the face of the secret police, is a new and fraught development in Jordan. "An organization dedicating itself to gaining power through violence has to be stopped," McCain told me. He noted that the Muslim Brothers in Jordan have publicly sworn off violence, but he said he doubts their sincerity. "Everybody says that the Muslim Brotherhood is being deceiving in adopting a much more moderate image." The king, McCain said, had taken his point. "He got it. He's smart."

The Jordanian monarchy represents the sort of regime the United States finds itself defending. It is not the most difficult regime in the Middle East to defend—throughout the early stages of the Arab revolt, Bahrain's royal family, engaged in the often violent suppression of the country's Shia majority, was the problem child of the American monarchy-maintenance program—but Jordan is still governed in a manner inconsistent with the spirit of Tahrir Square, a spirit appropriated by President Obama and Secretary Clinton whenever they speak of the Arab desire for democracy.

Hillary Clinton, as one would expect, doesn't think much of the charge that the administration is engaged in a sustained campaign of hypocrisy. As the administration's point person on the entire set of issues roiling the Middle East, she is perceived in dramatically divergent ways. In Cairo, many democracy activists believe she was overly coddling of Mubarak; at the same time, she is the object of an intense lobbying campaign by leaders of the Arab states of the Persian Gulf, who fear, according to ambassadors and foreign ministers I have spoken with, that she has become some sort of moralizing neoconservative. One Gulf official I spoke with asked me earnestly if Paul Wolfowitz, the leading neoconservative theoretician of the previous presidency, was now serving as her adviser. I mentioned to Clinton that she is seen in some quarters as a kind of wild-eyed Wolfowitz. "Oh, no, not that!" she said. "Call me wild-eyed, but not that."

When I asked her how she squares the inconsistency—working to build democracies in some countries while keeping incompetent monarchs on their thrones in others—she rejected its very existence.

"I wouldn't accept the premise," she said. "I think we believe in the same values and principles, full stop. We believe that countries should empower their people. We believe that people should have certain universal rights. We believe that there are certain economic systems that work better for the vast majority of people than other systems. I think we're very consistent."

The U.S. needs to work with the monarchies to help them stay ahead of the unrest brewing in their kingdoms, Clinton said, but even if they don't take American advice—and she was adamant (and the record does, in fact, show) that Hosni Mubarak was offered a great deal of advice that he consistently ignored—the administration will live with what she refuses to see as inconsistencies.

"We live in the real world, and there are lots of countries that we deal with because we have interests in common, we have certain security issues that we are both looking at," she said. "Obviously, in the Middle East, Iran is an overwhelming challenge to all of us. We do business with a lot of countries whose economic systems or political systems are not ones we would design or choose to live under. We encourage consistently, both publicly and privately, reform and the protection of human rights. But we don't walk away from dealing with China because we think they have a deplorable human-rights record. We don't walk away from Saudi Arabia."

I noted that the Chinese seem frightened by the possibility that the forces unleashed by the suicide of a Tunisian peddler could reach Tiananmen Square. "They're worried," she said. "They're trying to stop history, which is a fool's errand. They cannot do it, but they're going to hold it off as long as possible."

If it is true, to cite one of President Obama's favorite Martin Luther King Jr. quotations, that the moral arc of the universe is long, but it bends toward justice; and if it is true that history will sooner or later catch up with the Chinese Communist Party, then why isn't it also true that history will soon catch up with a collection of superannuated desert monarchs? The answer came, elliptically, when I asked Clinton whether she would be sad to see the disappearance of the regime of Syrian President Bashar al-Assad. Not long ago, Clinton had been criticized for suggesting that Assad himself might be a "reformer," though she acknowledges that Assad is anti-American in some very consequential ways (and not only in his service to Iran). "Depends on what replaces it," she said, her answer combining disdain for Assad with a real-politik understanding that some things out there are, despite the promise of the Arab Spring, potentially more dangerous to U.S. interests than certain dictatorships. For people who have known only dictatorship and who yearn for democracy, this is a hard swallow.

Striking this balance—understanding when the United States absolutely must support leaders it dislikes intensely—will remain the key foreign-policy challenge for the Obama administration, and perhaps its successors, in the coming years. Managing Saudi Arabia's pre-modern royal family alone is a herculean task. But the United States will ultimately fail if it forgets its fundamental responsibility to people who are living under the boot of repression, and seek the freedoms Americans already have.

On my most recent visit to the Middle East, I traveled from country to country asking essentially the same question of many different people: How could the United States best serve the interests of democracy and stability? Not a single person I spoke with believed that America was in decline; to a person, everyone agreed that American power was potent. Salafists believed it was potent and malevolent; secular democracy activists believed it could be marshaled benevolently. The most eloquent answer came from Ali Salem, a free-thinking Egyptian playwright whose plays and essays were periodically banned by the ancien régime. I met Salem in a café in the Mohandessin neighborhood of Cairo, on the west bank of the Nile. While we talked, various cartoonists, columnists, and Libyan resistance leaders joined us. Salem is an unusual figure, even among democracy activists in Cairo—he is frankly Americaphilic, in part because he was brought to the United States as a young man through a State Department visitors program. He was bursting with ideas about the roles the U.S. could play in the Middle East—in education, in agriculture, but mainly in teaching leaders about how power corrupts, and about building political systems that resist that corruption. "I believe you have a great thing," he said. "The great thing is, you have a president

for four or eight years, and then out. If you are an enemy of the minister of culture and he bans your plays, you will be banned for only four or eight years. The beautiful idea is to limit the damage one human being can do to another. It's a beautiful idea. Do you know how beautiful it is?"

Critical Thinking

1. What happens if Arab democracy means the rise of radical Islamism?
2. How do the Arab revolutions affect the U.S. policy of containing Iran?
3. What has been the role of the Muslim Brotherhood in the Arab revolutions?

From *The Atlantic*, June 2011, pp. 46–54. Copyright © 2011 by The Atlantic Media Co. Reprinted by permission of Tribune Media Services. www.theatlantic.com

Bangladesh's Quest for Political Justice

"Stints in power have been occasions to wipe out opponents, justice has meant vengeance, and egregious abuses have been legalized through immunity."

JALAL ALAMGIR

B rimming with optimism and displaying its resilience, Bangladesh at the end of 2008 launched democracy anew. Colorful festoons lined town and village streets. Neighborhoods buzzed with the rallies of candidates and the frantic chatter of young voters. Television screens in crowded bazaars broadcast the din of 24-hour news channels. Millions of text messages relayed election updates in a country now networked densely with cell towers. The general aspiration, it seemed, was to overcome Bangladesh's troubled political past once and for all with the casting of ballots.

When the Awami League (AL) assumed office in January 2009, voted in by a landslide, it first had to temper the high expectations of jubilant Bangladeshis who had suffered under the former regime. In the previous two years a military junta, fronted by a "caretaker government" in civilian garb, had ruled under a state of emergency. All fundamental rights were suspended, and the repressive forces enjoyed, by official decree, immunity for their actions.

The authorities arrested half a million citizens, holding many without charges. Torture and extrajudicial killings were rampant. The intelligence services monitored academics and the media. By the time the elected government took over, hundreds of political leaders had been put away for lengthy prison terms, typically on corruption convictions handed down by special tribunals.

Bangladeshis expected not just political deliverance but economic deliverance as well. Food price inflation had reached its highest level in decades. The poor were hurting badly, but could not protest under the military-backed regime without risking physical harm. Commerce had decelerated: Traders were wary of arbitrary repression by the regime's dreaded Rapid Action Battalion and an Anti-Corruption Commission headed by a former army chief. Electricity, the mainstay of both industrial production and agricultural irrigation, was in short supply.

In early 2009 Bangladesh's economy faced threats stemming from the global recession, and the new government braced for two related blows. First, remittances from migrant workers were expected to shrink because many construction and labor-intensive projects had come to a standstill in the Middle East, a region that in 2008 supplied 60 percent of the $9 billion that Bangladeshi workers sent home. The second blow was expected in exports. Credit had dried up in America and Europe, reducing in those regions the consumer funds available to be spent on Bangladesh's exports, including its $12 billion worth of garment shipments.

The threat of militant Islamism also remained a worry. Many Islamist organizations are intimate with the Bangladesh Nationalist Party (BNP), a large right-wing political organization. In the first half of the 2000s, the BNP and its main ally, the Islamist party Jamaat-e-Islami, had orchestrated or condoned many gruesome attacks on AL leaders and progressive activists. By 2006, the exploits of the BNP-Jamaat alliance had pushed a fairly moderate Muslim democracy toward what some observers called "Pakistanization"—a violent, unpredictable, fractured political order.

The instability that developed during that time, along with rampant corruption, explained why loud cheers had greeted the military's power grab in 2007. And yet Jamaat was the only major political faction that was left largely untouched by the two-year military interlude. The continuing partnership between religious fundamentalists and right-wing nationalists, combined with the belligerence typical of Bangladeshi politics, was certain to make governance difficult for the AL, a center-left party that advocates religious freedom and socially progressive policies.

So Far, So Good

In spite of the challenges, the "Grand Alliance" government led by the AL has made a decent showing thus far. Remarkably, it has been able to retain the level of popular support that won it victory in the elections. All major surveys conducted recently show positive ratings. Two-thirds of citizens are either satisfied or very satisfied with the new government's performance. A similar proportion believes the country is headed in the right direction. As one analyst has noted, this share is higher than the percentage of votes that the alliance received in the elections, so apparently the governing coalition has been able to convert some skeptics into supporters.

The Grand Alliance proposed a "Charter for Change" with specific policy targets, the foremost of which was to curb food price hikes. Overall inflation fell from a 10 percent annual rate in July 2008 to around 5 percent by October 2009, in part because of falling global commodity prices, but also because of improved local food production. Diplomatic initiatives in the Middle East have helped reduce the layoffs of migrant workers. In fact, remittances have increased, compensating for losses in garment exports. And three government stimulus packages, including incentives for exporters, have cushioned the global recession's impact. Bangladesh expects GDP to grow by 5.5 to 6 percent this year.

The political development that surprised everyone most was the composition of Prime Minister Sheikh Hasina's cabinet: She appointed many young newcomers in place of party veterans. This was a gamble. Hasina earned kudos by recognizing the public's desire for change and its distaste for the same crop of politicians who were seen to have locked the country into endless feuds. On the other hand, the inexperience of the new ministers became quickly apparent, especially when it came to leading a bureaucracy politicized by years of authoritarian rule, interference, and irregularities in recruitment and promotions.

The government, animated by fresh thinking and a burst of populism, has taken up many expensive initiatives, from planning new airports, bridges, and highways, to extending subsidies and safety nets, to reforming the education system, to increasing pay across the state sector. But bureaucratic implementation has been slow and uncertain. In the first half of the 2009–10 fiscal year, spending in seven of the ten largest ministries was far behind budgetary allocations.

The government's strongest performance has been in agriculture, the sector that dominates rural Bangladesh, where more than two-thirds of the population resides. Hasina's government has extended credit and subsidies. It has also ensured increased supplies of raw materials, and, very importantly, diesel fuel and electricity for irrigation, in spite of a nationwide power shortage. Food grain production in 2009 exceeded that of previous years, and is expected to continue a record upward trend.

As befits the agenda of a center-left party the government has also given considerable attention to education and health. In fact, Bangladesh's big strides in human development are mostly due to the state's extensive presence and programs in these sectors. The government's key plan here is to increase school retention rates. To that end, it has printed 190 million textbooks to be provided free of cost to all primary and secondary students.

Over the past year, efforts on behalf of the poor have offered the clearest demonstration of the difference between an insulated authoritarian regime and a responsive democratic government. They also have helped cement the AL-led government's broad political support.

History of Violence

The Grand Alliance's biggest challenge, however, is the pursuit of political justice. Grave transgressions of human rights have plagued Bangladesh from the moment of its violent birth. In 1971, the Pakistani army and its collaborators committed a genocide in which at least a million died. Hundreds were assassinated in coups and counter-coups after independence. Thousands have been killed and maimed in political violence. And since the late 1990s Islamist terrorism has been added to the mix.

This state of affairs has continued because political crime in Bangladesh is rarely prosecuted successfully. The perpetrators, regardless of the regime, almost always find powerful interests to protect them. In the absence of political commitment and legal enforcement, rage, resentment, dismay, and vendettas have accumulated in the political culture. To control the consequent violence, the state continues to strengthen its repressive apparatus, which commits further crimes with impunity—and the cycle goes on.

Rage, resentment, dismay, and vendettas have accumulated in the political culture.

Unlike other parties, the Grand Alliance has pledged to prosecute political crimes as a matter of national policy. The first step was to restart the investigation into a deadly assault on an AL rally in August 2004. The attackers had positioned themselves in high-rise buildings in downtown Dhaka. When an ensemble of AL leaders came into sight, they hurled grenades and fired bullets into the crowd. Twenty-two were killed, including senior party members. Hundreds were injured.

The audacity of the attack, the weaponry used, and the ease with which the attackers disappeared all pointed to complicity by the BNP-Jamaat government in power at that time. But the original investigation slowed, finally yielding nothing of substance. In reopening the case, detectives have begun to uncover a full-scale criminal conspiracy by some BNP-Jamaat bosses. The plotters recruited extremists from banned organizations and helped to finance and provision them. They worked under the aegis of the office of Prime Minister Khaleda Zia's son, with logistical support from Bangladeshi and even Pakistani intelligence agencies.

After crimes such as these were carried out, the political sponsors typically would step in to thwart any investigation. The conspirators worked with a wide nexus of players who had various motivations—money, political supremacy, religious bigotry, business rivalry, international intrigue. They arrayed an impressive pool of resources, too potent for local law enforcement to obstruct—except once, in 2004, when an inquisitive junior officer chanced on a suspicious shipment in the port of Chittagong. It turned out to be 10 truckloads' worth of arms and ammunition, headed for distribution among insurgents in India's northeast and Islamist extremists in Bangladesh. Most such transactions were never discovered.

Despite public consternation, neither the grenade attack nor the arms haul was prosecuted successfully. With such prominent political crimes neglected, it was no accident that a surge in terrorism marked the 2001–2006 tenure in power of the BNP-Jamaat coalition. By contrast, in the 1990s, many individuals, from local academics to US President Bill Clinton, liked to praise Bangladesh—the third-largest Muslim-majority country in the world—as a virtuous marriage between democracy and Islamic identity. The country's first major incident of Islamist terrorism occurred in 1999, when a bomb killed 15 at a concert in a provincial town. By 2005, an average of 40 significant attacks was taking place annually, with the targets including cultural events, movie theaters, courts and government offices, minorities, progressive writers and journalists, and opposition politicians.

Among these, the only major case to be investigated to completion was a series of bombings by Jamaat-ul-Mujahideen (JMB), a radical organization coordinated by a militant named Siddiqui Islam, who was believed to have fought alongside Osama bin Laden during his mujahideen days in Afghanistan. Intense local and international pressure forced the government to apprehend JMB leaders and put them on trial. Until that point, the government had even insisted that Siddiqui Islam was a figment

dreamed up by the media, though dozens of JMB attacks claimed 64 lives between 2000 and 2005.

The Abusive Caretaker

Coming on the heels of the discredited BNP-Jamaat administration, the 2007–08 caretaker government adopted a tough antiterrorism stance. It executed Siddiqui Islam and five associates. But the *Daily Star,* the country's largest English-language newspaper, summarized public qualms by noting that "a veil of mystery" still clouded the case: The militants were never allowed to reveal publicly the names of their political kingpins.

The caretakers were embroiled in crimes of their own. The Directorate General of Forces Intelligence, an intelligence agency that, according to the International Crisis Group, was "the driving force behind military rule," operated secret torture chambers in Dhaka. Among many atrocities, the case of Choles Ritchil especially shocked the pro-democracy community. Ritchil was an indigenous activist who protested the setup of a commercial "eco-park" in an area inhabited by the Garo people, an indigenous minority. Infuriated, an army major and his accomplices arrested Ritchil, who was then reportedly dragged to an army camp, tied down, and tortured to death. His captors plucked out his eyes, smashed his testicles, pulled out his fingernails and toenails, burned his back, cut his flesh, and then dumped the corpse at a local church.

The army's aversion to indigenous peoples is well known in Bangladesh. The military committed many atrocities in the Chittagong Hill Tracts area while it fought a decades-long insurgency by the local Pahari (hill) peoples, who resisted being colonized by Bengali settlers. But that was thought to be a thing of the past. Ritchil's gruesome murder brought it to the fore. Yet the government did not bring the perpetrators to justice in any of the torture cases, including Ritchil's.

The agency responsible for the largest number of civilian killings is the Rapid Action Battalion (RAB), a virtually unaccountable paramilitary force that the BNP-Jamaat government created in 2004 to clamp down on violence. Conveniently, every successive administration, including the AL-led Grand Alliance, has used this force on a regular basis. Since its inception, the RAB has killed over 1,200 citizens. The government routinely claims that the victims were caught in "crossfire," as though they were not targeted. Political observers in the country know otherwise. According to an investigation by Human Rights Watch, "a large proportion of these killings are in fact extrajudicial executions carried out after the victim had been taken into custody."

Thus, a long litany of crimes, politically sanctioned and protected, burdens Bangladesh's democracy. This is what the AL needs to confront, since it is the only large party whose values are founded on secular human rights. The new government's declarations of intent are a welcome step. But the coalition has not matched rhetoric with committed action. Its promise to eliminate extrajudicial killings has so far proved hollow. In 2009, the citizenry suffered more than 140 extrajudicial killings at the hands of government agents.

Toward the Rule of Law

In this troubled setting, two trials—one completed, one planned—could redefine the discourse and practice of political justice and human rights in Bangladesh.

The first, completed trial was for the assassination of Sheikh Mujibur Rahman and his family. A mercurial personality known affectionately as Bangabandhu (Friend of Bengal) and as Sheikh Mujib, he led the country's independence movement in 1971 and became its first prime minister. The movement for independence established him among the Third World's dissident vanguard, earning him the respect of Salvador Allende and Fidel Castro, as well as the animosity of Henry Kissinger.

But Mujib struggled to balance multiple goals: rebuilding an economy destroyed by war and then battered by cyclones; ensuring security in a country that had been liberated by millions of armed guerillas; nurturing effective foreign relations under cold war realpolitik; and crafting the identity of a Muslim nation that had just rejected, through violent tenacity, the idea that Islam could hold together otherwise different cultures.

Mujib in 1975 opted to replace the vagaries of democracy with one-party authoritarianism. A few months later, in August 1975, he was gunned down by a group of army officers. They also killed most of his family that night, including his 9-year-old son. Only two lived: his daughters Sheikh Hasina and Sheikh Rehana-and only because they happened to be in Germany.

Incredibly, the men who usurped power rewarded Mujib's assassins with officially legislated immunity from prosecution. General Zia ur-Rahman, who rose to power through a series of coups and eventually founded the BNP, not only extended the indemnity through a parliamentary act, but also appointed the masterminds to diplomatic posts abroad. This came to symbolize all that was wrong with political justice in Bangladesh. If the assassins of the country's founding father could be protected and pampered in this way, no one was safe. With impunity instituted as the norm, Islamist fundamentalists positioned themselves as a political force, with the military

dictators General Zia and General Hussein Muhammad Ershad as their patrons.

Bangladesh became a multiparty democracy in 1991, and the AL won elections in 1996, with Sheikh Hasina as prime minister. Her government repealed the indemnity act and initiated the trial of Mujib's assassins. Representatives of the BNP and Jamaat-e-Islami abstained from voting for the repeal. The next elections were won by the BNP-Jamaat coalition—which suspended the trial. Not a single hearing was held during its tenure. The trial resumed in 2009 when the AL returned to power. After all appeals were exhausted, five of the assassins were hanged in January 2010. Six others remain at large abroad.

The trial of Mujib's assassins was a watershed in Bangladesh's political history. It was exceptional in its transparency and procedural integrity. In the past, whenever the country's rulers had opted for political "justice," they usually pursued quick fixes: new laws, special tribunals, exemplary punishment—all outside regular judicial processes.

The most recent such example was the war against corruption by the military-led caretaker government. Its cases against politicians, corrupt or not, were marred by violations of due process. Military agents routinely intimidated lawyers, produced dubious witnesses, and bullied judges. Special speedy tribunals were formed, which proceeded to award the same lengthy sentence to every senior politician regardless of the charge. (My father, Muhiuddin Khan Alamgir, a senior AL member and former minister of planning, was among those imprisoned and tried on trumped-up charges. Last year, the country's High Court declared his conviction illegal. In February 2010, the High Court also threw out a conviction in absentia against me. A special tribunal had sentenced me to three years in prison for being one day late in submitting a statement of assets to the Anti-Corruption Commission.)

This has been the modus operandi in Bangladesh: Stints in power have been occasions to wipe out opponents, justice has meant vengeance, and egregious abuses have been legalized through immunity. Indemnity laws enacted in 1975 and 1978 protected Mujib's killers. In 2003, the BNP-Jamaat government enacted the Joint Drive Indemnity Act, which gave impunity to members of the armed forces for an anticrime initiative in which thousands were arrested, many were tortured, and at least 50 people were killed in custody. In 2007, the military-led caretaker government proclaimed emergency powers that prohibited legal challenge against any action taken by its security forces. All these assaults, taken together, have shattered the idea of the rule of law, so vital for the deepening of democracy.

The trial of Mujib's murderers bucked the trend. Sheikh Hasina did not opt for legal shortcuts, even though she had lost almost all of her family in the killings. The civilian police conducted the investigation; local lower courts heard the charges; and the detailed initial hearings, public and transparent, took two years to complete. Tellingly, the government did not rush unduly even though elections approached. The case eventually moved up to the higher courts, following appropriate procedure to the letter. The most prominent trial in Bangladesh's history thus set a precedent for achieving political justice through fair, legal means.

Genocide on Trial

The second major trial, which has yet to take place, will be much larger and more complex in scope, will be limited in its results, and will have tricky foreign implications. The government is seeking justice and closure for war crimes committed during the 1971 war of liberation against Pakistan. The AL-led government last year began consultations on a legal framework for trials, and has vowed to initiate them in 2010.

Nothing rouses the country's emotions more than the collective failure to hold accountable those who organized genocide against Bengalis. In 1971, the West Pakistani leadership decided to crush the ethnic Bengalis' demand for autonomy and democracy by unleashing a brutal crackdown, which soon degenerated into genocide. Between March and December 1971, the Pakistani army and its local collaborators slaughtered at least 1 million Bengalis; some estimates put the toll as high as 3 million. Bengali men and boys were killed en masse. Hindus were targeted specifically. Between 250,000 and 400,000 women were sexually violated. Hundreds of the most prominent Bengali intellectuals, artists, and cultural icons were rounded up and executed.

After Bangladesh became independent, foreign policy reality combined with arbitrary decision making to extend impunity to the war criminals. India, which had helped liberate Bangladesh, repatriated 90,000 Pakistani soldiers held as prisoners of war. Optimistic Bengalis expected that the ringleaders would be tried; they were not. India was keen to move on and Pakistan, bifurcated by secession and shamed by surrender, had no intention of damaging the morale of its surviving warriors by charging them criminally. Pakistan also had a strong ally in the United States, which, under Kissinger and President Richard Nixon's direction, had continued to supply arms to the Pakistani military knowing well that they were being used for genocide. Bangladesh, new to foreign relations and reeling from mass destruction, did not have the diplomatic prowess to push the issue internationally.

Still, the scars ran deep. So the newly formed Bangladeshi government decided to focus on the local war

collaborators. In 1973 it passed the International Crimes (Tribunals) Act and arrested several thousand suspects. By that time, however, economic ruin, insecurity, and political instability had set in. In the interest of preventing further turmoil, Mujib abruptly issued an amnesty order. Most collaborators were released.

Many who suffered in the war saw this award of amnesty as an unjust, dictatorial decision, the "original sin" in the vortex of political injustices into which the country eventually sank. The local collaborators were led by members of the Jamaat-e-Islami, adamant to preserve the unity of a Muslim country regardless of cost. Jamaat members had organized death squads that carried out mass executions. Some Jamaat leaders fled after independence, when the party was banned from politics. Mujib's assassination allowed them to consider a return. Then, President Zia's policy of reasserting the country's Muslim identity gave them a concrete opening.

Jamaat leaders helped Zia cultivate connections in the Middle East, and as quid pro quo, Zia permitted the Jamaat to resurface as a formal political party to take part in his staged elections. The political patronage of General Zia and General Ershad between 1978 and 1991 allowed the Jamaat to spread nationwide. It won converts through a combination of Islamic rhetoric, funds, and social services. By 1991 the Jamaat, still led by perpetrators of the genocide, had become a major political party. Even the AL, engrossed in electoral calculations, worked with the Jamaat for a brief period.

The ascent of political Islam in Bangladesh is, thus, not simply a natural turn of events. It is intertwined with a sense of injustices on several levels: the original sin that absolved war criminals, a second sin that reinstated the criminals into politics, and a third, deeper one that integrated Islamic symbols and discourse into the official state narratives of a country that had earlier rejected, at the cost of genocide, nationhood based on religion.

In the absence of a meaningful state response, many independent secular progressives joined hands under Jahanara Imam, who had lost one of her sons to an Islamist death squad in 1971. They assembled evidence, compiled a list of war criminals, and organized a "People's Court" to try them. The BNP-led government persecuted the group, charging it with disrespect for the country's existing judicial system.

The injustices deepened when the BNP-Jamaat alliance came to power a second time, in 2001. Two Jamaat leaders, including an alleged war criminal, were named to the cabinet. The Jamaat, using its position of power, urged the country's youth to forget the past and look to the future, and began to recast the "Liberation War" as a "civil war," thus reducing the genocide to a simple armed conflict in which both sides might have been equally responsible.

Islamists Under Fire

This proved to be a mistake. The insult mobilized front-line commanders from 1971. They launched a movement that mushroomed into a nationwide demand for war crimes trials. The AL-led Grand Alliance endorsed the idea, which helped it win 263 out of 300 seats in the parliament in the 2008 elections. Voters crushed the Jamaat: The party managed to win just 2 seats, compared to the 17 that it had captured in the previous elections as a BNP ally.

War crimes trials will certainly damage the Jamaat and its leadership further. The position of political Islam in Bangladesh will likely weaken for the first time since the 1980s. Public support in favor of the trials is overwhelming—86 percent, according to one recent survey. This support will embolden the Grand Alliance, and open and fair trials will go a long way toward establishing political justice for Bengalis' deepest national trauma.

Difficulties lie ahead. Public support must not tempt the government to take legal shortcuts. The primary basis for the trials will be an updated version of the International Crimes (Tribunals) Act. The government needs to ensure that the revision defines the specific crimes and criminal responsibility clearly. Furthermore, the trials will have limited scope: Only significant local collaborators will be held accountable, and none of the Pakistani masterminds will be tried. The government, therefore, will have to carefully manage public expectations, which are lofty right now.

The Grand Alliance has secured support from the European Union and the United Nations. The UN has recommended four of its war crimes experts to the government. But for the trials to be internationally acceptable, the government must remove any provision for capital punishment, however locally unpopular that might be.

The trickiest challenges relate to Pakistan, the Middle East, and the United States. Although Pakistanis will not be on trial, the responsibility of their erstwhile government and generals for the bloodbath will certainly be a persistent theme. So the current Pakistani government is on a diplomatic offensive, seeking allies in the Middle East. The Nixon administration also has blood on its hands. Declassified documents show that Nixon forbade "all hands" to restrain General Muhammad Agha Yahya Khan, Pakistan's president. To skirt a Congress opposed to funding genocide, Kissinger even channeled arms to Pakistan using third countries, like Jordan and Iran. Bangladesh should counter potential American discomfort through a principled yet tactful stand that positions the trials as necessary for longer-term stability in a Muslim democracy riven by fundamental injustices.

The Fate of Democracy

Will the search for political justice deepen democracy? Bangladesh's foremost political achievement has been the institutionalization of free and fair elections. But two basic ingredients of democratic consolidation have been missing: commitment to human rights and equality before the law. Their absence is manifest when murderers are granted legal immunity and their sponsors enjoy political immunity, both unaccountable for the subversion of everyday democratic ethics. The end of impunity for the 1971 war criminals and the 1975 assassins of the Mujib family will likely bolster demands for justice for other political crimes, including extrajudicial killings. Such killings have been the ugliest blot on the democratic performance of all major parties.

Coming days may tempt the government to use extrajudicial force against Islamists. The conviction of Jamaat leaders as war criminals would likely provoke a violent reaction. In the four democratic elections that Bangladesh has held so far, Islamists have won a consistent 5 to 7 percent of the vote. Violent protests against war crimes trials, the single issue that unites an overwhelming majority of Bangladeshis, will only reduce the Islamists' appeal further, as long as the government can stay on high moral ground and practice procedural integrity.

The injustices that will prove the most difficult to resolve concern the military. Its recent stint in power left it with a financially profitable but politically bitter experience. It was hard to govern at gunpoint a citizenry accustomed to the messy freedoms afforded by democracy. Two specific questions linger from the caretaker period. First, can accountability be established for the human rights abuses that occurred? Second, will corruption be investigated, especially large state contracts awarded without oversight?

The answers will remain negative for the foreseeable future. In a country that has suffered decades of military rule, most recently in 2007–08, any civilian government will naturally be on guard and adopt prudence over idealism, a policy of "live and let live." Thus, the military will stay largely outside the jurisdiction of civilian justice. But uneasy spillovers continue. About half of the extrajudicial killings under the current government's watch have occurred during military interrogations of suspected participants in a brutal mutiny in February 2009, in which paramilitary border guards killed several dozen army officers.

Complexities and compromises notwithstanding, Bangladeshis are optimistic. According to a recent survey, 54 percent detect a positive change in the political culture. A massive 82 percent believe that "old political practices" will not return. One such practice is the boycott of parliament by the opposition. Citing a series of grievances, the BNP boycotted most parliament sessions in 2009. For its part, the AL, enjoying an electoral preponderance, has lapsed occasionally into that old practice called "tyranny of the majority."

But three developments encourage the optimists. First, parliamentary committees have asserted themselves, grilling officials about executive decisions and at times putting the government on the defensive. Second, the BNP decided to join in parliamentary oversight in 2010, after repeated surveys showed that three-quarters of Bangladeshis did not approve of its boycott. And in this rests the third basis for optimism: Relentless media scrutiny, television talk shows, and the growing frequency of public opinion polls have made political parties more responsive.

If such everyday democratic procedures complement the longer-term goal of attaining political justice, the future bodes well for Bangladesh.

Critical Thinking

1. Why does the threat of militant Islamism remain a worry in Bangladesh?
2. Why weren't the perpetrators of the 1971 genocide held accountable for their actions?
3. What has been the role of the military in Bangladesh's democratization?

JALAL ALAMGIR is an assistant professor of political science at the University of Massachusetts, Boston, and a fellow at the South Asia Initiative at Harvard University. He is the author of *India's Open-Economy Policy: Globalism, Rivalry, Continuity* (Routledge, 2008).

From *Current History,* April 2010, pp. 151–157. Copyright © 2010 by Current History, Inc. Reprinted by permission.

The Great Democracy Meltdown
Why the World Is Becoming Less Free

JOSHUA KURLANTZICK

As the revolt that started this past winter in Tunisia spread to Egypt, Libya, and beyond, dissidents the world over were looking to the Middle East for inspiration. In China, online activists inspired by the Arab Spring called for a "jasmine revolution." In Singapore, one of the quietest countries in the world, opposition members called for an "orchid evolution" in the run-up to this month's national elections. Perhaps as a result, those watching from the West have been positively triumphalist in their predictions. The Middle East uprisings could herald "the greatest advance for human rights and freedom since the end of the cold war," argued British Foreign Secretary William Hague. Indeed, at no point since the end of the cold war—when Francis Fukuyama penned his famous essay *The End of History,* positing that liberal democracy was the ultimate destination for every country—has there been so much optimism about the march of global freedom.

If only things were so simple. The truth is that the Arab Spring is something of a smokescreen for what is taking place in the world as a whole. Around the globe, it is democratic meltdowns, not democratic revolutions, that are now the norm. (And even countries like Egypt and Tunisia, while certainly freer today than they were a year ago, are hardly guaranteed to replace their autocrats with real democracies.) In its most recent annual survey, the monitoring group Freedom House found that global freedom plummeted for the fifth year in a row, the longest continuous decline in nearly 40 years. It pointed out that most authoritarian nations had become even more repressive, that the decline in freedom was most pronounced among the "middle ground" of nations—countries that have begun democratizing but are not solid and stable democracies—and that the number of electoral democracies currently stands at its lowest point since 1995. Meanwhile, another recent survey, compiled by Germany's Bertelsmann Foundation, spoke of a "gradual qualitative erosion" of democracy and concluded that the number of "highly defective democracies"—democracies so flawed that they are close to being failed states, autocracies, or both—had doubled between 2006 and 2010.

The number of anecdotal examples is overwhelming. From Russia to Venezuela to Thailand to the Philippines, countries that once appeared to be developing into democracies today seem headed in the other direction. So many countries now remain stuck somewhere between authoritarianism and democracy, report Marc Plattner and Larry Diamond, co-editors of the *Journal of Democracy,* that "it no longer seems plausible to regard [this condition] simply as a temporary stage in the process of democratic transition." Or as an activist from Burma—long one of the world's most repressive countries—told me after moving to Thailand and watching that country's democratic system disintegrate, "The other countries were supposed to change Burma. . . . Now it seems like they are becoming like Burma."

Twenty or even ten years ago, the possibility of a global democratic recession seemed impossible. It was widely assumed that, as states grew wealthier, they would develop larger middle classes. And these middle classes, according to democracy theorists like Samuel Huntington, would push for ever-greater social, political, and economic freedoms. Human progress, which constantly marched forward, would spread democracy everywhere.

For a time, this rosy line of thinking seemed warranted. In 1990, dictators still ruled most of Africa, Eastern Europe, and Asia; by 2005, democracies had emerged across these continents, and some of the most powerful developing nations, including South Africa and Brazil, had become solid democracies. In 2005, for the first time in history, more than half the world's people lived under democratic systems.

Then, something odd and unexpected began to happen. It started when some of the leaders who had emerged in these countries seemed to morph into elected autocrats once they got into office. In Venezuela, Hugo Chávez is now essentially an elected dictator. In Ecuador, elected President Rafael Correa, who has displayed a strong authoritarian streak, recently won legislation that would grant him expansive new powers. In Kyrgyzstan, Kurmanbek Bakiyev, who led the 2005 Tulip Revolution, soon proved himself nearly as authoritarian as his predecessor. And, in Russia, Vladimir Putin used the power he won in elections to essentially dismantle the country's democracy.

But it wasn't just leaders who were driving these changes. In some cases, the people themselves seemed to acquiesce in their countries' slide away from free and open government. In one study by the Program on International Policy Attitudes, only 16 percent of Russians said it was "very important" that their nation be governed democratically. The regular Afrobarometer survey of the African continent has found declining levels of support for democracy in many key countries. And in Guatemala, Paraguay, Colombia, Peru, Honduras, and Nicaragua, either a minority or only a small majority of people think democracy is preferable to any other type of government. Even in East Asia, one of the most democratic regions of the world, polls show rising dissatisfaction with democracy. In fact, several countries in the region have developed what Yu-tzung Chang, Yunhan Zhu, and Chong-min Park, who studied data from the regular Asian Barometer surveys, have termed "authoritarian nostalgia." "Few of the region's former authoritarian regimes have been thoroughly discredited," they write, noting that the region's average score for commitment to democracy, judged by a range of responses to surveys, has recently fallen.

East Asia has seen a rise in "authoritarian nostalgia."

But what about the middle class? Even if large segments of the population were uninterested in liberal democracy, weren't members of the middle class supposed to act as agents of democratization, as Huntington had envisioned? Actually, the story has turned out to be quite a bit more complicated. In country after country, a familiar pattern has repeated itself: The middle class has indeed reacted negatively to populist leaders who appeared to be sliding into authoritarianism; but rather than work to defeat these leaders at the ballot box or strengthen the institutions that could hold them in check, they have ended up supporting military coups or other undemocratic measures.

Thailand offers a clear example of this phenomenon. In 2001, Thaksin Shinawatra, a former telecommunications tycoon turned populist, was elected with the largest mandate in Thai history, mostly from the poor, who, as in many developing nations, still constitute a majority of the population. Over the next five years, Thaksin enacted several policies that clearly benefited the poor, including national health insurance, but he also began to strangle Thailand's institutions, threatening reporters, unleashing a "war on drugs" that led to unexplained shootings of political opponents, and silencing the bureaucracy. In 2005, when the charismatic prime minister won another free election with an even larger mandate, the middle class revolted, demonstrating in the streets until they paralyzed Bangkok. Finally, in September 2006, the Thai military stepped in, ousting Thaksin. When I traveled around Bangkok following the coup, young, middle-class Thais, who a generation ago had fought against military rulers, were engaged in a love-in with the troops, snapping photos of soldiers posted throughout Bangkok like they were celebrities.

The middle class in Thailand had plenty of company. In 2001, urban Filipinos poured into the streets to topple President Joseph Estrada, a former actor who rose to power on his appeal to the poor, and then allegedly used his office to rake in vast sums of money from underworld gambling tycoons. In Honduras in 2009, middle-class opponents of populist President Manuel Zelaya began to protest his plans to extend his power by altering the constitution. When the military removed him in June of that year, the intervention was welcomed by many members of the urban middle class. An analysis of military coups in developing nations over the past two decades, conducted by my colleague David Silverman, found that, in nearly half of the cases—drawn from Africa, Latin America, Asia, and the Middle East—middle-class men and women either agitated in advance for the coup, or, after the takeover, expressed their support in polls or prominent press coverage.

Even as domestic politics in many developing nations has become less friendly to democratization, the international system too has changed, further weakening democratic hopes. The rising strength of authoritarian powers, principally China but also Russia, Saudi Arabia, and other states, has helped forestall democratization. Moscow and Beijing were clearly rattled by the "color revolutions" of the early and mid-2000s, and they developed a number of responses. First, they tried to delegitimize the revolts by arguing that they were not genuine popular movements but actually Western attempts at regime change. Then, in nations like Cambodia, Ukraine, Georgia, Kyrgyzstan, and Moldova, Moscow and Beijing intervened directly in attempts to reverse democratic gains. The Kremlin's youth group, Nashi, known for its aggressive tactics against democracy activists, launched branches in other Central Asian nations. In Kyrgyzstan, Russian advisers helped a series of leaders emulate the Kremlin's model of political control. In part because of this Russian influence, "[p]arliamentary democracy in Kyrgyzstan has been hobbled," according to the International Crisis Group. China and Russia even created new "NGOs" that were supposedly focused on democracy promotion. But these organizations actually offered expertise and funding to foreign leaders to help them forestall new color revolutions. In Ukraine, an organization called the "Russian Press Club," run by an adviser to Putin, posed as an NGO and helped facilitate Russia's involvement in Ukrainian elections.

But China and Russia are only part of the story. In many ways, the biggest culprits have actually been stable democracies. Consider the case of Myo, a Burmese publisher and activist who I met four years ago in a dingy noodle shop in Rangoon. The educated son of a relatively well-off Burmese family, he told me he had been working for a publishing company in Rangoon, but had to smuggle political messages into pieces he published in magazines that focused on safe topics like soccer or Burmese rap. "It's kind of a game everyone here plays," he explained, "but after a while it gets so tiring."

When I next met Myo, it was in Thailand two years later. He'd finally grown weary of trying to get his writing past the censors and left for India, then for Thailand. "I'd heard that, before, India had been very welcoming to Burmese activists, particularly after 1988," Myo said, referring to a period of anti-government rioting in Burma. At one time, Indian officials had assisted Burmese democracy activists, and India's defense minister from 1998 to 2004 was George Fernandes, a prominent human rights advocate who even gave some Burmese exiles shelter in his family compound. By the time Myo came to India, however, Delhi had stopped criticizing the Burmese junta. Instead, it had reversed itself and was engaging the generals under a policy called "Look East." When Than Shwe, the Burmese junta's leader, paid a state visit to India, he was taken to the burial site of Mahatma Gandhi, a cruelly ironic juxtaposition that Amnesty International's Burma specialist called "entirely unpalatable." For Myo, India's chilly new pragmatism was a shock. "I expected China to work with Burma," he said. "But to see it from India, it was so much more disappointing."

Like Myo, many Western officials had expected that stable developing-world democracies like India, Indonesia, South Africa, Brazil, and Turkey would emerge as powerful advocates for democracy and human rights abroad. But as they've gained power, these emerging democratic giants have acted more like cold-blooded realists. South Africa has for years tolerated Robert Mugabe's brutal regime next door in Zimbabwe, and, in 2007, it even helped to block a U.N. resolution condemning the Burmese junta for human rights abuses. Brazil has cozied up to Iranian dictator Mahmoud Ahmadinejad and to local autocrats like Cuba's Castros. When a prominent Cuban political prisoner named Orlando Zapata Tamayo held a hunger strike and eventually died, former Brazilian President Luiz Inácio Lula da Silva seemed to ridicule Tamayo's struggle, likening the activist to a criminal who was trying to gain publicity.

There are exceptions to this trend. Poland, for one, has used its influence to support reformers in other post-Soviet states like Belarus. But Poland is unusual, and by playing a limited—or hostile—role in international democracy promotion efforts, countries like South Africa or Brazil or Turkey have made it easier for autocratic leaders to paint democracy promotion as a Western phenomenon, and even to portray it as an illegal intervention.

Why have regional democratic powers opted for this course? It seems hard to believe that a country with, say, Brazil or South Africa's experience of brutal tyranny could actively abet dictators in other nations. But it now appears that the notion of absolute sovereignty, promoted by authoritarian states like China, has resonated with these democratic governments. Many of these emerging democratic powers were leading members of the non-aligned movement during the cold war and weathered Western efforts to foment coups in their countries. Today, they feel extremely uncomfortable joining any international coalition that could undermine other nations' sovereignty, even if potentially for good reason. And many of these countries, such as Turkey and Indonesia and India, may simply be eager to avoid criticism of their own internal human rights abuses.

Then there is the United States, still the most influential nation on earth. Its missteps, recently, have been serious. Barack Obama's efforts to distance himself from the Bush

administration—which greatly undermined America's moral authority—have combined with the country's weakened economic position to downgrade the importance of democracy promotion in U.S. foreign policy. While Obama has delivered several speeches mentioning democracy, he has little obvious passion for the issue. When several prominent Iranian dissidents came to Washington in the summer of 2009, following the uprising in their country, they could not obtain meetings with any senior Obama administration officials. Rabeeya Kadeer, the Uighur version of the Dalai Lama, met with Bush in 2008 but found herself shunted off to low-level State Department officials by the Obama administration.

More substantively, the administration has shifted the focus of the federal bureaucracy. Though it has maintained significant budget levels for democracy promotion, it eliminated high-level positions on the National Security Council that, under Bush, had been devoted to democracy. The administration also appointed an assistant secretary for democracy, human rights, and labor who in his previous work had been mostly focused on cleaning up America's own abuses. This was not a bad thing—the Bush administration indeed left major issues to resolve—but it meant that he had far less experience than many of his predecessors with democracy promotion abroad.

To be fair, the White House has to grapple with an increasingly isolationist American public. In one poll taken in 2005, a majority of Americans said that the United States should play a role in promoting democracy elsewhere. By 2007, only 37 percent thought the United States should play this role. In a subsequent study, released in late 2009, nearly half of Americans told the Pew Research polling organization that the United States should "mind its own business" internationally and should let other nations work out their challenges or problems themselves. This was the highest percentage of isolationist sentiment recorded in a poll of the American public in four decades.

There is an obvious appeal to the constantly touted notion that the march of human freedom is inevitable. But not only is it simple-minded to treat history as a story with a preordained happy ending; it is also, for those who truly want to see democracy spread, extraordinarily dangerous. After all, if democracy is bound to triumph, then there's no reason to work too hard at promoting it. This overconfidence can spread to developing nations themselves, lulling democrats into a false sense of security once an election has finally been held, and dissuading them from building the institutions that are necessary to keep a country free over the long-term. Democracy is not a simple thing: It's a complex system of strong institutions and legal checks. Very few nations have mastered it fully. And sustaining it is a never-ending effort.

Stopping the global democratic reversal, then, will require giving up the assumption that democracy will simply happen on its own—and instead figuring out what we can do to promote it. At the most basic level, the United States can be much less abashed in its rhetorical advocacy of democracy and much more consistent. Condemning autocracy in places like Bahrain and Saudi Arabia—where the United States has significant strategic interests—would help to counteract the notion that democracy is merely a concept the West wields to serve its own geopolitical aims. In addition, the United States and its allies should do more to make democracy promotion pay off for emerging powers. New democratic giants, like Brazil, should be granted more power in international institutions like the United Nations—if, that is, they show a commitment to helping expand human rights and free government around the globe.

Right now, few of these lessons have been learned. Instead, we seem content to watch events unfold across the world and assume that things will work out for the best, because history is invariably headed in the direction of freedom. We should stop telling ourselves this comforting story and instead do what is needed to give democracy a fighting chance.

Critical Thinking

1. Why has East Asia seen a rise in authoritarian nostalgia?
2. Why is the process of global democratization not moving forward?
3. Why haven't stable developing world democracies emerged as powerful advocates for democracy promotion abroad?

JOSHUA KURLANTZICK is Fellow for Southeast Asia at the Council on Foreign Relations.

Failed States
The 2011 Index

Three African states—Somalia, Chad, and Sudan—once again top this year's Failed States Index, the annual ranking prepared by the Fund for Peace and published by *Foreign Policy* of the world's most vulnerable countries. For four years in a row, Somalia has held the No. 1 spot, indicating the depth of the crisis in the international community's longest-running failure.

The new edition of the index draws on some 130,000 publicly available sources to analyze 177 countries and rate them on 12 indicators of pressure on the state during the year 2010—from refugee flows to poverty, public services to security threats. Taken together, a country's performance on this battery of indicators tells us how stable—or unstable—it is. And the latest results show how much the 2008 economic crisis and its ripple effects everywhere, from collapsing trade to soaring food prices to stagnant investment, are still haunting the world.

Somalia's unending woes are the stuff hopelessness is made of. But elsewhere in the top 20, some countries showed improvement, even as others fell further behind. Afghanistan and Iraq both moved down the ranks, suggesting slight gains for the two war-torn countries as the United States seeks a sustainable exit strategy. Kenya moved out of the top 15, showing that the country continues to recover from its bloody post-election ethnic warfare of recent years. Liberia and East Timor, wards of the United Nations, largely stayed out of trouble. But Haiti, already a portrait of misery, moved up six places on the index, battered and struggling to cope with the aftermath of January 2010's tragic earthquake, which left more than 300,000 dead. Another former French colony, Ivory Coast, rejoined the top 10, grimly foreshadowing its devastating post-election crisis this year, while fragile Niger leapt four spots amid a devastating famine.

Africa's promise and peril are likely to figure prominently again this year, with 27 African countries scheduled to hold presidential, legislative, or local elections throughout 2011. As much as elections can contribute to democratic progress, they are often a flashpoint for conflict—conflicts that invariably send already fragile states back up the ranks of the index. Uganda's incumbent President Yoweri Museveni won reelection in February, but the opposition has cried foul and his inauguration was met with violent protests. In Nigeria, steady in the rankings this year at No. 14, post-election rampages in April killed as many as 800 people. Sudan's closely watched referendum in January on an independent southern state was surprisingly free of bloodshed, but the country continues to hover on the brink of new violence.

As if its traumas last year weren't horrific enough, Haiti in 2011 is again proving to be a hard test for the world, with billions of dollars in donation pledges left unfulfilled and thousands still living in squalid tent camps, battling a cholera epidemic that has killed more than 4,600. After a fraud-marred first round, a presidential runoff election in March brought to power an untested stage performer nicknamed "Sweet Micky."

Perhaps the biggest challenge of all for 2011 will be dealing with the global fallout of the Arab revolutions, which began in Tunisia and quickly spread to Egypt, Bahrain, Libya, Yemen, and Syria. Few could have predicted that a street vendor's humiliation would be the spark that set an entire region ablaze, with consequences that may reach far beyond the Middle East. After all, if peaceful protesters can unseat an entrenched dictator in Cairo, why can't they take to the repressed streets of Tashkent or Rangoon?

Rank		Score	Change in Rank
1	Somalia	113.4	—
2	Chad	110.3	—
3	Sudan	108.7	—
4	Dem. Rep. of Congo	108.2	↑
5	Haiti	108.0	↑
6	Zimbabwe	107.9	↓
7	Afghanistan	107.5	↓
8	Central African Republic	105.0	—
9	Iraq	104.8	↓
10	Ivory Coast	102.8	↑
11	Guinea	102.5	↓
12	Pakistan	102.3	↓
13	Yemen	100.3	↑
14	Nigeria	99.9	—
15	Niger	99.1	↑
16	Kenya	98.7	↓
17	Burundi	98.6	↑
18	Burma	98.3	↓
18	Guinea-Bissau	98.3	↑
20	Ethiopia	98.2	↓
21	Uganda	96.3	—
22	North Korea	95.6	↓
23	East Timor	94.9	↓
24	Cameroon	94.6	↑
25	Bangladesh	94.4	↓
26	Liberia	94.0	↑
27	Nepal	93.7	↓
28	Eritrea	93.6	↑
29	Sri Lanka	93.1	↓
30	Sierra Leone	92.1	↓

Rank		Score	Change in Rank
31	Kyrgyzstan	91.8	↑
32	Republic of the Congo	91.4	↓
33	Malawi	91.2	↓
34	Rwanda	91.0	↑
35	Iran	90.2	↓
36	Togo	89.4	↑
37	Burkina Faso	88.6	↓
38	Cambodia	88.5	↑
39	Tajikistan	88.3	↓
39	Uzbekistan	88.3	↓
41	Equatorial Guinea	88.1	↑
42	Mauritania	88.0	↓
43	Lebanon	87.7	↓
44	Colombia	87.0	↑
45	Egypt	86.8	↑
46	Laos	86.7	↓
47	Georgia	86.4	↓
48	Syria	85.9	—
48	Solomon Islands	85.9	↓
50	Bhutan	85.0	—
50	Philippines	85.0	↑
52	Angola	84.6	↑
53	Israel/West Bank	84.4	↑
54	Papua New Guinea	84.2	↑
55	Zambia	83.8	↑
55	Comoros	83.8	↓
57	Mozambique	83.6	↑
58	Madagascar	83.2	↑
59	Bolivia	82.9	↓
60	Djibouti	82.6	↑

Critical Thinking

1. What is the significance of the Failed States Index?
2. Why is Somalia number one on the Failed States Index?
3. What region of the world ranks the highest on the Failed States Index?

UNIT 3

Foreign Policy and Terrorism

Unit Selections

Learning Outcomes

After reading this Unit, you will be able to:

- Define "grand strategy."

- Describe President Obama's grand strategy.

- Explain what factors would prevent President Obama from implementing his grand strategy.

- Define humanitarian intervention.

- Explain why the U.S. engaged in humanitarian intervention in Libya.

- Explain the implications of the changes in the Middle East for U.S. Foreign Policy.

- Determine what changes can be expected in the war against terror since Osama bin Laden's death.

- Determine what branches or franchises of Al Qaeda pose a threat to Western interests.

Student Website

www.mhhe.com/cls

Internet References

The National Security Archive
    www.gwu.edu/~nsarchiv
Office of the Coordinator for Counterterrorism
    www.state.gov/s/ct
U.S. State Department
    www.state.gov

It has been about four years since President Obama took office, and this provides the opportunity to take stock of his foreign policy since he assumed his office in 2008. There were elements of continuity between the foreign policy of president Obama, and that of his predecessor, President Bush. This not surprising given that a more liberal vision of world order may succumb to some of the constraints on presidential foreign policy. These constraints stem from the structure of the international system and the position, which the United States occupies as a leader, if not a global hegemon, in a system characterized by emerging multipolarity. President Obama's National Security Strategy, issued in May 2010, also recognized the multipolar nature of the system. It recognized the importance of "emerging centers of influence," such as the BRIC countries. President Obama's foreign policy recognized the importance of multilateralism in a globalized world, as a component of diplomacy and the necessity to work with international institutions such as the United Nations. Obama's foreign policy between 2008–2012, was a mixture of liberal idealism and pragmatism. The rhetorical emphasis was on soft power, but there was no reluctance to use hard power or military force. A major change from the policy of the Bush administration was the effort to improve relations with Russia, to reverse the deterioration of relations that had set in following the Russian invasion of Georgia in 2008, although the preservation of the sovereignty and territorial integrity of Russia's neighbors was recognized in the National Security Strategy of 2010. The centerpiece of the resetting of relations between Russia and the United States was the negotiation of a new START (Strategic Arms Reduction Talks) between the two countries to replace the Cold War START Treaty that had lapsed in December 2010. Another step in the direction of improving relations between the United States and Russia took place when the Obama administration reversed the Bush administration's decision to deploy missiles in Poland, along with a radar system in the Czech Republic, ostensibly to deal with an Iranian nuclear missile threat to Europe in the future. The decision to deploy missiles instead in the Black Sea state of Romania, however, was still seen as a threat to its national security by Moscow.

The question is whether President Obama does have a grand strategy as he deals with such thorny issues as the wars in Iraq and Afghanistan, working with Washington's alliance partners in NATO, peace between Israel and the Palestinians, the nuclear weaponization efforts of Iran and North Korea, and mass atrocities in the Sudan. Daniel Drezner argues that the Obama administration does have a grand strategy of responding to international provocations and balancing against rising threats. For example, clearly the rise of China in the Pacific, has resulted in a U.S. policy of not only engaging China, but counterbalancing it as well. As Drezner points out, the biggest problem with Obama's grand strategy is the troublesome domestic politics of the United States. Obama's National Security Strategy placed a great deal of emphasis on the importance of a strong economic base for the implementation of U.S. foreign policy. A strong economic base clearly is lacking, evidenced by the possibility that the United States might have defaulted on its debts

© Pete Souza/The White House

before an agreement was reached on raising the ceiling of the national debt in July 2011.

The promotion of democracy has always been a consistent theme of U.S. foreign policy, as illustrated by Woodrow Wilson's goal of making the world safe for democracy, when the United States entered the First World War in 1917. However, as Michael Singh points out, the United States must now readjust its policies in a Middle East that is going through enormous change. Washington must protect its interests by persuading those allies that have not done so, to engage in political reform. Even though the promotion of democracy was a central theme in the National Security Strategy of the Obama administration, clearly more emphasis in the document was placed on the importance of Egypt as a strategic ally, rather than emphasizing the need for the Mubarak administration to democratize.

One of the central themes of the president's National Security Strategy was the destruction of al Qaeda and its affiliates. A special forces operation of Navy Seals resulted in the killing of Osama bin Laden in Pakistan in May 2011. The special forces raid, which resulted in the death of Osama bin Laden, further strained relations between the United States and Pakistan because it was clear that Osama had lived in Pakistan for several years, and must have had some support from elements in the Pakistani military or intelligence services. Relations between the United States and Pakistan were also strained because as far as can be determined, the raid had been conducted on sovereign Pakistani territory without the permission of the government in Islamabad. "After Osama bin Laden," in the *Economist* discusses what can be expected after the death of bin Laden. The killing of bin Laden will not stop the activities of al-Qaeda, even if it is smaller and less capable of carrying out operations in the West. Affiliated Islamic terrorist organizations, such as al-Qaeda in the Arabian peninsula (AQAP), al-Qaeda in Iraq (sometimes referred to as al-Qaeda in Mesopotamia), and al-Qaeda in the Islamic Maghreb, can be expected to continue their terrorist activities.

However, the emphasis on Islamic fundamentalist terrorism overlooked the dangers of indigenous terrorists who felt threatened by the growth of Muslim communities in their own countries. The Norwegian massacre that took place in Norway in July 2011 shook the serenity of Oslo. Contrary to initial beliefs, the bombing of government buildings in Oslo was not the work of al-Qaeda, but the work of a Norwegian who had written a 1,500-page manifesto, which he had posted online, arguing that he was engaged in a crusade against Muslim communities that had settled in western Europe, protesting its "Arabization."

Although from a liberal point of view, President Obama's administration began with an effort to engage the Muslim world in a dialogue, the administration was persuaded to use force in the form of air power, along with its NATO allies, to aid the Libyan uprising against Gadaffi, that erupted in February 2011. Jacob Heilbrunn writes about the role Samantha Power, a key presidential advisor, played in convincing Obama to support military intervention in Libya. The military intervention in Libya was based on Power's view that the United States should not fail to prevent another genocide like the genocides that had occurred in Rwanda and Darfur.

Does Obama Have a Grand Strategy?

Why We Need Doctrines in Uncertain Times

Daniel W. Drezner

As the U.S. military intervenes in Libya, a fierce debate has erupted over the possible existence of an Obama doctrine, with a chorus of foreign policy observers bemoaning the United States' supposed strategic incompetence. Last fall, the columnist Jackson Diehl wrote in *The Washington Post*, "This administration is notable for its lack of grand strategy—or strategists." In *The National Interest* this January, the political scientist John Mearsheimer concluded, "The root cause of America's troubles is that it adopted a flawed grand strategy after the Cold War." The economic historian Niall Ferguson took to *Newsweek* to argue that alleged U.S. setbacks in the Middle East were "the predictable consequence of the Obama administration's lack of any kind of a coherent grand strategy, a deficit about which more than a few veterans of U.S. foreign policymaking have long worried." Even the administration's defenders have damned it with faint praise. *The National Journal*'s Michael Hirsh argued that "the real Obama doctrine is to have no doctrine at all. And that's the way it's likely to remain." Hirsh, at least, meant it as a compliment.

But is it true that President Barack Obama has no grand strategy? And even if it were, would that be such a disaster? The George W. Bush administration, after all, developed a clear, coherent, and well-defined grand strategy after 9/11. But those attributes did not make it a good one, and its implementation led to more harm than benefit.

Grand strategies are not nearly as important as grand strategists like to think, because countries tend to be judged by their actions, not their words. What really matters for great powers is power—national economic and military strength—and that speaks loudly and clearly by itself. Still, in times of deep uncertainty, a strategy can be important as a signaling device. In these moments, such as the present, a clearly articulated strategy matched by consistent actions is useful because it can drive home messages about a country's intentions to domestic and foreign audiences.

Despite what its critics say, the Obama administration has actually had not just one grand strategy so far but two. The first strategy, multilateral retrenchment, was designed to curtail the United States' overseas commitments, restore its standing in the world, and shift burdens onto global partners. This strategy was clearly articulated, but it delivered underwhelming policy results.

The second, emergent grand strategy is focused on counterpunching. More recently, the Obama administration has been willing to assert its influence and ideals across the globe when challenged by other countries, reassuring allies and signaling resolve to rivals. This strategy has performed better but has been poorly articulated. It is this vacuum of interpretation that the administration's critics have rushed to fill. Unless and until the president and his advisers define explicitly the strategy that has been implicit for the past year, the president's foreign policy critics will be eager to define it—badly—for him.

Sound and Vision

A grand strategy consists of a clear articulation of national interests married to a set of operational plans for advancing them. Sometimes, such strategies are set out in advance, with actions following in sequence. Other times, strategic narratives are offered as coherent explanations connecting past policies with future ones. Either way, a well-articulated grand strategy can offer an interpretative framework that tells everybody, including foreign policy officials themselves, how to understand the administration's behavior.

All this sounds terrifically important, but most of the time it is not. For grand strategies to matter, they have to indicate a change in policy. And trying to alter a state's foreign policy trajectory is like trying to make an aircraft carrier do a U-turn: it happens slowly at best. The tyranny of the status quo often renders grand strategy a constant rather than a variable, despite each administration's determined efforts at intellectual differentiation and rebranding.

Power is the true reserve currency in international affairs, and most countries simply lack the power to make others care about their intentions. The rest of the world is not waiting up nights to learn about Belgium's grand strategy (although a government would be nice). The same applies to nonstate actors. After 9/11, a cottage industry of analysts emerged to deconstruct every statement issued by al Qaeda's leadership. As the group's operational tempo, capabilities, and ideological appeal eroded, however, its statements garnered less and less interest. Unless Osama bin Laden's successors demonstrate their continued ability to wreak havoc, only a narrow slice of specialists will care about their ideology or strategy. This is why the debate over U.S. grand strategy is less important than the debate over how to rejuvenate the U.S. economy.

Even for powerful actors, moreover, actions speak louder than words. George Kennan may have articulated the doctrine of containment, but in his formulation, the strategy did not require protecting South Korea. "Containment" gained the meaning it did because a series of presidents fleshed out Kennan's concept in their own distinct ways. As the historian Melvyn Leffler has documented, the core elements of George W. Bush's National Security Strategy—preventive war and democracy promotion—were not new, having appeared in the official discourse of prior administrations. What was different about Bush was that unlike his predecessors, who treated the concepts as boilerplate rhetoric, he acted.

Critics and analysts stress the importance of choosing the right grand strategy and the catastrophic implications of selecting the wrong one. History suggests, however, that grand strategies do not alter the trajectory of great-power politics all that much. Consider the United States. Even radically imperfect strategies have not fundamentally affected its rise and fall. The United States should have taken a more active role in world affairs after World War I but instead retreated into isolationism. Successive presidents bought into the domino theory of communism and expanded U.S. involvement in the Vietnam War beyond what any other strategic logic would have dictated. The Bush administration launched a war of choice against Iraq that was designed to inject a stable democracy into the region while bolstering nuclear nonproliferation. The actual result was a $1 trillion-plus diversionary war and a global wave of anti-Americanism.

All three of these strategic mistakes were rooted in coherent strategic narratives popular with both policymakers and the public. What is striking, however, is that none of these missteps altered the trajectory of U.S. power. The United States eventually assumed the responsibilities of primacy after World War II. The country's overstretch in Vietnam did not change the outcome of the Cold War. Operation Iraqi Freedom was costly, but public opinion data demonstrate that the harm done to the United States' standing quickly faded. In all three cases, the institutional strengths of the United States forced appropriate corrections to the grand strategy. New leaders in the White House, Congress, and the Pentagon made the country adopt a leadership role in the postwar era, refrain from post-Vietnam interventions, and reform its counterinsurgency doctrine in the face of setbacks in Iraq. These course corrections prevented strategic miscues from becoming permanent reversals.

When Ideas Matter

If grand strategies are so overrated, why the furious debate? For two reasons, one petty and one substantive. The petty reason is that everyone in the U.S. foreign policy community secretly hopes to be the next Kennan. When a commentator bewails the failings of the United States' grand strategy, it is usually because he has scribbled down his own set of musings on the topic. Indeed, complaints about grand strategy have plagued every U.S. administration since the end of World War II for precisely this reason. Grand strategies are easy to devise—they are forward-looking, operate in generalities, and make for great book tours. Whenever a foreign policy commentator articulates a new grand strategy, an angel gets its wings.

> **Whenever a foreign policy commentator articulates a new grand strategy, an angel gets its wings.**

The more substantive reason is that there are moments when grand strategies really do count: during times of radical uncertainty in international affairs. Ideas matter most when actors are operating in uncharted waters. They can function as cognitive beacons, guiding countries to safety. During normal times, decision-makers will extrapolate from current capabilities or past actions to predict the behavior of others. In novel times, however, grand strategies can signal to outsiders the future intentions of a country's policymakers, reassuring or repulsing important audiences.

Two kinds of events can trigger the kind of radical uncertainty necessary for a grand strategy to matter. One is a massive global disruption—a war, a revolution, or a depression—that rejiggers countries' interests across the globe. In this situation, when everybody is unsure about what comes next, grand strategies can provide a functioning road map for how to interpret current events and the appropriate policy responses. The other is a power transition, which can also lead to profound uncertainty. When a fading hegemonic power is confronted by a rising challenger, countries want to know how each of the two governments views its role in the world. States in relative decline can respond in a myriad of ways, from graceful retrenchment to preemptive conflict. Rising powers, for their part, can be revisionist states, like Germany in the 1930s, or status quo powers, like Japan in the 1980s. Other actors will assess the statements and actions of rising powers carefully to parse out their intentions.

The current era, interestingly, is marked by both sets of uncertainties. The Great Recession has rocked the global economy, and commodity prices have gyrated wildly. The international system has had to cope with a welter of natural disasters, technological changes, and incidents of diplomatic turmoil. Revolution has spread across the Middle East with dizzying speed and with an uncertain effect on the global system.

At the same time, China's relative power has increased and the United States' has shrunk. The International Monetary Fund currently estimates that, based on purchasing power parity, China's economy will surpass the United States' in five years. This shift has led to genuine confusion as to the relative power of both countries right now. In April 2010, a Pew Global Attitudes survey asked global respondents to name "the world's leading economic power." In many developing countries, including Brazil and India, majorities picked the United

States. The results looked dramatically different in the developed world. In five of the original G-7 countries, including Germany, Japan, and the United States, strong pluralities named China as the world's leading economic power. In other words, the developing world still largely believes that the United States has retained its hegemony, whereas the developed world thinks that primacy has shifted to China. Something is clearly going on, but people disagree about what it is. It is precisely in such a world of radical uncertainty that intentions matter, and this is where grand strategy comes in.

When operating in unfamiliar terrain, officials in charge of making and executing national policy can infer what to do from their government's strategy documents. Actors abroad can also develop expectations about the future from them. In these circumstances, foreign governments will care about how much a country's proposed response to uncertainty seeks to revise or reinforce the status quo. Countries prefer the devils they know. Even during uncertain times, grand strategies that advocate wholesale revisions of the international order will make other countries nervous. The Bush doctrine of preemptive intervention had this effect, as did China's more recent statement that the South China Sea represents a "core national interest."

One other aspect of grand strategy will pique everyone's interest: whether a country's strategic vision appears to promote public or private goods. All great powers have their own ideas about how to buttress a stable world order: strict recognition of Westphalian sovereignty, nuclear nonproliferation, counterterrorism, more multilateralism, greater global development, democracy promotion, and so forth. Some of these ideas advance goods that clearly benefit the rest of the world as well as the great power itself; in other cases, the benefits to others seem less clear. When a great power puts forward a grand strategy that appears to focus on its own interests, it will trigger a backlash from other countries. For example, the Bush administration believed that democracy promotion was in the greater good, but other countries viewed that goal in combination with preemptive intervention as a license for the United States to bypass multilateral institutions. Not surprisingly, this grand strategy resulted in significant short-term costs for the United States.

Much of the handwringing about U.S. grand strategy has been overblown—but the Obama administration has inherited a world of great uncertainty. Does it have a grand strategy to respond? Actually, it has had two.

Strategy Switch

Obama came into office with three firm strategic convictions. First, domestic rejuvenation was crucial for any long-term grand strategy, a point he has stressed in all his foreign policy speeches. "[We have] failed to appreciate the connection between our national security and our economy," Obama said in his December 2009 address on Afghanistan. "Our prosperity provides a foundation for our power. It pays for our military. It underwrites our diplomacy." Second, the United States was overextended in all the wrong places, fighting two counterinsurgencies and a war on terrorism in the Middle East while

neglecting other parts of the globe. Third, the Bush administration's mistakes had pushed the United States' standing in the world to an all-time low. Ben Rhodes, Obama's deputy national security adviser for strategic communications, recently explained the administration's strategic vision to *The New Yorker:* "If you were to boil it all down to a bumper sticker, it's 'Wind down these two wars, reëstablish American standing and leadership in the world, and focus on a broader set of priorities, from Asia and the global economy to a nuclear-nonproliferation regime.'"

Obama's first grand strategy, as explained in various speeches and administration initiatives in his first year, was to make lemons out of lemonade. As Secretary of State Hillary Clinton put it, a multipolar world was actually a "multipartner" world, in which the United States would call on other countries—rivals as well as allies—to assist it in preserving global order. The Obama administration attempted to "reset" relations with Russia. With China, there was talk of the U.S.-China Strategic and Economic Dialogue becoming a "G-2" that would echo the summitry of the Cold War. The administration embraced the G-20 to supplant the G-8 as the premier international economic forum, in the belief that more partners would mean more effective partnerships. Rather than aggressively push for democracy, a more reserved United States would lead by example.

This mixture of words and actions represented a clear strategic concept, but the results fell short of the administration's expectations. China reacted to Obama's outstretched hand with bellicose rhetoric and grander regional aspirations. Russia continued to be truculent in its dealings with the United States. Traditional allies resisted making greater contributions in Afghanistan and elsewhere. The G-20's achievements have not matched its aspirations. Meanwhile, isolationist sentiment inside the United States reached a 40-year high.

What went wrong? The administration, and many others, erred in believing that improved standing would give the United States greater policy leverage. The United States' standing among foreign publics and elites did rebound. But this shift did not translate into an appreciable increase in the United States' soft power. Bargaining in the G-20 and the UN Security Council did not get any easier. Soft power, it turns out, cannot accomplish much in the absence of a willingness to use hard power.

Obama erred in believing that improved international standing would give the United States greater policy leverage.

The other problem was that China, Russia, and other aspiring great powers did not view themselves as partners of the United States. Even allies saw the Obama administration's supposed modesty as a cover for shifting the burden of providing global public goods from the United States to the rest of the world. The administration's grand strategy was therefore perceived as promoting narrow U.S. interests rather than global public goods.

In response, the administration reset its policies after its first 18 months in office, pivoting toward a second, more assertive grand strategy. One remaining constant is that the administration is still focused on restoring American strength at home, but it has been increasingly comfortable using the specter of rising foreign powers as a motivational tool. This is why Obama called for a "Sputnik moment" in this year's State of the Union speech and why he has tried to boost public investment in education, science, and clean energy.

At the same time, the administration switched from a strategy of retrenchment to one of counterpunching. In response to international provocations, the United States has signaled that it can still rally allies and counter rising threats. For example, the United States tightened its economic and security relationships with most of China's neighbors in the Asia-Pacific region, forcing Beijing to rethink its strategy. In demonstrating a willingness to balance against rising threats, the United States has reassured its allies that it will not be retreating into isolationism anytime soon. Similarly, reacting to the unrest in the Middle East, the United States used its leverage over the Egyptian military to assist in bringing about a mostly peaceful regime change in Egypt.

Finally, and contrary to the claims of many Republican operatives, Obama linked U.S. foreign policy to American exceptionalism. Clinton has become much more vocal in criticizing China's human rights abuses, and in responding to the revolutions in the Arab world, Obama has evinced an appreciation for promoting U.S. values as well as U.S. interests. When explaining his decision to intervene in Libya, he said, "To brush aside America's responsibility as a leader and—more profoundly—our responsibilities to our fellow human beings under such circumstances would have been a betrayal of who we are. . . . Born, as we are, out of a revolution by those who longed to be free, we welcome the fact that history is on the move in the Middle East and North Africa, and that young people are leading the way. Because wherever people long to be free, they will find a friend in the United States." These are not the words of a man who believes only in realpolitik.

Trouble at Home

As a set of ideas, Obama's new grand strategy holds together in most parts of the globe. The United States' key allies in Europe and the Pacific Rim appear to have been reassured. Its rivals now understand that the administration cannot be pushed around. But the administration's embrace of democratic ideals has not gone down as well in Saudi Arabia or Israel; those countries prefer the devils they know, and the United States again seems like a revisionist power in the region. The administration's reticence to intervene in Bahrain or Syria should ameliorate their concerns.

But whereas the new counterpunching doctrine is sustainable internationally, the same is not true on the domestic front. The most significant challenge to Obama's grand strategy is likely to emerge at home rather than abroad. Viable grand strategies need to rest on a wellspring of domestic support. The biggest problem with Obama's new grand strategy is its troublesome domestic politics.

The biggest problem with Obama's new grand strategy is its troublesome domestic politics.

One issue is the mismatch between the complexity of the global system and the simplicity of U.S. foreign policy rhetoric. Politicians do a fine job talking about "friends" and "enemies," but have great difficulty discussing "rivals," a more nuanced category. It is difficult for the administration to use rising powers as a threat to goad the United States into further action without it leading to excessive demagoguery about China. Official rhetoric is at least partly to blame for inflated public fears about Chinese power.

A more serious problem is that by focusing on renewing the United States' domestic strength, the Obama administration has introduced more partisan politics into the equation. There is still some truth to the aphorism that politics stops at the water's edge. But if the administration argues that the key to U.S. foreign policy is the domestic economy, then it increases the likelihood of domestic discord. Based on the tenor of the debates about the rising levels of U.S. debt, the possibility that the president can hammer out a grand bargain over fiscal and tax policies is looking increasingly remote. These difficulties reinforce the argument, made by the political scientists Charles Kupchan and Peter Trubowitz, that demographic and political shifts within the United States (including the right's rejection of multilateralism and the left's rejection of power projection) are making it harder and harder to build support for a grand strategy based on liberal internationalist principles.

But none of this explains why Obama has done such a bad job explaining his grand strategy to the American people. To be fair, the long economic downturn has soured Americans on engaging with the rest of the world, making any activist foreign policy a tough sell. That said, the administration has done itself few favors in this area. Indeed, the most well-known phrase that articulates current U.S. grand strategy is "leading from behind," which is a politically disastrous wording.

Why has the Obama administration not been more up-front about its grand strategic redesign? First, changing course implies an admission that the previous course was incorrect, and no administration likes to do that. Second, the administration takes pride in its foreign policy pragmatism, but that makes it difficult to promote a new grand strategic vision. Finally, military actions tend to crowd out attention to other dimensions of a foreign policy. And although the Libyan intervention might be justified on its own terms, it does not fit perfectly with Obama's new grand strategy. Libya, by the administration's own admission, is not a core national interest. This has left Obama in the awkward position of trying to explain his foreign policy while de-emphasizing the use of blood and treasure to prosecute the first war he started. Simply labeling it a "kinetic military action" has not helped.

All this is a problem because politics abhors a rhetorical vacuum. If the president is not clear about his grand strategy, foreign policy critics and political opponents will be happy to define it for him, using less than flattering language. Until the Obama administration does a better job of explaining its grand strategy to the American people, it will encounter significant domestic resistance to its policies.

After some initial wrong turns, the Obama administration seems to have found a useful strategic map, but it still needs to persuade the other passengers in the car. Clear communication is rarely a cure-all. In the wake of bin Laden's death, however, the administration has a golden opportunity to explain its revised grand strategy. In taking the risk of sending U.S. Special Forces into Pakistan to eliminate bin Laden, Obama earned a significant bump in public support for his foreign policy. If he articulates his counterpunching strategy soon, he will be doing it from a position of domestic strength rather than weakness. By better explaining his grand strategy to Americans, Obama can show them—and the rest of the world—that he knows where to go and how to get there.

Critical Thinking

1. What is the relationship between grand strategy and national interest?
2. What is Obama's grand strategy for dealing with China?
3. What was the grand strategy of the Bush administration?

DANIEL W. DREZNER is Professor of International Politics at the Fletcher School of Law and Diplomacy at Tufts University and the editor of *Avoiding Trivia: The Role of Strategic Planning in American Foreign Policy.*

Samantha and Her Subjects

Jacob Heilbrunn

Humanitarian intervention—the conviction that American presidents must act, preemptively if necessary, to avert the massacre of innocents abroad—is steadily acquiring a new prominence in the Obama administration. For America's foreign-policy elite, it is a precept that provides a way to expiate the sins of the past, either bellicose action (Vietnam) or complacent inaction (Rwanda). It not only holds out the expectation of protecting endangered civilians but also the promise of acting multilaterally to uphold international laws.

Yet the consequences of such intervention have rarely been more vexing. As the world's leading military power—it devotes more to defense than the next ten biggest-spending countries combined—America finds itself lurching from conflict to conflict, often with little idea of how they will end, other than the hope that the forces of righteousness will prevail, even as Washington becomes progressively more enmeshed in local disputes. In its quixotic quest to create a global and irenic order by force, it is flouting Shakespeare's admonition that it is best to "fling away ambition: By that sin fell the angels."

This is particularly so in the Middle East, where the Obama administration and, to a lesser degree, Europe face nothing less than a potential cataclysm of engagements, until the entire region is in tumult. The result is a self-reinforcing doctrine of permanent revolution. In creating, or abetting, chaotic conditions, it becomes necessary to intervene again and again, all in the name of averting further chaos.

These incursions embrace the idea—some more, some less—of humanitarian intervention. The conceit is that when America intervenes, it is not doing so on the basis of sordid national interests but, rather, on the grounds of self-evidently virtuous human rights or, in its most extreme case, to prevent genocide. This development—to call it a mere trend would be to trivialize its true import—has been a long time in the making.

Indeed, in an essay published in *The National Interest* (now reprinted in *The Neoconservative Persuasion*), Irving Kristol contended that human rights had become a kind of unquestioned ideology. Kristol traced its origins back to the debates between William Gladstone and Benjamin Disraeli over intervention in the Balkans, when the Turks massacred some twelve thousand Bulgarians. The realist Disraeli, who sought to check Russia, was unmoved by Gladstone's humanitarian appeals to endorse self-determination for the Balkan states. But perhaps an even earlier instance came in the lead-up to British involvement in the Crimean War, revolving as it did around the "Eastern Question"; the Turks and Russians could fight it out for influence in the Mediterranean—and the French could get in their squabble over Catholics, without much bother to the Brits. As liberal politician John Bright argued on March 31, 1854, in his great speech to Parliament against squandering power in foolish adventures abroad:

> How are the interests of England involved in this question? . . . it is not on a question of sympathy that I dare involve this country, or any country, in a war which must cost an incalculable amount of treasure and of blood. It is not my duty to make this country the knight-errant of the human race, and to take upon herself the protection of the thousand millions of human beings who have been permitted by the Creator of all things to people this planet.

Transforming the United States into a knight-errant, though, is at the heart of liberal internationalism. As in nineteenth-century Britain, so in modern America; just as with Gladstone, the current manifestation of this impulse first became apparent in the Balkans, when NATO established a no-fly zone there, during the bombings of 1995. And so a new generation of liberal hawks emerged, overcoming the discomfiture associated with the use of force in Vietnam, seeing themselves as divine intervenors for mistreated ethnic minorities abroad. It amounted, in some ways, to a multicultural foreign policy, or at least one that sees America as key to creating a new democratic order. Madeleine Albright, for example, announced during the Clinton administration, "If we have to use force, it is because we are America. We are the indispensable nation. We stand tall, and we see further than other countries into the future."

The hubris of ascribing a unique percipience to the United States was hardly confined to Albright. It also amounted a fortiori to the credo of the George W. Bush administration, which witnessed a fusion of neoconservatives and liberal hawks. "Damn the doves," Christopher Hitchens announced in the conservative London *Spectator* in 2001 as the United States readied to topple Saddam Hussein. While in *Dissent*, Michael Walzer declared that the Left was being "stupid, overwrought, grossly inaccurate" and should accept America's imperial status, modeling any opposition to the Iraq invasion on the Little Englanders during the Boer War.

Then, as the insurgency developed, the alliance melted away. A notable defector was Peter Beinart, who first wrote a book calling for a nationalistic Democratic Party, then issued a second one taking it all back.

Now the alliance between liberal hawks and neocons is returning, epitomized in an open letter sent to the White House in February 2011 by the Foreign Policy Initiative (successor to the Project for the New American Century), demanding that President Obama act to avoid a humanitarian disaster in Libya. Signed by Paul Wolfowitz and William Kristol as well as Martin Peretz and Leon Wieseltier, the old gang was back together again. Robert Kagan declared Obama's speech on Libya to be "Kennedy-esque," the ultimate term of neocon approbation. Intellectuals as a class have become habituated to demanding military action to make up for America's failure to prevent various atrocities and genocides. As David Rieff observed with vexation:

> This war—let us call it by its right name, for once—will be remembered to a considerable extent as a war made by intellectuals, and cheered on by intellectuals. The main difference this time is that, particularly in the United States, these intellectuals largely come from the liberal rather than the conservative side.

No doubt the Obama team was itself torn on the issue of intervention. It entered office emphasizing realist tenets. Now it is jettisoning them. The intellectual incoherence of the White House was epitomized by a statement from Deputy National Security Adviser Ben Rhodes:

> What we are doing is enforcing a resolution that has a very clear set of goals, which is protecting the Libyan people, averting a humanitarian crisis, and setting up a no-fly zone. Obviously that involves kinetic military action, particularly on the front end.

But Washington is not "getting into an open-ended war, a land invasion in Libya."

The plan, however, seems to be for America to act as an arsenal of freedom rather than to promote its own domestic welfare. Today this Wilsonian doctrine is sold as a form of atonement for past wrongdoings—that, unless we intervene decisively in what is often a civil war to tip the balance of the scales to one side, America will once again have blood on its hands. Never again, in other words, will become ever again.

It would be hard to think of a more ardent promoter of this doctrine than Samantha Power. Power is not just an advocate for human rights. She is an outspoken crusader against genocide. She has referred self-deprecatingly to herself as the "genocide chick." She has made it her life's mission to shame American statesmen into action and to transform U.S. foreign policy. And as she seeks to create a new paradigm, she is becoming a paradigmatic figure. She is a testament to the collapse of the old foreign-policy establishment and the rise of a fresh elite. This elite is united by a shared belief that American foreign policy must be fundamentally transformed from an obsession with national interests into a broader agenda that seeks justice for women and minorities, and promotes democracy whenever and wherever it can—at the point of a cruise missile if necessary. The same century-long progressive expansion of the democratic franchise that has taken place at home is also supposed to occur abroad. She is, you could say, the prophet armed.

Power is not just an advocate for human rights. She is an outspoken crusader against genocide. She is, you could say, the prophet armed.

Along with Secretary of State Hillary Clinton and UN Ambassador Susan Rice, Power has become closely—and publicly—identified as one of the advisers most responsible for pushing Obama to intervene in Libya. It is a stunning turnabout. Power served then-Senator Obama as a top aide on foreign policy, taking a leave of absence from the Kennedy School at Harvard. But during the presidential campaign, Power announced that Hillary Clinton (not yet in Barack's employ), who had been relentlessly bashing her boss, was a "monster." A furor erupted. Power resigned. Her career with Obama was over.

Only it wasn't. The late diplomat Richard Holbrooke, a close friend, called her "mesmerizing." Once Obama was elected, she landed a post as a senior adviser on the National Security Council, where she has become an increasingly influential and distinctive voice. Her rise there is even more astonishing given that National Security Adviser Tom Donilon was a deputy to Warren Christopher in the Clinton administration—and Power bitterly assailed that secretary of state for his dithering over Bosnia.

Power, unlike many liberal hawks, was an opponent of the Iraq War. When I hosted a panel with her in 2004 at UCLA that included journalist James Mann and scholar Chalmers Johnson, I asked how she was able to reconcile her espousal of humanitarian intervention with failing to put a stop to Saddam Hussein's depredations. Her response? The Bush administration was not acting multilaterally and Saddam's actions, at that point, didn't meet the definition of genocide even if they had in the past. It is an answer that I never found fully satisfactory, at least for someone who was otherwise championing the cause of stopping mad and bad dictators around the world.

Indeed, absent Power, Obama may not have intervened in Libya. Obama now uses arguments to justify the intervention that are somewhat redolent of Bush's about Iraq. Power has almost single-handedly revived the alliance between liberal hawks and neocons; as one of the chief promoters of the Iraq War, Fouad Ajami, declared in the *Wall Street Journal:*

> In Bosnia, as in Libya a generation later, the standard-bearer of American power had a stark choice: It was either rescue or calamity. Benghazi would have been Barack Obama's Srebrenica, the town that the powers had left to the mercy of [General] Ratko Mladic.

Power has almost single-handedly revived the alliance between liberal hawks and neocons.

An icon among the human-rights lobby, she has made it her personal crusade to ensure that American presidents act decisively to forestall, impede or halt the murder of civilians abroad. When President Obama gave his speech at the National Defense University in March, he explained military action in Libya protected the innocent; he was channeling Power:

> To lend some perspective on how rapidly this military and diplomatic response came together, when people were being brutalized in Bosnia in the 1990s, it took the international community more than a year to intervene with air power to protect civilians.

In fact, a few hours before Obama's speech, Power herself told an audience at Columbia University, in words that anticipated Obama's, that "in the Balkans it took three years for the international community to use air power to prevent heavy weapons from firing on civilians. In Libya it took a little more than a month."

The invocation of Bosnia was not adventitious. It has become the siren song of liberal interventionists. Part of the legend of Power is her first mission to Bosnia, where she filed reports for the *Boston Globe* and other publications about Serbian belligerence and Western inaction. Power became the anti–Rebecca West—where West lionized the Serbs standing up to fascism in the 1930s in her book *Black Lamb and Grey Falcon,* Power became a heroine chastising America and Europe for their lassitude in confronting contemporary fascist impulses from West's former freedom fighters. This was, at bottom, a new Spanish Civil War for Power and her cohort—a chance to choose sides, to experience good and evil, not vicariously but up close, and to denounce it. It is important to remember that when Power traveled to Bosnia, she frequently met with and chastised government officials, including Ambassador Peter Galbraith, for not doing more against Serbian iniquities (a favor he returned as Obama hesitated about intervention in Libya). Not for her the Weberian Wertfreiheit, or objectivity, that American newspapers inculcate. Power epitomizes an older model—the crusading journalist.

But Power's journalistic triumphs were a dress rehearsal for her next career as a professor and author of *"A Problem From Hell": America and the Age of Genocide,* which won a Pulitzer Prize.

It is a bold effort. Stylishly written, packed with vignettes and sharp portraits, it essentially rewrites much of twentieth-century American history in the shadow of genocide. She observes that, again and again, Western powers looked away from massacre. The problem, she famously declared, wasn't that America's policy failed. It was that it worked. Reticence about protesting mass murder was a constituent part of America's hard-nosed, realist approach to foreign affairs. What is missing from

Power's work, however, is a political context. There seems to be the assumption that Washington can always be on the right side of history—that American presidents can ignore domestic and international considerations simply to plunge into conflicts on the side of the beleaguered whenever they feel like it.

It is also notable that Power, in her extended case studies of genocide, ignores some of the biggest examples of the past century. There is no mention of Stalin's man-made Ukrainian famine. There is no mention of Mao's Cultural Revolution, which killed tens of millions.

Perhaps this is because these cases don't quite fit with her theory that the American government's deliberate indifference has invariably been key in the failure to stop mass deaths. Rather, many on the American and British left were bedazzled by what they saw as Communist dictatorships greatly leaping forward, whatever the human toll might be. It was active blindness on the part of these intellectuals, a shameful historical legacy that nothing can efface. As Saul Bellow once observed, "A great deal of intelligence can be invested in ignorance when the need for illusion is deep."

The true strength of Power's book is as a literary work, a ringing and idealistic call to arms. It does not merely recount. It instructs its reader what is to be done. Power's work begins with a bang—the 1921 assassination in Berlin of Mehmed Talat, the former Turkish interior minister who presided over the massacre of Armenians. It was one of the few actions, as Power notes, taken to punish the Turks. Woodrow Wilson, eager to remain neutral in World War I, had resisted the calls of his ambassador to the Ottoman Empire, Henry Morgenthau, to protest the killings of Armenians. Power castigates Wilson for refusing to "declare war on or even break off relations with the Ottoman Empire." She would have taken America onto the European battlefields—and into the bloodbath—far earlier. In going to war against Germany, Wilson told Congress, "it seems to me that we should go only where immediate and practical considerations lead us and not heed any others." According to Power, "America's nonresponse to the Turkish horrors established patterns that would be repeated."

What Power does not discuss is Wilson's conduct of the war, namely his decision to intervene after he had promised Americans he would not. If anything, Wilson, who promised the war to end wars, was wildly idealistic, anything but a hardened realist, someone who was bamboozled during the Paris peace negotiations by his French and British counterparts, the champion of the League of Nations, whose headquarters in Geneva became a testament to fecklessness during the 1930s. It seems peculiar to condemn Wilson for not having been idealistic enough.

When it comes to World War II, Power has a far stronger case to make. The wartime Allies, confronted with the crime of the century, focused on battling Nazism rather than exposing its genocidal campaign against the Jews and other ethnic and religious minorities. Her hero is the Polish-Jewish lawyer Raphael Lemkin who invented the neologism "genocide." He was pivotal to the new United Nations' adoption of a convention declaring genocide a violation of international law, though America refused to sign it for four decades. Now it provides a basis for military intervention.

Which returns us to Bosnia yet again. Power does an excellent job of limning the reluctance of the George H. W. Bush administration to intervene. As then–Secretary of State James Baker famously put it, "We don't have a dog in this fight." Instead, to quell charges of its heartlessness, the White House sent American troops to Somalia in a humanitarian venture—a disastrous decision that got America bogged down in a bloody civil war. Next, the Clinton administration came under fire for doing the same sort of hand-wringing over Bosnia as its realist predecessor—surely the Left could be counted on for compassion? Yet then it remained reticent about Rwanda, allowing the Hutus to conduct mass killings of hundreds of thousands of Tutsis.

Power's verdict is withering:

> The real reason the United States did not do what it could and should have done to stop genocide was not a lack of knowledge or influence but a lack of will. Simply put, American leaders did not act because they did not want to. They believed that genocide was wrong, but they were not prepared to invest the military, financial, diplomatic, or domestic political capital needed to stop it.

Power hopes to once and for all turn the tide against American lassitude, against the Democratic slogan propounded by presidential hopeful George McGovern in the 1972 campaign—"Come Home, America." Liberals were then opposed to Ronald Reagan's support for the Nicaraguan contras, even though he portrayed that partly as a humanitarian venture, pointing to the human-rights abuses perpetrated by the Sandinistas. Reagan, for all the bellicosity, was loath to send American troops into combat, withdrawing them from Lebanon after the bombing of the Marine Corps barracks in 1983. What Power overlooks, or minimizes, is the political context of a country in which the term "no more Vietnams" carried, and continues to carry, great political weight. It is these old thought patterns that Power wants to refashion, turning the United States into a nation that wields force wherever it deems fit—not for security, but for the betterment of others, secure we will not squander resources because of the justness of our cause.

Power has a penchant for dramatizing history through people rather than considering broader forces. She states in the acknowledgments to *"A Problem From Hell"* that a friend from Hollywood advised her to create a drama by telling the story through characters. And that is what she did.

As her other tome about the United Nations official Sergio Vieira de Mello—*Chasing the Flame: One Man's Fight to Save the World*—makes clear, however, Power champions her own kind of great-man history in which a lonely hero stands up for truth, justice and the international way. She produces a morality play rather than a conventional history. In a sense, Power, you could argue, is addicted to hero worship, beginning with Raphael Lemkin and ending with Obama. In fact, in her acknowledgments, she observes that she offered "whatever help I could to Barack Obama, the person whose rigor and compassion bear the closest resemblance to Sergio's that I have ever seen."

This seems excessive. Vieira de Mello was a Brazilian United Nations bureaucrat. He served the UN in a number of hot spots—East Timor, Rwanda, Cyprus, Cambodia, Lebanon and the Balkans (where Power first met him in her capacity as a journalist). He was a UN high commissioner for human rights and was murdered along with twenty other members of his staff in August 2003 when he was the secretary-general's special representative in Iraq. He served bravely. Perhaps he would have become secretary-general. But to elevate him, as Power does, into the stuff of legend defies credulity. For her Vieira de Mello serves as a beacon, a symbol of what true internationalism might accomplish.

As Power portrays it, Vieira de Mello is everything the United States was not under George W. Bush—dignified, restrained, attentive to local conditions, eager to negotiate with foreign tyrants. His death in the bombed-out Canal Hotel serves as a sign of the blundering malignancy of the land of the free. Obama, like Vieira de Mello, is supposed to personify the better side of America. He represents patience and understanding, and a readiness to negotiate with authoritarian leaders when necessary rather than refusing to deal with them at all.

But as Michael Massing observed in an incisive review in the June 9, 2008, issue of the *Nation,* Vieira de Mello actually reflected many of the worst traits of the UN. According to Massing:

> While she presents him as embodying the UN system at its best—its dedication to humanitarianism, multilateralism and dialogue—a strong case can be made, based on the evidence she presents, that he represented the UN system at its worst—its timidity, mediocrity and zeal for self-protection.

Instead of being a crusader, Vieira de Mello was ready to compromise. For example, Power writes that when it came to protecting the rights of Vietnamese boat people,

> he could have gone to greater lengths to use his pulpit at [the UN's refugee agency] UNHCR to try to ensure that the Vietnamese were more fairly screened in the camps and were better treated en route back to Vietnam. This was the first of several prominent instances in his career in which he would downplay his and the UN's obligation to try to *shape* the preferences of governments. By the 1980s he had come to see himself as a UN man, but since the organization was both a body of self-interested governments and a body of ideals, he did not seem sure yet whether serving the UN meant doing what states demanded or pressing for what refugees needed.

Such tentative statements, as Massing observes, are acutely at odds with the fire-breathing Power of *"A Problem From Hell."* There she denounced statesmen for doing what Vieira de Mello did. This raises the question of whether Power is willing to make any accommodation necessary to cater to her own new boss.

Nor did the role that Vieira de Mello played in Bosnia turn out any better. It's hardly a secret that the UN disgraced itself in the Balkans, where it served as a de facto accomplice to the

Serbs. Power recounts that Vieira de Mello was touring the former Soviet Union while Serbian General Ratko Mladic

presided over the systematic slaughter of every Bosnian man and boy in his custody, some eight thousand in all. When the Serb mass graves were discovered six weeks later, Vieira de Mello was stunned. "I never thought Mladic was this stupid," he said, projecting his own reverence for reason onto one who clearly observed different norms. "The massacre was totally unnecessary."

(What massacre, incidentally, is necessary?) In this telling, Vieira de Mello, who sought to curry favor with leading Serbs, sounds less like an international statesman than a gullible technocrat. Power's implicit criticisms of Vieira de Mello suggest, as Michael Massing notes, that she is wrestling with the contradictions of espousing an idealistic credo and implementing a policy. (Such would seem to be the case, for example, when she defends Obama administration policy on Guantánamo Bay, wildly at variance as it is with the president's promises circa 2008 to shutter the detention facility promptly.)

Power recounts other less-than-inspiriting episodes. She notes that in 1999, after the *Washington Post* reported that several UN weapons inspectors in Iraq were sending information to the Clinton administration, Vieira de Mello almost resigned. Fabrizio Hochschild, his special assistant, thought that some kind of démarche to Richard Butler, the head of the UN inspections team, was required. But he was, Power reports, "taken aback when he saw Vieira de Mello greet Butler on his next visit as if nothing had happened. No matter how great his outrage, Hochschild noted, Vieira de Mello remained as reluctant as ever to make an enemy." There can be no doubting that Vieira de Mello's extensive experience in war zones would have made him a valuable adviser, if the Bush administration had been disposed to listen to his advice, which it was not. He had, as Power observes, frequently "watched as promising postwar transitions collapsed because of a failure to fill the security void."

Power's assumption appears to be that given the right approach, Iraq might not have degenerated into sectarian warfare. There can be no doubting that the Bush administration botched the occupation. But it is unclear such interventions ever turn out well. It is not just the hubristic evildoers on the right who fail to build up new and better societies in the wake of war; incursions of this sort may simply be doomed. Doesn't Iraq, in fact, cast further doubt on the efficacy of so-called humanitarian ventures?

Now Power is behind the rush to fill the security void in Libya. As Secretary Clinton told ABC News in March:

We learned a lot in the 1990s. We saw what happened in Rwanda. It took a long time in the Balkans, in Kosovo to deal with a tyrant. But I think . . . what has happened since March 1st, and we're not even done with the month, demonstrates really remarkable leadership.

Power provided the tutorials these past years, both to Obama and to an entire class of liberal hawks. She may be the most influential journalist-turned-presidential-adviser since a young Walter Lippmann drafted the Fourteen Points for Woodrow Wilson, only to become a chastened realist after the Treaty of Versailles made a mockery of Wilsonianism and the internationalist dream.

Perhaps Power's next destination is to become United Nations ambassador. Maybe she will follow in the footsteps of Madeleine Albright and ultimately become secretary of state. In his memoir, *The Audacity of Hope,* Obama observed that Power "combed over each chapter." Now she has begun to exercise the same influence over his approach to foreign affairs. Obama entered office, like George W. Bush, promising to repudiate the arrogance of his predecessor, only to be seduced by the lure of militant democracy.

> ## Obama entered office, like George W. Bush, promising to repudiate the arrogance of his predecessor, only to be seduced by the lure of militant democracy.

Power's argument that there is a coincidence between humanitarian intervention and American national interests marks a profound shift in justification for military action. Rhetorically, she espouses a move away from fighting Islamic terrorism to battling aggressors under the banner of humanitarian intervention. This is supposed to mark a fundamental break with the Bush administration, whose approach to confronting terrorism she denounced in a lengthy essay in the *New York Times* in 2007. Whether it amounts to one in practice is another matter.

Even Obama didn't try to argue that genocide was taking place in Libya. Instead, this was a preemptive strike (ah, how redolent again of the 2003 Iraq invasion) against a potential massacre, one that would have profound implications for the region. It was in America's national interest to intervene. And so he plunged the United States into a new conflict. Where does Power draw the line? The bar for preventing genocide may well have been set too high in the past, as she argues. But she, in turn, may be setting it too low, providing an ideological smokescreen for the use of American military force in dubious circumstances, something she never adequately addresses. She runs the risk of exposing America to the charge of hypocrisy for not intervening in countries where brutal mistreatment of the local population is taking place, as in Zimbabwe, while providing a validating and dangerously palatable logic for American overextension. Power's solution to the conundrum that has bedeviled the Democratic Party since Vietnam—when to sanction the use of force abroad—is to support wars of national liberation. This is likely not a solution at all.

In a speech in 2006, Power told graduating students at Santa Clara University Law School "to demand that our representatives are attentive to the human consequences of their decision making." The new round of engagements abroad by the Obama administration may well come to be seen as the last glimmerings of American hubris. "Kings can have subjects," George F. Kennan once observed, "it is a question whether a republic can."

It would be no small irony if, in her zeal to reshape American foreign policy in the image of liberal internationalism, Power were to usher in its demise.

Critical Thinking

1. Was NATO justified in intervening in Libya?
2. What is the relationship between genocide and the decision of the Obama administration to intervene in Libya?
3. What are the international legal implications of NATO's intervention in Libya?

JACOB HEILBRUNN is a senior editor at *The National Interest*.

Change in the Middle East
Its Implications for US Policy

Michael Singh

To say that the Middle East has reached a turning point would be missing the point. The Middle East is hurtling in a new direction, and the United States must catch up or be left behind. The remarkable events in Tunisia, Egypt, Libya, Bahrain, and elsewhere have shaken a regional order that has stood relatively undisturbed since 1979 and thrown into disarray US interests that only a few months ago seemed secure. These events call into question Washington's post-Cold War approach to the Middle East and demand a reevaluation of US policy in the region.

During the Cold War, Washington supported authoritarian regimes in the Middle East as part of a broader strategy to defeat the Soviet Union and global communism. At stake in this contest, as far as US policymakers were concerned, was not simply geopolitical preeminence, but the fate of human liberty. Opposition movements were frequently seen, rightly or wrongly, as cat's paws for Moscow, and the local depredations of friendly dictators were excused for support in the global struggle. When the Soviet Union was defeated, the overarching Cold War objective had vanished, yet the US approach to the region did not change. Authoritarian regimes maintained a rough alignment of interests with the United States, while Washington did little to address the deficit of human and political rights across the region.

US policymakers have long recognized the problems inherent in this approach. It places our interests in opposition to our values. Even the benefits to our interests are questionable; it has long been recognized that over the long term democracies are more reliable and peaceful allies than are autocracies. It was this contradiction that led Secretary of State Condoleezza Rice to observe, in 2005, that "for 60 years the United States pursued stability at the expense of democracy in the Middle East—and we achieved neither." Yet, with few exceptions, US policymakers have found it difficult to navigate the short-term tradeoffs necessary to truly elevate the promotion of democracy and human rights in the Middle East to the top of the policy agenda.

Yet, in failing to take the opportunity afforded by the fall of the Soviet Union to shift toward greater support for political reform and democratization in the region, the United States planted the seeds of its current dilemma. Washington's support for leaders such as former Egyptian President Hosni Mubarak and Tunisia's Ben Ali, widely viewed as harshly repressive by their citizens, fostered anti-Americanism. And US policymakers' failure to build a broader foundation of support in these and other countries meant that US interests in the region were placed in the hands of individual leaders and their circles, with few ardent advocates otherwise. Taken together, these choices have increased the chances that the political turmoil in the region will at least for a time set back US interests. For this reason, recent events in the region represent not an intelligence failure, as some analysts and members of Congress have suggested, but a policy failure. As is so often the case in foreign policy crises, US policymakers were aware of the potential problem—prospects for serious domestic turmoil afflicting authoritarian regimes—but they did not treat the issue with urgency, subordinating it instead to other matters. Such was the road that led to the Obama administration's hesitation and inconsistency when faced with the ouster of erstwhile authoritarian allies in Tunis and Cairo.

With this context in mind, the United States must act amid the region's turbulence to put its interests on a more sustainable trajectory. This requires that Washington devise an approach that better accounts for the risks posed by persistent authoritarianism and the rampant corruption and economic maladies that accompany it. Even with policies in place to address these issues, however, the turmoil currently gripping the Middle East may persist for some time, and the affected governments may be weakened commensurately. As a result, the United States will need to redouble its efforts to address threats to its interests and conflicts in the region, alongside both local partners and allies in Europe and elsewhere. US interests in the Middle East have not fundamentally changed, but the risks to them may be greater, and the path to advancing them more tortuous than President Obama and his advisors previously understood.

> . . . the United States will need to redouble its efforts to address threats to its interests and conflicts in the region, alongside both local partners and allies in Europe and elsewhere.

Political Reform

Perhaps the clearest implication of recent events in the Middle East for US policy is the need to place greater emphasis on political reform and liberalization in the region. Pressing for such reform is not simply a moral imperative for the United States, and it is not charity; rather, it reflects a recognition that sustainable alliances must be with peoples, not just governments. In democracies this distinction is moot, but in autocracies and fragmented societies it is vital.

The popular uprisings in Tunisia, Egypt, Libya, and elsewhere generated significant sympathy among US officials, but they also caused a great deal of anxiety due to the possibilities of violence or political openings for extremist groups. It is important to recognize, however, that the ultimate cause of such prospects for instability is not the demand for political reform, but the prior absence of such reform. As Kenneth Wollack outlined in these pages in December 2010, US and European democratic assistance is based on the premise that democracy overseas not only delivers better for those foreign populations, but also enhances our own national security. Recent events in the Middle East underscore that this logic must motivate policy not just over the long term, but should also push political reform up Washington's near-term foreign policy agenda.

This is not to say that each country requires the same reforms on the same timetable; it is just as true now as it was prior to the uprisings in the region that each country faces unique challenges and will move at its own pace. Indeed, the uprisings themselves have demonstrated the importance of institutional differences between countries. For example, in Egypt the military remained unified and served as a stabilizing force, and perhaps forced the hand of Hosni Mubarak and his inner circle; in Libya, however, the armed forces quickly splintered. These differences are important and should inform US efforts, but recent events make clear that they should not be used to excuse or explain away the absence of political and human rights.

When it comes to advancing political reform, there are three broad categories of countries in the Middle East. For countries currently undergoing a political transition, such as Tunisia, Egypt, and Libya, US efforts will need to follow two primary lines of action. The first is to help create space for genuine political debate and deliberation. This means preventing internal or external extremists from using violence or intimidation to influence outcomes, as addressed in greater detail below. It also means making available tools—whether technological, such as broadcast media or Internet applications, or traditional, such as political training provided by international NGOs—where necessary to facilitate political discourse. The second line of action in these countries should be the provision of the technical and financial assistance required to build political institutions, conduct sound elections, and take the other steps required to carry out sustainable reform.

With respect to countries which are neither democratic nor US allies, such as Iran and Syria, the challenges facing Washington are very different. The United States has longstanding conflicts with these countries, many of which, like Iran's pursuit of nuclear weapons, are not directly affected by regional uprisings. Nevertheless, Tehran in particular has touted the revolutions as "Islamic awakenings" and as a repudiation of pro-Western leaders, heedless of the similarities between the demands of opposition movements in the affected countries and those of Iran's own opposition. In addition to ensuring that Tehran and Damascus do not move beyond such rhetoric to actual meddling in countries such as Egypt and Tunisia, the United States should seize the opportunity to increase international attention to human rights abuses and the absence of political freedom in Iran and Syria by increasing the prominence of these issues in international forums and diplomatic interactions with Iran. After an initially anemic response to the Iranian opposition protests that erupted in June 2009, Washington has increased its own focus on human rights in Iran, such as placing sanctions in February 2011 on Iranian officials involved in repression. The Obama administration should seek to broaden both the scope of these efforts—including the targeting of Syria—and multilateral support for them.

The most difficult challenge Washington faces is how to press non-democratic allies to enact political reforms. However great US sympathy for pro-democracy activists, Washington will be loath to strain its ties with its remaining regional allies, who in turn are reportedly unhappy with what they see as Washington's failure to support Ben Ali and Mubarak, and are looking for signals of continuing US support. The case that the United States must make to these allies is that political reform is in the interest of their countries as well as themselves. As Secretary of State Hillary Clinton asserted in a speech in Doha in January 2011, stability in Middle Eastern countries requires that these leaders respond to their countries' legitimate needs for political and economic reform. What caused the ignominious fall of Hosni Mubarak was not the withdrawal of US support—after all, Washington has been criticized for being slow to support the protesters—but his own refusal over many years to allow a significant political opening or respond to demands for change from Egyptians or calls to reform from Washington such as the one delivered by Secretary Rice in 2005.

The case that the United States must make to these allies is that political reform is in the interest of their countries as well as themselves.

Reform and Corruption

While political reform in the Middle East is important, it is not sufficient to address the discontent that gave rise to this year's uprisings. In a February 2011 poll of Egyptians conducted by the Washington Institute for Near East Policy and Pechter Middle East polls, it was revealed that the top three reasons given for the protests—by a wide margin—were "poor economic conditions," "corruption," and "unemployment." The data bears out these concerns. According to the CIA, unemployment was 30 percent in Libya in 2004 and 15 percent in Bahrain more recently, and almost certainly higher among the youth who formed the core of the recent uprisings. In Egypt, one-fifth of the population lived below the poverty line, and in Libya one-third was poor. As Wollack pointed out, economic development and democratic governance are intertwined; while critics of democracy are quick to point to the "China model" or other related examples of economic growth in the absence of political reform, there are far more cases of countries in which political repression, economic stagnation, and corruption go hand-in-hand.

Nevertheless, political reform will not in itself solve those obstacles to economic development; indeed, the turmoil in countries like Egypt and Tunisia, where tourism is an important contributor to GDP, may initially deepen rather than alleviate economic challenges. Democratization also does not automatically address corruption; it has been frequently asserted, for example, that Russia's reversion to authoritarianism was fueled in part by perceptions of oligarchical corruption in the immediate post-Communist period.

To help countries in the region overcome these economic challenges, the United States should consider several steps. These include, but are not limited to, the provision of macroeconomic advice and technical assistance, lowering or removing barriers to trade and investment, broadening usage of anti-kleptocracy sanctions, and urging oil-rich states to invest more in their poorer neighbors to reinforce the economic fabric of the region. In addition, the United States should review its approach to economic aid to these countries to ensure that assistance does not foster dependency but instead encourages entrepreneurship and local economic growth. In recent years, the United States has retooled its approach to economic aid via such vehicles as the Millennium Challenge Corporation, which vets potential recipients according to a strict set of criteria in order to encourage local reform and build indigenous skills and capabilities.

Threats and Conflicts

While a greater emphasis on smart political and economic reforms is essential to put US interests in the Middle East on a secure footing, the implications of the recent uprisings in the region are much broader. In the immediate term, the situations in Egypt, Libya, Tunisia and elsewhere are far from settled, and could just as easily descend into chaos or revert to authoritarianism as progress toward democracy remains elusive. In the longer term, US military planners and intelligence analysts will need to revisit their assumptions and judgments, which will have implications for the US posture in the region for years to come.

To grapple with these new challenges as well as longstanding threats, Washington will need to strengthen its partnerships with remaining allies. Contrary to conventional wisdom, bolstering our alliances and pushing for reform are not mutually exclusive. A firm commitment to allies' security and prosperity cements the trust necessary to effectively advocate for reform, and allays suspicions that the United States is acting imprudently. Indeed, the US alliances with Israel, the Palestinian Authority (PA), and some Arab states were strained even prior to the revolutions in Tunisia and Egypt, not over the question

of reform, but due to what our allies saw as poor approaches to regional issues such as the Middle East peace process and Iran. The challenge is different and perhaps more complex in countries undergoing transition, where the United States must rebuild relationships with individuals who may be skeptical of the benefits of cooperation with the West. Together with allies old and new, the United States will need to confront several challenges, including the three detailed below.

First, the transitions in Tunisia, Egypt, and Libya, and the unrest in the region more broadly, will provide openings that extremist groups will be eager to exploit. Much has been made, for example, of the possibility that the Muslim Brotherhood will benefit from a transition to democracy in Egypt. The extremist threat has two aspects, each of which demands a different response. The first is the possibility that extremist groups, alone or in conjunction with state sponsors of terrorism such as Iran, will seek to exploit the weakened condition of states in the region to foment chaos and violence and subvert movement toward participatory government in places like Tunisia and Egypt. The historical examples are bracing—the Bolsheviks in revolutionary Russia, partisans of Ayatollah Khomeini in Iran in 1979 and thereafter, or Hamas' forcible takeover of government in Gaza following its electoral victory in 2006. Addressing this threat requires that the United States redouble its vigilance in the region to monitor and counter terrorist groups and their supporters, all while enjoying a likely degraded level of counterterrorism cooperation from Egypt, Libya, and Tunisia.

The second challenge posed by extremist groups is that, by virtue of their size, resources, and organizational strengths relative to secular competitors, they will command a role in government that may exceed their true level of popular support. This fear is particularly acute in Egypt. According to the Washington Institute/Pechter poll, the Muslim Brotherhood's "approval" rating is just 15 percent in Egypt, and its leader receives just 1 percent support in a presidential straw poll. Nevertheless, the group captured 20 percent of seats in Egypt's parliament in 2005, and its leaders have estimated that it would enjoy 30 percent support in a free election.

To counter the possibility that the Muslim Brotherhood or similar groups will command disproportionate representation in government, the international community can aid in the development and training of secular alternatives, and advise Egypt's transitional authorities on designing a constituency-based electoral system that favors accountability over ideology.

Events in the region will also have implications for Israel and the Palestinians. Israel views the upheavals across the region, especially the revolution in Egypt, as potentially threatening to its security. Although Israel enjoyed neither peace with nor even recognition from many of its neighbors, it had nevertheless settled into a relatively stable relationship with them far preferable to the period of intermittent war between 1948 and 1973. Egypt's revolution not only calls into question the future status of the peace treaty and political relations between Israel and Egypt, but the security of Israel's southwestern border and the flow of arms to Hamas in Gaza. This is not merely a concern about the Muslim Brotherhood; secular politicians such as

Ayman Nour have also called for reevaluating the Camp David Accords. Israel also worries about its foes in the region being emboldened by the fall of Hosni Mubarak, who was reliably committed to peace with Israel. That Iran and its allies see this as a moment to act boldly was underscored by the passage of two Iranian ships through the Suez Canal on February 22, the first such transit by Iranian vessels since 1979.

As serious as the pressure on Israel resulting from recent events may be, the pressure on the Palestinian Authority (PA) may be more severe. Like Israel, the PA is negatively affected by the fall of Hosni Mubarak, who was a staunch supporter of the PA against Hamas, far more so than many other Arab leaders. Unlike Israel, however, the PA may also be subject to internal pressure from its own people, and find itself in the unenviable position of having to engage in domestic reform at a time of reduced regional support. To address the increased insecurity of both Israel and the PA, the United States will need to step up its support to both. In the case of Israel, this means not simply military assistance, an area in which the bilateral relationship is healthy, but also political support, which has frayed of late. In the case of the Palestinians, this means both the sort of financial and security assistance currently provided by the United States and others, as well as diplomatic backing to maintain or increase the political and other support from the region upon which the PA depends. Securing such support may be more difficult for American diplomats in the current regional context, but it is also more necessary than ever.

Given the loss of an ally in Egypt, and the pressure being placed on other friendly rulers such as King Abdullah of Jordan, both Israel and the PA should also reevaluate their current approach to the Israeli-Palestinian peace process. While now is hardly a propitious moment for progress on that front for many reasons, the recent changes in the region underscore that neither side can count on indefinite regional support for a two-state solution. New governments in Cairo and Tunis may or may not support initiatives like the Saudi Peace Initiative of 2002, which was far from perfect but, most importantly, held out the prospect of Arab normalization with Israel. And if Islamist parties gain increased sway, those governments may not even support Palestinian negotiations, preferring instead the path of violent "resistance" offered by Hamas and already endorsed by Iran, Syria, Turkey, and others. Both Israel and the PA should look to take advantage of what may be a shrinking window of regional support for their efforts.

Finally, as a result of the recent uprisings and other events, the United States will need to deal with an increasingly confident (perhaps overconfident) Iranian regime. As previously noted, Tehran sees the revolutions across the region as working in its favor and has thus acted boldly. Even before these events, however, the Iranian regime believed events in the region were going its way due to Hezbollah's ascendancy in Lebanon, the apparent recovery of Iran's uranium enrichment program, and rising oil prices, among other developments. When the Iranian regime feels emboldened, it has a tendency to engage in provocative behavior, as its ships' Suez transit demonstrates. To prevent Tehran from escalating this behavior or seeking to influence the direction of political transitions across the region, the United States should not lose sight of the need to continually deal new blows to the Iranian regime in the form of sanctions or other forms of pressure. Diplomatic bandwidth is not an infinite resource, but some must be found even amid efforts to deal with turmoil elsewhere in the region to curtail Iran's enthusiasm for troublemaking. Given the failure of the P5 + 1 (the five permanent members of the UN Security Council—the United States, United Kingdom, France, Russia, and China, plus Germany) to make progress in the latest round of nuclear negotiations with Iran in Istanbul, the West has been focused in any event on devising new means to pressure Tehran.

The recent wave of political turmoil that has swept across the Middle East has presented the United States with a host of challenges and demands that US policy in the region be reevaluated. However, the uprisings have also swept away the outdated notions that people in the Middle East do not want or are not ready for democracy. That these revolutions will result in democracy, or even that they will represent a net gain for their authors or for US interests, is far from inevitable. However, it can no longer be called into question that populations in the Middle East value and desire the same liberties that their counterparts in the West have long enjoyed. Those shared values, so frequently called into question, hold out the prospect for a renewed, revitalized, and enduring relationship between the people of the United States and the people of the Middle East.

Critical Thinking

1. How do the changes in the Middle East affect United States interests in the region?

2. Is there danger of a revival of authoritarianism in the Middle Eastern revolutions?

3. How do the changes in the Middle East affect United States policy toward Iran?

Michael Singh is managing director of the Washington Institute and a former senior director for Middle Eastern affairs at the National Security Council. Previously, Mr. Singh taught economics at Harvard University. He is currently serving as a term member of the Council on Foreign Relations.

From *Harvard International Review*, Spring 2011, pp. 17–21. Copyright © 2011 by the President of Harvard College. Reprinted by permission via Sheridan Reprints.

After Osama bin Laden
They Got Him

What the death of the movement's figurehead means for al-Qaeda, Pakistan, Afghanistan—and the West.

Woken by the deafening thump of rotor blades, Haji Bashir Khan crept on to his roof and watched, under a warm and moonless sky, as American special forces stormed his neighbour's compound. "Yes, we were scared. We don't have terrorism here," says the middle-aged restaurateur. He heard shooting and screams, then felt an explosion as a grounded helicopter was destroyed. The blast broke his bedroom window and strewed blackened bits of the chopper over a nearby wheat field.

Mr Khan and others in Abbottabad, a garrison town north of Islamabad, say the raid that killed Osama bin Laden lasted for 40 minutes. In the Situation Room at the White House, where Barack Obama and his staff gathered to watch reports of progress . . . , it seemed to last for very much longer. But in the end—in the very early hours of May 2nd, Pakistan time—American Navy Seals shot to death the man who had plotted the murder of nearly 3,000 people on September 11th 2001 and who had become the symbolic leader of global *jihad* against the West.

America's first lead came four years ago. Thanks to information acquired by interrogating detainees, officials identified one of the few al-Qaeda couriers trusted by Mr bin Laden. Two years later, they pinpointed the area of Pakistan in which he operated. But it was not until last August that they worked out precisely where this man and his brother lived: in a large house built in 2005 on what were then the outskirts of Abbottabad. It was surrounded by walls up to 18 feet high. Though large and expensive, it had no phone or internet connection, and few outward-facing windows. In addition to the two brothers, a third family was in residence. After careful analysis the Americans concluded that this family was Mr bin Laden's.

Pakistan's government, bracing itself for public anger and revenge attacks, grimly declared that it was caught unawares by the raid. Much harder to swallow are its claims that Pakistan's blundering spies had no idea that Mr bin Laden had been kept, probably for years, not in a remote cave on the Afghan frontier but cradled in the arms of retired and serving generals in a pleasant hillside town. It prefers to plead incompetence, since admitting to the alternative is far more painful: that the Inter-Services Intelligence directorate (ISI), or rogue elements in it, had long harboured Mr bin Laden and that Pakistan's leaders acquiesced in his killing, if at all, only moments before it was done.

That seems, to many, the likelier explanation. Mr bin Laden's prolonged stay, with many of his relatives flocking in from Yemen, required a network of help. That he had relatively few guards on the spot also suggests he trusted others for security. Ordinary residents of Abbottabad were expected regularly to show their ID cards.

Usually smooth-talking ISI men have been giving garbled accounts of what they and their government were up to. Pakistan's president, Asif Ali Zardari, pleaded innocence in an op-ed article in the *Washington Post,* arguing that Pakistan had as much reason to despise al-Qaeda as any other country. More telling is the gobsmacked silence of General Ashfaq Kayani, the powerful army chief, who had long denied that Mr bin Laden was hidden in Pakistan. Only on April 23rd he had brushed away American grumbles that too little was being done to fight terrorists, saying blithely that they would soon be beaten. All the more galling for him, he spoke at Abbottabad's military academy, within waving distance of the most wanted terrorist in the world.

A Waning Star

Ever since evading his pursuers in the Tora Bora mountains of Afghanistan in November 2001, Mr bin Laden's slipperiness in the face of America's efforts to find him had inspired jihadists everywhere. In the crowded field of Islamist terrorism it also preserved al-Qaeda, his loose-limbed organisation, as the leading brand.

Yet there were, and are, many cracks in this apparently bold façade. According to some observers, al-Qaeda is under severe pressure: smaller in numbers than it has been for years, short of money, and much less capable of carrying out big operations against the "far" enemy in the West (as opposed to the "near" enemy, usually defined as corrupt Muslim states). And in the Middle East, in particular, al-Qaeda's star has long been waning.

Mr bin Laden's death proved that. Although newspapers across the region splashed it over their front pages, and TV talk shows rattled on into the wee hours parsing the implications, interest faded quickly. Aside from a few odes to martyrdom posted on obscure jihadist websites, and sniffy complaints that Mr bin Laden's burial at sea offended Muslim tradition, scarcely a tear was shed.

Neither Mr bin Laden nor al-Qaeda ever held sustained appeal for most of his fellow Arabs and Muslims. To many he was a scourge and a criminal, responsible not only for thousands of deaths but for bringing notoriety to Muslims everywhere. Others regarded him as a romantically defiant figure, a man who, despite the evident brutality of his methods, harboured the good intention of freeing Muslims from Western tutelage. Yet even to many of his admirers, the thrill of seeing the American lion's tail violently yanked proved short-lived.

As time passed, it was clear that the goals of Mr bin Laden's *jihad*—especially ridding Muslim lands of infidel occupiers—were getting no closer. On the contrary, his belligerence excused further Western trespass into Iraq and Afghanistan, bolstered Western backing for Muslim allies in the war on terror, and starkly amplified Muslim divisions, such as those between Sunnis and Shias. Even before this year's surge of popular revolts upended regional politics, al-Qaeda had faded to the margins. Mr bin Laden's acolytes thrived only in remote, lawless zones such as the mountains of Yemen and Pakistan, the deserts of the Sahel and the badlands of Afghanistan and Iraq, where what sustained them was resistance to the foreign invasions they had helped to provoke. The constant hounding of security forces kept the leaders in hiding, increasingly unable to communicate with each other or the world.

As a result, "core" al-Qaeda, roughly defined as the remnants of the organisation led by Mr bin Laden and his Egyptian deputy, Ayman al-Zawahiri, which found refuge in the tribal areas of Pakistan after its expulsion from Afghanistan, is in a poor state. Mounting numbers of missile strikes by CIA-controlled Predator drones on its camps in North Waziristan have succeeded in killing many al-Qaeda fighters and operatives, some quite senior, over the past two years. These attacks have been so effective (at least militarily; they are loathed by ordinary Pakistanis, who too often end up as unintended victims) that they have led to some al-Qaeda commanders murdering each other, convinced they have been betrayed from within.

Such is the fear that their communications are being monitored that discarded mobile-phone sim cards have been found littering the ground around al-Qaeda and Taliban camps. According to intelligence sources, Mr Zawahiri "went dark" in late 2009 and has not been heard of since. The drones also gather huge amounts of real-time information, which has allowed General David Petraeus, the coalition commander in Afghanistan, to use special forces to attack Taliban and al-Qaeda bases, at times, almost nightly. Recent estimates suggest that al-Qaeda's active membership in Afghanistan and Pakistan is now little more than a couple of hundred, plus foreign fighters who come and go.

Franchises and Offshoots

The number of terrorist threats identified by Western intelligence agencies as coming from the region has declined, although not by as much as might have been expected. A few years ago more than 75 percent of the threats originated in South Asia; now the split with the rest of the world is about even. And yet the network has one proven advantage: its protean ability to adapt to circumstance.

Another result of the concerted pressure on al-Qaeda's core has been its mutation from the hierarchical pyramid organisation it was in 2001 into what Leah Farrall, author of the blog *All Things Counter-Terrorism,* describes as a "devolved network hierarchy, in which levels of command authority are not always clear, personal ties between militants carry weight and, at times, transcend the command structure between [al-Qaeda's] core, branch and franchises." In this model the core leadership is largely relieved of direct operational responsibilities, which devolve to the branches and franchises. Instead, the core exercises command and control only over strategy and ideology.

This is not a particularly recent development. In fact, the September 11th attacks were themselves intended to draw in disparate jihadist groups that had resisted Mr bin Laden's attempts to unify the movement—both through the huge propaganda impact of the deed itself, and also in reaction to America's anticipated military response. The tactic worked.

The first manifestation of the new structure was the activation by Mr bin Laden of al-Qaeda in the Arabian Peninsula (AQAP). According to Ms Farrall, AQAP, which has bases in south and east Yemen and was founded primarily to destabilise the Saudi regime, should be seen as an offshoot from the core organisation rather than a franchise operation.

The biggest and most powerful example of the latter is still al-Qaeda in Iraq (AQI), which was created in 2004 when Abu Musab al-Zarqawi pledged the allegiance of his terror group, Jamaat al-Tawhid wal-Jihad (JTJ), to Mr bin Laden. JTJ had more fighters and was perpetrating many more well-publicised acts of violence than al-Qaeda, but such was the strength of the al-Qaeda brand that Zarqawi, who died in an American air strike in 2006, had no hesitation in linking himself to Mr bin Laden.

Before he died, Zarqawi was instrumental in bringing another terrorist organisation, the Algerian-based Salafist Group for Preaching and Combat (known as GSPC), under the al-Qaeda umbrella. In late 2006 Mr Zawahiri announced a "blessed union" between GSPC and al-Qaeda. A few months later the group was renamed al-Qaeda in the Islamic Maghreb (AQIM), identifying France (the former colonial power) and America as the two "far" enemies on which it would focus.

The next outfit likely to become an al-Qaeda franchise is Shabab, a fast-growing militant group that operates in Somalia and has close ties to nearby AQAP—if it can reconcile its differences with Hisbul Islam, another Islamist insurgent group in Somalia with links to al-Qaeda. After bitter fighting between the two, Hisbul Islam submitted to a Shabab takeover at the end of last year, but tensions persist. Shabab has been particularly successful in recruiting foreign fighters and Somali exiles.

Some of these franchise groups are very small. AQAP is reckoned by Yemeni officials to be able to field about 400 men. In 2007 al-Qaeda in the Islamic Magreb had perhaps 200–300 fighters. Many surviving members of al-Qaeda's affiliates have drifted into smaller Sunni factions under no centralised command. Even tinier, isolated cells exist elsewhere in the region, erupting perhaps once a decade.

Global Reach

Attacks Attributed to Al-Qaeda Outside Afghanistan and Iraq, 1992 to 2008[†]

Date		Location	Description	Number Killed*
1992	December	Aden, Yemen	Hotel bombing	2
1993	February	New York	World Trade Centre bombing	6
	October	Mogadishu, Somalia	Ambush of US forces	18
1994	June	Mashad, Iran	Shiite shrine bombing	27
1995	November	Riyadh, Saudi Arabia	Truck bomb	7
1998	August	Kenya and Tanzania	US embassies bombed	301
2000	October	Aden, Yemen	*USS Cole* bombing	17
2001	September	New York, Virginia and Pennsylvania	9/11 attacks	3,000 approx.
2002	April	Djerba, Tunisia	Synagogue bombing	21
	May	Karachi, Pakistan	Hotel bombing	10
	June	Karachi, Pakistan	US consulate bombing	11
	October	Yemen coast	*Limburg* oil tanker bombing	1
	October	Bali, Indonesia	Nightclub bombings	202
	November	Mombasa, Kenya	Hotel bombing	15
2003	May	Riyadh, Saudi Arabia	Expatriate compound bombing	35
	May	Casablanca, Morocco	Multiple bombings	45
	August	Jakarta, Indonesia	Hotel bombing	16
	November	Riyadh, Saudi Arabia	Car bombs	17
	November	Istanbul, Turkey	Synagogues bombed	57
2004	February	Philippines	Ferry bombing	116
	March	Madrid, Spain	Train bombings	191
	April	Riyadh, Saudi Arabia	Government building bombing	3
	May	Yanbu, Saudi Arabia	Refinery attack	5
	May	Khobar, Saudi Arabia	Expatriate compound attack	22
	December	Jeddah, Saudi Arabia	US consulate attack	5
2005	July	London	Underground/bus bombings	56
	July	Sharm el-Sheikh, Egypt	Resort bombings	88
	November	Amman, Jordan	Hotel bombing	63
2007	April	Algiers, Algeria	Car bombs	33
2008	June	Islamabad, Pakistan	Danish embassy bombing	6

Sources: Press reports; Congressional Research Service   *Including perpetrators   †Later information unavailable

Yet the size of these groups may be misleading. AQAP, for example, is by far the most energetic part of al-Qaeda at present. Under the leadership of Nasser al-Wahayshi, a former close aide of Mr bin Laden's, and Anwar al-Awlaki, a charismatic American-Yemeni cleric, AQAP has been the instigator of several recent terrorist plots aimed at America: among them the Fort Hood shootings carried out by Nidal Malik Hasan, the attempted destruction of a passenger plane by Umar Farouk Abdulmutallab (the Christmas Day "underpants bomber") and the highly sophisticated plot last October to blow up two Chicago-bound cargo planes with almost undetectable bombs disguised as printer cartridges.

Internet monitoring also shows that far greater numbers of sympathisers follow jihadist literature, suggesting a broad pool of potential recruits. Many of these come from the wider Salafist trend of puritan Islam, much of which has traditionally rejected violent *jihad,* largely on tactical grounds, in favour of quiet proselytising.

Alex Gallo, of West Point's Combating Terrorism Centre, says that core al-Qaeda has evolved a most effective and flexible approach, a bit like Michael Porter's theory of the value chain. Core al-Qaeda, he argues, has de-emphasised the resource-intensive part of violent activity—training, equipping and deploying fighters around the world—in favour of acting as a kind of consultancy, providing strategic direction, ideological coherence and financial advice. According to him, "al-Qaeda understands that, given the constrained context in which it operates today, it is able to provide more robust and enduring value to the global jihadist movement through its unique infrastructure and expertise in . . . marketing and services."

Al-Qaeda manages its franchises by allowing them considerable autonomy against the "near" enemy, while insisting on some direct influence over their out-of-area operations against traditional al-Qaeda targets in the West. These include public-transport networks (the old obsession with airlines is undiminished), government buildings and vital infrastructure (top of the list would probably still be an attack on a nuclear plant). How much of a directing role al-Qaeda plays is uncertain. Large operations or those involving new tactics, such as an attack using a radiological device, appear to require permission from the top, usually transmitted by the more operationally active second-tier leadership.

British intelligence sources describe AQAP as the most innovative of the al-Qaeda franchises, thanks to the grafting on to a formerly parochial organisation of a small group of well-educated people who understand the West and its weak points.

But, disconcertingly, counter-terrorism agencies admit that not enough is known about the location of AQAP's Yemen bases to mount successful drone attacks against them.

Internal Divisions

Even with Mr bin Laden dead, most counter-terrorism professionals expect that little will change. The next few weeks will almost certainly see more strikes against high-value al-Qaeda targets as the Americans sift the information gathered from the raid in Abbottabad, a treasure trove of documents and computer hard drives, and put it to use before it goes stale. The leadership of core al-Qaeda will pass to Mr Zawahiri, who was always more operationally involved than Mr bin Laden. His first task will be to work out what aspects of the network may have been compromised and to make repairs. Less popular within the organisation than Mr bin Laden, Mr Zawahiri will have to show that he can be a unifying figure. If he cannot manage it, he will fairly soon be replaced.

In recent years hints of discord have appeared in the jihadists' own internet traffic. Even members of the historic leadership of al-Qaeda have criticised Mr bin Laden's strategy. Perhaps, say some dedicated jihadists, it would be better to

---

Assassination
A Messy Business

When a State Kills its Enemies Remotely, the Law Gets Tangled

Killing quickly in combat, when large numbers of soldiers are fighting according to the laws of war, is sad but legal. Change any of those parameters, and things get tricky. Some lawyers have denounced the killing of Mr bin Laden, unarmed and in his home, as an extra-judicial murder. Others see it as a wholly legitimate military operation.

Every country allows soldiers to use lethal force against a declared enemy in wartime, just as police may, in some circumstances, kill criminals. But America is at war with an organisation, not a country, and though al-Qaeda is not a state it is (by its own account) at war with the United States. Purists argue that the criminal law is the right weapon for defence against terrorists; pragmatists would differ.

In any case, America's armed forces have legal backing for their actions against al-Qaeda. Though a presidential order of 1976 bars assassinations by America's spooks, an act of Congress in 2001 authorised the president to use "all necessary and appropriate force" against the perpetrators of the terrorist attack in September of that year.

Next comes the category of person killed. Deliberately targeting civilians in any conflict is illegal. But al-Qaeda has a quasi-military structure, and plenty of precedents exist for killing enemy commanders in wartime: in April 1943 America ambushed Admiral Isoroku Yamamo-to, the Japanese naval commander, on the express order of President Franklin Roosevelt. Critics of America's actions are arguing that

Mr bin Laden was no longer the effective commander of al-Qaeda. But that would be hard to prove.

Location can be controversial too. Russia sees the émigré Chechen leadership, for example, as legitimate targets and has killed them in places such as Qatar, to the fury of the local authorities. The assassination of Mahmoud al-Mabhouh, a Hamas commander, in Dubai in January 2010, presumably by Israel, aroused similar ire. But Pakistan has itself used lethal force against al-Qaeda and allowed American drone attacks, for all its loud complaining now.

Timing complicates the question further. Bombing soldiers in a hospital, or shooting them after they have surrendered, is a war crime. Soldiers are under no legal duty to give their opponents a chance to surrender, though if the white flag is shown it must usually be honoured. Nobody has suggested that Mr bin Laden tried to surrender. But his shooting while unarmed raises questions about the nature of his resistance. Any video footage of the attack will be closely scrutinised to see whether he was a combatant, rather than a prisoner.

Behind the controversy is a change not in the laws of war but in the means of waging it. Drone strikes were measured in dozens under George Bush. They number many hundreds under Barack Obama. They allow an official sitting in America to kill someone thousands of miles away. Such killings usually escape scrutiny—and controversy—because they preclude any chance of surrender. Killing someone in the same room is always going to be more complicated.

work on consolidating gains, and appealing to like-minded Muslims, rather than eternally plotting new attacks. Perhaps the priority should be the "near enemy", rather than America.

Such doubts from within have recently grown stronger. Unlike the war on terror, which in many ways bolstered the jihadists' paranoid vision of Islam as a faith locked in mortal combat with an unrelenting foe, the wave of democratic change now sweeping the region risks undermining it altogether. Not only has it already succeeded where Mr bin Laden failed, in knocking down such "apostate regimes" as those of Egypt and Tunisia. It has done so through the peaceful mobilisation of ordinary people, inspired not by religious fervour but by secular demands.

The chain of Arab uprisings also subtly puts into question the relevance of al-Qaeda's ambition to rid Islam of foreign interference. This is most obviously true in Libya, where jihadist radicals, including former close associates of Mr bin Laden, have cheered NATO air strikes against the regime of Muammar Qaddafi as loudly as anyone. Mr Zawahiri, by contrast, called on Libyans both to fight Colonel Qaddafi and to attack the "infidel" NATO forces. Egypt's Muslim Brotherhood, a mainstream Islamist group whose global following is immensely greater than al-Qaeda's, dismissed this as "a desperate attempt by al-Qaeda to impose itself as a force for change amid the huge popular and international support for non-violent revolutions across the Arab world." It seems that, eventually, the central idea that Mr bin Laden stood for may simply be superseded.

The speculation that al-Qaeda will want to lash out to avenge its fallen leader may not be correct. One of its characteristics is patience: wide-ranging plots can take years to implement, and prematurely activating sleepers for "lone wolf" attacks may waste valuable assets. It is more likely that the next attacks, when they come, will instead simply be relabelled as retribution for Mr bin Laden's death. In the longer term, without his unifying prestige, the network could become even more dispersed. But that will only make the job of Western intelligence agencies harder.

And Now, Pakistan

Certainly it will be harder in Pakistan, where the government, and especially the ISI, now looks humiliated. India's hawks mock that their bitter rival can never again be trusted; noisier American congressmen want Pakistan's $3 billion military and civilian aid budget slashed. President Zardari and other civilian leaders have floundered for a response. Relations with America were already chilled, especially between spy agencies, and have turned icy as criticism of the ISI grows.

Spooked, the Pakistanis are already warning the Americans not to consider more such raids. But that is clearly a temptation. An obvious next target would be Mullah Omar, the ageing Afghan Taliban leader, whom the ISI is also accused of protecting. American agents snooping in Pakistan's cities in the past year may well have turned up other useful leads, but chosen not to act until Mr bin Laden was dealt with. Some conspiracy theorists even fret that the Americans may go after Pakistan's nuclear arsenal next.

Mr Obama bent over backwards after the raid not to rub Pakistan's face in the embarrassment of it all. His administration did not warn Pakistan that it was about to launch an attack deep inside its territory, as if there was no trust there. Nonetheless, Mr Obama said, "it's important to note that our counterterrorism co-operation with Pakistan helped lead us to bin Laden and the compound where he was hiding."

Jay Carney, the president's spokesman, fielding reporters' questions on May 3rd, admitted that relations with Pakistan were "complicated". America's problem with the Pakistanis, remarked Lindsey Graham, the senior Republican senator from South Carolina, was that "you can't trust them, and you can't abandon them."

Many foreign leaders agree. Britain's prime minister, David Cameron, who spoke on May 3rd, wants continued help for Pakistan's civilian leaders while, at the same time, demanding that its military chiefs come clean about their spies.

Winding Down a War

Any Western pressure will be calibrated with the war next door, in Afghanistan, in mind. It is unclear how much will change there after the beheading of al-Qaeda. Optimists see glimmers: for example, the hope that America may at last push Pakistan to start a long-postponed campaign against the Haqqani network, which attacks Western forces in east Afghanistan from Pakistani bases.

If the more powerful Taliban accept that Mr bin Laden is dead, they may feel excused from their Pashtunwali honour code about protecting guests and disavow their ties with al-Qaeda. A Western demand for them to do so has been the biggest block to the planned peace talks. Equally important, the Taliban may be spurred towards talks themselves, fearing that whatever support they get from inside Pakistan is now in jeopardy.

Yet it is not clear that the Taliban will grow any more amenable just yet, and such talks might not get far. Too many disparate groups would have to be involved. The Taliban's leaders will watch to see if Mr bin Laden's death softens Westerners' already flagging will to fight on in Afghanistan, and whether plans harden to get many of the troops out within the next three years.

Plenty of Americans fervently hope they will be. After almost ten bloody years, the war in Afghanistan is unpopular, especially in Mr Obama's own party. Many Democrats were appalled by his decision in 2009 to send 30,000 more troops. Now they see an unexpected opportunity. Since it was the search for Osama bin Laden that drew America into Afghanistan, isn't his elimination the perfect moment for America to declare victory and pull out?

For the present, there is little evidence that the president himself sees things that way. The official word from the White House and from America's ambassador in Kabul is that NATO still has plenty of hard work to do before handing the war over to the Afghan government and army in 2014 as planned. Under the president's current plan, the White House was already primed to start a review of the war in the coming weeks, to be followed in July by the start of a drawdown of some of its 100,000 soldiers in Afghanistan.

The exact number would depend on the outcome of the review. Before Mr bin Laden's death most insiders in Washington expected that this would be modest—a few thousand or so. Mr Carney, the press spokesman, insists stoutly that nothing has changed: Mr Obama's original plan was "very much in place", and the pace of the withdrawal would depend on conditions on the ground in Afghanistan. But on Capitol Hill and in Washington's think-tanks, some are more impatient.

Not all are Democrats. Senator Richard Lugar, the ranking Republican on the Senate Foreign Relations Committee, says that with al-Qaeda mostly gone from Afghanistan, decamped to Pakistan and Yemen, it is folly for America to keep 100,000 troops there at a cost of $100 billion a year, and to indulge in "grand nation-building ambitions". John Kerry, the committee's Democratic chairman, said the killing created the possibility of "re-evaluating what kind of transition we need in Afghanistan".

There are, however, many voices on the other side of the debate. Senator Graham said it would be a "huge mistake and a catastrophic blunder" to think that killing Mr bin Laden ended the need for American action in Iraq and Afghanistan. "You don't win the war by killing terrorists," he said. "Over time, you win the war by investing in those who will live in peace with us." Joe Lieberman, chairman of the Senate's Homeland Security Committee, said that to withdraw quickly would be to repeat the mistake America made when it abandoned Afghanistan to the Taliban after the Soviets departed.

It is impossible to be sure which way Mr Obama will jump. On the one hand, the raid on Abbottabad has delivered an immediate boost in the polls, including, according to the Pew Research Centre, a 17-point leap in the number of Americans who approve of his handling of the war. That, says Paul Pillar, a former CIA analyst for the Middle East and South Asia, gives the president some additional wiggle room if he wants to bring home more troops in July than he previously intended. But Mr Obama is also bound to be wary of doing anything that might squander his new-found standing as a potent warrior against America's enemies. Quite aside from the merits of the case, a dash for the exit might provoke a clash with his top brass, who are wary of leaving Afghanistan in disorder.

His Unseen Face

This has been a triumphant week in the fight against al-Qaeda. But the very success of the daring raid on Abbottabad has raised a host of fresh questions. Some are about the raid itself, and the details of Mr bin Laden's death—details the Obama administration has decided to part-conceal by not releasing photographs of his body, shot through head and chest, in case they inflame his supporters.

The most important question, however, concerns the form that global *jihad* will now take. Al-Qaeda may be in retreat in many ways, but it is far from beaten. It has adapted before, and is still changing. A movement that prizes "martyrdom" will not let the propaganda opportunities of its symbolic leader's execution be wasted. Indeed, Mr bin Laden's value as a recruiting sergeant for disaffected young Muslims may be even greater in death than in life.

Critical Thinking

1. Was it just to kill Osama bin Laden?
2. Should Osama bin Laden have been captured and then put on trial?
3. Are drone attacks on terrorists legal?

UNIT 4

War, Arms Control, and Disarmament

Unit Selections

Learning Outcomes

After reading this Unit, you will be able to:

- Describe the trend with regard to the amount of warfare in the international system.

- Determine whether or not the surge in Iraq has been successful.

- Explain why Iraq's future as a stable country remains problematic.

- Determine whether or not the surge in Afghanistan has been successful.

- Explain why the balance of power favors the insurgents in Afghanistan.

- Describe some of the challenges faced by the newly independent state in southern Sudan.

- Discuss some of the steps that can be taken to strengthen the nuclear nonproliferation treaty.

Student Website
www.mhhe.com/cls

Internet References

The Bulletin of the Atomic Scientists
    www.thebulletin.org
The Correlates of War Project
    www.correlatesofwar.org
International Crisis Group
    www.crisisgroup.org
International Security Assistance Force
    www.nato.int/ISAF
National Defense University
    www.ndu.edu
Peace Research Institute at Oslo
    www.prio.no
Stockholm International Peace Research Institute
    www.sipri.org

War is a method of conflict resolution that has been institutionalized over the centuries, according to the classical realist view of international relations. Some political scientists also argue that there is a relationship between the internal regime of a state and war, so that liberal democracies do not wage war on other liberal democracies. Neorealists, such as Kenneth, waltz argue that it is the international political structure within which states function, that explains the phenomenon of war. Wars can also result from the miscalculations and misperceptions of the opposing sides. For example, Robert Jervis writes that "Misperception . . . includes inaccurate inferences, miscalculations of consequences, and misjudgements about how one will react to one's policies." Leaders may underestimate or overestimate the intentions and threats of their rivals. In a crisis situation, foreign policy decision-making elites may be overloaded with information, have difficulty screening it, and also may be subject to the phenomenon of cognitive dissonance. Cognitive dissonance occurs when an individual is so overwhelmed with so much information, that he/she reverts to stereotypes that reinforce preexisting beliefs.

The end of the Cold War was marked by an outbteak and an intense flare-up of regional conflicts, characterized by ethnic and tribal wars. However, contrary to the popular perception about the amount of armed conflict in the international system, the number of armed conflicts has actually been declining, according to recent studies by the Oslo International Peace Research Institute, although the number of foreign interventions in armed conflicts has increased, as seen by NATO's intervention in Libya in 2011. In connection with this, the Uppsala Conflict Data Program (UCDP), which is one of the most reliable sources of data on armed conflicts around the world, found a total of 30 armed conflicts in the world in 2010, a reduction from 36 in 2009. According to the UCDP, four of the armed conflicts—in Iraq, Afghanistan, Pakistan, and Somalia—could be categorized as wars, since each experienced at least 1,000 battlefield deaths throughout the year, a definition of war commonly used by political scientists.

Nonetheless, the United States has found itself involved in expensive asymmetrical wars in Iraq and Afghanistan. The main concern in the United States revolves around when it can extricate itself from Iraq and Afghanistan. President Obama has downsized the United States force in Iraq by about 100,000 troops, while the jury is still out as to whether the "surge" has worked in Iraq. For example, on August 15, 2011, over 40 attacks occurred throughout Iraq, killing over 80 people and wounding over 300. Al Qaeda in Mesopotamia is claiming responsibility for the attacks and has vowed revenge for the killing of Osama bin Laden. The attacks occurred not long after the Iraqi government and the United States engaged in talks about keeping some United States troops in Iraq past the deadline for withdrawal, as serious questions still remained about the ability of the Iraqi military and security forces to maintain order. Emma Sky observes that "Iraq still has a long way to go before it becomes a stable, sovereign and self-reliant country" and fears that "Iraq could once again dissolve into violence without continued US support." As the United States downsized its military presence

© U.S. Air Force photo by Staff Sgt. Shane A. Cuomo

in Iraq, President Obama added about 30,000 troops to the military presence in Afghanistan, hoping that a surge in troop strength would effectively counter the resurgence of the Taliban in the country. General Petraeus, who had been responsible for the surge in Iraq, was placed in charge of the troops in Afghanistan. The President also set a target date for withdrawal from Afghanistan. However, Gary Bowman argues that the generals have provided poor advice to President Obama, because they ". . . oversold the troop surge's potential to quickly and sustainably alter the balance of forces in Afghanistan" which had resulted in "an irresolvable dilemma about how to leave the country conceding the country to the Taliban insurgents." The author concludes that "the surge has led to demonstrable military progress, but it will be squandered unless combat troops remain in place in 2012." Furthermore, under Obama, the number of drone attacks against the Taliban and Al-Qaeda targets has increased, but also has resulted in a rise in the level of tension with the civilian population and the Afghan and Pakistani governments, as more civilians were killed as "collateral damage" in the drone attacks. Also, following the killing of Osama bin Laden on May 2, 2011, the pressure on President Obama to hasten the withdrawal of troops from Afghanistan increased. President Obama announced in the summer of 2011 that he would start withdrawing some of the troops he sent to Afghanistan as part of the surge there.

Many of the armed conflicts that intensified after the end of the Cold War, were of an ethnic or tribal nature, as illustrated by the conflict in Darfur in the Sudan, which resulted in genocide and the killing of hundreds of thousands of people who belonged to the tribes targeted for extinction by the government. On July 9, 2011, the southern part of the Sudan finally achieved its independence. However, the independence of southern Sudan was marked by armed conflict as armed forces from the North and South fought each other over contested boundaries, and access to and control of oil, most of which is located in the southern part of the Sudan. Richard S. Williamson, in "Sudan on the Cusp," provides valuable background for this conflict, as he observes that "Many challenges lie ahead for the new independent nation and for what remains of the old Sudan, as well as for the neighboring countries, the wider region, and the international community . . ."

During the Cold War, even though the SALT (Strategic Arms Limitation Talks) and START (Strategic Arms Reduction Talks) reached between Moscow and Washington resulted in the destruction of nuclear weapons and delivery systems, the non-nuclear weapon states did not think enough had been done. The New START treaty concluded between Washington and Moscow during the Obama administration provides an opportunity for the non-nuclear weapon states, as well as other nuclear weapon states, to move forward in stopping the proliferation of nuclear weapons through, among other things, the strengthening of the nonproliferation treaty. James Goodby writes in "A World Without Nuclear Weapons Is a Joint Enterprise," that "With the entry into force of the New Strategic Arms Reduction Treaty (NEW START) between Russia and the United States, the time has come to widen the conversation about eliminating nuclear weapons to include other nuclear-armed states and states with advanced civil nuclear weapons programs."

Iraq, from Surge to Sovereignty

Winding Down the War in Iraq

EMMA SKY

By September 2008, when General Raymond Odierno replaced General David Petraeus as the top commander of the Multi-National Force–Iraq, there was a prevalent sense among Americans that the surge of additional U.S. forces into the country in 2007 had succeeded. With violence greatly reduced, the Iraq war seemed to be over. In July 2008, U.S. President George W. Bush had announced that violence in Iraq had decreased "to its lowest level since the spring of 2004" and that a significant reason for this sustained progress was "the success of the surge."

The surge capitalized on intra-Shiite and intra-Sunni struggles to help decrease violence, which created the context for the withdrawal of U.S. forces from Iraq. With U.S. troops on pace to depart entirely by December 2011, Iraqis held successful national elections last March and, after nine months of wrangling, eventually formed a broadly inclusive government in December 2010. But Odierno—for whom I served as chief political adviser—understood that the surge had not eliminated the root causes of conflict in Iraq. As we realized then, the Iraqis must still develop the necessary institutions to manage competition for power and resources peacefully. Iraqi elites across the political spectrum felt that the Obama administration was focused more heavily on leaving Iraq than on supporting the country's attempt to build a democratic system of government. The withdrawal of U.S. forces from Iraq should mark an evolution in the U.S.-Iraqi relationship, not Washington's disengagement. Without continued U.S. support, there is a real danger that Iraq may not succeed in using the opening provided by the surge to strengthen its stability and achieve its democratic aspirations.

Iraq could once again dissolve into violence without continued U.S. support.

One Last Try

By the end of 2006, Iraq appeared to be teetering on the edge of civil war. Tens of thousands of Iraqis had fled their homes, and Baghdad had degenerated into armed sectarian enclaves.

Insurgent groups, criminal gangs, and militias of political parties used violence to achieve their particular objectives. Neighboring countries backed them with funding, paramilitary training, and weapons, further fomenting instability. Meanwhile, back in the United States, public support for the war was waning. The prevailing U.S. strategy of attempting to transfer responsibility for security to the Iraqi security forces (ISF) seemed, in the words of U.S. Army Colonel H. R. McMaster, "a rush to failure."

The question became whether the United States would leave Iraq as quickly as possible or attempt to implement a new strategy to reduce the violence—raising U.S. troop levels and employing different tactics. Joe Biden, who was then a U.S. senator, adamantly opposed such a troop buildup, arguing in early 2007 that "a surge of up to 30,000 American troops cannot have any positive effect except for only temporary." Yet Bush, U.S. Senator John McCain, and others believed that a troop surge could provide enough security against sectarian violence to allow for political reconciliation. They were convinced that a withdrawal of forces under such circumstances would cause an all-out civil war that could spread into neighboring countries, jeopardizing oil exports across the region. Proponents of a surge also believed that abandoning Iraq would gravely harm the global reputation of the United States, boost the morale of Islamic extremists, and crush the spirit of the U.S. military.

In a televised address in January 2007, Bush announced that the United States would implement a surge of U.S. forces "to help Iraqis carry out their campaign to put down sectarian violence." Petraeus—who became commanding general of the Multi-National Force–Iraq in January 2007—and Odierno, who was his second-in-command, shared responsibility for developing the new strategy on the ground. Serving as operational commander, Odierno proposed sending U.S. troops out into Iraqi population centers to protect civilians. This marked a break from the previous U.S. approach, which had U.S. troops targeting insurgents from bases on the outskirts of Iraqi cities and then quickly withdrawing, leaving the unreliable ISF in their place. Additional U.S. forces were sent to the Sunni-dominated Anbar region—an erstwhile stronghold of al Qaeda whose tribes were beginning to abandon the terrorist group and ally with the United States—as well as to the outskirts of Baghdad, which insurgents sought to control in order to launch attacks into the city.

Petraeus and Odierno agreed that the essence of the struggle in Iraq was (and remains) a competition between communities for power and resources. By filling the power vacuum, the U.S. military sought to buy the time and space for the Iraqi government to move forward with national reconciliation and improve its delivery of public services. U.S. troops showed that they were willing to emerge from their bases and place the defense of the Iraqi people above all else, which sent a clear message to the Iraqi public that U.S. forces would not be defeated. Many Iraqis stopped providing passive sanctuary to armed groups and, assured that the United States would protect them from reprisal, offered intelligence that enabled U.S. troops to target insurgents more accurately. Meanwhile, the United States reached out to previously hostile tribal and factional leaders, coaxing them to turn against al Qaeda and participate in the political process.

The surge accompanied and fostered other crucial internal changes. It coincided with and benefited from tectonic shifts within the Sunni community, as the Sunni nationalist insurgency and al Qaeda began competing for dominance. Al Qaeda's efforts to impose a puritanical form of Islam angered the Sunni population, and the Sunni tribes, in a time-honored fashion, retaliated when their members were killed. At the same time, the Sunnis realized that they were losing ground to the Shiite militias and came to see Iran as a greater threat than the United States. These factors drove the Sunni tribes in Anbar to turn to the United States for support in a phenomenon known as the Sunni Awakening, which spread in similar ways to other parts of the country. When the Iraqi Shiites observed that the Sunnis were battling al Qaeda themselves and preventing insurgent attacks on the Shiite community, they became less tolerant of the Shiite death squads and militias, whose legitimacy rested on their defense of Shiites against Sunni aggression. This shift reached its climax in March 2008, when Iraqi Prime Minister Nouri al-Maliki felt that his government was being so undermined by the behavior of Jaish al-Mahdi, the Shiite militia led by the Iraqi cleric Muqtada al-Sadr, that he ordered military operations against it in Basra and Baghdad. The U.S.-supported operations decimated Jaish al-Mahdi, enhancing Maliki's standing and earning him the respect of Iraq's Sunnis as well.

In short, the surge succeeded in changing Iraq's political environment, encouraging the Shiites and the Sunnis to bring the civil war to an end. The improvement in the security situation convinced partisans on both sides that they could achieve their political goals only by joining the political process.

The surge succeeded in changing Iraq's political environment but did not eliminate the root causes of conflict.

Securing the Surge

The unexpected drop in violence convinced many Americans that the war in Iraq had been won. The surge had undoubtedly met its stated aim of buying the time and space necessary for the Iraqi government to advance national reconciliation and, at least in theory, develop the capacity to provide adequate public services. Yet Iraq's parties did not take advantage of the opportunity to turn progress at the local level into national reconciliation. When Odierno replaced Petraeus in September 2008, the greatest threat to Iraq's stability had become the legitimacy and capability of the government, rather than insurgents. Research and opinion polls showed that as the violence dropped, jobs and public services replaced security as the number one concern, and the government was not able to meet the public's growing expectations. I advised Odierno that we needed to meet these new hopes by preserving the fragile security gains and, at the same time, ensuring that our actions did not infringe on Iraqi sovereignty.

To quicken the pace of national reconciliation, Odierno attempted to integrate the ISF, which until that time had been predominately Shiite. From my close relationship with Maliki's advisers, I understood that the government remained suspicious of the Sunni Awakening and feared that by supporting it, the United States was creating a Sunni army that would overthrow the country's Shiite leadership. We sought to allay these concerns by pressuring the Iraqi government to place Sunni Awakening soldiers on its payroll, legitimizing them as local police forces and improving the ISF's sectarian balance. U.S. troops closely trained and monitored ISF troops, reporting instances of misconduct to the Iraqi government. As the ISF became more diverse and professional, the country became more secure.

Yet the annual United Nations Security Council resolution authorizing the presence of U.S. forces in Iraq was set to expire in December 2008, raising the possibility that the United States would have to depart the country immediately or remain there illegally, both of which would have threatened the gains made by the surge. To prevent either scenario, the U.S. and Iraqi governments entered negotiations over the U.S.-Iraq Status of Forces Agreement (SOFA), which would define the future of U.S. engagement in the country.

Iraqi officials bargained tenaciously during the SOFA negotiations and extracted significant concessions from the United States. They insisted on and won greater control over the actions of U.S. forces and secured a promise of their departure from population centers by the end of June 2009 and their total withdrawal by the end of 2011. The Bush administration even allowed Iraq the "primary right to exercise jurisdiction" over U.S. military members who committed "grave premeditated felonies," such as rape, and agreed that all suspects arrested by U.S. troops would be detained under warrant and held in Iraqi facilities. To the Iraqis, this meant that U.S. forces would be operating under the rule of law rather than the rule of war, as they had been since 2003.

The U.S. military reacted apprehensively to these demands, uncomfortable with the idea of U.S. soldiers falling under foreign legal authority and worried that the announcement of concrete dates for the troop withdrawals would boost insurgent morale. Some Iraqis expressed discomfort with the deal, too. For some of them, the idea of a security agreement permitting continued foreign occupation recalled the bitter memory of a century of colonial intervention in the country's affairs.

The political elites, for their part, feared that Maliki was becoming increasingly authoritarian and was consolidating his power through higher oil revenues and the ISF's growing capacity. They suspected that the SOFA would bring U.S. forces under Maliki's control, preventing the United States from playing a brokering role or guarding against sectarian and undemocratic behavior.

As expected, politicians allied with Sadr voted against the agreement in the Iraqi parliament. Some Sunni leaders also opposed the SOFA, afraid that a U.S. pullout would increase Iran's influence over Iraq and expose the Sunni community to further attacks from Shiite elements in the ISF. Despite doubts among both the U.S. military and Iraqi factions, Iraq's parliament reached a consensus to sign the agreement once its various parties felt they had achieved three important conditions: passing a resolution that demanded political reform, securing a commitment to hold a national referendum on the SOFA in July 2009, and receiving letters of assurance from the United States that repeated Washington's commitment to protect the democratic process. Meanwhile, Maliki boosted his reputation by taking a hard line in the negotiations, establishing U.S. forces as guests of the Iraqi government rather than occupiers under a UN resolution.

The SOFA was signed along with a strategic framework agreement, which provided a possible glimpse of the future of U.S.-Iraqi ties. It affirmed "the genuine desire of [Iraq and the United States] to establish a long-term relationship of cooperation and friendship" across a range of areas, including culture, health, trade, energy, communications, security, and diplomacy. Together with the SOFA, the Strategic Framework Agreement solidified the coming shift in the United States' relationship with Iraq, from one of patronship to one of partnership.

Embracing Iraqi Sovereignty

On taking office, President Barack Obama followed his campaign pledge to end the Iraq war while honoring the SOFA signed with Iraq's government under the Bush administration. He engaged in an extensive policy review with Odierno, taking into consideration the opinions of those who thought that only a small residual force was necessary in Iraq as well as the ideas of those who argued that a defined pullout date would simply encourage the insurgents to lie low until U.S. forces departed. Obama chose the middle ground, ordering the end of combat operations and the reduction of U.S. troops to 50,000 by August 2010. The decision gave Odierno the flexibility he desired, within set deadlines, to determine the pace of the troop withdrawal so that he could respond to any military or political contingencies, such as parliamentary delays in holding elections or forming a goverment. Odierno implemented Obama's plan by shifting the mission of the remaining U.S. forces from counterinsurgency to stability operations, focusing on bolstering the ISF's capacity to protect the Iraqi people on their own.

The U.S. military required significant physical and strategic restructuring to accomplish this transformation. As we discussed how to make those necessary adjustments, Odierno and I began with the premise that the struggle in Iraq was

essentially political. We agreed that the U.S. military could assist by training the ISF and preventing conflict but that only the Iraqis themselves could solve the underlying issues plaguing their country: tensions between Arabs and Kurds, Shiites and Sunnis, and local provinces and the national government. Although security in Iraq had greatly improved, the country had merely gone from being a failed state to being a fragile state, still beset with poor public services and subject to the pervasive influence of armed groups and foreign powers. As a result, Odierno instructed his commanders that the troop drawdown should not become the overriding focus of their mission. The United States had to help the Iraqi government develop the necessary state institutions to function properly on its own. Brigades were reorganized to further that goal, enabling U.S. State Department–led transition teams to build administrative capacity in provincial and local governments throughout Iraq.

Odierno provided his subordinates with the flexibility to determine when conditions in their respective areas were ripe for the shift. U.S. troops had to embrace Iraqi assertions of sovereignty as a sign of progress, even when they sometimes conflicted with U.S. advice. They also had to accept that the ISF were never going to be as proficient as U.S. troops. Odierno explained that the United States sought a strategic partnership with Iraq and that the way in which U.S. forces left the country would influence the long-term relationship between the U.S. and the Iraqi governments.

Odierno traveled the country to obtain on-the-ground progress reports from his commanders, considering it a success when they showed an in-depth understanding of what could cause instability in their areas and when they reported on how they were working closely with their U.S. civilian colleagues to address those issues through reconstruction project funds and technical assistance. Odierno encouraged his commanders to describe progress being made by the ISF in terms of the forces' relations with the local population, the operations they conducted, the circumstances in which they had requested U.S. assistance, and what further training they required.

As I prepared to depart Iraq in August 2010, it was clear that the close partnership between the U.S. military and the ISF had paid dividends. Accompanying Odierno as he toured the country to review the progress, I witnessed U.S. and ISF soldiers celebrating each time the United States transferred one of its bases to Iraqi forces, conducting ceremonies in which U.S. commanders symbolically delivered the keys to their Iraqi counterparts. The strong individual and institutional relationships between the two forces contributed to a growing sense of security across the country.

Changing Roles

U.S. forces surveyed their respective regions for disruptive elements that could undermine the calm. Communal struggles persisted between Arabs and Kurds and Shiites and Sunnis; state institutions remained weak, as the central government and the provinces negotiated power-sharing arrangements; foreign powers, especially Iran (as well as Syria and Turkey), continued to meddle in Iraqi politics; and extremist groups, such as the remnants of al Qaeda and lingering Shiite militias, continued to foment trouble. Odierno understood that the very presence of U.S. troops could fuel instability, as groups would attack them in an attempt to gain credit for the impending U.S. withdrawal.

By viewing post-surge Iraq through this prism, the U.S. military focused its actions to provide the necessary resources and advice to those Iraqis attempting to smooth the points of friction. In September 2008, for instance, tensions arose between Arabs and Kurds in the northern Iraqi region of Diyala, and followed several months later in Kirkuk and Ninewa. The two sides came close to armed conflict over control of disputed territories in northern Iraq, which the Kurdistan Regional Government was seeking to incorporate within its federal region. The ISF and the Kurdish Pesh Merga (security forces) viewed each other with increasing suspicion and focused their energies on each other, allowing al Qaeda to exploit the situation by attacking various religious minority groups, including Christians, Shabaks, and Yezidis. Only mediation by U.S. officers prevented fighting from breaking out between the ISF and the Pesh Merga. At the request of Maliki and Massoud Barzani, president of the Kurdistan Region, Odierno devised a system of cooperation among the ISF, the Pesh Merga, and U.S. troops in operational centers, at checkpoints, and during patrols. This helped establish relationships between the leaders of the various forces, building mutual trust and confidence and restoring stability to the disputed territories.

As the June 2009 deadline for U.S. soldiers to leave Iraqi cities approached, Odierno accompanied Iraq's minister of defense, Abdul-Kader al-Obeidi, and minister of the interior, Jawad al-Bolani, around the country to assess the security situation and the ISF's performance. It was clear that security was continuing to improve and that joint operations with U.S. forces were hastening the ISF's development. After some initial growing pains, communication and collaboration between the U.S. military and the ISF had allowed Iraqi soldiers to take the lead, with U.S. forces largely providing background support. Although conditions varied across the country—in Basra, the ISF had largely taken command, whereas in Ninewa, U.S. soldiers compensated for a lack of adequate Iraqi forces by continuing their combat operations against al Qaeda—nearly all U.S. units had undertaken the transition from counterinsurgency to stability operations by early 2010, months ahead of schedule.

The implementation of the SOFA proceeded far more smoothly than either Iraqi or U.S. leaders had anticipated. In order to be ready to address potential violations of the agreement, the U.S. and Iraqi governments had established a number of joint committees covering a spectrum of security issues, including military operations, detainee affairs, and airspace control. There were only a few initial complaints issued by Iraqis about suspected U.S. violations of the agreement. Despite the initial fears of the U.S. military leadership, no U.S. soldier was ever arrested by the ISF and no issues of jurisdiction arose regarding U.S. soldiers. Meanwhile, the United States adhered strictly to the withdrawal timeline established by the SOFA, showing the Iraqis that the United States had no intention of occupying their country indefinitely. The deadline forced the U.S. military to relinquish power and allowed the Iraqis to assume command more quickly than might otherwise have happened. The United States demonstrated that it would leave with dignity, in partnership with the Iraqi government rather than under fire from insurgents.

The development of strong individual and institutional relationships between U.S. and Iraqi troops will likely continue as the two countries work to establish a long-term relationship. The rights and wrongs of the Iraq war will be debated for years to come. What will not be disputed, however, is the way in which the U.S. military learned from its initial blunders, adapted, retrained and reeducated its soldiers, transitioned seamlessly from counterinsurgency to stability operations, and strengthened the capacity of Iraqi forces.

The Struggle Continues

Despite the successful transition from the surge to sovereignty in Iraq, challenges remain on the horizon for internal Iraqi politics and the U.S.-Iraqi relationship. The fraught formation of a governing coalition following Iraq's March 2010 national elections revealed how fragile the country's political institutions remain. Although Iraq's 2009 provincial elections had brought the Sunnis into local government and promoted reconciliation, the 2010 contest saw friction once again. Maliki accused former elements of Saddam Hussein's Baath Party, along with Syria, of masterminding continued attacks in Iraq. Some Shiite politicians, supported by Iran, sought to weaken the nationalist, nonsectarian Iraqiya Party, led by Ayad Allawi, by attempting to disqualify its candidates as former Baath Party members.

The Iraqiya Party overcame these challenges and narrowly won the election, with 91 seats, gaining the votes of most Sunnis and of a sizable proportion of secular Shiites. Maliki's Dawa Party came in a close second, with 89 seats, and for the next nine months, the two factions left Iraq in political limbo, with each side seeking to secure a majority in parliament in order to form a coalition government. Ironically, both the United States and Iran supported Maliki's bid to remain prime minister; U.S. leaders sought to broker a power-sharing arrangement between the two parties to keep Sadr's followers out of the government and strengthen reconciliation, whereas Iran hoped for a Shiite-dominated coalition. Maliki and Allawi grudgingly came to terms this past December, with Maliki retaining his post as prime minister and Allawi becoming head of the newly created National Council for Higher Policies, the purview of which remains uncertain.

Although a government has been formed, Iraq's political factions sadly missed an opportunity to secure the public's belief in the democratic system. Instead of demonstrating a peaceful transition of power and unity, the process revealed the lingering mistrust within Iraqi society, particularly among the ruling elites, who appeared ready to elevate their personal interests above the national good. Meanwhile, Iraqis remain skeptical of the large and unwieldy coalition assembled by Maliki, which enjoys few points of agreement and will have difficulty grappling with politically sensitive issues, such as federalism, the sharing of oil revenues, and the demarcation of internal borders.

True reconciliation among Iraq's ethnic and religious groups thus remains elusive, and what progress has been achieved so far could unravel.

Meanwhile, the Obama administration's rhetorical emphasis on the troop withdrawal—meant for a domestic audience—has largely overshadowed the quiet but burgeoning strategic partnership between Iraq and the United States. Washington needs to devote adequate attention and resources to furthering the Strategic Framework Agreement, which established the basis for possible long-term cooperation between the two countries. Iraqi politicians from all communities, save the Sadrists, have voiced concern that the United States is too focused on withdrawing from Iraq, placing stability before democracy and strengthening Maliki's ability to maintain control of the country through the ISF rather than through the consent of Iraq's politicians or public. They have also expressed concern about Iran's ambitions and aspirations in Iraq—an issue that will loom over the country for years to come.

Iraq still has a long way to go before it becomes a stable, sovereign, and self-reliant country. Continued engagement by the United States can help bring Iraq closer to the American vision of a nation that is at peace with itself, a participant in the global market of goods and ideas, and an ally against violent extremists. Under the terms of the Strategic Framework Agreement, the United States should continue to encourage reconciliation, help build professional civil service and non-sectarian institutions, promote the establishment of checks and balances between the country's parliament and its executive branch, and support the reintegration of displaced persons and refugees. U.S. assistance is also needed to bolster Iraq's civilian control over its security forces, invest in the country's police units, and remove the Iraqi army from the business of policing. Should Washington fail to provide such support, there is a risk that Iraq's different groups may revert to violence to achieve their goals and that the Iraqi government may become increasingly authoritarian rather than democratic—undermining the United States' enormous investment of blood and treasure.

Critical Thinking

1. Has the surge eliminated the root causes of the conflict in Iraq? Why or why not?
2. What is the relationship between Iraqi sovereignty and the surge?
3. What are the prospects for stability in post-surge Iraq?

EMMA SKY served as Chief Political Adviser to General Raymond Odierno, Commanding General of the Multi-National Force–Iraq from 2008 to 2010.

From *Foreign Affairs,* March/April 2010, pp. 117–127. Copyright © 2010 by Council on Foreign Relations, Inc. Reprinted by permission of Foreign Affairs. www.ForeignAffairs.com

Will America Lose Afghanistan—Again?

"In an apparent effort to box President Obama into a long-term commitment to the war, the generals oversold the troop surge's potential. . . ."

GARY M. BOWMAN

S pring has come to Afghanistan and in a few weeks, after the wheat, marijuana, and poppy crops have been planted, and the grape fields and pomegranate orchards have greened to provide concealment for combatants, the traditional Afghan fighting season will begin again. As a July 2011 deadline approaches for starting the withdrawal of US forces introduced as part of a 2009 "surge," President Barack Obama and his senior civilian advisers should examine carefully the advice they receive from senior military officers about the pace of the drawdown.

On one hand, the generals have often provided poor counsel to Obama and his predecessor George W. Bush. This has led to a consistent under-resourcing of the war, which has brought America to an almost irresolvable dilemma about how to leave Afghanistan while not conceding the country to Taliban insurgents. In an apparent effort to box President Obama into a long-term commitment to the war, the generals oversold the troop surge's potential to quickly and sustainably alter the balance of forces in Afghanistan.

On the other hand, the surge has led to demonstrable military progress, and this progress will be squandered unless the combat troops currently on the ground remain in place at least through 2012. If the limited progress that has been achieved is reversed in the next two fighting seasons, the United States will have cemented the Bush administration's strategic failure and added insult to the injury that Americans suffered when terrorists operating out of Afghanistan attacked on 9/11.

Hasty Plans

On September 20, 2001, when President Bush before a joint session of Congress described the nation's response to the 9/11 assault, the US Central Command (CENTCOM), which is responsible for conducting military operations in the Middle East and Central Asia, possessed neither a plan for conventional ground operations in Afghanistan nor the information necessary to develop such a plan. This was so even though Al Qaeda had previously bombed US embassies in Africa and attacked the USS Cole, and it was well known that the group was based in Afghanistan.

The hasty preparation of a plan for ground combat in Afghanistan was based on assumptions about the Soviet experience in that country. According to Air Force General Victor Renuart, the CENTCOM director of operations, the planners were concerned that a large force might unify the Afghans against the Americans as foreign invaders. They considered it important not to become "pinned down to big installations that could become easy targets" and that "we not be seen as occupiers in the early stages because that would draw the same reactions that the Brits and the Russians drew."

The initial planning for the invasion did not include the deployment of a large conventional force. According to General Tommy Franks, the CENTCOM commander at the time, his staff originally came up with only three military options in response to the 9/11 attacks: Tomahawk missile strikes; Tomahawk strikes followed by aerial bombing; and Tomahawk strikes, aerial bombing, and the insertion of Army Special Forces units to provide intelligence and coordinate air support for proxy Afghan fighters—primarily the Northern Alliance, a collection of anti-Taliban militias. Franks wrote in his memoirs that he also proposed a fourth option: "the first three [options] simultaneously, as the lead-in for the deployment of conventional American ground combat forces."

The final CENTCOM plan presented to Secretary of Defense Donald Rumsfeld included the fourth option—deploying approximately 10,000 soldiers and Marines to "exploit the gains" made by the Afghan fighters and defeat remaining Taliban and Al Qaeda forces. But Rumsfeld and Franks recommended to the president the third option, involving no conventional ground combat forces, and Bush approved the plan on September 21.

On October 7, 2001, Bush announced the commencement of military operations in Afghanistan. He said that the "carefully targeted actions are designed to disrupt the use of Afghanistan as a terrorist base of operations and to attack the military capability of the Taliban regime. . . . Our military action is also designed to clear the way for sustained, comprehensive, and relentless operations to drive them out and bring them to justice."

A small group of Central Intelligence Agency officers and American special operating forces, bolstered by US airpower and working with Afghan fighters of the Northern Alliance, quickly toppled the Taliban regime, whose leaders fled across the border to Pakistan. Thus, the United States quickly achieved a number of Bush's stated goals. A generally permissive environment was created for foreign nationals, journalists, diplomats, and aid workers from 2001 through most of 2005, and terrorist training camps were eliminated from Afghan territory.

Nevertheless, as measured by the strategic objectives that Bush established, the United States lost the war. The conflict succeeded at the tactical level as a punitive expedition against the Taliban government, which no longer ruled Afghanistan. However, the Al Qaeda perpetrators of the 9/11 attacks escaped and the Taliban too were allowed to escape; both subsequently reconstituted within sanctuaries in Pakistan. This was a major strategic failure that the senior military leadership should have anticipated.

Unobstructed Exit

There have been two decisive battles of the war so far—"decisive" in the sense that Al Qaeda and the Taliban might have been permanently disabled—and the United States lost both of them because it lacked sufficient conventional forces.

The first decisive event was an unimpeded exodus by the Taliban's hard core along a highway from the southern city of Kandahar to Quetta, Pakistan. By December 5, 2001, two Afghan militia groups, working with US Special Forces, were outside Kandahar, the seat of the Taliban government. One militia group was led by Hamid Karzai, who had been named interim chairman of the Afghan Interim Authority at an international conference in Bonn, Germany. Karzai's group had moved toward Kandahar from the north. The other, led by Gul Agha Shirzai, had moved on the city from the south.

Karzai had selected Mullah Naqib to lead negotiations with the Taliban. Naqib, a leader of the Alokozai tribe and an important power broker in Kandahar province, had let the Taliban into the city in the first place. The Taliban did negotiate with Naqib and Karzai, but abruptly pulled out before reaching a surrender agreement, leaving Kandahar an open city. Naqib told National Public Radio "The Taliban declared they were not going to wait two days to pull out, they were going to leave tomorrow. Then, that very same night, they called me on the satellite phone and announced: 'Our people are going.' I wasn't ready. I didn't have enough men. I spread the 40 or 50 fighters I had around town." A convoy of cars and trucks loaded with Taliban leaders and hard-core followers drove down Highway 4 to Pakistan.

This account of the Taliban and Al Qaeda escape from Kandahar was partly corroborated by the American commander present outside Kandahar at the time, Army Lieutenant Colonel David G. Fox, who told the Public Broadcasting Service: "I am sure that key Taliban leaders escaped during negotiations for the surrender in the south. I am absolutely certain that Karzai knew nothing about it. What I believe is that the Taliban believed if they kept Karzai at bay in the south, [with] negotiations and a set date to surrender, this gave them the time to pick up, get in their vehicles, and drive off."

Karzai directed that Naqib become the governor of Kandahar province and that Shirzai stay outside the city and take control of the airport. Both Naqib and Shirzai were accompanied by US Army Special Forces advisers. Fox was with Karzai. However, the Army captain who commanded the Special Forces team accompanying Shirzai advised Shirzai to move into the city in advance of Naqib, whom the Americans did not trust because of his prior involvement with the Taliban.

Once Shirzai occupied the governor's residence he was able, because of US support, to take power in Kandahar against Karzai's wishes. This became a root of the corrupt governance in Afghanistan's south; Shirzai ruled as a warlord, resuming many of the abuses that had allowed the Taliban to rise in the first place and preventing President Karzai's government from establishing legitimacy.

Insufficient Force

At approximately the same time, the battle of Tora Bora—the second decisive event of the war—took place. As special operations teams and Northern Alliance fighters pushed south toward Kabul, Taliban and Al Qaeda fighters retreated in front of them, fleeing toward sanctuary in Pakistan. They were able to retreat because the Americans did not insert conventional ground forces to block their flight.

By December 1, 2001, many Taliban and Al Qaeda fighters had gathered in the Tora Bora valley, where Al Qaeda had maintained well-defended and well-developed caves that contained large stocks of supplies. Osama bin Laden himself was at Tora Bora. The main US force at Tora Bora was an 11-man Army special operations team commanded by a master sergeant, who linked up with a band of Afghan fighters that the Americans referred to as the "Eastern Alliance." The US team was ordered to support the Afghans, who at that point were delegated sole responsibility for conducting offensive operations in the valley.

On December 9, a task force consisting of 50 Americans and a team of British special operations soldiers arrived in Tora Bora, also authorized to conduct offensive operations. However, the small size of the force required that the Afghans control the pace of the operation, and the decisive factor became Ramadan, the Islamic month of fasting: The Afghans fought during the day and retreated at dinnertime.

Many Al Qaeda operatives were killed at Tora Bora, the most dedicated of them fighting to the last to cover the retreat of their leaders and comrades over the mountains into Pakistan. As Gary Berntsen, a former CIA officer, recalled in his book *Jawbreaker*, the CIA paramilitary operatives at Tora Bora pleaded with the conventional military commanders to release a battalion of Army Rangers to block the Al Qaeda escape, but the Rangers were not inserted into the Tora Bora fight.

Over the next two months, while "post-victory" planning for redeploying US forces proceeded, approximately 1,000 Al Qaeda fighters who had not been driven from Afghanistan took shelter in a traditional mujahideen sanctuary in the Shahi Kowt Valley in Paktia province, on Afghanistan's eastern border with Pakistan. The commander of Special Operations Forces in Afghanistan at the time, Colonel John Mulholland, recognized that: "It was beyond my ability with my small force to do something about it because we were confident there was a sizable concentration of bad guys in there."

Eventually, in the spring of 2002, an Army infantry brigade (consisting of three US battalions and one Canadian) was deployed to the Shah-i-Kot Valley, in what was called Operation Anaconda. Coalition forces encountered a number of difficulties, such as insufficient helicopter support to move troops, a lack of close air support, and a misreading of the enemy's intentions. Planners assumed the Al Qaeda fighters would attempt to flee in mass out of the valley; instead, standard-core group stood and fought, maintaining a rear guard to cover the retreat of most of their forces into Pakistan.

Tactically, Operation Anaconda was a successful operation: By applying sufficient conventional force, the US-led coalition destroyed the last vestiges of Al Qaeda's training bases in Afghanistan. But it was too little, too late. Moreover, all of the conventional forces that fought in Operation Anaconda were redeployed from Afghanistan within five months.

Overall, the United States made a fundamental strategic error by relying exclusively on special operations teams and Afghan fighters to drive the Taliban from power. The failure to deploy conventional forces to block Taliban and Al Qaeda escape routes led directly to the ability of both groups to reconstitute themselves in Pakistan—which resulted in the situation we see today, in which the Taliban destabilize Afghanistan from sanctuaries in Pakistan.

The basic premise of coalition planning—that the Soviet experience demonstrated that the deployment of a large conventional force would lead to a successful insurgency—was invalid: As perceptive analysts have pointed out, the Soviet experience demonstrated merely that a conventional force using conventional tactics could be defeated by Afghan insurgents. This was not a justification for failing to deploy sufficient light conventional forces to pursue the enemy and block its escape.

Some commentators have argued that conventional forces could not have reached Afghanistan in time to close the Taliban and Al Qaeda escape routes into Pakistan. The evidence does not support this conclusion. An airbase in Uzbekistan was available to the United States by early October 2001, and Army Rangers and a brigade of the 101st Airborne Division began arriving in Afghanistan that same month. The unique strength of the US military is its ability to project power quickly anywhere in the world. The Americans simply applied insufficient power to prevent the terrorists and their supporters from finding sanctuary in Pakistan.

The Americans applied insufficient power to prevent the terrorists from finding sanctuary in Pakistan.

Obama's Surge

It is well known that the United States treated the Afghanistan war as an "economy of force" mission during the period from 2002 through 2009. The war in Iraq consumed American resources and attention instead.

The brigade is the basic building block of land combat power. Under current policy, an Army brigade may deploy only once every three to five years. The number of brigades required in Iraq left the United States at least three brigades short in Afghanistan. By mid-2006, the United States had only 20,400 troops in Afghanistan and had no combat power allocated to the southern part of the country. The coalition relied on less capable British, Canadian, Dutch, and Romanian forces to stem the Taliban reinfiltration of the south.

During this period, the United States and its allies pursued the course that General Renuart had said the Soviet experience warned against. The coalition pinned its forces on two big bases, at Bagram and Kandahar. It did not apply the forces that were in the country to deny the Taliban access to the people and the territory from which they had launched their original drive to power in the 1990s. Thus the Taliban, having reconstituted in Pakistan, gradually reentered Afghanistan, and over the course of approximately five years regained control over much of the south and east of the country.

By 2009, the security situation in southern Afghanistan had become a crisis. The government controlled only the population centers, while the Taliban controlled or threatened to control almost all rural areas. The insurgents isolated towns and villages, conducted attacks at will on the main highway that circles the country, and undermined confidence that the government could protect the population centers—even the city of Kandahar—from the Taliban. Official corruption further reduced support for the Karzai government.

Washington's goals for Afghanistan were also substantially diminished compared to Bush's ambitious pronouncements soon after 9/11. Following extensive assessments, strategy reviews, and debate among senior national security officials, Obama personally dictated a number of "operational objectives" for the military surge he approved on November 29, 2009.

Those objectives included: "reversing the Taliban's momentum;" "denying the Taliban access to and control of key population and production centers and lines of communication;" "disrupting the Taliban in areas outside the secure area and preventing Al Qaeda from gaining sanctuary in Afghanistan;" and "degrading the Taliban to levels manageable by the Afghan National Security Force," which would be increased in size "so we can transition responsibility for security to the Afghan government on a timeline that will permit us to begin to decrease our troop presence by July 2011."

To achieve his operational objectives, Obama authorized an extended surge of 68,000 troops (21,000 combat troops authorized in March 2009, with 13,000 accompanying support troops; 4,000 trainers; and 30,000 additional combat troops authorized in November 2009) during the period from July 2009 through July 2011.

There was little science behind the number of troops included in the surge. The Army Field Manual on Counterinsurgency that was written under the direction of General David Petraeus, the commander of US forces in Afghanistan, states that 20 counterinsurgents per 1,000 residents "is often considered the minimum troop density required" for effective counterinsurgency operations. In order to achieve this troop density throughout Afghanistan, the coalition would require 654,760 security forces (including any combination of US, coalition, and Afghan soldiers and Afghan police).

Today, at the height of the surge of foreign forces, approximately 140,000 coalition troops are in Afghanistan, together with a total of 256,000 Afghan security forces. That is about 60 percent of the number required by military doctrine. And we are now approaching the July 2011 crossover point at which the number of US forces is supposed to decline and the number of Afghan forces will increase, resulting in, at best, the same size force.

To be sure, the doctrinal ratio of security forces to population may not be a good guide in Afghanistan. Population statistics for the country are not reliable, and the security forces can be concentrated in areas of Taliban influence rather than in areas already under government control.

Yet the number of US surge forces was not based on a military strategy, either. The military staffs in Afghanistan did not first have a plan as to how they would defeat the enemy in the contested southern area of the country, even though such a plan should have dictated the number of forces required. Instead, they developed a plan based on the number of forces they would get—after they found out how many forces were coming.

In reality, as journalist Bob Woodward has detailed in *Obama's Wars,* the number of surge forces was determined by political negotiation between the president and the senior military leadership. The military leaders then said that they could achieve the president's operational objectives, which included a drawdown beginning in July 2011, with the force that was provided.

It is clear that Vice President Joseph Biden was against a surge of conventional forces, and Obama himself was reluctant to approve it, but, as Lieutenant General Douglas Lute, the National Security Council Coordinator for Afghanistan-Pakistan, suggested to Woodward, the president "had to do this 18-month surge just to demonstrate, in effect, that it couldn't be done. . . . Obama would have given the monolithic military its day in court and the United States would not be seen as having been driven off the battlefield."

Tenuous Progress

At this point, the president's calculation that the surge might help the United States facilitate a drawdown while avoiding the appearance of being "driven off the battlefield" has not yet been vindicated.

The surge's stated goals, expressed in the language of counterinsurgency, are to "clear" population centers of the Taliban; "hold" these centers to prevent the insurgents from returning; maintain security to allow Afghans to "build" a minimal government and economic structure; and then "transfer" security responsibilities over these areas to the Afghan government. Currently, all the surge brigades have been deployed to southern Afghanistan—but their efforts have not reached the point in the "clear-hold-build-transfer" sequence that would allow US forces to transfer security responsibility to the government.

In Helmand province, US Marines have cleared key districts of Taliban influence, but not sustainably. For example, they

deliberately cleared the Marja district in the south of Helmand in February 2010, during the winter lull in fighting, creating a temporary appearance of security there. In May, however, the Taliban began to reinfiltrate the area and intimidate the population. The Marines fought all summer to create and defend an expanding number of small bases that allowed them to patrol the surrounding villages.

On April 16, 2010, Obama asked General Stanley McChrystal, then the commander in Afganistan, about the status of Marja and the Nawa and Garmsir districts in Helmand that were initially cleared in the summer of 2009. McChrystal described them as in the "hold" phase, not yet ready for transfer. Today, those districts are still in the hold phase. This does not mean military progress is not being made—an increasing number of districts in Helmand province have been cleared, or are being cleared, through hard fighting, which is definitely military progress. It is simply not progress to the transfer phase, which was the condition that was supposed to allow the "thinning" of US forces beginning in July 2011.

Similarly, the three Army surge brigades in Kandahar have cleared that province's key districts. Access to the provincial capital has been regulated through a ring of checkpoints around the city, and the army has blocked Taliban access to Route 1, allowing commerce to proceed. The soldiers also have created a new network of bases from which they, like the Marines in Helmand, can patrol throughout the adjacent villages and deny the Taliban access to their infiltration routes, support bases, and weapons caches.

In key parts of Kandahar province, the number of security forces (including US forces) exceeds the population they are protecting. At this point, the rural population in which the Taliban have thrived appears to be willing to accept and support the Afghan government and deny sanctuary to the Taliban because the residents believe that the forts built in their neighborhoods are a sign that the Americans are there to stay.

However, the military progress is tenuous. The gains in security have been made during the traditional winter lull in Afghan fighting; as demonstrated last year in Marja, the Taliban likely will come back in the spring. Moreover, the dense concentration of forces in certain areas requires that vast regions of the country, including areas of Kandahar province, are essentially unprotected.

The Taliban have demonstrated that they will resort to alternative methods of violence, such as suicide bombings, attacks on civilians, and assassinations, to intimidate the population and undermine the government—and these tactics are not easily mitigated with military force. If the Americans begin to abandon their forts in rural Kandahar and Helmand by drawing down this year, Afghan villagers will recognize that the United States is not going to stay. In the absence of any other governing force capable of assuring security, they will be irretrievably lost to the Taliban.

Obama, senior officials in his administration, and General Petraeus have repeatedly said that the withdrawal of forces beginning in July 2011 will be "conditions-based." But the president and the generals have different interpretations of this phrase. The political leadership construes the phrase to mean that forces will be withdrawn, while the military leadership interprets the phrase to mean that forces may not be withdrawn.

Mission Unaccomplished

Right now, conditions in Afghanistan have been stabilized. The coalition forces are not losing the war, and some of Obama's goals have been achieved: The Taliban's momentum has been reversed; the insurgents no longer have access to and control of key population and production centers and lines of communication, and they have been disrupted in areas outside the secure areas; and Al Qaeda has been prevented from gaining sanctuary in Afghanistan.

However, the conditions necessary for American forces to withdraw are not present. The premise of the counterinsurgency strategy is that it will make possible the transfer of security and governance responsibilities to the Afghan government; American forces create an "ink spot" of security that spreads as US units secure one area and move on to a new area to establish security there. Yet the Afghan government is not prepared to assume security and governance responsibility in any of the areas that the US surge forces have cleared and so far held. None of the American surge forces (with perhaps a small exception in Nawa, in Helmand province) have been able to transfer ground to the Afghan government and move on to a new area, thereby spreading the ink spot.

The conditions necessary for American forces to withdraw are not present.

Ideally, the generals on the ground should be able to make sound judgments regarding risk and incrementally move forces to expand the ink spot with the forces that are now available. But this endeavor is too serious to be left to the generals. The Taliban and Al Qaeda, after all, would not have escaped to Pakistan if force had been applied prudently in late 2001. The generals' record of judgment in using forces available to them to achieve lasting effects in this war does not warrant gambling on their ability to hold on to the current gains with fewer forces. In fact, a reduction in forces this year risks allowing military leaders to say that the administration stabbed them in the back due to the president's concern about the 2012 election.

The generals' record of judgment does not warrant gambling on their ability to hold on to the current gains with fewer forces.

The only way for the United States to achieve Obama's goals in Afghanistan is to wait until all of his operational objectives have been accomplished, including increasing the size and capability of Afghan security forces and building the capacity of the Afghan government. Unfortunately, no one can tell how long it will take for the country's security forces to be ready to have security responsibility transferred to them. They clearly are not ready now. The American objectives will not be met "on a timeline that will permit us to begin to decrease our troop presence by July 2011."

No one involved in the surge decision thought the objectives would be met by July 2011. The goals may not even be accomplished by 2014. But if the United States allows the Taliban to return in the wake of US troops' departure, which would likely happen with a thinning of the surge, the Americans will have been "driven off the battlefield" by arbitrary self-imposed constraints, and 9/11 will remain unavenged.

Critical Thinking

1. Are conditions for the withdrawal of American forces from Afghanistan present?
2. Why was it possible for the terrorists to find sanctuary in Pakistan?
3. Will the United States achieve its military objectives in Afghanistan by 2014? Why or why not?

GARY M. BOWMAN, a colonel in the US Army Reserve, has served on active duty for the past four years as the senior Army historian in Iraq and Afghanistan. This article does not reflect the views of the Department of Defense.

From *Current History*, April 2011, pp. 150–155. Copyright © 2011 by Current History, Inc. Reprinted by permission.

Sudan on the Cusp

"The appointed date for southern Sudan's separation fast approaches. . . . Once separation does take place, both north and south will still face a multitude of stress points, risks, and challenges."

RICHARD S. WILLIAMSON

I f events go as planned, southern Sudan in just weeks will separate from the north and the world's newest nation, the Republic of South Sudan, will be born. However, serious impediments to a peaceful separation still must be addressed. And even if an uneventful separation does take place, that will not be the end of the story—it will be the end of the beginning. Many challenges lie ahead both for the new independent nation and for what remains of the old Sudan, as well as for neighboring countries, the wider region, and the international community.

Seared in my memory is a visit I made in May 2008 to Abyei, a border town contested by north and south Sudan. Just days earlier thousands of families had lived, laughed, and loved there. On the day of my visit I saw only remnants of lives lost. The town's dirt roads stood empty except for three teenage soldiers wearing flip-flops and carrying Kalashnikov rifles. I saw burned-out huts, blackened chairs and bed frames, scattered fragments of clothes, the occasional charred skeleton of a truck, and the contorted remains of a child's bicycle. Here and there rose wisps of smoke, the pungent smell hanging heavy in the air.

An unknown number of innocents had been killed in the spring of 2008, and many more forced to flee their homes, in a terrible flash of violence carried out by nomadic Misseriya Arabs while Sudan's armed forces stayed in their barracks and allowed the carnage to rage on. Tens of thousands of people lost the lives they had known. They were only the latest victims of the endless violence in Sudan, a nation that has suffered more trauma and tragedy than any society could possibly digest.

Weeks later I visited Agok, a day's walk from Abyei, where over 50,000 displaced people who had fled the Abyei destruction had settled temporarily. It was the rainy season. The people were crowded under plastic sheets hung between trees. My feet sank three inches into the mud as I walked from shelter to shelter to visit the victims of yet another spasm of senseless destruction. These people, kept alive by humanitarian aid, were hurt and angry, but determined to return to their homes and rebuild.

The final disposition of Abyei—whether it becomes part of the new Republic of South Sudan or remains part of the north—has yet to be determined. This question is one of the many consequential matters still unresolved as we approach the scheduled separation date of July 9, 2011. Abyei is just one example of how fragile things are and of how much work remains to be done before a peaceful separation can proceed.

At the Margins

Throughout much of Sudan's painful history, Arab Muslims at the center have been favored while the non-Arab, non-Muslim people at the periphery have been marginalized. Indeed such discrimination—in the economy, politics, healthcare, and education—has defined Sudan's past 200 years. The country's divisions are deep and its injustices significant; no vision unites Sudan, no sense exists that various groups share a stake in the nation, no agreement pertains on what it is to be Sudanese.

Under the Ottoman Empire in the nineteenth century and the British Empire during the first half of the twentieth century, the Arab Muslims at the center were partners in ruling this diverse land, where nearly 600 ethnic groups and tribes speak almost 400 languages. When the British left in 1956, political power was transferred to the Arab Muslims and, not surprisingly, they continued the patterns of marginalization practiced by their former imperial rulers.

Economic deprivation, political discrimination, and injustice naturally produced deep resentments. Periodic efforts by Khartoum to assert greater control over the periphery, coupled with attempts to impose sharia, led to rebellions and warfare.

No acceptable narrative for a broader Sudan has ever existed; nor a sense of nationhood; nor the harmony and tranquility associated with a normal state. Instead the country has experienced discrimination and division, strain and struggle, fragmentation and friction, bickering and brutality. These were the underlying causes of the long north-south Sudanese civil war, a conflict that began in 1955, stopped in 1972, then resumed in 1983. It was Africa's longest war, claiming 2.5 million lives and displacing more than 4 million people.

A 2005 peace agreement ended the worst violence of that war and created a six-year path toward self-determination and the independence of the south. But it is important to understand that the people of the south are not the only group on the periphery that has long been marginalized. Peoples of the east, of the central Nuba Mountains, of Darfur in the west, and elsewhere have suffered similar injustices and have rebelled from time to time. The fundamental problems between them and Khartoum will not end with the south's independence. Indeed, the danger of violence between Khartoum and these other peripheral areas may well increase.

Yes and No

President George W. Bush and Jack Danforth, a former senator and my predecessor as Bush's special envoy to Sudan, took the lead in trying to end Sudan's north-south civil war. Negotiations were long and difficult, and involved Khartoum; Juba (the city in southern Sudan that is now slated to be the capital of the new republic); countries belonging to the Intergovernmental Authority on Development, a regional grouping; and other stakeholders, such as Norway and the United Kingdom. The result was the Comprehensive Peace Agreement (CPA) between Khartoum and the leadership of the southern rebels, the Sudan People's Liberation Movement. The agreement was signed in January 2005.

Implementing the pact has been difficult and imperfect. Low-intensity fighting has continued and casualties persist. The north after the agreement was reached failed to live up to some important commitments. Leaders in southern Sudan, meanwhile—especially Salva Kiir, the president of the south—proved patient, skilled, and disciplined. They refused to respond proportionally to violence sponsored by Khartoum. They kept their focus on the prize of self-determination.

The CPA, while often in danger, proved resilient, and the parties moved toward the January 2011 referendum on southern independence that was specified in the agreement. The vote was deemed credible. Over 99 percent of southerners chose independence.

Still, it is worthwhile to examine some CPA commitments that have not been honored—for example, regarding border areas contested between the north and south. In the agreement, both parties committed to accept a border demarcation to be drawn by the Abyei Border Commission, a body of international experts who were to rely on various specified criteria.

The commission gathered information and rendered its judgment. The south did not get everything it had hoped for, but nonetheless met its obligation and accepted the border decisions. The north, however, abrogated its commitment by refusing to accept the commission's decision.

After the May 2008 flare-up in Abyei, both the north and the south made various commitments, outlined in a document called the Abyei Road Map Agreement. This agreement specified that, among other things, the contested border issues would be referred to the Permanent Court of Arbitration in The Hague and that both sides would abide by whatever decision this international body reached. In essence, the south agreed to let the north have a second bite at the apple.

Filings were made, documents were entered into evidence, and arguments were tendered to the court. The court made its decision. The new border demarcation was somewhat less favorable to the south than that rendered by the Abyei Border Commission; nonetheless, consistent with its commitment, Juba accepted the decision. The north, again in violation of its commitment, refused to accept.

Similarly, the north did not disarm and demobilize its proxy Arab militias as it had committed to do in the CPA. The north did not fully integrate joint security forces, nor did it provide transparent accounting for the sharing of oil revenues as agreed to in the CPA. The list goes on. The point is that Khartoum's failure fully to live up to its commitments has created various negative consequences.

First, the south has developed a deep distrust of Khartoum's reliability; it appears to be the north's conscious strategy to give little weight to fulfilling its obligations. Second, other marginalized peoples in Sudan have witnessed this record and taken note. Third, the international community has developed a poor record of inducing the north to honor its commitments and of holding Khartoum accountable for its breaches.

While serving as special envoy, and working with Sudan's prominent personalities and watching the maneuvering of the north, I came to believe that Khartoum had decided there was little cost to abrogating commitments. Rather, the leaders in the capital saw value in a strategy that drew things out. They liked to set up elaborate processes for consideration of critical matters. Then they would discuss, deliberate, debate, and delay. Meanwhile, the international community's attention would wander to some other pressing issue somewhere else in the world. So Khartoum would escape the immediate crisis and kick the can down the road.

Shifting Leverage

Before a peaceful separation can occur in July, a number of pressing issues must be resolved. These issues have been understood for more than six years. That they remain outstanding is a testament to the north's success at controlling the pace of deliberations.

The north's thinking seems to be that its leverage will grow as July 9 draws closer. I suspect that Khartoum believes Juba will increasingly feel that it must make a deal as that date approaches; that the south will make concessions and the north will win more-than-equitable terms on key issues.

Furthermore, given the Barack Obama administration's tilt away from Juba and toward Khartoum, the north might calculate that the United States will pressure Juba to make concessions. Based on the US government's posture over the past 28 months, that seems a reasonable perspective. But if Washington were to act in this way, it would be a grave mistake, and might imperil any chance for stability after the south's independence.

Key issues include Abyei and five other contested border areas, citizenship, various treaty commitments, security guarantees, and sharing of oil revenues. All of these matters are consequential, but the two most critical are oil-revenue sharing and the future of the Abyei region.

When President Omar Hassan al-Bashir and his regime came to power in 1989 in a coup d'état, total exports from Sudan amounted to around half a billion dollars a year. Thanks to oil, current Sudanese exports are about $9.8 billion per year. That enormous growth has helped prop up the regime, bought security, paid for various armed conflicts, and made many people in Khartoum rich. However, 70 to 80 percent of the oil comes from the south.

Southern Sudan is the size of Texas. It has no paved roads outside the capital.

Naturally, the north does not want to lose that revenue stream. The viability of the regime might even be endangered if it lost all its revenue from oil in the south. I believe the reason that the five contested border regions remain unresolved is not that Khartoum harbors a deep desire for more land, or that it feels particular loyalty to Arab nomadic tribes in those areas (some of whom have served as proxy militias for Khartoum), but because of the oil that lies under the ground.

The south, understandably, does not want to share its oil with the north, which has marginalized and brutalized it for so long. It wants the oil revenue to help build the south, to develop its economy, and to provide the peace dividend its people are hoping for. But the south has a problem. The pipeline through which the oil flows (built by the Chinese) goes through the north to oil storage facilities (also built by the Chinese); from these facilities, located near Port Sudan, the oil is exported to world markets. There is no alternative route. The south has few paved roads and receives about 50 inches of rain a year, making truck transport unfeasible. Building a pipeline to the sea through neighboring countries would take at least three years.

Consequently, both north and south have reasons to reach some accommodation, at least for the short term. The south has said it will not share revenue from the oil that rightfully belongs to the south; however, the south also has said it would be willing to pay a fee for use of the north's pipeline. So the basis for an agreement is available.

As of this writing, however, no deal has been struck. Various international partners, including the United States, are working as facilitators to help the north and south reach agreement on this and other issues. No reason exists that an agreement cannot be reached, but we can expect the north to overreach and the south to be parsimonious. The facilitators must act as honest brokers to guide the parties to a sustainable resolution of this crucial issue.

The Abyei area—a region on the border between the north and south—presents a different sort of challenge, one charged with emotion and political significance, and complicated as well by oil issues. It is the home of the Ngok Dinka, the tribe to which many of the most prominent personalities in southern Sudan belong. However, the nomadic Misseriya Arabs graze cattle there and consider it part of the north. It has been the site of clashes over the years, including the terrible violence of May 2008.

Abyei did not take part in the January referendum because the north and south could not agree on who there should have

the right to vote. Since the referendum Abyei has seen some scattered clashes, as well as major armed violence in late February and early March that claimed hundreds of lives. Each side accuses the other of starting these clashes. Additional United Nations peacekeeping troops have been sent to the area. The situation remains tense, with both sides drawing lines in the sand and refusing to compromise.

Bashir's adviser for security affairs, Salah Abdallah Gosh, has warned that Abyei will remain part of the north whether through a bilateral agreement or war. For Bashir, any compromise on Abyei would be a major political victory, while for Kiir it would be a major defeat. Nonetheless, some agreement must be reached. Otherwise, it is difficult to see a path toward a peaceful separation.

Hedging Bets

Nine countries share borders with Sudan. Most, while hedging their bets, have favored unity as the safest and most stable outcome. They are concerned about the contagion of instability and the possibility of terrorists exploiting power vacuums. They also are concerned that separation might set an example for resolving disputes within their own states. In various ways, large and small, most neighboring states in the past have found ways to be supportive of Khartoum during its various clashes with marginalized peoples on Sudan's periphery.

However, each neighbor has charted its own course, and in fact most have been active within Sudan's borders. Ethiopia has generally supported Khartoum but also has provided training for the southern Sudan People's Liberation Army. Uganda, plagued by rebels known as the Lord's Resistance Army (LRA)—who have gained some support from Khartoum and found safe haven within Sudan—has supported separation in the expectation that an independent southern Sudan will be less hospitable to the LRA.

Egypt, where some Sudanese refugees have flowed, is concerned about treaties and other arrangements regarding the Nile River, which flows through southern Sudan's vast marshland, and consequently has tilted heavily toward unity. Chad has served as a safe haven and a launching site for the Justice and Equality Movement (JEM), a Darfuri rebel group. In retaliation, Khartoum has provided safe haven and a launching pad for rebels in Chad. Libya's Muammar el-Qaddafi has provided support for various Darfuri rebels. The list goes on.

The south does not want to share its oil with the north, which has marginalized and brutalized it for so long.

Within the past year, however, things reached a tipping point. In part because of a diplomatic surge by the Obama administration last fall, it became clear that separation was inevitable. Since then neighboring countries have increasingly focused on nurturing a peaceful separation supporting a stable outcome. Of course, this is better for the Sudanese people as well as their neighbors.

The African Union (AU) has long favored unity. Most African nations are multiethnic and many face ethnic and regional stresses of their own, which has led to AU concerns about Sudan splitting into two states. While it never openly opposed the CPA, for a long time the AU was neither enthusiastic about it nor particularly helpful regarding its implementation. In more than one meeting at AU headquarters in Addis Ababa, I heard concerns about the dangers of elections, referendums, and the splintering of a country.

Over time, however, the wider region has come to accept the inevitability of separation, and African nations have recently sought to help with maintaining stability. This has been a very constructive development. Such regional help could prove invaluable in the immediate aftermath of separation, when both the north and the newly independent south will confront enormous internal stresses as well as the threat of violence.

The international community beyond Africa has been divided in its dealings with Sudan. Washington, the European Union, and most others have been committed to full implementation of the CPA. These countries have spoken out about violations of the CPA, supported mechanisms for implementation of the agreement, and provided humanitarian assistance and development aid to southern Sudan in preparation for possible separation. Norway in particular has been helpful, providing expertise on a range of oil-related matters.

Some countries, however, have been less helpful. Those that sell weapons to Sudan and those that purchase its oil have favored Khartoum in ways that have not always promoted full implementation of the CPA. China in particular has been singled out as having provided cover for Khartoum when the UN Security Council has considered the slow-motion genocide in Darfur and the violence and other problems in southern Sudan. The problematic nations, however, including China, seemed at some point last year to accept the probability of the south's secession and to behave more favorably toward stability in Sudan and development of the south.

High Stress

If the key issues—revenue sharing, Abyei, the five other contested border areas, citizenship, security, and so on—are resolved so that separation can proceed as scheduled in July, a number of major problems will still have to be overcome if sustainable peace is to be achieved.

Khartoum will face a crisis of legitimacy. Some will challenge the regime on the grounds that it allowed dismemberment of the country. Opposition political parties in the north are already in consultations about unifying to challenge Bashir's National Congress Party (NCP). Khartoum will also have to contend with a substantial drop in revenues because so much oil money will go to the newly independent south. This economic shock will feed further political turbulence.

Furthermore, the political unrest that began in Tunisia and proceeded to Egypt and elsewhere has bled into Sudan. While Egypt boiled over, demonstrations took place in Khartoum. The protests were not as large or sustained as they have been in many other Arab nations, but further unrest and political turmoil could ensue. Some commentators have suggested that this may lead the NCP to take a more Islamist tack. Many observers suspect that Bashir's recent declaration that he would not seek reelection in 2015 is a response to the unrest running through the Arab world.

During this time of great stress in the north, various rebel movements in Darfur and elsewhere may seize on Khartoum's weakness and renew demands for greater autonomy or independence. Especially problematic may be the JEM, which in May 2008 successfully advanced all the way to Omdurman, just across the Nile from Khartoum. This is the only time that any rebel group has been able to penetrate the defenses of Sudan's armed forces and strike near the heart of the regime.

From my many discussions with senior officials of the NCP, I know healthy concern exists about the military capabilities of the JEM. This may explain efforts that Khartoum has recently made to relieve tensions with Chad, Sudan's neighbor on the Darfuri border, and may also explain the deployment of more Sudanese troops to the Darfur region.

Indeed, Khartoum may be planning attacks of its own in Darfur. This would add more names to the long list of Darfuri victims, including those of innocent civilians. Moreover, attacks by Khartoum would make it very difficult if not impossible for the Obama administration to lift sanctions on Khartoum, as it has promised to do, if separation proceeds peacefully. After all, the most restrictive sanctions were imposed not because of the north-south struggle but because of the carnage in Darfur.

The south will also face enormous stress immediately after separation. President Kiir has a long history as a successful rebel general, but he is an accidental president. The dominant personality and unifier of southern Sudan's rebel movements was John Garang, the charismatic and skillful warrior-politician who drove the negotiations for the CPA, and who, it was assumed, would be the country's leader when the CPA was fully implemented. Tragically, soon after implementation began, Garang was killed in a helicopter accident—and his quieter vice president, Kiir, rose to the presidency.

I have enormous respect for Kiir. For almost six years he has been the indispensable man in keeping the CPA's implementation on track, often at considerable political cost. But he does not have a dominant personality—and during the long transition period, many other aspirants to the top post have been submerging their own ambitions. After independence, many constraints will be gone. The unifying force of a common enemy, Khartoum, will disappear, and personal ambitions will be unleashed. The jockeying for power, prestige, and position will be considerable, and Kiir's own position will be fragile.

For Peace's Sake

For the sake of stability, this natural political competition must occur within normal nonviolent boundaries. If the United States and others in the international community press Kiir to make excessive concessions on the final resolution of Abyei, or to concede too much to the north regarding oil revenues, such actions would invite a political crisis that would gravely endanger stability.

Furthermore, the new government of the Republic of South Sudan must deal with widespread expectations among southerners that a significant peace dividend will flow from independence. Southern Sudan is the size of Texas. It has no paved roads outside the capital. Most southerners live on less than a dollar per day. And while the United States and the international community have provided massive humanitarian assistance to the south, very little development has occurred.

Things must change and change quickly. Governance capacity is urgently needed. Improved education and health care are required, as are roads, bridges, and other infrastructure. And to move toward economic viability, the south must expand beyond oil extraction—it must exploit other mineral resources, establish small-scale manufacturing, and, most urgently, achieve sustainable agricultural development. For this, multilateral and bilateral development assistance is required. Assistance must be targeted and effective if stability is to be achieved in this land that for generations has been a cauldron of conflict and humanitarian crisis.

The appointed date for southern Sudan's separation fast approaches. But a great deal must be done for separation to occur peacefully. And once separation does take place, both north and south will still face a multitude of stress points, risks, and challenges. The Sudanese people, having suffered greatly, yearn for an end to the violence. It is in the interest of Sudan's neighbors, the region, and the international community to help them attain the diplomatic and material means to achieve the sustainable peace they desire.

Critical Thinking

1. Is the Sudanese government committing genocide in southern Sudan?

2. What has been the policy of the Obama administration toward Sudan?

3. How has the conflict in southern Sudan affected the conflict in Darfur?

RICHARD S. WILLIAMSON, a former US ambassador to the United Nations Commission on Human Rights, served as President George W. Bush's special envoy to Sudan from 2007 to 2009.

From *Current History,* May 2011, pp. 171–176. Copyright © 2011 by Current History, Inc. Reprinted by permission.

A World without Nuclear Weapons Is a Joint Enterprise

JAMES GOODBY

With the entry into force of the New Strategic Arms Reduction Treaty (New START) between Russia and the United States, the time has come to widen the conversations about eliminating nuclear weapons to include other nuclear-armed states and states with advanced civil nuclear programs. Their support for creating the necessary conditions for achieving a world without nuclear weapons is essential in practice as well as in principle.

Russia and the United States have urgent unfinished business: reductions in the number of nuclear weapons beyond those scheduled in New START, including warheads associated with short-range delivery systems. Yet, talks limited to Russia and the United States alone cannot succeed in creating conditions conducive to achieving a world without nuclear weapons. The U.S. Senate, in its resolution of ratification for New START, "calls upon the other nuclear weapon states to give careful and early consideration to corresponding reductions of their own nuclear arsenals." That is good advice.

The nuclear weapons programs of other countries are major barriers to sustained Russian-U.S. reductions in nuclear weaponry and can encourage further proliferation in the absence of solid signs of commitment to the goals of the nuclear Nonproliferation Treaty (NPT). These programs are cited again and again in critical commentary on the feasibility and even desirability of the goal of eliminating nuclear weapons. If other states that possess nuclear weapons were to join in a reduction and elimination program, even with small initial steps, the effect on Russia and the United States would be catalytic. It would energize their efforts to move toward deep reductions and ultimately the elimination of nuclear weapons. It also would help with nonproliferation efforts around the world.

A Relic of the Cold War

Historically, the involvement of other nuclear-armed states in nuclear reductions negotiations has not been a high priority for the United States. The focus has been on U.S. negotiations with Russia because those two countries account for about 90 percent of the world's nuclear weapons. The involvement of other states has been seen as an obstacle in an already complex, bilateral U.S.-Russian negotiation. Furthermore, expanding the roster of countries in the negotiations has been seen as complicating U.S. relations with its allies, France and the United Kingdom. These arguments are now relics of Cold War circumstances.

Four years ago, an op-ed published in *The Wall Street Journal* revolutionized thinking in the United States and elsewhere about the future of nuclear weapons. George Shultz, William Perry, Henry Kissinger, and Sam Nunn wrote that "reassertion of the vision of a world free of nuclear weapons and practical measures toward achieving that goal would be, and would be perceived as, a bold initiative consistent with America's moral heritage."[1] They warned that the world is at a tipping point in its capacity to avoid nuclear catastrophe. The article identified several "agreed and urgent steps" that should be taken to create the conditions for a world without nuclear weapons. Even before listing those steps, the authors called "first and foremost" for "intensive work with leaders of the countries in possession of nuclear weapons to turn the goal of a world without nuclear weapons into a joint enterprise."

During his first year in office, President Barack Obama accepted the goal of a world without nuclear weapons and the step-by-step method of achieving it. On September 24, 2009, he presided over a summit meeting of the UN Security Council on nuclear nonproliferation and nuclear disarmament. In Resolution 1887, the council resolved "to create the conditions for a world without nuclear weapons" and called on parties to the NPT "to undertake to pursue negotiations in good faith on effective measures relating to nuclear arms reductions and disarmament."

The United States and Russia acted together to comply with that mandate. Obama and Russian President Dmitry Medvedev signed New START on April 8, 2010. On December 22, 2010, the Senate gave its assent to ratification of the treaty. The Russian legislature followed suit on January 26, 2011. On February 5, 2011, New START entered into force with the exchange of instruments of ratification between Secretary of State Hillary Rodham Clinton and Russian Foreign Minister Sergey Lavrov.

Roles for All States

The Security Council resolution did not exclude other nuclear-armed countries when it called for an undertaking by NPT parties to pursue negotiations relating to nuclear arms reduction and disarmament. No state was excused from the task of helping to create the conditions necessary for a world without nuclear weapons. The purpose was not to urge Russia and the United States to reduce their nuclear arsenals while other states looked on. In fact, the resolution called "for further progress on all aspects of disarmament to enhance global security."

In a 2010 essay published by the American Academy of Arts and Sciences, Scott Sagan quite correctly pointed out that all parties to the NPT have a "shared responsibility" for disarmament and nonproliferation. Indeed, the treaty's Article VI states that "[e]ach of the Parties to the Treaty"—not just the nuclear-weapon states—"undertakes to pursue negotiations in good faith on effective measures relating to cessation of the nuclear arms race at an early date and to nuclear disarmament, and on a treaty on general and complete disarmament under strict and effective international control."[2]

One of the first things that states can do is promote enhanced transparency. The final document of the 2010 NPT Review Conference welcomed "efforts towards the development of nuclear disarmament verification capabilities that will be required to provide assurance of compliance with nuclear disarmament agreements for the achievement and maintenance of a nuclear-weapon-free world." It noted the cooperation between Norway, a non-nuclear-weapon state, and the United Kingdom on establishing a system for verifying the dismantlement of nuclear warheads.

Transparency is a crucial part of moving toward a nuclear-weapon-free world. The five countries that the NPT recognizes as nuclear-weapon states—China, France, Russia, the United Kingdom, and the United States—held a meeting addressing that issue in London in 2009 and are expected to meet again in Paris later this year. Transparency, however, is a global requirement. Exchanges of data on nuclear programs and on holdings of fissile materials by all countries could be conducted on a regional basis, or they could be managed through the International Atomic Energy Agency (IAEA) on a global basis. If the nuclear-armed states entered into an agreement not to use fissile material to build more nuclear weapons, an exchange of data would be an essential part of the verification process. Furthermore, Sidney Drell and Christopher Stubbs have suggested that the Open Skies Treaty has provided a successful framework for addressing verification challenges and that its membership should be expanded and its suite of sensors modernized. This could be an important feature of transparency programs related to production of fissile material.[3]

Agreed and Urgent Steps

These kinds of transparency and confidence-building measures might be necessary precursors to other, more concrete advances toward a nuclear-weapon-free world because reductions of weapons stockpiles likely would not be the first step

that the owners of smaller nuclear arsenals would take. They would need to build more mutual confidence than currently exists and gain experience in working together. A wide array of cooperative actions is available to nuclear-armed states and to states with advanced civil nuclear programs. Many of these actions could be pursued without delay. They would block further nuclear proliferation, an essential element in the effort to eliminate the nuclear threat.

Entry into force of the Comprehensive Test Ban Treaty (CTBT) was one of the "urgent" steps suggested in the *Wall Street Journal* op-ed. It would be a powerful nonproliferation tool. Adherence by all states to an IAEA additional protocol, a step that would promote international confidence that a country was not pursuing a covert nuclear weapons program, is another practical and realizable step. Several practical steps taken by individual states were identified in the documents emerging from the 47-state Washington nuclear security summit in April 2010. The work plan that emerged from the summit committed the countries to support the International Convention for the Suppression of Acts of Nuclear Terrorism, the Convention on the Physical Protection of Nuclear Material, UN Security Council Resolution 1540, and several IAEA initiatives. The experience of working together to tighten controls over nuclear materials is in itself a confidence-building measure.

Important early progress could be accomplished by a declaration among countries that have advanced civil or military nuclear programs that "fissile materials removed from nuclear weapons being eliminated and excess to national security requirements will not be used to manufacture nuclear weapons; no newly produced fissile materials will be used in nuclear weapons; and fissile materials from or within civil nuclear programs will not be used to manufacture nuclear weapons."

This language appears in a declaration issued by Russian President Boris Yeltsin and U.S. President Bill Clinton in 1995.[4] Early agreement on these points by all states with advanced nuclear programs would be a signal that they are determined to create the conditions for a world without nuclear weapons. A coalition of states acting in this fashion would accelerate agreement by Russia and the United States on deeper cuts in their nuclear arsenals.

Discussions about a treaty with a similar intent that would be applicable evenhandedly to all countries have been under way in the Geneva-based Conference on Disarmament, the UN forum for multilateral arms control negotiations, for several years. No serious negotiations have ever occurred, and the prospect for change in that situation is bleak. Nonetheless, these talks should continue. A binding and verifiable treaty should be negotiated, if possible, but the declaration described above would be much more than a stopgap measure. It would have value as a bridge to a vigorous joint enterprise to eliminate nuclear weapons.

Building a Coalition

International cooperation on sensitive nuclear issues should become easier if all nuclear-armed states visibly decided to opt out of nuclear weapons programs and states with advanced civil or military nuclear programs endorsed the CTBT and the declaration to disavow use of fissile material in future production of nuclear weapons. Russian and U.S. leadership will be required in measures such as these, but regional initiatives obviously must come from states in those regions. The other permanent members of the UN Security Council—China, France, and the United Kingdom—will have to assume leadership roles in a nonproliferation coalition if the global enterprise is to become a reality. However, this work should not be limited to the five permanent members of the UN Security Council.

Some of the measures are complex and therefore would require some time to negotiate; the relevant countries should start discussions now. Just beginning such talks would be a symbol of their intent and would tend to establish a nonproliferation coalition. These more complex measures include:

Settlement of regional disputes. Global agreements on nuclear weapons will not be sufficient in areas of the world where conflicts between regional powers have been deep-seated and intractable. A resolution of these differences will take a long time and will be multifaceted. One initial action could be regional negotiations on military confidence-building measures such as those that were negotiated as part of the Helsinki process in Europe. Restraints on conventional military operations could be negotiated, followed by protocols affecting weapons of mass destruction to augment existing global agreements, such as the Biological Weapons Convention and the Chemical Weapons Convention (CWC). These might entail "adversarial" inspections between rival states. Israel has supported the concept of a zone free of weapons of mass destruction in the Middle East. This procedure is probably the best way to deal with such weapons in that region; reliance only on global agreements is not likely to be sufficient. A final stage in this progression from regional first steps would be agreements not to permit nuclear weapons, built locally or elsewhere, within the borders of a treaty-defined region. In such cases, rules regarding permissible nuclear activities might be applied, consistent with rules worked out in broader international negotiations.

Global agreements on nuclear weapons will not be sufficient in areas of the world where conflicts between regional powers have been deep-seated and intractable.

Multilateralizing uranium-enrichment programs.[5] An international norm that sensitive parts of the nuclear fuel cycle should be subject to multinational ownership, providing opportunities to invest and participate in the management of such facilities while protecting the technology involved, could reduce incentives for states to acquire their own national facilities. All plans for new commercial enrichment facilities should be based on the presumption that the facilities will be owned multinationally and their operations safeguarded by the IAEA. The Nuclear Suppliers Group (NSG) should give preference to

such facilities when considerations about selling enrichment equipment and technology emerge. Selling enrichment technology is a rare event, but it would become even rarer if the NSG agreed on this approach. Existing commercial facilities or those under construction that are not already owned multinationally should be encouraged to convert to multinational ownership, with their operations safeguarded by the IAEA.

International interim storage sites for spent nuclear fuel. The storage of spent fuel in cooling pools adjacent to the reactors in which the fuel was used is a common practice, in the United States and elsewhere. Events following the earthquake and tsunami in Japan showed the hazards that are inherent in this practice. Developing and funding a program for storing spent fuel in dry casks is a necessity. The back end of the nuclear fuel cycle has attracted considerable attention in the United States, partly because the Obama administration set aside plans to send U.S. utilities' spent fuel to the Yucca Mountain repository in Nevada. "Cradle-to-grave" fuel services that would provide for leasing and take-back arrangements currently are seen as an attractive option in Washington although the United States has been reluctant to serve as a site for returned spent fuel. Regional, interim spent-fuel centers make a great deal of sense. Undersecretary of State for Arms Control and International Security Ellen Tauscher, in a presentation at Stanford University's Hoover Institution in January 2010, discussed the idea, pointing out that spent fuel could be stored at reactor sites while it was cooling and then be moved to an international interim-storage facility to await a decision on ultimate disposition.[6] (As the recent Japanese experience shows, at-reactor storage must be carefully planned; the location of reactors and associated spent-fuel cooling ponds is a critical issue.)

The idea of an interim storage facility should be pursued with a greater sense of urgency in light of the dangers shown in the case of Fukushima Daiichi. Moreover, in connection with turning the goal of a world without nuclear weapons into a joint enterprise, an effort to create regional interim-storage facilities deserves a high priority. It would contribute to nonproliferation objectives by providing international safeguards for material that can be turned into weapons. Also, it visibly would strengthen the practice of shared responsibility.

Unilateral or parallel reductions or freezes in nuclear weapons stockpiles. New START provides a treaty basis for reductions in the nuclear arsenals of Russia and the United States. France and the United Kingdom have unilaterally reduced their nuclear weapons stockpiles. A freeze at present levels on the part of China, India, and Pakistan would be a welcome contribution by those countries to the joint enterprise. In contrast, a buildup of nuclear weapons by those states would make it difficult, if not impossible, for the United States and Russia to move beyond New START. A good beginning in providing reassurance on this score would be the suggestion above for a joint statement regarding nonuse of fissile material for weapons modeled after the 1995 Clinton-Yeltsin declaration.

Continued work with Iran to block that country's development of a nuclear weapons capability and with North Korea to freeze and then roll back its nuclear weapons program will be essential. In fact, a failure to accomplish that level of cooperation with new or nascent nuclear-weapon states almost certainly will doom the whole nonproliferation project.

Required Conditions

At some relatively early point in a joint enterprise to reduce and eliminate nuclear weapons, future Russian-U.S. reductions would become part of a multilateral framework. No longer would Russia and the United States proceed with nuclear reductions in the absence of some kind of limits on the nuclear forces of other countries. This is not the place to discuss the many models of multilateral nuclear arms reductions. Such models are not valid predictors of actual reductions, but they do provide a framework for examining key security issues that countries will face as they approach and enter the end state, i.e., no assembled nuclear weapons. Among the issues that the nuclear-armed states and the countries with advanced civilian nuclear programs could usefully discuss at an early date is the conditions that should be met before nuclear weapons are completely eliminated. This exercise should help them realize that the goal is a difficult one to reach, but by no means is it a fantasy. It should help to validate the goal and strengthen the commitment to proceed, step by step, to a world without nuclear weapons, and it should help them design the kinds of practical safeguards they would want to have in any program intended to eliminate nuclear weapons.

At this point, it appears that four key conditions will need to be met during the course of reducing nuclear arsenals:

Procedures for challenge inspections to search for concealed warheads should have been established and satisfactorily exercised. U.S.-Russian agreements following New START are to deal with nondeployed warheads. Methods for monitoring declared nondeployed warheads have been studied for many years. These include the use of chain-of-custody techniques, such as tags and seals and perimeter and portal monitoring. Searching for concealed warheads is a different matter, and procedures akin to those used by the IAEA under its additional protocol or in the CTBT or CWC would come into play. This would require short-notice visits to suspect sites and some kind of managed inspections with agreed types of instrumentation.

As Sidney Drell and Raymond Jeanloz point out, "[I]t is not feasible to sustain a concealed stockpile of effective and reliable nuclear weapons by passive means."[7] Activities conducted by a state that tried to conceal a viable cache of nuclear weapons would be a tip-off to the likely location of undeclared concealed warheads. Such activities would justify a request for an on-site inspection on short notice. Effective operation for some years of a monitoring system that included short-notice visits on demand would be one condition for proceeding to eliminate all assembled weapons.

Warheads scheduled for elimination should have been dismantled under conditions that would assure that their actual dismantling can be confirmed, with the nuclear components placed in secure and monitored storage, pending final disposition. The United States and Russia have discussed the mechanics of doing this at least twice, once bilaterally and later with

the participation of the IAEA.[8] Techniques have been proposed that would protect especially sensitive design information while confirming that the nuclear components of a weapon were inside a container queuing up for dismantling. The Nunn-Lugar program, adopted by the U.S. Congress under the leadership of Senators Richard Lugar (R-Ind.) and Nunn (D-Ga.), provides funding and expertise to promote nonproliferation activities, originally in the states of the former Soviet Union. Under this program, the United States supported Russia in the construction of storage facilities for dismantled warheads. The irreversibility of dismantling would be assured by U.S. and Russian inspectors at storage sites in each country. IAEA involvement also might be useful. Methods that have been developed by the United States and Russia might not be directly transferred in every detail to other states. In each country that has started the process of eliminating nuclear weapons, however, arrangements very similar to the U.S.-Russian ones should have been put in place before agreement to complete the elimination process.

Delivery vehicles scheduled for elimination should have been verifiably destroyed and procedures should be in place to confirm that dual-use systems—those capable of delivering conventional or nuclear warheads—have not been armed with nuclear warheads. This condition is necessary to assure that countries cannot break out rapidly from an agreement to eliminate nuclear weapons. It is an essential element of the preceding two conditions. Techniques for eliminating delivery vehicles such as bombers and ballistic and cruise missiles have been applied in the original START and the Intermediate-Range Nuclear Forces Treaty and will be applied in New START.

The complication presented by the use of conventional high-explosive warheads with delivery vehicles typically associated with nuclear weapons has been resolved until now by counting all such delivery vehicles as nuclear armed. That will not be appropriate as nuclear weapons are reduced to zero and a relatively large number of delivery vehicles are equipped with conventional warheads. A procedure wherein all nuclear-capable delivery vehicles are inspected to confirm the absence of nuclear weapons will be required. Previous agreements also have banned nuclear weapons storage sites within specified distances of missile sites. Some variation on this arrangement also will be necessary, as well as new cooperative measures designed to facilitate detection of illicit movement of nuclear warheads.

Compliance mechanisms should have been established to enforce nuclear agreements. Commissions designed to discuss and, if possible, resolve questions that arise in the process of implementing arms reduction treaties have been organized as integral parts of U.S.-Soviet/Russian nuclear reduction agreements; a similar commission is part of New START. Those consultative instruments are essential to the management of treaty compliance and probably would be adopted by other countries that have been engaged in bilateral adversarial relationships. As nuclear weapons reductions become a multilateral enterprise, bilateral or regional oversight of implementation will have to be supplemented by international arrangements by entities such as the IAEA or the UN Monitoring, Verification and Inspection Commission, established in December 1999 and terminated in June 2007, to monitor Iraq's compliance with UN Security Council resolutions calling for elimination of all Iraqi weapons of mass destruction.

Creating a strengthened international capacity to enforce treaty compliance will be a daunting challenge, but it is one of the conditions that should have been met before countries get rid of the last of their nuclear weapons. There generally will be ambiguities about specific issues of compliance. For that reason, the basic requirements of a verification system are the capacity to present credible, preferably ironclad, evidence regarding any violations of a treaty. That means that an enforcement organization must have the technical expertise, the international legitimacy, and the freedom of access that will permit it to convincingly tell the public what it has discovered. Armed with that evidence, the UN Security Council, if necessary, can authorize actions under Chapter 7 of the UN Charter. If one of the permanent members of the council is involved, other nuclear-weapon states can take actions to reconstitute nuclear arsenals that they had dismantled. This form of nuclear deterrence is likely to be the enforcement mechanism for many, perhaps most, cases of potential violations.

Progress should have been made in addressing and resolving regional disputes that threaten to trigger military actions. One of the merits of making the elimination of nuclear weapons a truly international enterprise is that it shines a spotlight on "frozen conflicts," disputes that have festered for so long that they have become accepted as inevitable. Such disputes will have to be addressed and at least ameliorated, if not completely resolved, if global progress in the elimination of nuclear weapons is to be anything more than a lovely dream. Russia and the United States are very unlikely to consider reducing their stocks of nuclear weapons to the 500 level, one of the targets often cited, while Pakistan continues to build nuclear warheads as has been alleged recently. Other countries that might be contemplating increasing their inventories should consider the impact on the global holdings of nuclear weapons and the potential for accelerated proliferation of national nuclear weapons programs. If a resolution of nuclear issues in Iran and North Korea cannot be found, the world certainly will tip toward the expectation, almost certainly a correct one, that the NPT no longer will be a serious factor in international relations.

The regional disputes in the Near East, South Asia, and Northeast Asia have profound implications for any effort to save and extend the nonproliferation regime that has been in place since the 1970s. The news on those fronts is not so bad. Recently, India and Pakistan tentatively agreed to renew talks. The vague outlines of a possible settlement in the Korean peninsula and Northeast Asia more broadly have been discernible for many years. Recent democratic revolutions in the Near East have unsettled that region, but they point toward a focus on internal reform rather than external adventures.

Summing Up

The days when the interests of two superpowers dominated the world's strategic nuclear agenda are over. The days when the five NPT nuclear-weapon states had a decisive voice in global nuclear weapons issues are fading fast. As Russian and U.S. nuclear forces are reduced, other countries' nuclear arsenals will loom larger in security calculations. Regional conflicts also generate their own sets of impulses that affect nuclear decisions. The political dynamics of Asia and Europe are different today than during the Cold War. Eliminating the threat posed by nuclear weapons requires that many states actively participate in negotiations to reduce all nuclear weapons programs anywhere in the world.

The level of nuclear forces that Moscow and Washington may try to reach in the next phase could be achieved without the participation of other nuclear-armed states. Russia and the United States still will have by far the greatest numbers of nuclear weapons in their arsenals even after additional reductions. In practice, however, unless there is a widely and, preferably, universally shared commitment to progressively eliminate all nuclear weapons, the momentum necessary to sustain further Russian-U.S. negotiations will be lost.

The recognized nuclear-weapon states and the countries possessing advanced civil or military nuclear programs should join together to begin the process necessary to create conditions for a world free of nuclear weapons. These conditions can be identified and discussed even now, and implementing the first steps will provide the necessary real-world experience to fulfill those conditions and achieve the vision of a nuclear-weapon-free world. A number of near- and mid-term measures are available and could be implemented in short order. Others are more difficult, but beginning to talk about them as a joint enterprise would be very important symbolically.

Endnotes

1. See George P. Shultz, William J. Perry, Henry A. Kissinger, and Sam Nunn, "A World Free of Nuclear Weapons," *The Wall Street Journal,* January 4, 2007, p. A15.

2. Scott D. Sagan, "Shared Responsibilities for Nuclear Disarmament," *Daedalus,* Vol. 138, No. 4 (Fall 2009), pp. 157–168.

3. Sidney Drell and Christopher Stubbs, "Realizing the Potential of Open Skies" (unpublished) (copy on file with the author).

4. American Presidency Project, "Joint Statement on the Transparency and Irreversibility of the Process of Reducing Nuclear Weapons," Moscow, May 10, 1995, www.presidency.ucsb.edu/ws/print.php?pid=51341.

5. For a fuller discussion of this concept, see James Goodby and Geoffrey Forden, "Proceedings of MIT's Workshop on Internationalizing Uranium Enrichment Facilities: Executive Summary," Massachusetts Institute of Technology, October 20–21, 2008, http://web.mit.edu/stgs/pdfs/SummaryUpdatedMarch2009.pdf. For other papers associated with the workshop, see http://web.mit.edu/stgs/WorkshopOct2008.html.

6. Ellen Tauscher, "Addressing the Nuclear Fuel Cycle: Internationalizing Enrichment Services and Solving the Problem of Spent Fuel Storage," Stanford, CA, January 19, 2010, www.state.gov/t/us/136426.htm.

7. Sidney Drell and Raymond Jeanloz, "Nuclear Deterrence After Zero," in *Deterrence: Its Past and Future,* ed. George Shultz, Sidney Drell, and James Goodby (Stanford, CA: Hoover Press, 2011), ch. 3.

8. For a discussion of the former, see Harold Feiveson, ed., *The Nuclear Turning Point* (Washington, DC: Brookings Press, 1999).

Critical Thinking

1. Has the nonproliferation treaty been a success? Why?
2. Has the nonproliferation treaty been a failure? Why?
3. What can be done to resolve regional conflicts that affect global agreements on nuclear weapons?

JAMES GOODBY is a research fellow at the Hoover Institution at Stanford University and a nonresident senior fellow at the Brookings Institution. He was involved in the creation of the International Atomic Energy Agency and the negotiation of the Limited Test Ban Treaty, the Strategic Arms Reduction Treaty, military transparency measures in Europe, and cooperative threat reduction. He is the author or editor of several books on international security. This article draws from his chapter in *SIPRI Yearbook 2010: Armaments, Disarmament and International Security.*

From *Arms Control Today,* May 2011, pp. 23–28. Copyright © 2011 by Arms Control Association. Reprinted by permission.

UNIT 5

International Organization, International Law, and Human Security

Unit Selections

Learning Outcomes

After reading this Unit, you will be able to:

- Explain why the United Nations (UN) is still an important actor in the international system.

- Explain why the International Criminal Court (ICC) has not turned out to be an effective institution.

- Discuss the role of the Prosecutor-General of the ICC.

- Explain the role which women played in the Egyptian revolution.

- Discuss the arguments in favor of the ratification of the Convention on the Elimination of All Forms of Discrimination Against Women (CEDAW) by the United States.

- Discuss the arguments against the ratification of the CEDAW by the United States.

- Explain why genocide continues to be a major problem for the international community.

Student Website

www.mhhe.com/cls

Internet References

Amnesty International
www.amnesty.org

Genocide Watch Home Page
www.genocidewatch.org

Human Security Gateway
www.humansecuritygateway.com

International Court of Justice (ICJ)
www.icj-cij.org

The International Criminal Court
www.icc-cpi.int/Menus/icc

International Criminal Tribunal for the Former Yugoslavia
www.icty.org

International Criminal Tribunal for Rwanda
www.unictr.org

United Nations Home Page
www.un.org

The United Nations (UN) was created as the successor to the failed League of Nations in 1945. The main purpose of the UN was to prevent another world war, through the application of the principles of collective security. Collective security was based on the idea that the organized power of the international community was supposed to be sufficient to deter and punish aggression. The Charter of the United Nations, which envisaged the construction of a just world order, was based on the principle of liberal internationalism. In the first decade of the twenty-first century, the UN continued to support the promotion of important world-order values, such as peace, economic security, the protection of human rights, and the protection of the environment, most of which fall under the rubric of human security. However, it has been over six and a half decades since the United Nations was created, and very few changes have taken place within the organization to reflect the changes that have taken place in the international system. For example, the Security Council is the most important organ of the UN, because it has been entrusted with the responsibility for the maintenance of international peace and security. Most third-world members of the United Nations support the reform of the Security Council, so that it could function as a more democratic and representative organization. Although the UN has increased its membership from the original 51 to 193, the number of permanent members of the Security Council has remained the same five states (the United States, Russia, China, the United Kingdom, and France) since 1945. The leading candidates for additional permanent seats in the Security Council are Germany and Japan. It has also been suggested that other permanent members should be added from the major regions of Africa, Asia, and Latin America. If new permanent members are added to the Security Council, the rationale for the veto would also have to be reviewed. This might add to the overall legitimacy of the organization, and strengthen its ability to function as a systems-affecting actor. Thomas Weiss, who believes that the organization still matters in terms of its norm-setting activites, writes that the UN needs to undergo a major transformation to deal with transboundary threats that pose a major threat to human survival and dignity.

© Comstock/Jupiterimages

The UN itself was embedded in a realist conception of international order, based on the Westphalian system, which rested on the fundamental principle of the primacy of state sovereignty. The primacy of state sovereignty has now been challenged by the doctrine of humanitarian intervention, which states that the sovereignty of the individual should take precedence over the sovereignty of the state when gross and mass violations of human rights take place. The central question is at what point should the "international community" engage in military intervention, as illustrated by NATO's intervention in Libya in 2011. Other questions associated with this issue are who should authorize military intervention, and how can one make sure that such military intervention is not designed to serve the national interest of a single state or group of states? Who determines when a threshold has been crossed by the government of a state and has committed gross and mass violations of human rights against its own people and triggers military intervention? How many people have to be killed before such intervention

occurs? In an effort to deal with this problem, the international community has moved in the direction of holding political leaders who commit war crimes, crimes against humanity, and genocide, accountable for their actions. In 1993, the UN Security Council created an ad hoc tribunal for the former Yugoslavia, and put on trial Slobodan Milosevic, the former President of Serbia, who was charged with committing genocide in the wars of the Yugoslavian succession. Unfortunately, Milosevic died while he was still in custody undergoing his trial. However, the tribunal for the former Yugoslavia, has custody of Radovan Karadzic, the former President of the breakaway statelet of Republika Srpska. Ratko Mladic, the commanding Bosnian Serbian general, who was accused of committing genocide in the Bosnian town of Srebrenica in 1995, was arrested by the Serbian government and turned over to the tribunal at the Hague for trial. The UN Security Council also created a special tribunal to punish war criminals who had been involved in the genocide that took place in Rwanda in 1994, which resulted in the slaughter of over

800,000 people, mostly Tutsis, at the hands of the Hutu majority. Further positive steps in the development of international criminal law took place when the international criminal court was created in 1998. The ICC (International Criminal Court) has focused on war crimes, crimes against humanity, and genocide in the armed conflicts that have taken place in Africa. There has been a fair amount of criticism about the effectiveness of the ad hoc tribunals for the former Yugoslavia and Rwanda, and the UN has put pressure on them to wind up their business. Although, as Kay points out, the two ad hoc courts that were created by the Security Council have been successful in developing international criminal case law with a number of successful convictions. On the other hand, "Who's Afraid of the International Criminal Court?" argues that Prosecutor, Luis Moreno-Ocampo has not been very effective, since the ICC has yet to win a case. For example, the ICC has issued an arrest warrant for President Bashir of the Sudan (the first international arrest warrant ever issued for a sitting president) on counts of committing war crimes, crimes against humanity, and genocide in the Darfur region of the Sudan. But the ICC has no means of enforcing its decisions, and President Bashir continues to remain at large. Kay argues that unless the ICC appoints an effective prosecutor to replace Luis Moreno-Ocampo, the court runs the risk of being marginalized by the international community. Furthermore, China, Russia, and the United States are not members of the ICC and Kay concludes that "The ICC's authority is inherently fragile—a big problem given that its effectiveness depends on the help of governments."

Genocide, the deliberate targeting of a group of people because they are members of a national, religious, racial, or ethnic group, is one of the most evil of crimes against humanity, and yet until 1948, the crime of genocide had no standing under, international law. After World War II, due in a large extent to the efforts of a Polish lawyer and linguist by the name of Raphael Lemkin, the international community adopted the Convention on the Prevention and the Punishment of the Crime of Genocide.

However since then, the international community has not been very effective in dealing with cases of genocide, the most recent examples being the genocides committed in the former Yugoslavia, Rwanda, and Darfur. In trying to get at the reasons for this, David Rieff, in "The Persistence of Genocide," engages in a very critical analysis of a report that was issued by the U.S. Institute for Peace's task force on genocide, in which he argues that the solutions the task force presented are not real solutions to the problem of genocide.

Since the founding of the UN in 1945, the international community has established a network of treaties and declarations on human security that are designed to protect the human rights of individuals and groups against violations by their own governments as well as aggressors. These instruments, which establish norms designed to guide the behavior of states, range from the Universal Declaration of Human Rights in 1948, to the 1966 International Covenants protecting civil and political rights as well as economic, social, and cultural rights. A number of conventions have also been adopted to protect the rights of women, such as the Convention on the Elimination of All Forms of Discrimination Against Women (CEDAW). In "Feminism by Treaty," Christina Hoff Summers, investigates the arguments that have been presented to explain why the United States has not ratified this convention. She points out that CEDAW is supported by the American Bar Association and Amnesty International, who argue that it will not overrule U.S. law, while opponents of the treaty maintain that it would threaten individual freedom in the United States. Finally, as far as women's rights are concerned, a critical question revolves around the position of women in Muslim countries, and the extent to which they have been engaged not only in the struggle to realize their human and political rights, but also in the popular revolutions that swept across the Middle East in 2011. For example, Robin Wright discusses the critical role that women played in the revolution which resulted in the downfall of the Mubarak regime.

A Pipe Dream?
Reforming the United Nations

Thomas G. Weiss

The year 2011 marks the beginning of retirement for many baby-boomers. The Beatles once asked: "Will you still need me/Will you still feed me/When I'm sixty-four?" This year the United Nations turns 66 and many think it should have taken early retirement. Withholding US contributions—one-fifth of the overall UN budget and a quarter of its peacekeeping costs—is a Republican perennial. And the new chair of the House of Foreign Affairs Committee, Ileana Ros-Lehtinen, began with a battle cry on the first day of commitee work in 2011: "Reform first, pay later."

Eyes glaze over at the mention of UN reform. Before becoming a minister in the last Labor government in the United Kingdom, Mark Malloch Brown headed the UN Development Programme and was deputy secretary-general under Kofi Annan. He quipped that the United Nations is the only institution where, over coffee or around water coolers, reform is a more popular topic than sex.

To be fair, more adaptation has taken place in the UN system than critics acknowledge. Indeed, the founders would probably not recognize the system whose foundations were laid in 1945. However, while it would be unfair to describe the United Nations as in a state of stasis, it also would be false to suggest that the UN system is more than woefully slow in reforming itself. Why does so little happen? What, if anything, can be done?

The Central Challenge

Why should anyone in Washington or elsewhere care? The short answer is that dramatic transformation of the world organization, and not mere tinkering, is required if we are to address transboundary problems that threaten human survival and dignity. Former UN Secretary General Kofi Annan frequently speaks of "problems without passports." Many of the most intractable challenges facing humankind are transnational—acid rain does not require a visa to move from one side of a border to another. These problems range from climate change, migration, and pandemics, to terrorism, financial flows, and proliferation of weapons of mass destruction. Effectively addressing any of these threats requires policies and vigorous actions whose scope is not unilateral, bilateral, or even multilateral, but rather global.

Ironically, the policy authority and resources for tackling global problems remain vested individually in the 192 UN member states rather than in the collective body. The fundamental disjuncture between the natures of growing global threats and the current inadequate structures for international problem-solving and decision-making goes a long way toward explaining fitful, tactical, and short-term local responses to threats that require sustained, strategic, and long-term global thinking and action.

The United States resembles most countries in opting in and out of the United Nations when it suits Washington's short term calculations of interests. Selective "à la carte multilateralism," however, is insufficient. More fundamental reforms of multilateral institutions must be made so that they work effectively and in the common interest.

The United Nations' Main Weaknesses

The United Nations too often suffers paralysis. Before prescribing how to fix it, we must understand three underlying causes of its woes.

The first is the enduring concept of the international community as a system of sovereign states—a notion dating back to the 1648 Treaties of Westphalia. "Organized hypocrisy," as former National Security Council director Stephen Krasner reminds us, is either 360 years old or 360 years young. As a result of the grip of sovereignty, the current international system functions in the middle of a growing divide between virtually all of the life-menacing threats facing the planet and the existing structures for international decisions to do something about them. Government officials and so-called realist scholars of international relations agree that narrowly defined vital interests are the only basis on which to make commitments or avoid them.

The calculated vital interests of major powers, particularly of the United States as the most powerful, obviously create obstacles to action by the United Nations, but newer and less powerful countries are as vehemently protective of their sovereign prerogatives as are the major powers. All states are loath to accept elements of overarching central authority and the resulting inroads that would interfere with their capacities to act autonomously. As such, the United Nations remains the last and most formidable bastion of sacrosanct state sovereignty even as technological advances, globalization, and transboundary problems proliferate, leaving national borders with less and less meaning. Thus, the domestic institutions necessary for providing public goods in functioning countries do not exist for the globe—there is no power to tax, to conscript, to regulate, or to quarantine.

> ... the United Nations remains the last and most formidable bastion of ... state sovereignty even as technological advances, globalization, and transboundary problems proliferate.

The second ailment stems from the diplomatic burlesque that passes for diplomacy on First Avenue in Manhattan or in UN gatherings elsewhere. The artificial divide between the aging acting troupes from the industrialized North and from the developing countries of the global South provides the drama. Launched in the 1950s and 1960s as a means to create some diplomatic space for negotiations by countries on the margins of international politics, the once creative voices of the Non-Aligned Movement and the Group of 77 developing countries have become prisoners of their own rhetoric. These rigid and counterproductive groups—and the artificial divisions and toxic atmosphere that they create—end up constituting almost insurmountable barriers to diplomatic initiatives. Serious conversation is virtually impossible; replaced by meaningless posturing in order to score media points back home. Marquee stars include former US ambassador to the United Nations John Bolton and Venezuelan President Hugo Chávez, and while former Canadian politician and senior UN official Stephen Lewis has written that "men and women cannot live by rhetoric alone," this characterization does not apply to UN ambassadors and officials.

The third malady is structural. The Australian logistics genius who moved goods to Malta and the Middle East in World War II and subsequently oversaw a number of key UN humanitarian operations, Sir Robert Jackson, began his 1969 evaluation of the UN development system by writing: "The machine as a whole has become unmanageable ... like some prehistoric monster." The lumbering dinosaur is now more than 40 years older but certainly not better adapted to the 21st century.

The structural problems arise not only from the overlapping jurisdictions of various UN bodies, the lack of coordination among their activities, and the absence of centralized financing for the system as a whole; they are also exacerbated by the nature of the staff and its leadership. The United Nations' various moving parts work at cross-purposes rather than in a more integrated, mutually reinforcing, and collaborative fashion. Agencies relentlessly pursue cut-throat fundraising for their expanding mandates, stake out territory, and pursue mission creep. While the UN organizational chart refers to a "system," implying coherence and cohesion, the organization in reality has more in common with feudalism than with a modern organization. Frequent use is made of the term "family"—like many such units, the United Nations is dysfunctional and divided.

A related disorder stems from the overwhelming weight of the UN bureaucracy, its low productivity, and the often underwhelming leadership within international secretariats. The stereotype of a bloated administration overlooks many talented and dedicated individuals. However, the world body's recruitment and promotion methods are certainly part of what ails it. When success occurs, it usually reflects personalities and serendipity rather than recruitment of the best persons for the right reasons and institutional structures designed to foster collaboration. Staff costs account for the lion's share of the UN budget, and the international civil service is a potential resource whose composition, productivity, and culture could change quickly. There is little hope in the short run, however, while the current lackluster leadership of Secretary General Ban Ki-moon continues this year and during a second five-year term.

In fact, Rube Goldberg would have trouble finding a better design for futile complexity than the current array of agencies, each focusing on a substantive area, often located in a different city from relevant UN partners and with separate budgets, governing boards, organizational cultures, and independent executive heads. Confronting such threats as climate change, pandemics, terrorism, and weapons of mass destruction requires multidisciplinary perspectives, efforts across sectors, firm central direction, and inspired leadership. The United Nations too rarely supplies any of this.

Some Palliatives If Not Solutions

If cures for the United Nations' ailments are politically unrealistic, are palliatives available? Is there surgery that is more than cosmetic and might mean remission? The answer is a tentative "yes" for all three weaknesses.

The first remedy requires building upon spotty yet significant progress in recasting national interests. The prescription for the Westphalian system consists of more energetic recalculations of the shared benefits of providing global public goods and respecting international commitments. Democratic member states, whether large or small, should theoretically find this pill relatively easy to swallow because they have a long-term, rational, and vital interest in, as well as a moral responsibility to promote, multilateral cooperation in the interest of their own citizens as well as those of countries farther afield.

There is a therapeutic as well as actual conceptual benefit from "good international citizenship," an expression coined by Gareth Evans, the former Australian foreign minister and one-time president of the International Crisis Group. Nothing better illustrates the relationship between the provision of basic rights and wider international security than the responsibility to protect (R2P), which redefines state sovereignty as contingent upon a modicum of respect for human rights rather than as absolute. While R2P imposes the primary responsibility for human rights on governmental authorities, it argues that if a state is manifestly unwilling or unable to honor its responsibility, or worse is the perpetrator of mass atrocities, then the responsibility to protect citizens shifts upward to the international community of states.

The history of international law demonstrates that states accept limits on the exercise of their sovereignty by ratifying treaties to constrain their margins of maneuver. The R2P doctrine illustrates how to move in the direction of redefining state sovereignty to include a modicum of responsibility, a values breakthrough after centuries of passively and mindlessly accepting the proposition that state sovereignty was a license to kill. Recalculating the benefits of global public goods and solemn international commitments is the way forward. It is not farfetched to imagine that the international community of states, including the United States, will see a gradual advance of intergovernmental agreements and powers along the lines that Europe as a whole has nurtured.

Chipping away at sovereignty is a long-term project, which explains why this palliative will undoubtedly have a "Pollyannaish" ring to American ears. But the other two weaknesses could be addressed more readily.

Moving beyond the North-South quagmire and toward issues-based and interest-based negotiations is essential. We need to have different country configurations for different problems and to stop thinking about fixed memberships, and especially universal participation, for every item on the international agenda. Fortunately, states have on occasion breached the fortifications around the North-South camps and forged creative partnerships that portend other types of coalitions that could unclog UN deliberations. Less posturing and role-playing is a prerequisite for the future health of the world organization and world politics. While they got a bad name during the Iraq War, serious international politics always involves "coalitions of the willing."

> We need to have different country configurations for different problems and to stop thinking about fixed memberships, and especially universal participation, for every item on the international agenda.

Examples of wide-ranging partnerships across continents and ideologies include those that negotiated the treaty to ban landmines and established the International Criminal Court (ICC). Landmines mobilized a diverse group of countries across the usual North-South divide as well as global civil society under the leadership of the World Federalist Movement and the usually reticent International Committee of the Red Cross. The idea of a permanent criminal court had been discussed since the late 1940s but received a push after the ad hoc tribunals for the former Yugoslavia and for Rwanda; however, the shortcomings (including costs and the burden of evidence) demonstrated the need for a permanent court that could also act as a deterrent for future thugs. The 60-country like-minded group gathered in Rome in 1998 represented a formidable and persuasive coalition that joined forces with the 700 members of a nongovernmental organization (NGO) coalition, and the ICC treaty moved ahead vigorously in spite of strong opposition from several permanent members of the Security Council. Another example, one from the economic arena, is the Global Compact, which brings civil society and transnational corporations into a more productive partnership with the United Nations; it moves beyond a shibboleth from the capitalist North that formerly had been rejected by the global South.

The G20 is a more recent example that, in the midst of the 2008–2009 financial and economic meltdown, shifted from being a photo-op for finance ministers to being serious. Decisions in spring 2009 not only resulted in the infusion of substantial funds into the IMF, but also gave life at the fund in Washington and at the World Bank to long-sought governance reforms that provide more representation for developing countries.

If this larger grouping were to formulate a common position on institutional reform, no international organization, including the United Nations, could easily resist. Complaints about the G20's illegitimacy are hollow if the outcome is a more stable global economic order from which all states benefit. Indeed, the one-state-one-vote interpretation is merely one way to frame the sovereign equality of states. With 70 percent of the world's population, 80 percent of world trade, and 90 percent of the world's gross domestic product, the argument that the G20 lacks legitimacy is farfetched. The G7 lacked legitimacy; the G20 does not.

A unified G20 stance on climate change or pandemics, for example, could jump-start UN negotiations. For years the global South, along with Japan and Germany, have sung in unison that the Security Council and other intergovernmental organizations represent the past and not the present. The G20 could help infuse the United Nations with the political dynamics of contemporary global power.

The third line of treatment would be to pursue the possibility of making the United Nations work with more cohesion, as advocated by "Delivering as One," one of the last sets of proposals published before Kofi Annan's departure as secretary-general. No previous reform has reduced turf struggles and unproductive competition for funds within the so-called UN system. But could one? Yes, but donors would have to stop talking out both sides of their mouths and insist upon the centralization and consolidation that they often preach before UN forums and parliamentary bodies, but upon which they never act.

A related therapy consists of taking steps to reinvigorate the personnel of the United Nations. There is an urgent need to revive the notion of an autonomous international civil service as championed by the second UN Secretary General, Dag Hammarskjöld. Competence and integrity should outweigh nationality and gender considerations as well as cronyism, which have become the principal criteria for recruitment, retention, and promotion. In fact, Hammarskjöld's ideal goes back to what the Carnegie Endowment for International Peace during World War II called the "great experiment" of the League of Nations.

Moving back to the future for the United Nations would involve recruiting people with integrity and talent. There are numerous ways to attract more mobile and younger staff members with greater turnover and fewer permanent contracts while providing better career development for the world organization of the 21st century. Regional or linguistic quotas could diminish the governmental influence resulting from national ones. In addition, as the expenditures for UN staff account for 90 percent of the organization's budget, strengthening performance and productivity should be at the top of any to-do list.

Conclusion

While revitalizing the United Nations may strike readers not only as far-fetched but also as a secondary priority in the midst of massive domestic problems, it should not be. Strobe Talbott, the president of the Brookings Institution and former deputy Secretary of State, recently wrote that mega-threats can only be avoided through multilateralism that extends beyond anything we currently have. That type of change requires US leadership like that in the aftermath of World War II, when the United States boldly led the effort to construct a second generation of international organizations on the ashes of the first, the League of Nations.

Expectations of the Barack Obama presidency were as impossibly high internationally as domestically, including reviving US leadership in multilateralism. His rhetorical contributions have been appreciable—not only his Cairo speech on tolerance, but also numerous others which indicated that the United States was rejoining the planet, prepared to reengage with both friends and foes, and considered multilateralism essential to US foreign policy. Many of his first steps were in the right direction—including repaying US arrears to the United Nations, funding programs for reproductive health, joining the Human Rights Council, moving ahead with nuclear arms reductions, and preparing to initial the Comprehensive Test Ban Treaty. Still, given the "shellacking" in November 2010 and the imperative to improve unemployment and growth, the failure to mention the United Nations in his State of the Union address was unsurprising.

Nonetheless, multilateralism must re-emerge as a priority for this administration. For example, the global financial and economic meltdown should have made clearer what previous crises had not—namely the risks, problems, and costs of a global economy without adequate international institutions, democratic decision-making, or powers to bring order and ensure compliance with collective decisions. Henry Kissinger, whose realist credentials are still intact, wrote that the financial collapse revealed the lack of global institutions to alleviate the shock and reverse the trend. To date, however, trillions of dollars, euros, and pounds have been used to paper-over the cracks. Business-as-usual remains the standard operating procedure.

But perhaps we can learn from history. In a recent book about the origins of American multilateralism, Council on Foreign Relations analyst Stewart Patrick makes a persuasive case that issues concerning US multilateralism are much the same as in the 1940s. Now as then, the United States enjoyed a semblance of global hegemony, but never has that hegemony eliminated the necessity to act multilaterally.

"Le machin" is what Charles de Gaulle famously dubbed the United Nations, thereby dismissing international cooperation as frivolous in comparison with the realpolitik. He conveniently ignored that the formal birth of "the thing" was not the signing of the UN Charter in June 1945, but rather the adoption of the "Declaration by the United Nations" in Washington, DC in January 1942. The 26 countries that defeated fascism also anticipated the formal establishment of the world organization as an essential extension of their war-time commitments. These were not pie-in-the-sky idealists. The UN system was not viewed as a liberal plaything to be tossed aside when the going got tough, but a vital necessity for post-war order and prosperity. Multilateral approaches to punishing horrific deeds and mitigating global threats, then and now, must be not only pragmatic and well-adapted to local realities but also spectacular and utopian.

Could that same far-sighted political commitment rise again under the Obama administration, certainly not in 2011, but after his reelection?

For all its warts, the United Nations still matters for its norms, legitimacy, and idealism . . . [and] urgently needs to reinvent itself . . . to be a vital force in global affairs.

Readers, and certainly classmates, will undoubtedly speculate that this author has been inhaling as well as smoking, but he is guardedly sanguine about affirmatively answering that question as well. Individuals and states can be as strong as the institutions that they create. There are plenty of things wrong, but many can be fixed. For all its warts, the United Nations still matters for its norms, legitimacy, and idealism. The world organization urgently needs to reinvent itself and to be a vital force in global affairs.

Critical Thinking

1. What limits the effectiveness of the United Nations?
2. Why should the UN Charter be revised?
3. Why is it so difficult to reform the UN Security Council?

THOMAS G. WEISS is Presidential Professor of Political Science and Director of the Ralph Bunche Institute for International Studies at the Graduate Center of the City University of New York.

From *Harvard International Review*, Spring 2011, pp. 48–53. Copyright © 2011 by the President of Harvard College. Reprinted by permission via Sheridan Reprints.

Who's Afraid of the International Criminal Court?

Finding the Prosecutor Who Can Set It Straight

DAVID KAYE

Last February, soon after Libyan leader Muammar al-Qaddafi unleashed his forces against civilian protesters, the United Nations Security Council unanimously voted to refer the situation in Libya to the International Criminal Court. Days later, the ICC's chief prosecutor, Luis Moreno-Ocampo, announced the launch of an investigation of members of the Qaddafi regime, promising, "There will be no impunity in Libya."

With the UN Security Council injecting the court into one of the year's biggest stories, the ICC may seem to have become an indispensable international player. It already is looking into some of the gravest atrocities committed in recent decades—in the Democratic Republic of the Congo, Sudan, and Uganda, among others—and its investigation into the 2007 election-related violence in Kenya is shaking up that country's elite. But a closer look suggests that the ICC's sleek office building on the outskirts of The Hague houses an institution that is still struggling to find its footing almost a decade after its creation.

The court has failed to complete even one trial, frustrating victims as well as the dozens of governments that have contributed close to $1 billion to its budget since 2003. The ICC's first trial was nearly dismissed twice. Its highest-profile suspects—Sudanese President Omar al-Bashir and Joseph Kony, the leader of the Lord's Resistance Army (LRA), the rebel group that has terrorized northern Uganda and neighboring areas—have thumbed their noses at the court and are evading arrest. And with all six of the ICC's investigations involving abuses in Africa, its reputation as a truly international tribunal is in question.

A rare opportunity to recapture the court's early promise lies ahead: at the end of the year, the 114 states that have ratified the Rome Statute, the ICC's founding charter, will elect a successor to Moreno-Ocampo, who is expected to step down as head of the Office of the Prosecutor (OTP) in mid-2012. As the ICC's driving force and its face to the world, the chief prosecutor has a critical job: choosing which situations to investigate, which senior officials to indict, and which charges to bring—all sensitive decisions with major political implications. In 2003, before Moreno-Ocampo was elected, then UN Secretary-General Kofi Annan rightly said that "the decisions and public statements of the prosecutor will do more than anything else to establish the reputation of the court." By this standard, Moreno-Ocampo's tenure has not been a success. Thanks partly to a management and decision-making style that has alienated subordinates and court officials alike, he has been dealt repeated judicial setbacks, which have overshadowed his office's modest gains.

The ICC needs a new leader who has not only the necessary prosecutorial, diplomatic, and managerial skills but also a keen sense of the importance of this moment in the development of the still fledgling institution. To achieve the ICC's promise as a global court, the parties to the Rome Statute must select a prosecutor who can meet the court's most serious challenges: concluding trials; convincing governments to arrest fugitives; conducting credible investigations in difficult places, such as Libya and Sudan; and expanding the ICC's reach beyond Africa. This may be a lot to ask for, but the future of the ICC depends on it.

Laying Down the Law

The ICC is the culmination of a decades-old movement to promote international criminal law. The movement started soon after World War II, with the creation of the international military tribunals at Nuremberg and Tokyo, and gained steam again in the early 1990s, when in the midst of the war in Bosnia, the UN Security Council set up the International Criminal Tribunal for the Former Yugoslavia (ICTY) and then, in the wake of the genocide in Rwanda, the International Criminal Tribunal for Rwanda (ICTR). The Security Council gave both tribunals the mandate to prosecute war crimes, crimes against humanity, and genocide, with the expectation that they would target the most senior political and military leaders. The early days were hard going. It took a year to find a chief prosecutor for the ICTY, and at first even supportive governments contributed only small amounts to the courts' budgets. Other states were obstructionist. The governments of Croatia and Serbia, alleging bias, refused to turn over war crimes suspects to the ICTY or share information with it—they relented only when cooperation became a precondition for membership in the European Union. NATO originally refused to carry out the ICTY's calls to arrest indictees in Bosnia for fear of endangering its forces in the country. Serbian President Slobodan Milosevic managed to drag out his trial for years, making the ICTY seem powerless in the face of his defiance. The work proceeded slowly: the ICTY handed down its first sentence in 1996; the ICTR, in 1998.

By now, however, the ICTY and the ICTR have held dozens of trials, including against senior political leaders, such as Milosevic and Radovan Karadzic, the president of Republika Srpska, and top military officials, such as Théoneste Bagosora of Rwanda. The ICTY has sentenced 64 defendants and acquitted 12, and the trials of another three dozen are on its docket; it has also transferred defendants and evidence to local courts in Bosnia. The ICTR has sentenced 46 defendants and acquitted eight, and the trials of two dozen more are on its docket. The two tribunals have significantly developed international criminal jurisprudence, and they have deeply influenced the training, if not the behavior, of military officers worldwide. They have contributed, although perhaps only modestly, to stability in several countries. The ICTY has not alleviated deep-seated animosities in Bosnia, but it can claim some credit for bringing a measure of reconciliation to Bosnia, Croatia, and Serbia. The ICTR has produced an authoritative historical account of the Rwandan genocide. The ICTY has triggered the development of a specialized war crimes chamber in the Bosnian courts, and the ICTR has inspired the widespread use in Rwanda of the traditional *gacaca* court system to deal with hundreds of thousands of lower-level perpetrators.

Thanks in part to these courts' relative success, the international criminal law movement continued to gain traction. By the early years of this century, the Special Court for Sierra Leone had been established to prosecute the war crimes and crimes against humanity committed in Sierra Leone since late 1996 (that court's highest-profile trial, against former Liberian President Charles Taylor, is winding down toward a judgment). After protracted negotiations, a mixed Cambodian-international tribunal was set up to try the surviving Khmer Rouge leadership. Meanwhile, under the heavy influence of international nongovernmental organizations and local civil-society movements, Western governments led an effort to draft a charter for a permanent international criminal court. In 1998, a UN-sponsored diplomatic conference in Rome adopted the Rome Statute, creating the first permanent international criminal institution. The ICC was tasked with investigating and prosecuting war crimes, crimes against humanity, and acts of genocide committed on the territories of its member states or by their nationals, or whenever asked by the UN Security Council. It would not look back to past injustices; it would have the power to go after crimes committed at or after its creation. And it would act only when national courts with jurisdiction over these crimes were "unable" or "unwilling" to do so themselves—meaning when governments lacked the necessary substantive law or legal infrastructure or when they were shielding culprits from responsibility.

The ICC became a reality after the 60th signatory to the Rome Statute ratified the treaty, in July 2002—just four years after the Rome conference. This was lightning speed by the standards of international treaty-making and a measure of the court's vast following. Still, it was only natural that the ICC, which sits at the intersection of war and peace, politics and law, would also attract enemies. China, Russia, and the United States have chosen not to join it, for instance, for fear that it might one day take aim at their own nationals. Washington has slowly been softening its position, but it remains wary. Earlier this year, in an unprecedented show of support for the court, it voted for the Security Council's referral of the Libya situation. (In 2005, it had abstained from voting on the Sudan referral regarding atrocities committed in Darfur.) But partly at the insistence of the U.S. government, the referral stipulated that the nationals of states that have not ratified the Rome Statute do not fall within the jurisdiction of the ICC. The idea was to protect them from prosecution by the ICC if they ever were to be suspected of committing crimes in the course of a foreign military intervention against Qaddafi.

In other words, unlike the ICTY and the ICTR, the ICC has very broad jurisdiction, both in time and space, but without enjoying the UN Security Council's unequivocal backing. This makes its authority seem inherently fragile—a big problem given that its effectiveness depends on the cooperation of governments. Prosecuting international crimes in countries where conflict is ongoing, or against sitting heads of state, is delicate work: it challenges not only accepted notions of state sovereignty but also the traditional territorial boundaries of criminal investigations. At the same time, the ICC relies on state authorities to arrest suspects and transfer witnesses, evidence, and intelligence, and most governments have done little to help. Some have stepped up in relatively simple situations: for instance, Belgium and France each arrested one Congolese suspect on their territory and transferred the two men to the ICC in The Hague. But Bashir, for one, has managed to travel around Africa and the Arab world, including to states that are parties to the Rome Statute, such as Chad and Kenya. The Security Council, the very body that referred the Sudan situation to the ICC, has not stood firmly behind the arrest warrant against Bashir; it could have increased the cost of doing business with Bashir by imposing sanctions on fugitive Sudanese officials and governments that flout the arrest warrant. The Security Council may deserve credit for making the referral, but it appears uninterested in giving the court the kind of support it needs. And it is unclear whether when the time comes to back up the recent referral on Libya, the Security Council will once more undermine the court even as it seems to be empowering it.

The ICC's authority is inherently fragile—a big problem given that its effectiveness depends on the help of governments.

Courting Trouble

Given that the ICC operates in a complicated, sometimes hostile political environment, it was bound to face serious problems. Yet many of its wounds have been self-inflicted. Management and personality clashes, for instance, have hindered its development. The court's leadership was in place by early 2003, with a triumvirate formed by the prosecutor, the court's president (the court's ceremonial head, who is responsible for external relations), and the registrar (the lead administrative officer). As impressive as the three principals were, they were mismatched. Moreno-Ocampo, interpreting the independence of the OTP broadly, challenged the registrar not to raid his bailiwick and continually picked battles with the registrar's staff on everything from human resources to witness protection. He also resisted coordination with the president. These petty battles over turf and resources undermined

the sense that the court's leaders were sharing a historic mission. Meanwhile, many of the ICC's prosecutors and investigators chafed under what they perceived to be Moreno-Ocampo's micromanaging and erratic decision-making. Some of the OTP's most experienced staffers quit; those who remain say that low morale continues to plague the court.

Worse, the OTP has not made enough concrete progress. It has yet to conclude a single trial. Its first case, which indicted the Congolese militia leader Thomas Lubanga Dyilo for recruiting and using children as soldiers, has faltered repeatedly. Some observers have chided Moreno-Ocampo for failing to charge Lubanga with any crimes of sexual violence, a scourge in the Ituri region while he was in charge—this was a lost opportunity, the critics argued, considering the extent of gender-based atrocities in Congo and elsewhere in Africa. During opening statements in the case, Moreno-Ocampo was seen repeatedly using his Blackberry, and he left the hearings, reportedly to attend the World Economic Forum in Davos, before the defense concluded its presentation. Twice, a three-judge panel ordered that Lubanga be released (he has been in custody since March 2006) because of serious concerns that the prosecution had failed to share potentially exculpatory information with the defense. And although both times an appellate chamber ordered that Lubanga stay in detention, it also harshly criticized the OTP's work. Throughout, the prosecution repeatedly failed to implement court orders, infuriating the judges. Even if Moreno-Ocampo's team occasionally got the law right, its brash behavior undermined the judges' confidence in its good faith and competence.

Six years after the UN Security Council referred the situation in Sudan to the ICC, not one suspect is in custody. In 2007, the court issued a warrant for the arrest of Ahmad Harun, a senior official in Bashir's government, and Ali Kushayb, a leader of the Janjaweed militias, for committing war crimes and crimes against humanity in Darfur. But instead of carefully plotting the two men's arrests, targeting other parties at the same level of responsibility, and carefully establishing the Sudanese government's broader policy of repression and violence, in 2008, Moreno-Ocampo requested that the judges issue a warrant for Bashir's arrest, charging him, too, with war crimes and crimes against humanity—and also with genocide. The move was supposed to be a bold demonstration of the court's purpose. But deciding what to do about the genocide charge—which had never been brought against a sitting head of state—held up the judges' decision for eight months. Finally, in 2009, came a warrant for war crimes and crimes against humanity; it took another year—and an appeal—for the warrant for genocide to be issued. And the damage was already done. Internal dissent at the court had been exposed, public confidence in the genocide charge was undermined, and Darfur activists disagreed bitterly over strategy. Alleging genocide would have been ambitious in even the best investigative circumstances: it is always difficult to prove the crime's requirement that the perpetrators specifically intended to destroy, in whole or in part, a national, ethnic, racial, or religious group. But in the case of the atrocities in Darfur, there were special difficulties. As one former senior ICC prosecutor put it, "It is difficult to cry government-led genocide in one breath and then explain in the next why two million Darfuris have sought refuge around the principal army garrisons of their province." Many atrocities have clearly been committed against civilians in Darfur; but whether Bashir intended to, and is responsible for trying to, destroy the region's ethnic communities remains a subject of intense debate. And so Moreno-Ocampo's big gesture backfired. The Sudanese government, which was already refusing to cooperate with the ICC, went into lockdown. It kicked most humanitarian workers out of Darfur and cracked down on the domestic opposition. The International Crisis Group, a strong supporter of the ICC, criticized Moreno-Ocampo's approach, accusing him of "risking politicizing his office" and taking a needlessly "confrontational" approach with Bashir. Today, progress on the Darfur file seems to have completely stalled.

A related problem has been the ICC's lack of legitimacy among some African leaders. Although 31 African countries have ratified the Rome Statute, many of them, as well as the African Union, have opposed the ICC's investigations in Sudan and Kenya. This may have something to do with self-serving politics—mutual back-scratching among the continent's leaders. But with all its formal investigations targeting African states—the Central African Republic, Congo, Kenya, Libya, Sudan, and Uganda—the court has also invited the charge that it is an agent for postcolonial Western interests.

This is unfortunate. For one thing, Africa is the setting for innumerable atrocities, and international attention to them should be welcomed, not shunned. For another, the ICC has been conducting preliminary examinations (inquiries that may or may not turn into formal investigations) outside Africa, including in Afghanistan, Colombia, Georgia, Honduras, and the Palestinian territories. Unfortunately, Moreno-Ocampo has failed to see these as easy opportunities to defang the opponents who call the OTP biased. He could have taken a more aggressive line regarding Colombia, for example, and launched a full investigation into war crimes and crimes against humanity committed by paramilitary officials with links to official government agencies. The facts called for it, and the circumstances allowed it: with the Colombian courts seeming unlikely to pursue any senior-level cases, the ICC had the jurisdiction to step in.

By commission and omission alike, the OTP has repeatedly made itself a target for charges of politicization. This has come as a surprise to those who applauded Moreno-Ocampo's decision early on to create within the OTC a special office to encourage cooperation from other international actors and ensure the ICC's complementarity with national courts. Moreno-Ocampo has undoubtedly faced significant pressure to go after senior leaders, but having chosen to pursue the big fish and failed to catch many, now he does not have much to show for his efforts. Particularly during its nascent phase, the ICC needed a more effective operator, institution builder, and diplomat.

> **By commission and omission alike, the prosecution's office has repeatedly made itself a target for charges of politicization.**

Trials and Tribulations

There are reasons to hope that the ICC can still become a viable agent against impunity, chief among them the desire of victims worldwide to see the court succeed. The upcoming election of the next prosecutor is an occasion to do right by them.

African leaders are understandably pushing for an African prosecutor. The continent has largely embraced the Rome Statute, and the ICC has focused on some of Africa's most conflict-riven states. Having an African lead the prosecution over the next decade could help inspire domestic and regional efforts at developing accountability and the rule of law by demonstrating that international justice is not a norm imposed by the West but one shared by top African jurists. An African prosecutor might also have a better sense of how to reach out to African communities that need to be convinced of the ICC's value. Yet a search for Moreno-Ocampo's replacement that starts and ends with a focus on Africa would only bolster the ICC's unwanted reputation as a single-minded, regionally focused court. Two well-regarded Gambian lawyers—Fatou Bensouda, the ICC's deputy prosecutor, and Hassan Jallow, chief prosecutor of the ICTR—are currently the front-runners. (The chief prosecutor of the ICTY, the Belgian Serge Brammertz, is thought to be a long shot, not least because much of the work will require leading prosecutions involving Congo, a former Belgian colony.) But as the parties to the Rome Statute begin to look for candidates—they have already established a search committee—they should dispel the impression that anyone already has a lock on the position. And they should consider candidates without any geographic constraints; the ICC deserves the prosecutor best able to meet its core challenges.

At the bureaucratic level, the next chief prosecutor will need to be a manager who can lead on multiple fronts. First among those must be an effort to gain back the confidence of the ICC's investigators, analysts, and other prosecutors. Recruiting and retaining the most highly qualified staffers means giving them substantial authority and providing them with guidance without micromanaging them. Another important task will be to rebuild the OTP's reputation with the court's judges. The next prosecutor will also have to bring several trials to conclusion, as well as conduct high-profile investigations in difficult environments, such as Libya.

In all these tasks, the next prosecutor will need to display political and diplomatic savvy. One pressing and thorny issue will be getting states to enforce arrest warrants, especially those against Bashir and the other Sudanese indictees. This will not be easy. Even key ICC supporters in Africa, such as Ghana, Senegal, and South Africa, have been unable to beat back the anti-ICC fever within the African Union. To many African Union members, arresting Bashir may seem less desirable than ever now that he appears to be accepting the fact of southern Sudan's secession, which was decided by referendum early this year. Some Western officials are reportedly in favor of getting the Security Council to defer enforcing the arrest warrant against him; the U.S. special envoy to Sudan, J. Scott Gration, has publicly stated his concern that the warrant has complicated peacemaking efforts. On the other hand, ignoring this warrant would likely undermine the credibility of the court's warrants generally.

In such a fraught political environment, the next prosecutor will not make any headway using confrontational or triumphalist rhetoric. The OTP would do better to rethink its top-down approach in Sudan and reopen investigations concerning other senior-level figures with potential liability for the atrocities committed in Darfur. The suspects are already known: a secret annex to the 2005 report of the UN's International Commission of Inquiry on Darfur is said to list over four dozen names. Focusing on suspected perpetrators at levels of seniority lower than Bashir's would allow ICC prosecutors to establish that the Sudanese government implemented a widespread policy to commit atrocities in Darfur. The ICC seems likely to prosecute two Darfur rebel leaders for attacking UN peacekeepers; bringing a viable case against Sudanese government figures in addition to those two would significantly bolster the ICC's credibility. Over the long term, holding one or several trials that establish Khartoum's involvement in the atrocities in Darfur could put pressure on governments that currently give Bashir assistance. It could also add to the pressure on Bashir himself, particularly if someone in his circle is found guilty.

The LRA leader Kony will continue to pose both a diplomatic and a military challenge. Since the warrants for the arrest of Kony and four of his lieutenants were issued in 2005, the Ugandan government has pushed the rebels out of northern Uganda, bringing a modicum of safety to the region's residents. But now the LRA is brutalizing civilians in bordering areas of the Central African Republic and Congo. Short of mounting a military operation aimed at arresting Kony and his commanders, which no government appears prepared to do, there may be no solution to this problem—at least none within the powers of the ICC prosecutor. When it comes to the LRA file, the main challenge for the next prosecutor will be to continue to press for arrests without appearing powerless in the face of ongoing atrocities.

So far, the threat of ICC prosecutions has helped generate some useful discussion about justice at the national level. In places as diverse as Colombia and Kenya, for instance, the court's activities have helped generate public calls—and, in Kenya, legislation—for domestic trials for war crimes and crimes against humanity. The next ICC prosecutor should take the task a step further, doing more than simply advocating for national efforts and instead playing a substantial role in shaping them. Moreno-Ocampo and court officials have said all the right things about the importance of national prosecutions, and there has been some interaction between prosecutors and investigators at the ICC and their national counterparts. But this activity has been treated as though it is tangential to the court's success. In fact, it is essential. The prosecution of senior officials in The Hague should support the prosecution of lower-level officials in national courts. Under the new prosecutor, the ICC should help build the capacity of national legal systems to try international crimes by sharing more strategy, tactics, and information, much as the ICTY has done to assist prosecutors throughout the Balkans.

Witness for the Prosecution

The new prosecutor will need to defend the ICC against charges that it brings too little accountability while standing in the way of peace and stability. Among other things, this will mean deploying the post's powers carefully, with a full awareness of their limits. At times, this could require considerable restraint: for instance, the OTP might be better off not seeking any warrants in the Libya case if the Security Council is unlikely to help with enforcement. The ICC prosecutor must be a forceful spokesperson for international criminal justice, of course, but that job also requires understanding that most governments see justice as only one priority among many. Not all international prosecutors have successfully handled this aspect of the role. Carla Del Ponte, the third chief prosecutor of the ICTY and the ICTR, regularly tussled with officials at the tribunals, government officials in the Balkans, and members of the UN Security Council—so much so that in 2003 the Security Council took back the ICTR half of her job. Louise Arbour, who held the dual position before Del Ponte, was just as firm in insisting that states cooperate with the courts, but she also managed both to get her hands dirty with investigations and prosecutions and to maintain the respect of the state leaders whose support she needed. Moreno-Ocampo is more Del Ponte than Arbour, and the ICC needs an Arbour.

Arbour herself once wrote that the international community's repeated failure to prevent atrocities "leaves criminal justice to meet the sometimes unrealistic expectations about the contribution that it can make to social peace and harmony, to the eradication of hatred, and to the reconciliation of previously warring factions." Substitute "the ICC prosecutor" for "criminal justice" in that sentence, and the difficulty of the job becomes clear. To be effective, the ICC's next chief prosecutor must share Arbour's healthy understanding of both the court's promise and its limitations.

Critical Thinking

1. Why doesn't the United States join the International Criminal Court (ICC)?
2. Why isn't the International Criminal Court more effective?
3. Would a different prosecutor-general make a difference in enhancing the effectiveness of the ICC? Why?

DAVID KAYE is Executive Director of the International Human Rights Law Program at the University of California, Los Angeles, School of Law.

The Pink Hijab

The Arab revolts of 2011 have transformed the image of the Islamic world. One young Egyptian woman's struggle reflects the scope of change—and shows how long it has been in coming.

ROBIN WRIGHT

The greatest wave of empowerment in the early 21st century has produced a new political chic. It has been shaped by conditions conspicuously ripe for unrest. A youth bulge altered the generational balance of power. Rising literacy spurred aspirations beyond daily survival, especially among women. And new technology tools—cheap cell phones with video capabilities, Internet access, social media, and some 500 independent satellite channels launched since 1996—gave ordinary Arabs a larger sense of the world and then allowed them to connect at a crucial juncture.

The new chic has been fashioned by a yearning for change that is at once democratic and indigenous. The restless young chafe at old ways and old leaders, but many who turned out in Cairo's Tahrir ("Liberation") Square this year do not aspire merely to imitate the West. They reject militant jihad and the rigid formulas of the Salafis, yet they fervently embrace their faith as a defining force in their future. They want new systems that are both fully representative and true to their religious values. Their quest, which began quietly long before the so-called Arab Spring, also helps illuminate what lies ahead.

The 21st-century believers are establishing their voice in hip-hop lyrics and bold comedy, subversive poetry and satirical plays. The cultural uprising is as critical as the political upheaval. The young in particular have been encouraged by a new generation of popular televangelists who preach a softer and more flexible form of Islam. The militant Muslim Brotherhood and its allies may play a powerful role in the new Egypt and elsewhere in the Arab world, but they will face strong countercurrents among young Muslims who have their own ideas. They will encounter people like Dalia Ziada.

Dalia Ziada was 29 when she joined the revolt against President Hosni Mubarak in Egypt. She had a particularly long journey to Liberation Square. It started when she was a little girl.

"I am a survivor of female genital mutilation," Ziada told me as she stirred a steamy espresso in a Cairo café. "In 1990, when I was eight years old, my mother told me to put on my best party dress. It was supposed to be some kind of surprise, a celebration. I found myself instead in a doctor's office. I shouted and refused, but the doctor gave me a shot. I woke up in terrible physical pain."

Ziada's first protest was within her family. As a teenager, she tried to prevent the genital mutilation of her sister and cousins. No female in her family had ever fought back. "And mostly," she conceded, looking up from her coffee, "I failed."

In Egypt, the practice of female genital mutilation spans millennia, dating back to the pharaohs. In 2005, a United Nations report found that 97 percent of Egyptian females between the ages of 15 and 49 had undergone one of four types of genital mutilation—clitoridectomy, excision, infibulations, or the miscellaneous pricking, piercing, incising, scraping, or cauterizing of the genital area. The practice is cultural rather than religious in origin, more African than Middle Eastern. Many Christian girls in Egypt have also been genitally mutilated.

In 2006, when she was 24, Ziada had a long debate with an uncle about her seven-year-old cousin Shaimaa, the family's youngest female child.

"We talked most of the night. He was shocked at the blunt discussion," she recalled. "I told him that he had no right to circumcise her. I said I'd cut off Shaimaa's finger if he went through with it. He looked at me with surprise and said that would ruin her life—and I said, 'Now you get it.' I thought I'd lost. But he called me the next day and said I'd convinced him. That's when I realized I could do things, because I had been able to save someone," she said. "I decided to see what else I could do."

Ziada, who comes from a traditional family, does not look the part of sex educator. She is doe eyed and wears no makeup, so her pale, chubby cheeks and colorless lips make her appear younger than she is. In public, she wears hijab coverings in bright florals, rich patterns, or fake designer prints; she changes her scarf daily. She is an observant Muslim, so not a wisp of hair shows. Judging from her eyebrows, her hair must be dark brown.

"Hijab is part of my life," she told me. "I would feel naked without it." She often jokes, with a robust laugh at herself, that her scarves are the most interesting part of her wardrobe. Yet her religious commitment defines her life.

Her goal, she wrote when she began her new blog in 2006, "is derived from the ultimate goal that any Muslim seeks; which is to please Almighty Allah."

Ziada soon became a leading activist among the pink hijab generation, young women committed to their faith, firm in their femininity, and resolute about their rights. With three college classmates, she launched a campaign to educate women about genital mutilation and domestic violence. Then she moved on to human rights. And she ended up at Liberation Square.

"When I grew up," she explained on her blog, "my personal interest in having more equal rights as a woman expanded to my country."

Her first big project was translating a comic book called *The Montgomery Story,* which recounts Martin Luther King Jr.'s civil disobedience campaign against racial segregation in 1955. King famously mobilized a bus boycott in Montgomery, Alabama, after Rosa Parks was arrested for refusing to give up her seat to a white man. Dozens of the boycott's leaders were arrested; a bomb was thrown into King's home, narrowly missing his wife and child. Yet the movement remained nonviolent. The Supreme Court ultimately ruled that bus segregation was illegal.

"When I read this story, I learned that someone must take the risk for others to follow," Ziada told me. "I wanted to be the Martin Luther King of Egypt!"

The Montgomery Story, originally an educational tool to promote civil rights among the young or mildly literate, ends with tips on nonviolent activism. One of several groups Ziada worked with distributed copies of her Arabic version across the Middle East.

"Finding a way to explain civil disobedience was very exciting. It was something new for ordinary people," she said. "Then I started looking for other ways to use nonviolence and civil disobedience for my own campaigns."

Her next major project was organizing the first human rights film festival in the Arab world. The Mubarak regime tried to block her. "The government reacted as if we were planning a terrorist attack," she said.

The authorities imposed a stiff fee for showing each film, which Ziada and her backers could not afford. So she cut back from dozens of films to seven. Then government censors denied approval of the films, even though she had avoided movies about Egypt. Undeterred, Ziada went to the censorship board's offices, waited by the elevator for its director, then rode up with him to plead her case.

"I think he was shocked that I would dare stop and question him," she told me with a chuckle. "We talked all the way up the elevator. In the end, he was laughing and he gave me approval. Security didn't believe it."

The harassment was not over, however. The authorities shut down the theater that had agreed to show the films. Ziada then hastily arranged for various nongovernmental organizations to host a different film and panel discussion every night for a week. "We stopped letting them always tell us no. We started making decisions for ourselves," she said.

In 2009, facing the same obstacles, Ziada managed to sneak in 20 movies for the second Cairo human rights film festival. To get around official obstacles, she provided the wrong schedule and imaginary venues. In a country with one of the region's most autocratic regimes, Ziada showed films such as *Orange Revolution,* about the 2004 uprising in Ukraine, and, most daringly, four Egyptian films. One dramatized a well-known incident in which police used a broomstick to sodomize a young man who had intervened when his cousin refused to pay the police a bribe. Another was a Romeo-and-Juliet tale about a young Christian boy who falls in love with a Muslim girl he can never marry. The most potent movie, however, was also the shortest. *Please Spare Our Flowers* is a one-minute film about female genital mutilation that shows ragged pinking shears slowly snipping off the tops of dozens of beautiful flowers, one by one by one, just as they're blooming—each producing a piercing scream from an unseen girl child or baby.

As the pink hijab generation gradually chisels away at centuries of restrictions, the young women are also redefining what it means to wear hijab—as a declaration of activist intent rather than a symbol of being sequestered. The change is visible in virtually every Muslim country. The young are shedding black and gray garb for clothing more colorful and even shape-revealing, albeit still modest. Pink is the most popular hue. Women in their teens, twenties, and thirties also flavor their faith with shades of pastel blue, bright yellow, and rustic orange, occasionally trimmed with sparkles, tassels, or even feathers. Hijab stores from Gaza to Jakarta now carry everything from long denim dresses with rhinestone designs to frilly frocks with matching scarves. *Hijab Fashion,* an Egyptian monthly magazine, was launched in 2004 for the pink hijab generation. It has nothing to do with religiosity. But it is also not just about fashion or vanity.

The Veiled—or al-Motahajiba—is one of Cairo's new fashion centers combining Islamic feminism and cool. When I visited the shop in 2009, hijab ware was as elegantly displayed on the glass shelves as designer scarves at Nieman Marcus. Shaimaa Hassan, a 20-year-old salesclerk, told me that her favorite color was turquoise. She handed me a booklet of fashionable new hijab styles. The latest fad was the Spanish wrap, so called because the scarf is tied with a large knot at the back, in an allusion to the hairstyles worn by flamenco dancers. As she demonstrated how to wrap it, Hassan explained that she had just finished vocational school in commerce and intended to open her own business someday.

Sabaya, which means "young girls" in Arabic, is a salon, boutique, and café in Cairo's trendy Heliopolis district. It was launched in 2008 by Hanan Turk, a famous Egyptian ballerina who was recruited for the cinema in 1991. The glamorous young actress appeared in more than 20 major films, both comedies and dramas, in which she often wore racy dresses or exposed ample décolletage. In 2005 she starred in the controversial film *Dunia* ("World"), about a young dancer who explores her sexual identity and resists pressures to hide her femininity. The director struggled to get it past Egypt's censorship board.

Shortly after finishing the film, however, Turk opted to don hijab. The reaction in Egypt's arts world was electric. "She must have gone crazy," said Yusef Chahine, the director who gave Turk her early break in cinema.

Turk was unfazed. "I had intended to take this step a long time ago," she declared, "but I never had the guts before." A year later, she announced plans to launch a religious magazine with a noted singer. They called it *Hajj,* after the Muslim pilgrimage to Mecca. Two years later, she opened Sabaya for fashionable hijabis. A sign in neon lights outside called it a place of "veiled beauty."

Turk remained a fashion plate, devising ways to dramatically drape her curves in stunning colors—and replicate them for other women. In many pictures, she looked even more exotic than she did before hijab. The wares in her store reflected her style.

"There's a tendency among people who don't know Islam to think of the veil as a sign of conservatism, ignorance, or backwardness," Nagwa Abbas, the store manager, told me over lattes at Sabaya's café. "It's just identification. Underneath, we wear what everyone else wears. We're all for women having every opportunity. Our aspirations don't change just because our clothing is different."

For many young women, hijab is now about liberation, not confinement. It's about new possibilities, not the past. It provides a kind of social armor that enables Muslim women to chart their own course, personally or professionally. For Ziada, hijab provides protective cover and legitimacy for campaigns she considers to be the essence of her faith—human rights and justice.

For many young women, hijab is now about liberation, not confinement.

"Families feel much more comfortable allowing their girls to be active, to get higher education, or jobs, or even to go out alone at night when they are wearing hijab," she told me. "It's a deal between a Muslim girl and society. I agree that I will wear hijab in order to have more space and freedom in return."

In its many forms, hijab is no longer assumed to signal acquiescence. It has instead become an equalizer. It is an instrument that makes a female untouchable as she makes her own decisions in the macho Arab world. It is a stamp of authenticity as well as a symbolic demand for change. And it is a weapon to help a woman resist extremism's pull into the past. Militants cannot criticize or target her for being corrupted by Western influence.

"The veil is the mask of Egyptian women in a power struggle against the dictatorship of men," explained Nabil Abdel Fattah, author of *The Politics of Religion* (2003), when I stopped to see him at Cairo's al-Ahram Center for Political and Strategic Studies. "The veil gives women more power in a man's world."

And Muslim women are increasingly assuming those powers as basic rights.

Education has been a key to the transformation. A 2008 Gallup poll not only found that literacy is the rule rather than the exception among Muslim women, but that they are a growing proportion of university students even in countries with strong religious sentiment. In Iran, 52 percent of women told Gallup they had at least some postsecondary education, while in Egypt, Saudi Arabia, and Lebanon about one-third did. Surprisingly, Gallup also reported that more women had postsecondary educations in Pakistan (13 percent) and Morocco (eight percent) than in Brazil (four percent).

"Now, it's hardly something worth noting that in Egypt, universities are filled with women, in some cases more than men, and they are excelling," one highly educated Egyptian woman told the Gallup researchers. "The valedictorians of Cairo's elite medical school are famously known to almost always be female."

Attitudes about female education have shifted markedly across the Muslim world, according to a 2009 Pew Global Attitudes survey, apart from obvious exceptions such as Afghanistan. In Egypt, 71 percent of those surveyed said it is as important to educate girls as it is boys (and to educate both sexes equally). In Lebanon, 96 percent agreed. One result of this broad change in attitudes is that young women entering universities across the Islamic world are no longer necessarily English-speakers or the children of Westernized families. Young women in their pastel hijabs are highly visible on every Egyptian campus, including the prestigious American University of Cairo.

Like many of the pink hijabis, Ziada has little taste for Islamist politics. She rejects the Muslim Brotherhood, the Islamic movement founded in Egypt in 1928 that now has more than 80 offshoots around the world. She considers the group hypocritical for promising to improve life for all Egyptians while also issuing a draft manifesto that said women and Christians should not be allowed to seek the presidency.

"So the only person who can run is a Muslim man," she told me angrily. "What the hell is this? They talk about democracy all the time, but look at the party's own structure. They don't have elections for leaders. There are no women, except in a women-only branch. And when people make petitions to challenge them on something, they don't get answers.

"You know, ordinary people are not stupid," she said. "We discovered that they're working for their own goals, not our interests. They don't understand the duality of young people who want to be faithful to their religion *and* live a modern life."

Last year, Ziada started organizing workshops for young Egyptians to encourage civil disobedience rather than confrontation. "Debate, don't hate," the promotion poster advised. Working with a Muslim civil society group, she coached activists from other Arab countries on moving from online activism to on-the-street action. Among the trainees were two Tunisian bloggers who, only months later, played critical roles in flashing the story of Mohamed Bouazizi's self-immolation in Tunisia across the Internet and beginning the Arab Spring.

132

"You can see," she told me in a phone call later, with great excitement, "it's paying off!" Ziada continued her campaign at Liberation Square earlier this year. After protesters set up a permanent camp there, she walked around the vast plaza distributing copies of *The Montgomery Story*.

"It was a good time," she told me, "to remind people of the techniques—and to remind them that there were people who did it before us, and we can do it too."

In every country, the message of the Arab street movements has been the same. "We want democracy. We want freedom," said a Libyan protester shortly after the uprising began against Moammar Qaddafi. "I want to go on the street feeling like nobody is looking after me, not looking over my shoulder."

But in Arab countries where rebellion has succeeded in ousting leaders (or will), painful makeovers still lie ahead. None will get through the change quickly. Most will stumble over daunting political and economic challenges. Some may fail. All will grapple to find the right blend of freedom and faith. Globalization—or the traumatic transition to it—may also intensify personal affiliations with faith, and backward-looking groups may profit from the change. Yet the uprisings are among the many signals that the Islamic world is no longer an exception to history's forces. A new generation is taking the helm. And the vast majority of Muslims are not attracted to the three major models that until recently defined political Islam's spectrum: Al Qaeda's purist Salafism, Iran's Shiite theocracy, and Saudi Arabia's rigid Wahhabism. All three have a singular vision. All three have no room for anything else.

The new movements are about pluralism and tolerance. The alternatives they create over time—perhaps a great deal of time—may not be liberal in the Western mode. Alcohol and pornography, for example, are not on the list of freedoms endorsed even by liberal Muslims (though hypocrisy is hardly unknown). But most of those who swept away the old order do want to end political monopolies and open up space—to play whatever music they want as well as to have a genuine choice of political parties.

"I'm worried about our future. There are not enough signs that tell you liberalism will be achieved or freedom is guaranteed," Ziada said shortly after she returned from a "protect the revolution" rally at Liberation Square six weeks after Mubarak's ouster.

"But I'm not afraid. I know now that I have power," she told me. "And I know what to do with it."

Critical Thinking

1. Why are Muslim women increasingly assuming their basic rights?

2. What is the relationship between the hijab and women's rights?

3. Why do most pink hijabis have little taste for Islamist politics?

ROBIN WRIGHT, the U.S. Institute of Peace–Woodrow Wilson Center Distinguished Scholar, is a journalist who has reported from abroad for *The Washington Post* and many other publications. This article is drawn from her new book, *Rock the Casbah: Rage and Rebellion Across the Islamic World.* Her other books include *Dreams and Shadows: The Future of the Middle East* (2008) and *The Iran Primer: Power, Politics, and U.S. Policy* (2010).

Feminism by Treaty

CHRISTINA HOFF SOMMERS

On November 18, 2010, a surprisingly large and boisterous crowd gathered in a U.S. Senate chamber to witness new hearings on a decades-old United Nations treaty. Guards had to caution the excited attendees to keep their voices down. Senator Richard Durbin, chair of the Senate Subcommittee on Human Rights and the Law, requested that another room be opened to accommodate the large gathering of feminist leaders, human-rights activists, lawyers, lobbyists, and journalists. "Women have been waiting for 30 years," said Durbin in his opening statement. "The United States should ratify this treaty without further delay."

The treaty in question—the Convention on the Elimination of All Forms of Discrimination against Women (CEDAW)—commits signatory nations not only to eliminating discrimination but also to ensuring women's "full development and advancement" in all areas of public and private life. The document was adopted by the General Assembly and submitted to UN member states in 1979. Since then, nearly every nation has ratified what many now call the "Women's Bill of Rights" or the "Women's Magna Carta." The only holdouts are three Islamic countries (Iran, Sudan, and Somalia), a few Pacific islands—and the United States. "Look at the company we are keeping in refusing to ratify this treaty," said a dismayed Senator Durbin. "We can do better."

In fact, America's failure to ratify the Women's Treaty has not been for lack of powerful support. President Jimmy Carter submitted it to the Senate for ratification in 1980, and many influential legislators of both parties have favored it over the years. In 1993, 68 senators, including Republicans Orrin Hatch, John McCain, and Strom Thurmond, urged President Bill Clinton to secure ratification. Nine years later, President George W. Bush's State Department told the Senate Foreign Relations Committee that it was "generally desirable" and "should be ratified." Its supporters have included not only political leaders and women's groups but also broad-based organizations such as the AARP, AFL-CIO, American Bar Association, and League of Women Voters. Even the Audubon Society has endorsed the Women's Treaty.

Some ascribe the U.S. failure to ratify the treaty to one man: the late Senator Jesse Helms of North Carolina. To Helms, CEDAW was a terrible treaty "negotiated by radical feminists with the intent of enshrining their radical anti-family agenda into international law." As chairman of the Senate Foreign

Relations Committee from 1995 to 2001, Helms refused even to hold hearings on the matter. In 1999, ten women from the House of Representatives marched into his committee room, disrupted a hearing, and demanded that he schedule CEDAW hearings. Pounding his gavel, Chairman Helms reprimanded the placard-carrying women for their breach of decorum. "Please be a lady," he said to the leader, Representative Lynn Woolsey from California. He then instructed the guards to eject the group from the room. (Among the shaken protesters was future Speaker of the House Nancy Pelosi.) Representative Woolsey would later tell the press that Helms "held CEDAW hostage so that women across the globe continued to be victimized and brutalized." But Senator Helms never wavered. At a 2002 Senate hearing, he described the treaty as harmful to women as well as a direct threat to American sovereignty. "It will never see the light of day on my watch."

Some ascribe the U.S. failure to ratify the treaty to one man: the late Senator Jesse Helms of North Carolina.

Helms's watch is now long over, and treaty supporters can see daylight. President Barack Obama and Vice President Joe Biden are strong supporters. So are key Senators John Kerry, chairman of the Foreign Relations Committee, and Barbara Boxer, chairwoman of the subcommittee with jurisdiction over it. Secretary of State Hillary Clinton is an enthusiast, as is Harold Koh, former dean of the Yale Law School and now the State Department's chief legal adviser. An influential advocate of "transnational jurisprudence," Koh invokes the sad irony that "more than half a century after Eleanor Roosevelt pioneered the drafting of the Universal Declaration of Human Rights, her country still has not ratified . . . CEDAW."

The Obama State Department has notified the Senate that ratification of CEDAW is its top priority among the many human-rights treaties the United States is considering. The prospects remained good even after the November 2010 elections. It is the Democratic Senate, not the newly Republican House, which provides advice and consent to treaties. In any event, the treaty has enjoyed Republican support in the past and will again.

So U.S. ratification of the treaty, followed by an inspirational address by President Obama in some international forum, may seem inevitable. Except that it is not. For many years, Senator Helms's adamant opposition to it made support an easy gesture for many senators who may have shared his qualms but not his temerity. Now that ratification has become a live prospect, there will be a real debate. The senators are going to have to confront the treaty itself—what it says and what signing it would mean. It is a complicated and problematic document, and there are many good reasons why the Senate has resisted ratification for more than 30 years.

U.S. ratification of the treaty, followed by a speech from the president, may seem inevitable. Except that it is not.

The question the Senate has to consider is not, as Chairman Durbin suggested at the November hearing, "Should the United States stand with oppressed women of the world?" Of course we should, and we do. No nation on earth gives more to foreign aid or has more philanthropies and religious groups dedicated to women's causes. Voters across the political divide welcome innovative programs to help women struggling with repressive governments and barbaric traditions such as child marriage, dowry burnings, genital cutting, and honor killings. What the senators have to answer are two more basic questions. One, is CEDAW a necessary and worthy addition to an already vibrant national effort to help the world's women? Two, for better or worse, how will ratification affect American life?

Supporters such as Durbin, Biden, Boxer, and Koh are emphatic about how the Women's Treaty would affect American rights and liberties—*not at all.* "CEDAW wouldn't change U.S. law in any way," said Durbin at the hearing. In a 2002 op-ed, Biden and Boxer reminded readers of the horrors of honor killings in Pakistan, bride burnings in India, and female genital mutilation in sub-Saharan Africa. By signing the treaty, they said, the United States would demonstrate its commitment to helping women secure basic rights and increase its leverage with oppressive nations. And, contrary to critics' fears, "ratification . . . would not impose a single new requirement in our laws—because our Constitution and gender discrimination laws already comply with the treaty requirements." On this view, CEDAW is a foreign-policy initiative—in Senator Boxer's words, "a diplomatic tool for human rights." CEDAW opponents see the treaty's consequences in exactly opposite terms. They say American ratification would do little to help women in oppressive societies. Signatories like Saudi Arabia, Yemen, and North Korea have done almost nothing to reform their laws, policies, and practices, even when admonished by the UN's CEDAW-monitoring committee. By contrast, the United States takes its international treaty obligations seriously: If we ratified CEDAW, we would consider ourselves morally committed to abide by its

rules. But many of those rules are antithetical to American values, and any good-faith effort to incorporate them into American law would conflict with our traditions of individual freedom.

A case in point is the central CEDAW provision that requires "all appropriate measures to modify the social and cultural patterns of conduct" of citizens in order to eliminate all practices based on "stereotyped roles for men and women." Under CEDAW, private behavior such as how couples divide household and childcare chores is subject to government regulation under the tutelage of the UN oversight committee. In written testimony for the November 2010 hearing, John Fonte, a senior fellow at the Hudson Institute, described how CEDAW could subvert our democracy "by taking political issues out of the hands of elected officials and transforming them into 'universal human rights' to be determined by judges on the basis of 'evolving norms of international law.'"

The pro-treaty side has heard complaints like this many times and has drawn up detailed refutations. The American Bar Association and Amnesty International, for example, insist that critics are wrong to suggest that CEDAW would supersede American law or traditions. On the contrary, they say the United States could ratify it subject to caveats. If some provision in the treaty conflicts with our laws, we can simply exempt ourselves from it. Furthermore, the treaty would not be "self-executing"—once ratified, it would not become the law of the land until our legislators took action to make it law.

The American Bar Association and Amnesty International insist that it is wrong to suggest that CEDAW would supersede American law.

The ABA and Amnesty International are correct that a nation can ratify a treaty with caveats called reservations, understandings, and declarations, or RUDs. The Clinton administration proposed nine such RUDs, including one that the United States "does not accept any obligation under the Convention to regulate private conduct except as mandated by the Constitution and U.S. law" and another that we do not accept an obligation "to put women in all combat positions." To protect American autonomy still further, the administration added, "No new laws would be created as a result of CEDAW." As the Amnesty International fact sheet says, "Such language upholds U.S. sovereignty and grants no enforcement authority to the United Nations." So, it seems, the critics are wrong: With the help of RUDs, we can show our support for women's rights abroad while protecting American sovereignty and liberties at home.

But here is the problem. Legal experts disagree about the power of RUDs to insulate a nation from provisions of a treaty it has committed itself to honor. The legitimacy and role of reservations to international human-rights treaties is one of the most contested areas of international law. CEDAW itself states,

"A reservation incompatible with the object and purpose of the present Convention shall not be permitted."

Legal experts disagree about the power of RUDs to insulate a nation from provisions of a treaty to which it has committed.

It is not even clear that the ABA, Amnesty, and other pro-treaty activists believe that RUDs offer genuine protection—at least not when they are talking among themselves. When the National Organization for Women met with several human-rights groups in 2009 to plan the current campaign to get the treaty passed, it expressed concern that RUDs would make it difficult to enforce treaty provisions in the United States. But as NOW somewhat indiscreetly reported on its website on August 31, 2009, "Representatives from groups who have advocated for ratification over the years suggest that RUDs have little meaning and could potentially be removed from the treaty at some point."

Even more telling, the UN Division on the Advancement of Women, the agency that monitors the treaty's implementation, is emphatic that the document is obligatory, not hortatory: "Countries that have ratified or acceded to the Convention are legally bound to put its provisions into practice." Moreover, many American legislators—and judges—will sincerely feel we are obligated to bring our laws in line with a treaty we have agreed to honor.

But, according to the ABA and Amnesty, as well as Durbin, Biden, Boxer, and Koh, these arcane questions of international law are irrelevant. Because American laws are already in full or near-full compliance with the treaty, it will have few if any domestic consequences. This argument brings us to the most striking feature of the discussion: the treaty's most engaged and knowledgeable proponents—activist women's groups— *disagree* with the for-export-only argument emphasized by public officials and human-rights groups like Amnesty. NOW, the Feminist Majority Foundation, and their sister organizations actually agree with conservative critics that CEDAW would have a dramatic impact on American laws and practices.

"U.S. women have endured denials of their basic human rights long enough—please do not make them wait any longer," wrote NOW President Terry O'Neil in a March 11, 2010, letter to President Obama urging immediate ratification. Feminist activists see the treaty as an opportunity for American women to secure rights the Constitution has not delivered. The Feminist Majority Foundation has released a video explaining how American women can use CEDAW to bring about a "sea change" in our laws. It shows Congress debating the 2009 "stimulus bill" and explains how CEDAW can lead to "gender-fair budgets." State-mandated quotas, the narrator explains, have led to gender-balanced legislatures in South Africa, Iraq, and Rwanda. Images of beaming women in the Rwandan parliament are juxtaposed with the sorry picture of the U.S. Senate, with only 16 women members out of 100. The video also juxtaposes images of young Afghan women hideously disfigured from acid attacks with those of corpses of American women brutally murdered by intimate partners. "Clearly we need CEDAW," says the narrator. Janet Benshoof, president of the Global Justice Center, speaks for many in the feminist establishment when she says, "If CEDAW were fully implemented in the United States it would revolutionize our rights . . . American women need legal tools to fight patriarchy."

The most detailed assessment of its potential effects on American law appears in a 50-page booklet, *Human Rights for All: CEDAW*, first published in 2001 by a consortium of more than 100 legal and philanthropic associations who support it. The publication includes seventeen pages that spell out how the treaty would transform the American legal system. For example, current American law promises equality of opportunity— but not equality of outcome. "How CEDAW would help?" ask the authors of *Human Rights for All*. Their answer is in bold, capitalized, red letters: "CEDAW Calls Upon State Parties to Adopt Temporary Special Measures Aimed at Accelerating De Facto Equality Between Men and Women." Without using the words "quotas" or "comparable worth," the authors make it clear that CEDAW could give new life to these policies. "U.S. laws," they explain, "do not create rights for women that are specific to their day-to-day reality." The new treaty would correct that. If this guide is to be trusted, treaty ratification will mean that women's groups can litigate all areas of American life that fail to evince statistical parity between the sexes.

Current American law promises equality of opportunity—but not equality of outcome. CEDAW could change that.

What is certain is that, after 67 consensus-seeking senators vote to ratify the treaty and turn to other legislative business, the feminist groups and lawyers who have forthrightly declared their ambitions would be in possession of a powerful new tool. "CEDAW . . . SEA CHANGE" is the refrain in a pro-ratification rap song put out by the Feminist Majority Foundation. To understand just what this sea change might entail, let us turn to the treaty's little-known intellectual provenance.

Back to the Future

The circumstances of CEDAW's creation are submerged in the current ratification debates but essential to making sense of those debates. The Women's Treaty is a product of a unique and unsettled moment in the American women's movement—a moment when a radical version of feminism was briefly ascendant but was soon to be eclipsed by its very success.

In the early 1970s, the UN General Assembly declared 1975 "International Women's Year" and authorized the first World Conference on Women. Thousands converged in Mexico City for both the official UN conference and a parallel conference, called the Tribune, held a few miles away. The UN conference was formal, orderly, and decorous. The Tribune, by contrast, was a raucous affair, attracting some 4,000 feminist activists, writers, and intellectuals. The 1,500 American participants included such feminist luminaries of that era as Betty Friedan, Gloria Steinem, Angela Davis, Jane Fonda, and Bella Abzug.

Foreign Affairs gave a detailed account of some of the many quarrels that broke out between Western feminists and women's activists from the developing world.[1] The Westerners believed that "all women are subject to colonization" and spoke of themselves as members of an inferior "caste." The Third World women were taken aback by facile comparisons between the sometimes-uncomfortable circumstances of privileged middle-class Americans and those of the impoverished, often essentially enslaved women in their own countries. And they were alarmed by the bitter gender politics.

When members of the official U.S. delegation from the UN conference came across town to visit the Tribune, the male delegates were harangued, shouted down, and driven out. One hapless fellow who identified himself as a population expert was unable to complete his remarks because the American feminists demanded to know whether he had had a vasectomy. When he said, "Yes," there was thunderous applause. At a later Tribune event, all men were banished from the room so the women could engage in an impromptu "consciousness-raising" session. "The Third World women were outraged," said *Foreign Affairs*. "Female chauvinism is the last thing we want," complained an Indian journalist. The women from the developing countries also accused the Westerners of "denigrating woman's maternal role" and weakening marriage. Soon women from the Soviet Union joined the fray and made it clear that they did not share the Western feminist goal of eliminating gender roles. In fact, they sought the "liberation of their femininity." Most of them had been forced into the workplace by the Communist system—yet they continued to do all the work at home. "They now want pleasure and beauty; they want to dress up and be courted, perhaps to emphasize motherhood and domestic life."

The disputes over femininity, family, and motherhood that erupted at the 1975 conferences were nothing new to the women's movement. Since the movement's beginning in the early 18th century, reformers have held radically different views on gender roles. "Egalitarian feminists" stressed the essential sameness of the sexes and sought to liberate women from conventional social roles. By contrast, "social feminists" were not opposed to gender distinctions. Indeed, they embraced them, looking for ways to give wives and mothers greater power, respect, and influence in the public sphere, as well as more protection from abuse and exploitation in their domestic roles.

Social feminism has always enjoyed a distinct advantage over its more egalitarian sister: great majorities of women like it. It clearly had a strong following among some of the non-Western and Soviet women at the Mexico conference in 1975. Indeed, an updated version of it informs the lives of most American women today. They want the same rights and opportunities as men—but few make the same choices as men. To give one example, according to a 2009 Pew survey, "A strong majority of all working mothers (62 percent) say they would prefer to work part time . . . An overwhelming majority [of working fathers] (79 percent) say they prefer full-time work. Only one-in-five say they would choose part-time work."

Social feminism has always enjoyed a distinct advantage over its more egalitarian sister: great majorities of women like it.

The rowdy egalitarian feminists at the 1975 Tribune included the leaders of the then-raging feminist revolution in the United States—the "Second Wave of Feminism" as it is now called, which had begun in 1963 with the publication of Betty Friedan's canonical *The Feminine Mystique*. Feminists like Friedan and Gloria Steinem urged American women to live "not at the mercy of the world, but as builder and designer of that world." Women listened, and by the 1980s, they were entering the workplace in record numbers; filling the colleges, law schools, and medical schools; starting businesses; joining sports teams; and generally enjoying freedoms and opportunities far beyond those of any women in history.

But then the women's movement suffered a serious setback. After scoring a series of landmark legal victories in the 1960s and early 1970s, they failed to pass the Equal Rights Amendment. In 1975 the ERA seemed to be on a fast track to ratification. But as the political scientist Jane Mansbridge explains in her meticulous study, *Why We Lost the ERA*, Americans became disenchanted when they began to understand the worldview of its feminist sponsors: radical sexual egalitarianism.

The egalitarian feminists who dreamed of a fully androgynous society are found today in university women's studies programs, law schools, and not least in a network of activist organizations that sprang into being in those heady days. They are relatively small in number, but they wield disproportionate influence. But without question, the defeat of the ERA was a serious setback from which they never really recovered. What these activists now see in CEDAW is a second chance in another venue. It is not for nothing that the Women's Treaty is sometimes called a "global ERA."

So, then, what does the treaty actually say? It requires signatory countries to remove all barriers that prevent women from achieving full equality with men in all spheres of life—law, politics, education, employment, marriage, and "family planning." It defines discrimination against women to be "any distinction, exclusion or restriction made on the basis of sex." Some of its more specific provisions are highly laudable, such as its requirement that signatories "suppress all forms of traffic in women and exploitation of prostitution." Others are, from an American standpoint, unexceptional, such as the requirement that signatories "accord to women equality with men before the law." But its central provision, Article 5(a), is pure 1970s egalitarian feminism, and is the key to understanding what the Women's Treaty envisages. It reads, in part: "States Parties shall take all appropriate measures . . . [t]o modify the social and cultural patterns of conduct of men and women, with a view to achieving the elimination of prejudices and customary and all other practices which are based on the idea of the inferiority or the superiority of either of the sexes *or on stereotyped roles for men and women*" (emphasis added).

The philosophy of Article 5(a) pervades the entire document. Throughout it, the drafters are determined to use its provisions to eradicate gender stereotypes, especially those that associate women with caregiving and motherhood. The treaty instructs signatories "to ensure that family education includes a proper understanding of maternity as a social function and the recognition of the common responsibility of men and women in the upbringing and development of their children." It also calls for the "elimination of any stereotyped concept of the roles of men and women at all levels and in all forms of education . . . in particular, by the revision of textbooks and school programmes." States are advised to provide paid maternity leave as well as "the necessary supporting social services to enable parents to combine family obligations with work responsibilities . . . in particular through promoting the establishment and development of a network of child-care facilities."

It is clear that CEDAW's drafters are determined to use its provisions to eradicate gender stereotypes.

And the battle against stereotypes requires special efforts to guarantee equal results in the workplace and in government. "Temporary special measures aimed at accelerating de facto equality between men and women," reads Article 4, "shall not be considered discrimination." The UN's CEDAW Committee interprets this as mandating "positive action, preferential treatment or quota systems to advance women's integration into education, the economy, politics and employment."

Signatory governments are also required to "take all appropriate measures" to ensure women's "right to equal remuneration . . . in respect of work of equal value." This means "comparable worth" policies, according to the CEDAW Committee, which effectively require the establishment of government agencies to determine the proper level of salary for differing kinds of work. "Comparable worth" was a concept much bandied-about in United States in the 1980s until its backers found it impossible to deny they were advocating a radical governmental intrusion into the workings of the private marketplace of an unprecedented kind. The treaty brings it back. And it would not just be American intermediaries that would be charged with figuring out how the U.S. is handling these matters.

The Committee

Indeed, if the United States were to ratify CEDAW, we would immediately be subject to an evaluation of how well we comply with the treaty's provisions. Such an evaluation is to be carried out by the CEDAW Committee—23 experts of "high moral standing and competence in the field covered by the Convention." They are elected by signatory nations including Cuba, Burma, and Nigeria. Countries under review submit detailed reports outlining their progress toward fulfilling the treaty's requirements. Their representatives then meet with the Committee every three years, when they are questioned, challenged, sometimes rebuked, and provided with official recommendations for improvement.

Today any country, no matter how free and democratic, is out of compliance with the treaty as long as significant gender roles are still discernible in its customs or institutions—both public and private. If, for example, more women than men routinely take care of children, the Committee recommends ways to turn things around, usually with government-imposed quotas and "awareness raising" campaigns. The UN publishes detailed accounts of exchanges between the Committee and countries under review. It is hard to read them and not conclude that the United States would be in for a rough time.

Today any country is out of compliance with the treaty as long as significant gender roles are still discernible.

Consider what happened during Iceland's formal CEDAW review in July 2008. Iceland has one of the most extensive gender-equity bureaucracies in the world; there are equity ministers, equity councils, equity advisors, and a Complaints Committee on Gender Equality whose rulings are binding. More than 80 percent of Icelandic women are in the labor force, and parents enjoy paid maternity and paternity leave, including one month of pre-birth leave. Iceland is ranked first in the World Economic Forum's 2009 Global Gender Gap Report. It would appear to be a paradigm of egalitarianism. Yet it falls short of the CEDAW Committee standards.

The Committee praised Iceland for its "strides" toward gender parity, but several members found it remiss in its efforts to stamp out sexism. Hanna Beate Schopp-Schilling, an expert from Germany, was concerned that for all the government's gender and equity committees, the Parliament itself had not formed a committee on gender equity. The expert from Algeria wanted to know why so few women were full professors at the University of Iceland. Magalys Arocha Dominguez, a gender authority from Cuba, was unhappy to find that many Icelandic women held part-time jobs and spent much more time than men taking care of children. She was also displeased by survey findings that Iceland's women were allowing family commitments to shape their career choices. She demanded to know, "What government measures have been put in place to change these patterns of behavior?"

Treaty proponents such as Senator Durbin, Vice President Biden, Senator Boxer, and Harold Koh praise its work with women in the developing world. But in practice the CEDAW Committee devotes disproportionate energies to monitoring democracies and urging them to realize egalitarian ideals in all spheres of life. It recently advised Spain to organize a national awareness-raising campaign against gender roles in the family. Finland was urged "to promote equal sharing of domestic and family tasks between women and men." Slovakia was instructed to "fully sensitize men to their equal participation in family tasks and responsibilities." Liechtenstein was closely questioned about a "Father's Day project" and reminded of the need to "dismantle gender stereotypes."

The Committee sounds far more reasonable when reviewing countries where women are truly oppressed, like Nigeria, Niger, Mauritania, or Yemen. Such nations often send delegates who present their homelands as models of gender equity. "Mauritanian women and men were equal before the law in all spheres," reported one. The Yemeni delegation spoke of legal reforms, new programs, and strategies for women's empowerment. To its credit, the Committee respectfully but firmly pressed these delegates on matters such as child marriage, polygamy, legal wife beating, stoning, female genital mutilation, and high maternal mortality rates. Members often give the delegations concrete ideas on how to improve women's lives. In its 2007 review, Niger was advised to offer families micro-credits for each daughter enrolled in school and to try to limit female genital mutilation by finding alternative employment for the older women who perform the procedure for a living. The same Committee that sounded so absurd when it rebuked Liechtenstein for recognizing Father's Day was impressive in its exchanges with Yemen about how to address female illiteracy.

The efficacy of these reviews of repressive countries is a matter of dispute. Most experts believe they do some good. They point out that these countries are getting a strong sense of where they stand in relation to a set of universal standards. Furthermore, the Committee issues a final report after each review, which it believes helps local women's advocacy groups foment change. But critics note that many of the world's most repressive nations show little or no intention of abiding by the treaty. Yemen ratified CEDAW in 1984 without reservations. It has undergone six Committee reviews. Yet in 2010, for the fifth year in a row, it came in last in the World Economic Forum's annual Global Gender Gap Report. Fifty-seven percent of females are illiterate, compared to 21 percent of males. Girls as young as eight years old can be legally married, and its penal code specifies that any man who kills a female relative suspected of adultery should not be prosecuted for murder. In the 2008 review, exasperated Committee members repeatedly asked the Yemeni delegation if its government understood the treaty or took any of its provisions seriously.

Is the treaty likely to improve the circumstances of women in places like Yemen (and for that matter Cuba)? Would U.S. ratification make it more effective? Are there better ways for America to advance women's rights than through a UN treaty? There is lots of room for argument on these points, and there are many disagreements among feminists and human-rights advocates. As for its effects on *American* life, however, there is no doubt: They would be momentous.

Fallout

If the United States ratifies CEDAW there will be a three-ring circus each time we come up for review. American laws, customs, and private behavior will be evaluated by 23 UN gender

ministers to see whether they comply with a feminist ideal that is 30 years out of date. The Committee will pounce on all facets of American life that fail to achieve full gender integration. That many American mothers stay home with children or work part-time will be at the top of their list of "discriminatory practices." Committee members like Cuba's Magalys Arocha Dominguez will want to know what our government has done to change our patterns of behavior. The American delegation will then enter a "consultative dialogue" with the Committee to develop appropriate remedies.

If the United States ratifies CEDAW there will be a three-ring circus each time we come up for review.

They will get plenty of help from organizations like NOW, the Feminist Majority, and the American Association of University Women. Groups of which Americans know little or nothing will take CEDAW as a legal mandate to implement their worldview. If ratified, the treaty would give these organizations a license to sue, reeducate, and resocialize their fellow citizens. Gender quotas, comparable-worth pay policies, state-subsidized daycare, and other initiatives that have failed again and again to win democratic support would instantly be transformed into universal human rights. And the women's groups would have new allies: UN officials and international NGOs would join them in cultivating American pastures under the legal and moral authority of the Women's Treaty.

At the November 2010 Senate hearing, one pro-CEDAW expert witness openly praised the Treaty for its impact at home. According to Marcia Greenberger, copresident of the National Women's Law Center, "No one would disagree that there is still progress to be made in the Unites States. . . . We like every other country in the world have our own challenges to confront." She is right, of course, but what she needs to explain is why an international treaty and a body of foreign experts is better at meeting the moral challenges of equity than our own democratic institutions.

For groups like NOW, the Feminist Majority, and the National Women's Law Center, life under CEDAW would be exhilarating and gratifying. For the majority of Americans who do not share their egalitarian agenda, it could be oppressive.

But let's say, just for the sake of argument, that the Obama administration and the U.S. Senate do ratify the Women's Treaty subject to various "understandings" that effectively protect our institutions from the ministrations of the Committee and deny the feminist network its "tool" to dismantle the American patriarchy. Should the United States be lending its authority to a human-rights instrument that treats the conventions of femininity as demeaning to women?

Few women anywhere want to see gender roles obliterated. The late Elizabeth Warnock Fernea was an expert on feminist movements in the contemporary Muslim world. In her travels through Saudi Arabia, Morocco, Turkey, and Iraq, she met great numbers of advocates working to improve the status of women—and who were proud of their roles as mother, wife, and caregiver. Fernea called it "family feminism," but it was classic social feminism—the style of women's liberation that hard-line egalitarians disdain but that great majorities of women find ennobling and empowering. The women of America are no exception.

Harold Koh suggests that by abjuring "the Women's Rights Treaty" Americans are betraying the legacy of Eleanor Roosevelt—the leader of the group that created the celebrated Universal Declaration of Human Rights of 1948. But Koh is confused about Roosevelt's legacy. She was a lifelong, dyed-in-the-wool social feminist, energetically committed to women's rights as well as to the protection of their social roles and callings. She saw men and women as equal, but decidedly different. No woman, she said, should feel "humiliated" if she gives priority to home and family. "This was our first field of activity," she said, "and it will always remain our most important one."

Gender experts at NOW or the NWLC will say that Roosevelt was captive to the prejudices of her time. Maybe so. But it is more likely that this deeply humane and large-souled woman, whose vision helped create the Universal Declaration of Human Rights, also had a clear vision of where women's emancipation might lead. Social feminism appears to be the universal feminism of women. By endorsing the treaty, the United States Senate would be canonizing a school of *egalitarian* feminism most women reject, one that is as likely to impede as to advance women's progress in societies where their current circumstances are most degraded.

CEDAW contains many worthy and indeed noble declarations, but its key provisions are 1970s feminism preserved in diplomatic amber. Releasing those aged provisions in 21st-century America would be strange at best, and at worst they could seriously compromise the privacy, well-being, and basic freedoms of Americans. At the November hearing, Senator Durbin called on his colleagues to "ratify this treaty without further delay." For the past 31 years, our legislators have wisely delayed ratification. Today's Senate should continue to follow that example.

Note

1. Jennifer Whitaker, "Women of the World: Report from Mexico City," *Foreign Affairs* 54:1 (October 1975).

Critical Thinking

1. What are the major treaties and conventions that have been adopted by the UN system to protect the rights of women?
2. Why doesn't the United States ratify CEDAW?
3. How successful has the implementation of UN norms been in protecting the rights of women?

CHRISTINA HOFF SOMMERS is a resident scholar at the American Enterprise Institute. Her books include *Who Stole Feminism* and *The War Against Boys*. She is coauthor of *One Nation Under Therapy* and editor of *The Science on Women and Science*. An early version of this paper appeared in the book *New Threats to Freedom*.

The Persistence of Genocide

DAVID RIEFF

According to the great historian of the Holocaust, Raul Hilberg, the phrase "Never Again" first appeared on handmade signs put up by inmates at Buchenwald in April, 1945, shortly after the camp had been liberated by U.S. forces. "I think it was really the Communists who were behind it, but I am not sure," Hilberg said in one of the last interviews he gave before his death in the summer of 2007. Since then, "Never Again" has become kind of shorthand for the remembrance of the Shoah. At Buchenwald, the handmade signs were long ago replaced by a stone monument onto which the words are embossed in metal letters. And as a usage, it has come to seem like a final word not just on the murder of the Jews of Europe, but on any great crime against humanity that could not be prevented. "Never Again" has appeared on monuments and memorials from Paine, Chile, the town with proportionately more victims of the Pinochet dictatorship than any other place in the country, to the Genocide Museum in Kigali, Rwanda. The report of CONADEP, the Argentine truth commission set up in 1984 after the fall of the Galtieri dictatorship, was titled "Nunca Mas"—"Never Again" in Spanish. And there is now at least one online Holocaust memorial called "Never Again."

There is nothing wrong with this. But there is also nothing all that right with it either. Bluntly put, an undeniable gulf exists between the frequency with which the phrase is used—above all on days of remembrance most commonly marking the Shoah, but now, increasingly, other great crimes against humanity—and the reality, which is that 65 years after the liberation of the Nazi concentration camps, "never again" has proved to be nothing more than a promise on which no state has ever been willing to deliver. When, last May, the writer Elie Wiesel, himself a former prisoner in Buchenwald, accompanied President Barack Obama and Chancellor Angela Merkel to the site of the camp, he said that he had always imagined that he would return some day and tell his father's ghost that the world had learned from the Holocaust and that it had become a "sacred duty" for people everywhere to prevent it from recurring. But, Wiesel continued, had the world actually learned anything, "there would be no Cambodia, and no Rwanda and no Darfur and no Bosnia."

Wiesel was right: The world has learned very little. But this has not stopped it from pontificating much. The Obama administration's National Security Strategy Paper, issued in May 2010, exemplifies this tendency. It asserts confidently that "The United States is committed to working with our allies, and to strengthening our own internal capabilities, in order to ensure that the United States and the international community are proactively engaged in a strategic effort to prevent mass atrocities and genocide." And yet again, we are treated to the promise, "never again." "In the event that prevention fails," the report states, "the United States will work both multilaterally and bilaterally to mobilize diplomatic, humanitarian, financial, and—in certain instances—military means to prevent and respond to genocide and mass atrocities."

Of course, this is not strategy, but a promise that, decade in and decade out, has proved to be empty. For if one were to evaluate these commitments by the results they have produced so far, one would have to say that all this "proactive engagement" and "diplomatic, financial, and humanitarian mobilization" has not accomplished very much. No one should be surprised by this. The U.S. is fighting two wars and still coping (though it has fallen from the headlines) with the floods in Pakistan, whose effects will be felt for many years in a country where America's security interests and humanitarian relief efforts are inseparable. At the same time, the crisis over Iran's imminent acquisition of nuclear weapons capability is approaching its culmination. Add to this the fact that the American economy is in shambles, and you do not exactly have a recipe for engagement. The stark fact is that "never again" has never been a political priority for either the United States or the so-called international community (itself a self-flattering idea with no more reality than a unicorn). Nor, despite all the bluff talk about moral imperatives backed by international resolve, is there any evidence that it is becoming one.

And yet, however at variance they are with both geopolitical and geoeconomic realities, the arguments exemplified by this document reflect the conventional wisdom of the great and the good in America across the "mainstream" (as one is obliged to say in this, the era of the tea parties) political spectrum. Even a fairly cursory online search will reveal that there are a vast number of papers, book-length studies, think tank reports, and United Nations documents proposing programs for preventing or at least halting genocides. For once, the metaphor "cottage industry" truly is appropriate. And what unites almost all of them is that they start from the premise that prevention is possible, if only the "international community" would live up to the commitments it made in the Genocide Convention of 1948, and in subsequent international covenants, treaties, and UN declarations. If, the argument goes, the world's great powers, first and foremost of course the United States, in collaboration with the UN system and with global civil society, would act decisively and in a timely way, we could actually enforce the moral standards supposedly agreed upon in the aftermath of the Holocaust. If they do not, of course, then "never again" will never mean much more than it has meant since 1945—which, essentially, is "Never again will Germans kill Jews in Europe in the 1940s."

Since 1945, "never again" has meant, essentially, "Never again will Germans kill Jews in Europe in the 1940s."

The report of the United States Institute for Peace's task force on genocide, chaired by former Secretary of State Madeleine Albright and former Secretary of Defense William Cohen, is among the best of these efforts. As the report makes clear, the task force undertook its work all too painfully aware of the gulf between the international consensus on the moral imperative of stopping genocide and the ineffectiveness to date of the actual responses. Indeed, the authors begin by stating plainly that 60 years after the United Nations adopted the Genocide Convention and twenty years after it was ratified by the U.S. Senate, "The world agrees that genocide is unacceptable and yet genocide and mass killings continue." To find ways to match words and "stop allowing the unacceptable," Albright and Cohen write with commendable candor, "is in fact one of most persistent puzzles of our times."

Whether or not one agrees with the task force about what can or cannot be done to change this, there can be no question that sorrow over the world's collective failure to act in East Pakistan, or Cambodia, or Rwanda is the only honorable response imaginable. But the befuddlement the authors of the report confess to feeling is another matter entirely. Like most thinking influenced by the human rights movement, the task force seems imbued with the famous Kantian *mot d'ordre*: "Ought implies can." But to put the matter bluntly, there is no historical basis to believe anything of the sort, and a great deal of evidence to suggest a diametrically opposing conclusion. Of course, history is not a straitjacket, and the authors of the report, again echoing much thinking within the human rights movement, particularly Michael Ignatieff's work in the 1990s, do make the argument that since 1945 there has been what Ignatieff calls "A revolution of global concern" and they call a "revolution in conscience." In fairness, if in fact they are basing their optimism on this chiliastic idea, then one better understands the degree to which the members of the task force came to believe that genocide, far from being "A Problem From Hell," as Samantha Power titled her influential book on the subject, in reality is a problem if not easily solved then at least susceptible to solution—though, again, only if all the international actors, by whom the authors mean the great powers, the UN system, countries in a region where there is a risk of a genocide occurring, and what they rather uncritically call civil society, make it a priority.

Since it starts from this presupposition, it is hardly surprising that the report is upbeat about the prospects for finally reversing course. "Preventing genocide," the authors insist, "is a goal that can be achieved with the right institutional structures, strategies, and partnerships—in short, with the right blueprint." To accomplish this, the task force emphasizes the need for strengthening international cooperation both in terms of identifying places where there is a danger of a genocide being carried out and coordinated action to head it off or at least halt it. Four specific responses are recommended, one predominantly informational (early warning) and three operational (early prevention, preventive diplomacy, and, finally, military intervention when all else has failed). None of this is exactly new, and most of it is commonsensical from a conceptual standpoint. But one of the great strengths of the report, as befits the work of a task force chaired by two former cabinet secretaries, is this practical bent—that is to say, its emphasis on creating or strengthening institutional structures within the U.S. government and the UN system and showing how such reforms will enable policymakers to respond effectively to genocide.

Preventing genocide is a goal that can be achieved with the right institutional structures, strategies, and partnerships . . .

However, this same presupposition leads the authors of the report to write as if there were little need for them to elaborate the political and ideological bases for the "can do" approach they recommend. Francis Fukuyama's controversial theory of the "End of History" goes unmentioned, but there is more than a little of Fukuyama in their assumptions about a "final" international consensus having been established with regard to the norms that have come into force protecting populations from genocide or mass atrocity crimes. It is true that there is a body of such norms: the Genocide Convention, the UN's so-called Responsibility to Protect doctrine, adopted by the World Summit (with the strong support of the Bush administration) in 2005, and various international instruments limiting impunity, above all the Rome Statute that created the International Criminal Court. And, presumably, it is with these in mind that the report's authors can assert so confidently that the focus in genocide prevention can now be on "implement[ing] and operationalizing the commitments [these instruments] contain."

It is here that doubt will begin to assail more skeptical readers. Almost since its inception, the human rights movement has been a movement of lawyers. And for lawyers, the establishment of black-letter international law is indeed the "end of the story" from a normative point of view—an internationalized version of *stare decisis,* but extended to the nth degree. On this account such a norm, once firmly established (which, activists readily admit, may take time; they are not naifs), can within a fairly short period thereafter be understood as an ineradicable and unchallengeable part of the basic user's manual for international relations. This is what has allowed the human rights movement (and, at least with regard to the question of genocide, the members of the task force in the main seem to have been of a similar cast of mind) to hew to what is essentially a positivist progress narrative. However, the human rights movement's certitude on the matter derives less from its historical experience than it does from its ideological presuppositions. In this sense, human rights truly is a secular religion, as its critics but even some of its supporters have long claimed.

Almost since its inception, the human rights movement has been a movement of lawyers.

Of course, strategically (in both polemical and institutional terms) the genius of this approach is of a piece with liberalism generally, of which, in any case, "human rights-ism" is the offspring. Liberalism is the only modern ideology that will not admit it is an ideology. "We are just demanding that nations live up to the international covenants they have signed and the relevant national and international statutes," the human rights activist replies indignantly when taxed with actually supporting, and, indeed, helping to midwife an ideological system. It may be tedious to have to point out in 2010 that law and morality are not the same thing, but, well, law and morality are not the same thing. The problem is that much of the task force report reads as if they were.

An end to genocide: It is an attractive prospect, not to mention a morally unimpeachable goal in which Kantian moral absolutism meets American can do-ism, where the post-ideological methodologies (which are anything but post-ideological, of course) of international lawyers meet the American elite's faith, which goes back at least to Woodrow Wilson if not much earlier in the history of the republic, that we really can right any wrong if only we commit ourselves sufficiently to doing so. Unfortunately, far too much is assumed (or stipulated, as the lawyers say) by the report's authors. More dismayingly still, far too many of the concrete examples either of what could have been done but wasn't are presented so simplistically as to make the solutions offered appear hollow, since the challenge as described bears little or no resemblance to the complexities that actually exist.

Darfur is a good example of this. The report mentions Darfur frequently, both in the context of a nuts and bolts consideration of the strengths and weaknesses of various states and institutions such as the UN and the African Union, which have intervened, however unsatisfactorily, over the course of the crisis, and as an example of how the mobilization of civil society can influence policy. "In today's age of electronic media communication," the report states, "Americans are increasingly confronted in their living rooms—and even on their cell phones— with information about and images of death and destruction virtually anywhere they occur. . . . The Internet has proven to be a powerful tool for organizing broad-based responses to genocide and mass atrocities, as we have seen in response to the crisis in Darfur."

The problem is not so much that this statement is false but rather that it begs more questions than it answers, and, more tellingly still, that the report's authors seem to have no idea of this. There is no question that the rise in 2005 and 2006 of a mass movement calling for an end to mass killing in Darfur (neither the United Nations nor the most important relief groups present on the ground in Darfur agree with the characterization of what took place there as a genocide) was an extraordinarily successful mobilization—perhaps the most successful since the anti-Apartheid movement of the 1970s and 1980s. Beginning with the activism of a small group of college students who in June 2004 had attended a Darfur Emergency Summit organized by the U.S. Holocaust Memorial Museum and addressed by Elie Wiesel, and shortly afterwards founded an organization called Save Darfur, the movement rapidly expanded and, at its height, included the U.S. Congressional Black Caucus, right-wing evangelicals, left-leaning campuses activists, mainline human rights activists, and American neoconservatives. But nowhere does the task force report examine whether the policy recommendations of this movement were wise, or, indeed, whether the effect that they had on the U.S. debate was positive or negative. Instead, the report proceeds as if any upsurge in grassroots interest and activism galvanized by catastrophes like Darfur is by definition a positive development.

In reality, the task force's assumption that any mass movement that supports "more assertive government action in response to genocide and mass atrocities" is to be encouraged is a strangely content-less claim. Surely, before welcoming the rise of a Save Darfur (or its very influential European cousin, SOS Darfour), it is important to think clearly not just about what they are against but what they are for. And here, the example of Save Darfur is as much a cautionary tale as an inspiring one. The report somewhat shortchanges historical analysis, with what little history that does make it in painted with a disturbingly broad brush. Obviously, the task force was well aware of this, which I presume is why its report insists, unwisely in my view, that it was far more important to focus on the present and the future more than on the past. But understanding the history is not marginal, it is central. Put the case that one believes in military intervention in extremis to halt genocide. In that case, intervening in late-2003 and early-2004, when the killing was at its height, would have been the right thing to do. But Save Darfur really only came into its own in late 2005, that is, well after the bulk of the killing had ended. In other words, the calls for an intervention reached their height after the moral imperative for such an intervention had started to dissipate. An analogy can be made with the human rights justification for the U.S. overthrow of Saddam Hussein. As Kenneth Roth, the head of Human Rights Watch, has pointed out, had this happened during Baghdad's murderous Anfal campaign against the Kurds in 1988, there would have been a solid justification for military intervention, whether or not Human Rights Watch would have agreed with it. But to intervene fifteen years later because of the massacre was indefensible on human rights grounds (though, obviously, there were other rationales for the war that would not have been affected by such reasoning).

The calls for an intervention in Darfur reached their height after the moral imperative for intervention had started to dissipate.

If you want to be a prophet, you have to get it right. And if Save Darfur was wrong in its analysis of the facts relevant to their call for an international military intervention to stop genocide, either because there had in reality been no genocide (as, again, the UN and many mainstream NGOs on the ground insisted) or because the genocide had ended before they began to campaign for intervention, then Save Darfur's activism can just as reasonably be described in negative terms as in the positive ones of the task force report. Yes, Save Darfur had (and has) good intentions and the attacks on them from de facto apologists for the government of Sudan like Mahmood Mamdani are not worth taking seriously. But good intentions should never be enough.[1]

In fairness, had the task force decided to provide the history of the Darfur, or Bosnia, or Rwanda, in all their frustrating complexity, they would have produced a report that, precisely because of all the nuance, the ambiguity, the need for "qualifiers," doubtless would have been of less use to policymakers, whose professional orientation is of necessity toward actionable policies. But when what is being suggested is a readiness for U.S. soldiers (to be sure, preferably in a multilateral context) in extreme cases to kill and die to prevent genocide or mass atrocity crimes, then, to turn human rights Kantianism against them for a change, it is nuance that is the moral imperative. Again, good intentions alone will not do. *Qui veut faire l'ange, fait la bete,* Pascal said. Who wishes to act the angel, acts the beast.

History, in all its unsentimentality, is almost always the best antidote to such simplicities. And yet, if anything, the task force's report is a textbook case of ahistorical thinking and its perils. The authors emphasize that, "This task force is not a historical commission; its focus is on the future and on prevention." The problem is that unless the past is looked at in detail, not just conjured up by way of illustrations of the West's failures to intervene that the task force hopes to remedy, then what is being argued for, in effect, are, if necessary, endless wars of altruism. To put it charitably, in arguing for that, I do not think the authors have exactly established their claim to occupying the moral high ground. If they had spent half the time thinking about history in as serious a way as they did about how to construct the optimal bureaucratic architecture within the U.S. government, then what the task force finally produced would have been a document that was pathbreaking. Instead, they took the conventional route, and, in my view, will simply add their well-reasoned policy recommendations to the large number that came before and, indeed, as in the case of the recent initiative of the Montreal Institute for Genocide and Human Rights Studies on the so-called Will to Intervene, have already begun to come after.

With the best will in the world, what is one to make of arguments made at the level of generalization of the following?

> Grievances over inequitable distribution of power and resources appear to be a fundamental motivating factor in the commission of mass violence against ethnic, sectarian, or political groups. That same inequality may also provide the means for atrocities to be committed. For example, control of a highly centralized state apparatus and the access to economic and military power that comes with it makes competition for power an all-or-nothing proposition and creates incentives to eliminate competitors. This dynamic was evident in Rwanda and Burundi and is serious cause for concern in Burma today.

The fact is that, vile as they are, there is actually very little likelihood of the butchers in Rangoon committing genocide—their crimes have other characteristics. It is disheartening that the members of the task force would allow the fact that they, like most sensible people, believe that Burma is one of the worst dictatorships in the world, to justify their distorting reality in this way, when they almost certainly know better. And since they do precisely that, it is hard not to at least entertain the suspicion—whose implications extend rather further than that and beg the question of what kind of world order follows from the task force's recommendations—that consciously or (and this is worse, in a way) unconsciously they reasoned that if they could identify the Rangoon regime as genocidal, this would make an international intervention to overthrow it far more defensible. If this is right, then, if implemented, the report (again, intentionally or inadvertently) would have the effect of helping nudge us back toward a world where the prevention of genocide becomes a moral warrant for other policy agendas (as was surely the case with Saddam Hussein in 2003, and was the case with General Bashir in Khartoum until the arrival of the Obama administration).

I write this in large measure because the task force's description of why mass violence and genocide occur could be a description of practically the entire developing world. Analysis at that level of generalization is not just useless, it is actually a prophylactic against thought.

It gets worse. The authors write:

> It is equally important to focus on the motivations of specific leaders and the tools at their disposal. There is no genocidal destiny. Many countries with ethnic or religious discrimination, armed conflicts, autocratic governments, or crushing poverty have not experienced genocide while others have. The difference comes down to leadership. Mass atrocities are organized by powerful elites who believe they stand to gain from these crimes and who have the necessary resources at their disposal. The heinous crimes committed in Nazi-occupied Europe, Cambodia, and Rwanda, for example, were all perpetrated with significant planning, organization, and access to state resources, including weapons, budgets, detention facilities, and broadcast media.

> There are also key triggers that can tip a high-risk environment into crisis. These include unstable, unfair, or unduly postponed elections; high-profile assassinations; battlefield victories; and environmental conditions (for example, drought) that may cause an eruption of violence or heighten the perception of an existential threat to a government or armed group. Sometimes potential triggers are known well in advance and preparations can be made to address the risk of mass atrocities that may follow. Poorly planned elections in deeply divided societies are a commonly cited example, but deadlines for significant policy action, legal judgments, and anniversaries of highly traumatic and disputed historical events are also potential triggers that can be foreseen.

I tax the reader's patience with such a long quotation to show how expertise can produce meaninglessness. For apart from the mention of poorly planned elections—a reference to Rwanda that is perfectly correct as far as it goes—the rest of this does not advance our understanding one iota. To remedy or at least alleviate these vast social stresses, the task force recommends "effective [*sic*] early prevention"! The authors themselves were obliged to admit that, "Such efforts to change underlying social, economic, or political conditions are difficult and require sustained investment of resources and attention." Really, you think? But about where these resources, as opposed to institutional arrangements, are to come from, they are largely silent, apart from emphasizing the need to target with both threats and positive inducements leaders thought likely to choose to commit such crimes. But the authors know perfectly well that, as they themselves put it, "early engagement is a speculative venture," and that "the watch list of countries 'at risk' can be long, due to the difficulty of anticipating specific crises in a world generally plagued by instability." Surely, people like Secretary Albright and Secretary Cohen know better than anyone that such ventures are never going to be of much interest to senior policymakers, just as the global Marshall Plan that would be required to effectively address the underlying causes of genocidal wars is never going to be on offer.

To a great power, and to the citizens of great power, powerlessness is simply an unconscionable destiny. The task force report, with its strange imperviousness to viewing historical tragedy as much more than an engineering problem, is a perfect illustration of this. Unsound historically, and hubristic morally, for all its good intentions, the task force report is not a blueprint for a better future but a mystification of the choices that actually confront us and between which we are going to have to choose if we are ever to prevent or halt even some genocides. My suspicion is that the reason that the very accomplished, distinguished people who participated in the task force did not feel obliged to face up to this is because the report gives as much weight to the national interest basis for preventing or halting genocide as it does to the moral imperative of doing so. As the report puts it:

First, genocide fuels instability, usually in weak, undemocratic, and corrupt states. It is in these same types of states that we find terrorist recruitment and training, human trafficking, and civil strife, all of which have damaging spillover effects for the entire world.

Second, genocide and mass atrocities have long-lasting consequences far beyond the states in which they occur. Refugee flows start in bordering countries but often spread. Humanitarian needs grow, often exceeding the capacities and resources of a generous world. The international community, including the United States, is called on to absorb and assist displaced people, provide relief efforts, and bear high economic costs. And the longer we wait to act, the more exorbitant the price tag. For example, in Bosnia, the United States has invested nearly $15 billion to support peacekeeping forces in the years since we belatedly intervened to stop mass atrocities.

Third, America's standing in the world—and our ability to lead—is eroded when we are perceived as bystanders to genocide. We cannot be viewed as a global leader and respected as an international partner if we cannot take steps to avoid one of the greatest scourges of humankind. No matter how one calculates U.S. interests, the reality of our world today is that national borders provide little sanctuary from international problems. Left unchecked, genocide will undermine American security.

A core challenge for American leaders is to persuade others—in the U.S. government, across the United States, and around the world—that preventing genocide is more than just a humanitarian aspiration; it is a national and global imperative.

Again, apologies for quoting at such length. but truthfully, is one meant to take this seriously? There is absolutely no evidence that terrorist recruiting is more promising in failed states than, say, in suburban Connecticut where the (very middle-class) Faisal Shahzad, son of a retired Pakistani Air Force vice-marshal, plotted to explode a car bomb in Times Square. Nor, in the U.S. case is there any basis for concluding that the main source of immigration is from places traumatized by war. To the contrary, most of our immigrants are the best and the brightest (in the sense not of the most educated but most enterprising) of Mexico, the Philippines, India, and China. The proportion of migrants from Sudan or Somalia is small by comparison. As for the costs of peacekeeping, are the authors of the report serious? Fifteen billion dollars? The sum barely signifies in the rubric of the military budget of the United States. And lastly, the report's claim that the U.S. won't be viewed as a global leader and respected as an international partner if it doesn't take the lead to stop genocide is absurd on its face. Not respected by whom, exactly? Hu Jintao in Beijing? Merkel in Berlin? President Felipe Calderon in Mexico City? To put it charitably, the claim conjures up visions of Pinocchio, rather than Theodore Roosevelt or Woodrow Wilson.

The report calls for courage, but courage begins at home. Pressed by Armenian activists at one of the events held to launch the report as to why they had both earlier signed a letter urging the U.S. not to bow to Armenian pressure and formally recognize the Armenian genocide, Secretary Cohen and Secretary Albright refused over and over again to characterize the Armenian genocide as, well, a genocide. It is true that the Armenian activists had come looking for a confrontation. But there can be little question that both secretaries did everything they could to avoid committing themselves one way or the other. "Terrible things happened to the Armenians," Secretary Albright said, refusing to go any further. The letter, she explained, had been primarily about "whether this was an appropriate time to raise the issue." For his part, Secretary Cohen, emphasized that angering the Turks while the Iraq war was raging could lead to Turkish reactions that would "put our sons and daughters in jeopardy." And, in any case, the task force was not "a historical commission."

This is a perfectly defensible position from the perspective of prudential realpolitik. The problem is that what the task force report constantly calls for is political courage. And whatever else they were, Secretaries Albright and

Cohen's responses were expedient, not courageous. There will always be reasons not to intervene—compelling pressures, I mean, not trivial ones. Why should a future U.S. government be less vulnerable to them than the Bush or Obama administrations? About this, as about so many other subjects, the task force report is as evasive as Secretary Albright and Secretary Cohen were at the press conference at which the Armenian activists confronted them. Doubtless, they had to be. For the solutions they propose are not real solutions, the history they touch on is not the actual history, and the world they describe is not the real world.

Note

1. Under attack from a number of quarters, the leadership of Save Darfur has claimed that they were never calling for a military intervention to overthrow the Bashir regime in Khartoum but rather for an international protection force to protect the people of Darfur. Leaving aside whether, in practical terms, this is a distinction without a difference (i.e., that the latter would have required the former, as other pro-Darfur activists like Eric Reeves and Gerard Prunier had the courage to acknowledge), the record of their statements belies this claim.

Critical Thinking

1. What are some of the defects of the task force's report on genocide?

2. What should the international community do to prevent genocide?

3. What is the definition of genocide?

DAVID RIEFF is a New York-based writer and policy analyst who has written extensively about humanitarian aid and human rights. He is the author of eight books, including *A Bed for the Night: Humanitarianism in Crisis* and *At the Point of a Gun: Democratic Dreams and Armed Intervention,* and is currently writing a book on the global food crisis.

From *Policy Review,* February & March 2011, pp. 29–40. Copyright © 2011 by David Rieff. Reprinted by permission of Policy Review, a publication of Hoover Institution, Stanford University, and David Rieff via The Wylie Agency.

UNIT 6

International Political Economy

Unit Selections

Learning Outcomes

After reading this Unit, you will be able to:

- Discuss how the international regulatory framework of the global financial system is being reshaped.

- Explain how the economic geography of global markets has changed since 2008.

- Explain how Greece contributed to the Eurocrisis in the Eurozone.

- Discuss the nature of the sovereign debt crisis in the Eurozone countries.

- Discuss the relationship between dependency and foreign aid.

- Discuss the problems a country like Haiti faces in recovering from a natural disaster.

- Explain the implications of the Eurocrisis for the future of the European Union.

Student Website
www.mhhe.com/cls

Internet References

Eurobarometer
http://ec.europa.eu/public_opinion/index_en.htm
Europa
http://europa.eu.int
International Monetary Fund
www.imf.org
World Bank
www.worldbank.org

As the United States wrestled with the problem of raising the national debt ceiling, which had reached over 14 trillion dollars in 2011, roughly equivalent to the annual gross domestic product of the country, the democratic president and the republican-controlled House of Representatives, found it difficult to agree on a plan to raise the ceiling over $2 trillion. Negotiations went right down to the wire, up to the deadline of August 2, in which the United States would be in default of its debts to its creditors. The republican speaker of the House of Representatives, faced a rebellion within the ranks of his own party, as the more conservative wing of the Republican party wanted a constitutional amendment to balance the budget included in any plan. There was considerable speculation as to what would happen if a default occurred, with the chairman of the Federal Reserve Board warning of catastrophic consequences. At the last minute, a short-term agreement was reached, through 2013, avoiding the issue in the upcoming 2012 elections. However, the instability surrounding the negotiations, contributed to a perception of the United States by other countries as a declining hegemon in the international system. One of the results of this was a downgrading of the United States' credit rating by Standard and Poor from AAA to AA+, although the other two major credit rating agencies, Moody's and Fitch Ratings, maintained the triple A credit rating for the time being. Given the inability of the United States to deal with its national debt problem until the last minute, there were fears that the dollar, as an international currency could weaken, raising concerns that the recovery from the 2008 recession would be placed in jeopardy. There was also concern that foreign investors in U.S. Treasury bonds, such as China, would seek to invest in a less riskier country. China urged that "The global community should improve the communication and coordination of their macro-economic policies to realize sustainable, stable and balanced growth in the world economy." Josef Ackermann, in "The Global Financial System and the Challenges Ahead," drew attention to the fact that ". . . the stabilization of financial markets is a precarious one . . ."

The U.S. financial crisis over the national debt in 2011, also merged with the financial crisis in the Eurozone. The term Eurozone refers to the 17 countries which are members of the European Union, that opted for the Euro to replace their national currencies. When the Euro was adopted, it was viewed as a critical step further in the direction of European integration. Stringent conditions were established for participation in the Eurozone. Obviously, not every country that is a member of the European Union opted for the Euro. For example, the United Kingdom preferred to keep its national currency. In 2010 and 2011, some of the more peripheral members of the European Union, such as Portugal, Ireland, Greece, and Spain, experienced serious financial problems in repaying the debts they had accumulated. The crisis involving the sovereign debt of these countries turned out to be much more difficult to deal with than anticipated. There were also concerns in 2011 that the financial crisis in the Eurozone was spreading to Italy, which had a massive debt, and which would even be beyond the capability of the resources of the European Union to deal with. This was particularly worrisome, given the fact that Italy possessed the seventh

© Comstock Images/Getty Images

largest economy in the world. Even France was in danger of being affected by the sovereign debt crisis in Greece, because some of the largest French banks had extended credit to the Greek government. The globalized nature of the European financial crisis was underscored by the fact that some French banks had also borrowed money from Asian banks. In 2011, some of the Asian banks, reviewing the financial situation, cut back in their loans to the exposed French banks, fearing that some of them might fail. French banks had also borrowed from American banks, further underscoring the globalized nature of the European financial crisis.

The European Union created a special financial facility to deal with spreading financial crisis in the Eurozone. The European Union extended a second financial rescue package to Greece to follow up the first rescue package it provided to Greece in May 2010. A second rescue package was conditioned on the adoption of austerity measures by the Greek government, whose implementation resulted in a considerable amount of turmoil in the country. The role of Germany, which has the most solvent economy in the European Union, is critical in helping to resolve the crisis in the Eurozone. There were differences of opinion between Germany and France, and Germany and the European Central Bank, as to the best way to go about dealing with the financial crisis. Furthermore, the other solvent members of the European Union, such as the Netherlands, Finland, and Austria, were rather reluctant to bail out the mostly southern European insolvent countries, and argued that private creditors should assume more of the financial obligations that were involved. There was some speculation that the future of the Euro itself was at stake, and perhaps even the European Union itself, unless the crisis was resolved in a satisfactory fashion, as the crisis in the Eurozone has called into question the whole European Union enterprise. In "One for All, All for One: The Euro in Crisis" Franco Pavoncello engages in an analysis of the origins of the Euro crisis and discusses how Greece's financial difficulties have called into question the future of the Eurozone.

The bulk of the world's population resides in the third world. Much of this population lives an existence of abject poverty, poor health, and in conditions in which their basic human needs for food, security, and adequate housing are not satisifed. Haiti, which is one of the least developed of the developing nations, suffered a devastating earthquake in January 2010, which killed over 200,000 people. Haiti has received a significant amount of foreign aid to help in its reconstruction efforts, but as Carol Adelman argues in "Haiti: Testing the Limits of Government Aid and Philanthropy," given its dependency on foreign aid, Haiti should focus on "new aid approaches that seek to work from the bottom up, including the local community and the local government."

The Global Financial System and the Challenges Ahead

JOSEF ACKERMANN

We all share an obligation to reflect intensively on the lessons to be drawn from the financial crisis of 2008, but also to find answers to help reduce the chances of a repetition of such events. First and foremost, of course, banks themselves have an obligation to rectify deficiencies revealed by the crisis. Next, it is up to regulators, supervisors, and other policy-makers to put the right framework into place. But to do this in an optimal manner we also need (1) a sound scientific foundation for all the changes to banks' risk-management systems and the regulatory framework, and (2) to make sure that managers have the right mind-set. In the following, I will present a few ideas on what is needed to put the global financial system on a firmer footing. Of course, the natural starting point for such an analysis is the current state of the international financial system.

The Global Financial System: Where Do We Stand?

The global financial system has recovered from the depth of the crisis. The extreme flight to quality observed in the autumn of 2008 has given way to a renewed interest in riskier, higher-yield assets. Stock markets have returned roughly to the levels they had in the summer of 2008. Markets have reopened for companies to issue debt and equity. In fact, at the end of September we witnessed the largest share issuance ever, amounting to USD 70 billion, by Petrobras—tellingly, a company based in an emerging-market country. More importantly, it is significant that even banks are able to tap equity markets again, as Deutsche Bank demonstrated with its EUR 10 billion rights issue in September 2010,[1] showing that investor confidence in financial institutions has returned. Even securitization markets have reopened.

Nonetheless, two observations should be made: first, the stabilization of financial markets is a precarious one. Market sentiment remains volatile and vulnerable to

bad news. Investors continue to be concerned about the strength and stability of the economic recovery. They are worried about lingering public debt crises, which in many countries have followed on the heels of the financial sector bailouts. There is widespread concern about the potential inflationary impact of the loose monetary policies currently pursued by some central banks. No doubt, the recent record-high price of gold reflects these concerns.

Second, and related to the first observation, the extent of stabilization varies. Clearly, concerns about public debt levels are more pronounced in some countries where debt levels are high or rising fast—Greece, Ireland, and Portugal spring to mind—whereas other sovereign issuers, such as Germany, enjoy record-low interest rates or, like many emerging-market sovereigns, are benefitting from substantial capital inflows on the back of rising investor interest in countries with sound finances and positive debt dynamics. Similarly, with regard to financial institutions, there is a growing dichotomy between banks that again have unlimited access to equity, debt, and money markets, and banks that still have to rely on liquidity support from central banks.

Parallel to these market developments, the institutional and regulatory framework for global financial markets is being reshaped. With regard to institutions, new supervisory bodies such as the systemic risk supervisors—the Financial Stability Oversight Council in the United States and the European Systemic Risk Board in the European Union (EU)—are taking up their work. Existing bodies, such as the International Monetary Fund, have reinvented themselves in terms of their tools and policy approaches and are undergoing changes in their governance structures. Moreover, the G20 has officially replaced the G7 as the premier forum for international policy coordination. In terms of rules, the fundamental overhaul of existing framework policies, such as the Basel capital and liquidity requirements, and the creation of entirely new regulatory elements, such as bank resolution and insolvency regimes, will reshape the structure of the financial industry and the way it does business.

Challenges for the Global Financial System

Based on this description of the global financial system, what are the challenges ahead and what is needed to put the global financial system on a firmer footing? Essentially, there are four challenges:

- How can we preserve the integrated nature of the system?
- What are the building blocks for a regulatory framework that is adequate for and commensurate with today's global financial markets?
- In this context, how can we address the question of balancing state intervention and market processes?
- Finally, how should we respond to the shifting economic and political geography in the global economy and, by extension, in global financial markets?

Preserving the Integrated Nature of the Financial System

Not everyone shares the view that preserving an integrated financial system is a desirable aim. Many argue that less market integration would be desirable to increase room for autonomous policy action and to shield national economies from the vagaries of international spillovers in the event of financial disruptions. This view has become increasingly fashionable—not only among the broader populace, but also in policy circles as part of a more general trend of rising opposition to internationalism.

These tendencies are highly disconcerting given that the benefits we draw from integration outweigh the risks by far. Capital market integration, if conducted within an adequate framework, allows for more efficient capital allocation, expands access to funds for firms and households, and lowers financing costs. It also offers people in aging countries faced with the prospects of declining growth rates an opportunity to engage in an intergenerational transfer of wealth by investing their high income of today in dynamic economies, so that they can draw on the returns on these investments in the future.

Capital market integration, if conducted within an adequate framework, allows for more efficient capital allocation, expands access to funds for firms and households, and lowers financing costs.

Last but not least, open, internationally integrated markets are an integral part of open societies. Intensifying links between countries, for instance by integrating capital markets, is one of the channels that binds not only economies, but also societies. Nowhere is this more evident than in the transatlantic arena: half of the foreign assets held by U.S. investors originate in Europe. Likewise, the share of EU investments in U.S. equity stands at almost 40 percent and in U.S. debt securities at nearly one-third of total foreign investments.

In light of these benefits, there is an urgent need to align regulatory approaches to the highest extent possible. It is necessary to create global rules and frameworks. Members of the G20 have solemnly committed themselves to take coordinated action. However, in the recent past, we have seen isolated actions on the part of individual G20 members, a behavior that should not become entrenched.

Building Blocks of the New Regulatory Framework

Saying that regulatory initiatives should be aligned does not, of course, address the question as to *what* is to be aligned. The process of reshaping the regulatory framework has taken almost two years now, and it seems that the key building blocks are now falling into place. A consensus is emerging that the overarching objective of all reforms should be to enhance the resilience of the global financial system. This, in turn, has two dimensions: (1) reduce the probability of shocks to the financial system, and (2) limit the repercussions of such shocks, should they occur.

A consensus is emerging that the overarching objective of all reforms should be to enhance the resilience of the global financial system.

Many of the initiatives currently being pursued do, indeed, follow this overarching objective. With the aim of reducing the likelihood of failure, toughening capital and liquidity requirements is at the heart of these efforts. Overall, it seems that the Basel regulators, with their proposals presented on September 12, 2010, struck the right balance between establishing greater stability through tougher rules and limiting the repercussions on the financial system's capacity to fund growth and innovation. There are still three concerns, though:

- First, the cumulative impact of all regulatory changes must not be underestimated. These changes, of course, go far beyond capital requirements, which are just one instrument that will weigh on banks' capital and profitability, alongside levies, reformed deposit insurance schemes, and higher collateral requirements in derivatives markets, to name only a few.

- Second, while regulators have commendably set long transition periods for attaining the new capital ratios, markets (i.e., investors, counterparties, and rating agencies) may not be so patient. It appears that they are not actually willing to wait until 2019 but want to see the requirements fulfilled as early as 2013. Clearly, this entails the risk that some banks might become overstretched and that the impact on the economy might be more severe than desired.

- Third, some of the measures, such as counter-cyclical buffers and surcharges for systemically important banks, have not been fully fleshed out yet, creating uncertainty as to their impact on banks and the economy.

Among the measures to limit the potential spillover from failures, strengthening market infrastructures is probably the most important one. Trade repositories and the use of central counterparties will make the distribution of risk within the financial system more transparent. In a crisis, this will help to avoid uncertainty, which was one of the causes for the freezing of the money markets and the sell-offs during the last crisis: market participants who are not sure about the health of potential counterparties shy away from trading at all. But stronger market infrastructures will also help when it comes to separating failed institutions from the rest of the system in an orderly fashion. In this sense, stronger market infrastructures complement other instruments—such as recovery and resolution regimes, insolvency regimes, and an obligation to redesign banks' organizational structures—so that systemically important parts (like payment activities, for example) can be easily split off.

Overall, then, there is a sound conceptual framework for increasing the resilience of the global financial system. It is true, as always, that the devil is in the details, but the broad thrust of the current regulatory efforts is right. Having said this, however, it is also undeniable that some of the elements in the current regulatory debate are essentially driven by politics and will contribute little, if anything, to making the financial system more robust. Limiting the size of banks is one such example, financial transaction taxes are another, and the Volcker rule is a third. Such measures may go down well with parts of the electorate but will do more harm than good in economic terms.

Balancing State Intervention and Market Processes

Designing new regulations inevitably entails the question of how to achieve the right balance between market forces and state intervention. It is fair to observe that this balance has shifted in the wake of the crisis toward a greater reliance on hard rules and more extensive intervention rights for the state. This definitely brings to a halt almost three decades of liberalization, deregulation, and a shift towards more principles-based regulation, all of which started in the 1980s.

How far the pendulum will actually swing back, though, remains to be seen. On the one hand, a return to state interventions in the financial markets certainly enjoys strong backing in wide parts of the population. Having gone through the trauma of the financial crisis, the electorate wants greater stability. During the crisis, people also observed that the state was the rock in a sea of market turmoil, the only institution that had the capacity to act in order to address panic and instability.

On the other hand, people are aware of the limits to the power of the state. They know that the financial crisis was preceded by state failure as much as by market failure. They realize that excessive debt increasingly limits a government's capacity to act. At the same time, governments themselves do not appear to be all too inclined to go back to being in command of the economy. This is evidenced, for instance, by their efforts to reprivatize the equity stakes taken in distressed banks as quickly as possible, not least with the aim of reducing their debt levels.

So, all in all, we may not be seeing a full swing of the pendulum, but rather only a partial adjustment. As the jury is still out on this, the final results may very well differ from country to country and will crucially depend on the final costs of the crisis as well as how they are perceived. In any case, we would be well advised to keep the close relationship between regulation and politics in mind, lest we end up with rules that shift the balance in an undesirable way.

In any case, we would be well advised to keep the close relationship between regulation and politics in mind, lest we end up with rules that shift the balance in an undesirable way.

Coming to Grips with the New Economic Geography

The crisis also produced a new economic geography. Anecdotal evidence of this regularly hits the headlines: just think of the reports on China, as the largest foreign creditor of the U.S. government, and how important their interests were in guiding the Bush administration's decisions to rescue government-sponsored entities.[2] Another example is the series of recent reports on how China used its powerful investment position to send a not-too-subtle message in the dispute on global currency issues, by apparently signaling its intention to buy Greek debt to underline its interest in a strong euro, in other words, in a multi-polar currency regime.[3] Or just think of hard facts, such as the USD 4 trillion in sovereign wealth funds, most of which are based in emerging markets. One need only look at the fact that the industrialized countries' share in global GDP has dropped to less than 50 percent—down from two-thirds as recently as the 1990s.

The new economic geography is, of course, not limited to the country level. It is also increasingly being felt at the company level. Six of the top 50 listed companies based on turnover are headquartered in emerging markets. Also, as a corollary to the rise of their home countries, banks from emerging markets are climbing the global league tables. Whereas at the end of 2006, before the start of the crisis, no bank from outside the U.S., Western Europe, or Japan had made it into the top-30 league based on market capitalization, by the end of 2009, banks from these industrialized regions accounted for only 70 percent of banks' global market capitalization. In their place, banks from China and Brazil have entered the top league. Today, four of the world's ten biggest banks by market value are Chinese—in 2004, there was not a single bank from China in that category.

Today, four of the world's ten biggest banks by market value are Chinese—in 2004, there was not a single bank from China in that category.

There is also an intellectual dimension to this, of course: the financial crisis, originating in what was once considered the world's most sophisticated financial market, has, in the eyes of many, severely undermined the credibility of the Western economic model. Paul Volcker got right to the point when he said in an interview in late 2009 that the crisis was "symbolic of the relative, less dominant position the U.S. has, not just in the economy but in leadership, intellectual and otherwise."[4]

What is the right way to deal with these challenges? At the individual company level, the answer remains the same as it always was—by being smarter, better, and more customer-focused than your competitor, whether old or new.

Of course, building a competitive edge also has a public policy dimension. A strong, profitable home base is the foundation of all internationalization strategies. In the European context, with its predominantly small economies, the need to preserve a strong home base highlights the importance of continuing the drive to build a single market for financial services in the EU. Europe must not waver in this effort if it wants to hold on to its chances to seriously compete in the global economy.

Furthermore, the new challengers make it even more important that we do not fall into a trap of our own making when designing new rules for the financial markets. Go-it-alone strategies that may be popular with voters but simply shift business elsewhere are vastly inferior to internationally coordinated approaches, even if these require greater efforts and are harder to achieve initially.

Go-it-alone strategies that may be popular with voters but simply shift business elsewhere are vastly inferior to internationally coordinated approaches, even if these require greater efforts and are harder to achieve initially.

Moving from the level of business and industry to the level of international politics, I believe it is important to integrate the new emerging-market powers into the new system. Broadening the membership in the Financial Stability Forum and the Basel Committee and transferring responsibility for economic governance from the G7 to the G20 were good steps in the right direction. They incorporate the new powers into the disciplined approach of these bodies and give them a proper forum to bring their views to the table. Even if not everything is running smoothly in this context, it is the best chance we have and we need to make the most of it.

Europe is aware of its responsibility in this context. As the largest economic area in the world and issuer of the globe's second most important currency, Europe's contribution to building a stronger, more resilient financial system is crucial. European countries have been the driving force in the G20 process and were also decisive in bringing plans for the International Monetary Fund's governance reform to a successful conclusion. Now, the realignment in governance will have to go hand-in-hand with greater responsibility on the part of emerging-market countries in the shared aim of promoting a healthy, open, and balanced global economy.

Conclusion

The financial crisis has been a watershed event in many respects. But it gives us a chance—or rather, an obligation—to participate in redesigning the global financial system with a view to enhancing its resilience and preserving its efficiency. The challenge is monumental, but it can be managed if we work on it together with drive and imagination, diligence and perseverance.

Endnotes

1. Ulrike Dauer, "Deutsche Bank Seeks EUR9.8B to Buy PostBank, Lift Ratios," *The Wall Street Journal,* September 12, 2010.

2. See, for example, Daniel Drezner, "Bad Debts: Assessing China's Financial Influence in Great Power Politics," *International Security* 34(2) (Fall 2009): 7–45.

3. Maria Petrakis and Natalie Weeks, "China Supports Stable Euro, Strong EU Ties, Wen Says," *Bloomberg Businessweek,* October 3, 2010.

4. James Tyson and Michael McKee, "Volcker Says China's Rise Highlights Relative U.S. Decline," *Bloomberg,* September 29, 2009.

Critical Thinking

1. What are the challenges for the global financial system?

2. What would be the building blocks of the new regulatory framework?

3. What is the role of China in the new economic geography?

JOSEF ACKERMANN is chairman of the management board and the group executive committee of Deutsche Bank. In 1996, Ackermann joined the board of managing directors of Deutsche Bank, where he was responsible for the investment banking division. Prior to Deutsche Bank, he was president of Schweizerische Kreditanstalt (SKA). He is chairman of the board of directors of the Institute of International Finance and a member of the supervisory boards of Shell, Siemens, and Zurich Financial Services.

One for All, All for One
The Euro in Crisis

FRANCO PAVONCELLO

When the Greek government suddenly revealed in late 2009 that it might not be able to honor its debts, a wave of panic spread through the European market: Other countries in distress—Ireland, Spain, Portugal—could suffer the same fate, and the euro and eurozone themselves could possibly collapse.

To avoid sovereign default and financial collapse, Greece needed the help of the European Union—reluctantly granted in a dramatic meeting of the European Council of May 2010, in exchange for a program of strict austerity measures by the Greek government. This meant slashing salaries and pensions, raising taxes substantially, and pushing unemployment to dramatic levels. As the Greek Parliament approved those measures in the spring of 2010, police battled enraged protesters outside in the streets of Athens. It served as a perfect snapshot of Europe's rude awakening.

Wobbling but not yet falling, Greece has raised questions that can't be put off any longer. What can we expect for the eurozone? Can the euro survive, and at what price? What kind of Europe is this crisis going to produce? How did we reach this point?

In the wake of the Second World War, leaders of victorious and defeated European countries alike faced an inescapable realization: If the nations of Europe could not find a way to cooperate, share resources, and prosper together, they would probably find themselves, sooner or later, in another—and this time possibly final—civil war. Thus the postwar integration of Europe began.

The lesson of the "beggar thy neighbor" policies of the 1930s, which turned into the "slaughter thy neighbor" policy of the 1940s, left an indelible image in the minds of all who had lived through it, particularly the founding fathers of modern Europe: Jean Monnet, Robert Schuman, Konrad Adenauer, and Alcide de Gasperi. A new and different Europe was no longer a dream; it was a necessity.

The goal was both strategic and political: to create a supranational entity watching over the destiny of Europeans. The means were economic, because it was by improving economic conditions that the self-interest of Europeans could be promoted without reawakening periodically the destructive nationalism of the various countries bunched so closely together on the continent. This was a strategy that Jean Monnet spelled out clearly when he said, "Europe will not be made at once, nor through a comprehensive architecture, rather it will be made through concrete achievements, creating first of all a sense of objective solidarity." The way to build the new union was through incremental steps toward economic integration that one day would lead to political integration.

The process was sparked by the United States, which made the implementation of the Marshall Plan for the postwar reconstruction of Europe conditional upon the creation of a European common authority to distribute the aid, according to criteria agreed upon by the recipient countries.

This successful collaboration emboldened visionaries like Monnet and Schuman to push forward new cooperative initiatives, most notably the creation of the European Coal and Steel Community, which put management of the iron ores of the Franco-German border under collective control, and which led to the milestone Treaty of Rome in 1957, which in turn set up the Common Market in an effort to establish a Customs Union among the treaty's six original signatories: France, Germany, Italy, Belgium, the Netherlands, and Luxembourg.

The Common Market created economic growth and social progress of unprecedented dimensions. (Italy saw its GDP grow by a stunning eight percent a year between 1958 and 1963.) Its success brought the founding countries closer, generated second thoughts among countries who had originally decided not to join—most notably Britain—and helped seed the collapse of Communism and the birth of globalization.

The process that started with the Treaty of Rome set in motion a constant drive to expand the areas and agenda of collaboration among the member states, producing what Walter Hallstein, the first president of the European Commission, has called "the bicycle theory of the European Union," according to which integration must always keep moving forward, becoming broader and deeper, at the risk of otherwise losing momentum and falling over. The bicycle's forward motion led to important developments regarding the size of the union, the number and scope of its institutions, and the depth of its economic integration. It also encouraged the various countries and European institutions to expand first and find a solution to the problems created by that expansion later.

By 1985, this brand of integration and expansion led to the signing of the Single European Act, which took effect in 1992, introducing the principle of free circulation of capital, services, and people within the union. But the further integration at the level of trade could hardly be achieved without some sort of coordination between the currencies of the countries involved. The open currency markets and the wide fluctuations those markets introduced, coupled with the tendency of the less diligent countries of the union to resort to competitive devaluations, made it increasingly necessary to improve the level of monetary coordination.

Early attempts to create this coordination, following the demise of the Bretton Woods system, had only been partially successful. The European Monetary System, put in place at the end of the 1970s, was seen as too subordinate to the interests of the Deutsche mark, creating serious difficulties for other currencies, which were easy prey to speculative attacks, as in the case of the British pound and the Italian lira in the early '90s. The creation of a single currency became the decisive means of keeping the European bicycle moving along.

The European Monetary System, put in place at the end of the 1970s, was seen as too subordinate to the interests of the Deutsche mark. The creation of a single currency became the decisive means of keeping the European bicycle moving along.

The decision to create a single European currency, implemented by the 1992 Treaty of Maastricht, was one of the most fateful steps taken by Europeans in their history. This decision, in principle strictly a financial one, had enormous political and social implications because it bound together in an unprecedented way the destinies of many European nations, who relinquished one of the most important functions of sovereignty—the control of their own currency and monetary policy—to a supranational entity located outside their national borders. There were two important provisions in the treaty. The first was that members of the European Union had in principle an obligation to join the euro system (except for certain countries, like Great Britain, that received a specific exemption), and that once in the eurozone countries could not leave the euro without also leaving the European Union. The second was that the process of financially bailing out individual countries was expressly forbidden, apart from "exceptional, most serious and temporary circumstances." This was a legal obligation that seriously limited the flexibility of the EU in dealing with potential financial problems.

The creation of the euro created overnight the largest trading area in the world, took away the uncertainty of national currency fluctuation, and made intra-European transactions much easier and cheaper, while also creating a friendlier borrowing environment. The euro also sent a clear message of political commitment and stability: major European countries now accepted a common monetary fate.

At the same time, however, the euro was based on some tenuous assumptions, e.g., that it would be enacted in an "optimal currency area," allowing for the seamless transfer of goods, labor, and capital from one area to the other—an assumption that turned out to be much too optimistic. Furthermore, a common currency among very different national economic realities ran the risk of creating a one-size-fits-all monetary policy, creating tensions between countries positioned along different phases of the economic cycle. In times of crisis, this could clearly lead to "asymmetric shock" that would significantly strain the system.

Whatever the potential problems, however, European countries understood clearly that failing to enter the monetary union would have condemned them to a destiny of instability and bar them from a massive market. The euro was a train they could not afford to miss, and many of these countries made truly heroic efforts to meet the criteria for entrance into the exclusive club. The more profligate candidate members made a commitment to follow a path of rigor and restructuring in order to meet the criteria set in the Maastricht Treaty: inflation up to no more than 1.5 percent a year, a maximum budget deficit of three percent of GDP, and a debt-GDP ratio of less than sixty percent. To reach these goals, many countries had to embark on a strict budgetary policy, cutting waste, reining in government expenditures, privatizing public companies, and extending taxes. The political price for those moves was too high for countries like Italy, Spain, and eventually Greece, and they entered the euro without that deep restructuring.

But the need to enforce the original "Maastricht criteria" was very high on the agenda of more diligent eurozone countries like Germany and the Netherlands, who feared that weaker countries, once they were in the euro, might not maintain the rigorous fiscal behavior they promised as an entry ticket. To mitigate this risk, Germany demanded and was granted a Stability and Growth Pact, which introduced rigid penalties for those states that deviated from the original admissions criteria. The meticulous control by the bureaucracies of Brussels and Frankfurt with respect to these fiscal criteria, which proved difficult to enforce, generated a false assurance in the union that as long as the criteria were respected all was well. In this they failed to see other structural problems that were potentially far more dangerous to the economic stability of the eurozone: the lack of control over the regulation of national financial institutions, the emphasis on demand-side economic expansion connected with financing bubbles, the subservience of national governments to the interests of strong national groups, the inexorable expansion of benefits, and finally the scant attention to the strengthening of productive, competitive sectors of the various eurozone economies.

Whatever the problems lurking down the road, the birth of the euro in January 1999 had the immediate effect of leveling borrowing rates in the various countries. Suddenly countries like Italy and Portugal, which had been able only to borrow at rates tied to those of Germany, found themselves able to borrow money at rates quite similar to those of their more diligent neighbors. The rationale was that, being eurozone countries, they had the weight of the entire continental superstructure behind them.

This created an unprecedented possibility for increased liquidity, with banks happy to lend money to countries selling bonds denominated in euros, gaining a small spread compared to Germany, and discounting those bonds at the European Central Bank. The euro, moreover, benefitted by emerging during a period of strong growth in the world economy, which, following the collapse of the Nasdaq bubble and the 2002 recession, witnessed a massive infusion of liquidity into the international financial system, with the major central banks bringing the cost of money close to zero.

This reinforced substantial global lending, and proved a bonanza for one of the main European growth areas: the banking sector, which in the eurozone is a national affair, regulated and managed on a country-by-country basis.

The various national banks went on a lending spree, to the point that eurozone bank-controlled assets have grown 3.5 times faster than GDP since the inception of the euro, leading to an amazing exposure of the European banking system, an exposure that has yet to be fully digested by the market. (According to Leto Research, as of February 2009, the eurozone banks had a financial exposure of $1.6 trillion to Eastern Europe, $2 trillion to other export-driven countries, and $4.1 trillion to Spain, Italy, Portugal, Greece, Ireland, and France.)

This massive infusion of liquidity and extensive borrowing had important effects for the economies of the eurozone. In particular, it led to a big confidence boost and an ensuing demand boom in the peripheral euro countries, accompanied by a significant rise in wages and benefits. However, the productive capacity of those countries remained imprisoned by rigid labor markets, low productivity, and a growing reduction of their economic competitiveness. Their increased economic activity was instead fueled mainly by the housing sector, which in countries like Spain and Ireland saw the formation of truly spectacular bubbles, with rising private indebtedness and skyrocketing real estate prices.

The end result was increased borrowing by many countries and an exponential growth in government spending aimed at satisfying the demands of labor for wage increases and retirement benefits. This strong, demand-led economic growth insured an increase of taxation that prevented governments from suffering from excessive deficits, allowing politicians to expand benefits to electorally important social groups, all financed by a toxic influx of capital liquidity.

The onslaught of the financial crisis in 2007 and 2008, along with the drying up of liquidity that followed, had devastating consequences for the more exposed eurozone countries. The housing boom ended overnight, leading to massive defaults and leaving European banks with enormous debt exposure and little hope of regaining their loans. The crisis led to a precipitous recession in those economies, a serious shrinking of economic activities, and a slim likelihood of solving the problem by increasing exports, since high labor costs and poor competitiveness made those goods far too expensive. The more vulnerable countries quickly found themselves with double-digit government deficits and public debt greater than their GDP.

The United States had reacted to the drying up of liquidity with a massive infusion of cash into the system to stabilize the financial institutions with much-needed capital. Toxic assets were eliminated from the banks' balance sheets. This was not how Europe reacted to the crisis. Faced with the collapse of the national financial systems, Europe lacked a culture of solidarity that could have made possible the massive influx of liquidity in problem areas; nor did it have a Department of Treasury to pump money into the system. Actually, the worry of the Central Bank at the height of the crisis had more to do with keeping Germany free from inflationary pressures than restoring liquidity to the rest of the eurozone.

Most important of all, because troubled countries could neither devalue nor inflate themselves out of debt, the euro turned out to be a straitjacket. The only way out of debt was thus through fiscal policy, i.e., the reduction of wages and benefits and of government spending, which meant a sharp reduction of demand and a growing recession. The austerity packages that had to be approved led to massive popular demonstrations, general strikes, and at times social unrest.

Although the current use of the acronym "PIGS" has had the effect of treating Portugal, Ireland, Greece, and Spain as various examples of the same problem, the paths those countries took to their financial crises were quite different, namely in terms of the weight of their respective economies within Europe, the dynamics which led to their crises, and their future economic prospects. Ireland is suffering a bank default crisis due to the collapse of the housing bubble and its decision to bail out its banking system with taxpayer money (a decision that led to shock on the part of bond investors who were trying to get rid of their bonds at fifty cents to the dollar). This particular choice has significantly damaged Ireland's fiscal health, quite strong until the crisis, and sent the country into a deep recession.

Spain is also paying the price for a burst housing bubble, along with heavy indebtedness and a consequent banking crisis associated with it—all on top of the loss of its economic competitiveness of the past decade. Portugal is suffering the consequences of a bloated public sector, which tended to buy social peace through debt, and a consequent lack of exporting competitiveness.

In a way, Greece is the extreme case of fiscal irresponsibility—indulging in a spending and consumption binge and granting rises in wages and benefits that were way beyond the economic capacity of the country. This led to spiraling government deficit and public debt, kept hidden through accounting manipulation. It's no wonder that news of Greece's true economic woes, and the government's cry for European help as the only way to avoid national financial disaster, sparked a market panic. Greece provoked the sudden realization that a default of sovereign debt by eurozone countries was possible, if not probable.

As the need for a bailout in Greece came to the table in early 2010, with other distressed countries soon to follow,

the reaction of the European Union, and of Germany in particular, was one of great hesitation and internal political division. The idea of bailing out the "PIGS" was seen as a violation of the Lisbon Treaty and the beginning of the "monetization" of debt in the eurozone with the introduction of collective financial responsibility—exactly what the founding euro treaties had sought to avoid. As a former Bundesbank officer said, "A bailout would be like jumping in a swimming pool without water." Important German ministers were starting to question the possibility and desirability of avoiding the Greek default (in this, echoing the opinion of the German public, which had no interest whatsoever in paying the bills of untrustworthy Southern Europeans who should not have entered the euro in the first place) and began drafting scenarios of a two-tiered European Union, one inside the euro and the other outside.

But the response of the markets to eurozone wavering in the face of potential collapse was hard to misinterpret. The euro declined precipitously, as markets quickly lost confidence in its long-term prospects; and there was a sharp increase of borrowing rates for the peripheral countries, with rates for Greece three times those of Germany.

The prospects of a eurozone breakup, and a taste of the financial consequences this would entail, quickly swept away any hesitation on the part of European leaders, in particular the German chancellor. Germany, with roughly 700 billion euros in loans to the distressed countries, had to put its money where its mouth was. At its historic May 2010 meeting, the European Council and the European Central Bank (ECB), in coordination with the IMF, set up a bailout fund of 750 billion euros, consisting of 440 billion euros in guarantees from eurozone states, an IMF contribution of 250 billion euros, and a 60-billion-euro European debt instrument, allowing the ECB to buy bonds on the open market. To run the operation, the EU set up a new organism, the European Financial Stability Facility (EFSF), with the authority to issue bonds based on those guarantees, and the mission "to provide loans to eurozone countries in financial difficulties, recapitalize banks or buy sovereign debt."

The prospects of a eurozone breakup, and a taste of the financial consequences this would entail, quickly swept away any hesitation on the part of European leaders, in particular the German chancellor. Germany, with roughly 700 billion euros in loans to the distressed countries, had to put its money where its mouth was.

The first loan went to Greece for a total of 110 billion euros, at a rate of five percent a year (rather high for a bailout), in exchange for significant fiscal tightening and budget cuts by the Greek government—truly draconian measures aimed at bringing the country's fiscal deficit in 2011 from thirteen to seven percent. This was stiff medicine for the Greek economy, sending the country deeper into recession and leading to widespread workers' demonstrations and civil unrest.

The enactment of austerity measures was carried out by all the eurozone countries in distress. Italy, Spain, and Portugal took important steps to cut their spending and bring their deficits within sight of the three percent limit by 2012. These measures sent these countries into a recession as well, but a much shallower one than Greece will face in the coming years, and proved sufficient to avoid the need for bailouts, at least for now.

Ireland also undertook a series of steps to cut down its public debt, which had skyrocketed following the government decision to bail out its own banks after the burst of the housing bubble and the bankruptcy of its banking system. The government enacted an unprecedented austerity plan aimed at reducing its fiscal deficit from thirty-two percent of GDP in 2010 to three percent in 2014. This seemed a recipe for misery that led many observers to question the decision to bail out the banking system, but it did not keep Ireland from becoming the second country to demand a bailout, in this case one of 85 billion euros.

The willingness of the larger countries of the eurozone to diverge from a policy of non-intervention in the sovereign debt of the individual members, however, did not come without stern and far-reaching demands.

Germany and France demanded that in return for the new 750-billion-euro aid package, the EU had to put in place much more effective controls on fiscal and broader economic discipline. The enhancement of financial support for member states in distress and increased fiscal and economic coordination and controls have been the two parallel evolving designs of the eurozone summits throughout 2010 and into 2011.

Thus, while there was an agreement to create the European Stability Mechanism, which will work as a sort of European Monetary Fund and will substitute for the EFSF starting in 2013, at the same time Germany and France have increasingly demanded stricter rules of control not only of national fiscal discipline, but also of wider economic policies and national financial institutions. They have seen that worrying about a three percent fiscal deficit while allowing national banks to produce private debt many times greater than a nation's GDP can lead to disaster. To avoid these problems in the future, the European Union in December 2010 created the European Systemic Risk Board to oversee risk in the financial system as a whole, including banks, funds, and other types of financial intermediaries.

At the February 2011 Euro Summit, Germany and France, while reiterating their unwavering support of the preservation of the euro and of honoring sovereign debts, presented a list of far-reaching reforms that gave the full sense of where they want to take the eurozone and the price they attach to their commitment to the financial stability of the European Union. They demanded rules not only for fiscal discipline but also for price competitiveness, including wage stability; minimum rates of investment in research, education, and infrastructure; European-wide rules for dealing with financial institutions at the national level; and a drastic request for a debt brake provision in national constitutions.

The EU has finally accepted, albeit still in a limited fashion, collective financial responsibility as a fundamental instrument to fight fiscal and economic crises. At the same time, the mere creation of a mechanism to offer limited guarantees for debt support might not be the comprehensive solution that Europe needs.

Countries like Greece, Ireland, Portugal, and Spain face a serious problem: now that the consumption and housing bubbles have ruptured, these countries will undergo a long period of recession while being forced to pay high interest rates on their sovereign bonds. This will make their debt situation even worse. It is thus vital for them to see those interest rates reduced. The prospect of spending many years without any hope of growth and better living conditions, while working very hard to send money to foreign creditors as debts keep piling up, will likely produce an untenable political and social situation in these societies. They might simply be forced out of the euro and the EU by sheer exhaustion and loss of hope, and this would be a tragedy for them as well as for the rest of Europe.

At the same time, default and unilateral debt restructuring cannot be tolerated by the eurozone, as it would introduce a level of mistrust and panic that would generate a run to the banks in all the countries of the zone, no matter what their solidity on paper.

The solution lies in finding a middle way between these two imperatives—creating a financial and political mechanism that will make it acceptable for the people of Europe to reduce the debt of countries in distress by replacing high interest bonds with cheaper ones and transferring the cost of this orderly operation to European taxpayers.

It is certainly hard to believe that Europe will allow the present crisis to lead to a demise of the euro. Greece and

Ireland, and more recently Portugal, each face a very difficult situation, and the jury is still out on their capacity to weather the storm politically and economically, but Spain has been able to avoid bailouts and appears to be edging toward stability.

One dividend of the present crisis is that it seems to have forced Europeans to confront the stark reality that a Europe without its Union is a continent without a dream, a fate without hope. Going back to national currency and trade wars, enmity and turmoil is hardly a future to propose to the generations of Europe to come, no matter how difficult the current national financial muddle might be.

Critical Thinking

1. Why was a single European currency created?

2. What were some of the tenuous assumptions on which the euro was based?

3. What are some of the major factors that have caused the crisis in the Eurozone?

FRANCO PAVONCELLO is a professor of political science at, and president of, John Cabot University in Rome. A frequent media commentator on Italian politics, his work has appeared in major international journals, including the *American Political Science Review,* the *British Journal of Political Science,* and the *Parliamentary Monitor.*

From *World Affairs,* May/June 2011, pp. 59–70. Copyright © 2011 by American Peace Society. Reprinted by permission. www.WorldAffairsJournal.org

Haiti: Testing the Limits of Government Aid and Philanthropy

Carol Adelman

aiti is testing the limits of foreign aid, both public and private; it remains to be seen whether successful innovations in philanthropy and public-private partnerships stand a chance on this long-devastated island. There has been a general reinvention of foreign assistance over the last decade that is playing out in countries across the globe. New players have emerged who are testing innovative ways of spurring long-term economic growth to free individuals and nations from dependence on the inefficiencies of foreign aid. Long-time players like major nonprofits and foundations are experimenting with bottom-up, technology-driven solutions that also seek to replace dependence with sustainability. Public-private partnerships are replacing donor-driven models in foreign aid. Many of these actors are also working to involve grassroots organizations in development efforts, believing that locally designed and driven strategies have a greater chance for success. While these new approaches in Haiti promise hope for the future, without much needed good governance, this impoverished country cannot expect long-term growth and prosperity.

What undergirds the new aid efforts in Haiti is the realization that private actors working with private dollars often have more flexibility to demand accountability flexibility and results than government donors have. Through its Index of Global Philanthropy and Remittances, the Center for Global Prosperity measures private financial flows from developed to developing countries. The report has shown that these flows—global philanthropy, remittances, and private capital investment—greatly exceed government aid. They account for some 80 percent of the developed world's economic dealings with developing countries. These private financial flows from the Organisation for Economic Co-operation and Developments (OECD) Development Assistance Committee donor countries amounted to $455 billion in 2009 (the most recent year for which data are available).[1]

What is clear from these numbers is that developed countries provide far more to the developing world through private actors than through government aid. This reflects the diverse, new world of international development where for-profits, nonprofits, religious organizations, universities, families, and individuals are contributing to economic growth in the developing world. The recession that began in 2008 has had a broad impact on global financial flows. Private capital investment fell dramatically in 2008 but recovered nicely in 2009, totaling $228 billion from developed to developing countries. At the same time global philanthropy and remittances remained steady, creating an important lifeline to the world's poor.[2]

The January 2010 earthquake that killed an estimated 230,000 people in Haiti demonstrated once again that global generosity seems to know no bounds. Significant humanitarian relief flowed from both public and private sources. Since the disaster, the United States government has provided $1.2 billion in aid to Haiti.[3] In March of 2010, more than 100 countries pledged $5 billion in short-term aid for Haiti and $10 billion toward long-term reconstruction.[4]

Money also poured into the Haitian relief effort from individuals and corporations around the world. Americans alone gave $774 million within the first five weeks of the earthquake. The response was also faster than ever thanks to SMS technology, which allowed the Red Cross to raise an unprecedented $32 million in $10 donations sent via text message.[5] By mid-May of 2010, private and voluntary organizations reported an astounding $1.1 billion in donations for Haitian relief and the total would eventually reach $1.4 billion.[6]

Of that $1.4 billion, some of the largest amounts went to traditional emergency humanitarian relief and health care organizations: the American Red Cross raised $444 million, Doctors Without Borders raised $124 million, and Partners in Health raised $70 million. Some of the largest donation totals were for faith-based organizations, many of which had a long history of working in Haiti: Catholic Relief Services raised $136 million, World Vision raised $41 million, and the United Methodist Committee on Relief raised $14.5 million.[7]

The disaster resulted in the formation of several philanthropic efforts especially designed to address the Haiti crisis. The Clinton Bush Haiti Fund, founded by former presidents Bill Clinton and George W. Bush, raised a total of $52 million.[8] The high-profile nature of many individuals involved in the relief effort helped raise money, as well as the profile of international philanthropy. The Hope for Haiti telethon, which was televised on numerous television stations in the United States and around the world, featured Hollywood celebrities and performances by Madonna and Bruce Springsteen, raising a total of $66 million. Movie stars also contributed; for example, Sandra Bullock and Leonardo DiCaprio each donated $1 million to the relief effort.[9]

> **What is clear from these numbers is that developed countries provide far more to the developing world through private actors than through government aid.**

Corporations also became involved in the relief effort. As of March 2010, the most recent time for which comprehensive statistics are available, corporations had donated $148 million to relief efforts, made numerous in-kind donations, and launched employee-matching programs. Abbott Laboratories donated $5 million and Bank of America donated $1 million and waived credit card fees on all donations to Haiti earthquake relief. Becton, Dickinson, and Company donated $5 million in medical supplies and GlaxoSmithKline donated $1.8 million in antibiotics. eBay set up a special site where individuals can buy, sell, or donate items with proceeds going to organizations involved in Haitian relief. Microsoft donated $1.25 million in cash, matched employee donations up to $12,000, and mobilized their employee response team to provide technical support to NGOs operating on the ground.[10]

While the outpouring of humanitarian relief for Haiti succeeded in its main goal of keeping many people alive who otherwise would have perished without food, water, or shelter in the aftermath of the disaster, the earthquake complicated an already complex development situation in the country. Prior to the earthquake, Haiti was already the poorest country in the Americas. Despite a constant stream of aid money, little progress has been made against seemingly intractable poverty. The problems that plague Haiti are well known: little economic development, no modern infrastructure, a corrupt and inefficient government, and a population overwhelmed by lawlessness and preoccupied with surviving day-to-day.

Decades of political instability and violence decimated the Haitian economy and left it with a barely functioning government prone to frequent upheavals and a legacy of inefficiency and corruption that permeates every facet of life. Haiti's unemployment rate is believed to be as high as 70 percent; there is little modern manufacturing, energy, or transportation infrastructure.[11] Agriculture is the largest segment of the economy, but most farmers operate at subsistence level. The World Bank ranks Haiti as the 162nd worst place in the world to do business out of 183 economies.[12] Transparency International routinely ranks Haiti as the most corrupt country in the Americas and one of the most corrupt in the world.[13] Approximately 54 percent of the population lives on less than $1 a day and 78 percent on less than $2 a day.[14]

In the aftermath of the earthquake, most of the NGOs in Haiti are still working on basic problems of food supply, sanitation, and shelter. The sheer scope of the disaster and the dual burdens of poverty and corruption have made progress toward recovery slow. The streets of Port-au-Prince are still piled with earthquake debris, although rubble removal is finally proceeding.[15] Stories abound of supplies languishing at the docks while payoffs are sought; endless red tape hampers the distribution of much needed medical and relief supplies. The relief camps that sprung up after the earthquake are still crowded. While structural damage to many homes in the capital was not as bad as first feared, many Haitians are afraid to return home in case of another earthquake. In addition, the camps, which offer schooling, security, clean water and health care, have become somewhat of a magnet in the destabilized country.[16]

Foreign aid, which does not include non-government aid from private sources, accounted for 13 percent of Haiti's GNI in 2008.

For the international development community, Haiti promises to be an interesting test case to see if grassroots entrepreneurial and technology-driven private development solutions will help break the development logjam. But it is clear that past aid solutions for Haiti, no matter how well intentioned, have not worked. Most essential is the

development of the local economy and jobs for the chronically under-employed Haitian population and the strengthening of government and civil institutions. However, a 2006 study by the National Academy of Public Administration calculated that Haiti received $4 billion in foreign aid from bilateral and multilateral sources between 1990 and 1993 with little to show for it in terms of improved governance or quality of life for the Haitian people.[17]

The National Academy of Public Administration (NAPA) study concluded that Haiti had become excessively dependent on foreign aid, which hampered its ability to develop its own economy. Foreign aid, which does not include non-government aid from private sources, accounted for 13 percent of Haiti's GNI in 2008, which is as high as some sub-Saharan African nations such as Congo and Ethiopia.[18] In 2003, per capita aid in Haiti was $23.70, as compared to an average of $9.90 for the Latin America and Caribbean region.[19]

A second problem identified by the NAPA study is the funneling of large amounts of aid through NGOs, which administer most foreign aid programs in Haiti because the government is so inefficient and corrupt. The study concluded that funneling aid through NGOs perpetuated the problem of poverty in Haiti by limiting government and civil capacity building in the country. It also noted that lack of government ownership of aid programs further eroded the legitimacy of government, led to government indifference about the success or failure of programs and contributed to "brain drain" in the country.[20]

The result of large amounts of aid being channeled through a multitude of NGOs in Haiti has led to the burgeoning of the nonprofit sector in the country. According to the World Bank, there were as many as 10,000 private voluntary organizations (PVOs) operating in Haiti before the earthquake, the highest number per capita in the world, leading to Haiti's nickname: The Republic of NGOs. These nonprofits provide the bulk of social services in the country, running everything from schools to hospitals. The National Academy of Public Administration study showed that NGOs were running 80 percent of the social services in the country, which severely limits the ability of the government and private professionals to develop the skills and capacity they need to run the programs themselves.[21] The result, according to the study, is a vicious cycle: donors funnel money through NGOs because they do not trust the government, which further erodes the capacity and legitimacy of the Haitian government, thereby suppressing the country of any chance to build its own future.

Jean Palerme Mathurin, an advisor to former Haitian Prime Minister Jean-Max Bellerive, recently charged that NGOs have "infantilized" Haiti.[22] For instance, Haiti already relies heavily on food imports, much of it funded by foreign aid, its own agricultural sector having been destroyed by cheaper imports, natural disasters, and poor management. The influx of food aid may only further hamper efforts to revive the agricultural economy. Of all the organizations that have flooded the capital since the earthquake, "NGOs are having a huge impact, distorting the economy," says Anne Hastings, CEO of Fonkoze, Haiti's largest microlending institution. Like many who complain about the distorting effects of so many NGOs in the country, she is looking for more transparency and better coordination of efforts.[23]

InterAction, which serves as an umbrella organization for many US based aid agencies, has launched an innovative effort to map the projects of 61 of its member organizations in Haiti. The interactive map sorts projects by geography and type of project. The mapping platform is expected to improve transparency and accountability, facilitate partnerships and coordination among NGOs, and help NGOs and other donors make more informed decisions about where to direct resources.

If there is any hope for Haiti, it may be in new aid approaches that seek to work from the bottom up, involving the local community and local government in planning and implementation, helping to build both ownership and capacity. Technology-driven solutions may also help overcome many of the infrastructure problems endemic to Haiti.

Microfinance is particularly promising in Haiti because there is a weak banking sector and little access to capital. Less than half of all Haitians have a bank account. Fonkoze, with 45 clients and 43 branches, is Haiti's largest microfinance provider. It is pioneering innovative microfinance solutions to help its customers recover from the earthquake and rebuild sustainable livelihoods. After the earthquake, Fonkoze used funding from the Red Cross, the MasterCard Foundation, and MercyCorps to write off the loans of 10,000 of its clients who lost their livelihoods. It gave each client a one-time payment of $125 to help with their recovery and will provide new loans when the clients are ready to resume their businesses. It has enlarged a special loan program that provides micro-micro loans of $25 for a short period of time and increased literacy and health classes to provide additional support to borrowers. For clients who are too poor to even qualify for the micro-micro loan program, it has created a program that gives clients goats or chickens so they can sell milk or eggs and provides them with a stipend of about $7 per week so they do not eat their businesses.[24]

The MasterCard Foundation is convinced that Fonkoze's approach to microfinance—which includes comprehensive mentoring, literacy training, and financial education—has the potential to make a real difference in Haiti. After the earthquake, it committed $4.5 million to the organization to help rebuild its devastated headquarters and staff and to extend its efforts to rural communities to help small businesses and local trading activities.[25]

According to David Owens, VP of corporate development for World Vision, "Haiti was a catalyst for American companies to look at broader and deeper ways they could partner with aid groups that are on the front lines." The US Chamber of Commerce's Business Civic Leadership Center (BCLC) has also seen an uptick in interest from corporations that are interested in being involved in Haiti's growth. "We have seen that Haiti rebuilding is a catalyst for corporations to offer both financial support as well as sector expertise," explained Stephen Jordan, BCLC's Executive Director. BCLC is working with Executives without Borders to establish the Haiti Business Corps to make it make it easier for companies to leverage their talent and expertise to contribute to the long-term redevelopment of Haiti.[26]

Coca-Cola has announced the $7.5 million Haiti Hope Project, which will bring together a team of business, government, and civil society partners to help 25,000 Haitian mango farmers increase production and access to markets. Coca-Cola's local bottling partner is the largest private-sector employer in Haiti. As part of the project, 100 percent of the profits from the new Odwalla Haiti Hope Mango Lime-Aid will go toward the effort. "The Haiti Hope Project exemplifies the innovative role that partnerships with the private sector can play in the reconstruction of Haiti," said former President Bill Clinton.[27]

NGOs are also harnessing technology to aid in rebuilding and long-term development. In the first step toward a national mobile money system in Haiti, MercyCorps is using cell phones to deliver aid wirelessly to earthquake victims. The national launch of the T-cash system is expected to greatly increase access to banking services for the 50 percent of the Haiti population that does not have access to bank accounts.[28] Fonkoze is also using mobile phones to help Haitians access financial services. It has developed a system to allow Haitians living in the United States to send unlimited remittances to their relatives back home using mobile phones. Haitians redeem the money at local Fonkoze branches, where they can deposit some of the money into savings accounts.[29]

If there is any hope for Haiti, it may be in new aid approaches that seek to work from the bottom up, involving the local community and local government

Traditional PVOs are also looking toward the future. Mindful of the impact of continued free food deliveries on the local economy, Catholic Relief Services has begun ramping up cash-for-work projects that allow Haitians to purchase food in local markets rather than rely on handouts. It is currently paying workers to clean out one of the major canals in Haiti and is employing 25 Haitians in building transitional housing for their fellow countrymen.[30] MercyCorps is using the cash-for-work approach to employ some 28,000 Haitians in Port-au-Prince's tent camps and in rural communities of the Central Plateau. Given Haiti's historic reliance on imports rather than locally produced goods, the program can only maintain the existing economy, however, and will not have the ability to contribute to the long-term development of a healthy economy. Mercy Corps currently has projects underway to rehabilitate market feed roads and improve farmland to establish the infrastructure Haiti needs to develop its agricultural economy. Mercy Corps is also starting a small and medium enterprise (SME) development program that will engage mentors from the Haitian diaspora and the international business community to provide support and training to 500 entrepreneurs around the country.[31]

While these approaches are promising, the National Academy of Public Administration concluded that little could be done to move Haiti forward in the absence of a stable, working government. In terms of projects that would help move the country forward, it recommended that donors fund sustainable projects, such as "creating an irrigation system that helps farmers compete in food markets, the returns from which allow farmers to maintain the irrigation system with their own resources."[32] It also recommended focusing on programs that build local capacity, fight corruption, and have measurable outcomes.

Innovative philanthropy and public-private partnerships, focusing on local ownership, entrepreneurship and creative new uses of technology may have some immediate answers for Haiti economic well being. However, without a transparent and accountable government even the most innovative projects will be hampered in creating long-term economic growth in Haiti.

Notes

1. Center for Global Prosperity, *The Index of Global Philanthropy and Remittances 2011* (Washington, DC: CGP, 2011), 15.

2. Ibid.

3. USAID Fact Sheet #6, Haiti-Earthquake, 19 November 2010, www.usaid.gov/our_work/humanitarian_assistance/disaster_assistance/countries/haiti/template/fs_sr/fy2011/haiti_eq_fs06_11-19-2010.pdf.

4. Howard LaFranci, "UN Haiti conference: more than 100 countries pledge $15 billion," Christian Science Monitor, 31 March 2010, www.csmonitor.com/USA/Foreign-Policy/2010/0331/UN-Haiti-conference-more-than-100-countries-pledge-15-billion.

5. Center for Global Prosperity, The Index of Global Philanthropy and Remittances 2010 (Washington, DC: Hudson Institute, 2010), 6.

6. "$1.1 billion donated for Haiti relief," *The Chronicle of Philanthropy*, 11 May 2010. The $1.4 total is as of 9 July 2010, the most recent date for which totals are available from the Center on Philanthropy at Indiana University. See www.philanthropy.iupui.edu/research/disaster.aspx.

7. "$1.1 billion donated for Haiti relief," *The Chronicle of Philanthropy*.

8. "Rebuilding for Strength to Survive and Thrive," Clinton Bush Haiti Fund, www.clintonbushhaitifund.org

9. Agnes Teh, "Boy, 7, raises $240,000 for Haiti appeal," CNN.com, 26 January 2010; Charlie's Fundraising for Haiti page, JustGiving, www.justgiving.com/CharlieSimpson-HAITI.

10. "Haiti Earthquake 2010: Corporate Citizenship in Action," Business Leadership Civic Center, accessed 27 December 2010, http://bclc.uschamber.com/programs/disaster/corporate-donations-response-earthquake-haiti.

11. "Haiti: Economy Overview," CIA World Factbook, accessed 28 March 2011, www.cia.gov/library/publications/the-world-factbook/geos/ha.html.

12. "Doing Business in Haiti," World Bank, accessed 28 December 2010, www.doingbusiness.org/data/exploreeconomies/haiti.

13. Transparency International, Corruption Perceptions Index 2009, accessed 28 December 2010, www.transparency.org/policy_research/surveys_indices/cpi/2010/results.

14. World Bank, "Country Brief: Haiti," http://web.worldbank.org/WBSITE/EXTERNAL/COUNTRIES/LACEXT/HAITIEXTN/0,,contentMDK:22251393~pagePK:1497618~piPK:217854~theSitePK:338165,00.html

15. Deborah Sontag, Weary of Debris, "Haiti Finally Sees Some Vanish," *New York Times*, 17 October 2010.

16. William Booth and Mary Beth Sheriden, "Funding delays, housing complexities slow Haiti rebuilding," *Washington Post*, 26 November 2010.

17. Terry F. Buss, *Why Foreign Aid to Haiti Failed* (Washington, DC: National Academy of Public Administration, 2006).

18. OECD Aid Statistics, Recipient Aid Charts, accessed December 10, 2010, www.oecd.org/dataoecd/62/26/1877775.gif; www.oecd.org/dataoecd/18/31/1901167.gif; www.oecd.org/dataoecd/21/7/1880804.gif.

19. Buss, *Why Foreign Aid to Haiti Failed*.

20. United States Institute of Peace, "Haiti: A Republic of NGOs?", accessed 20 November 2010, www.usip.org/files/resources/PB%2023%20Haiti%20a%20Republic%20of%20NGOs.pdf

21. Buss, *Why Foreign Aid to Haiti Failed*.

22. Jose de Cordoba, "Aid spawns backlash in Haiti," *Wall Street Journal*, 12 November 2010.

23. Tom Chiarella, "The NGO Conundrum: Is Haiti's Future a Republic of Aid?," accessed 15 November 2010, www.esquire.com/blogs/politics/haiti-ngo-coordination-bill-clinton#ixzz180P3RR5r.

24. Daniel Costello, "Can Microlending Save Haiti?," *New York Times*, 13 November 2010.

25. Reeta Roy, "Helping Haitians to Rebuild and Restart the Economy," *Philanthropy News Digest*, accessed 15 November 2010, http://foundationcenter.org/pnd/commentary/co_item.jhtml?id=301000001.

26. "Haiti Quake a 'Game Changer' for Corporate Philanthropy," *PR Newswire*, 31 August 2010, www.prnewswire.com/news-releases/haiti-quake-a-game-changer-for-corporate-philanthropy-101882143.html.

27. "The Coca-Cola Company Announces $7.5 Million Haiti Hope Project To Boost Incomes Of 25,000 Mango Farmers In Haiti," Coca-Cola press release, 31 March 2010, www.thecoca-colacompany.com/dynamic/press_center/2010/03/the-coca-cola-company-announces-75-million-haiti-hope-project-to-boost-incomes-of-25000-mango-farmer-1.html.

28. Cameron Peake, "Celebrating the Launch of Mobile Money in Haiti," accessed 15 December 2010, www.mercycorps.org/cameronpeake/blog/22893.

29. Nicholas Kristof, "I've Seen the Future (In Haiti)," *New York Times*, 4 December 2010.

30. Michael Hill, "Taking the Long View for Haiti," Catholic Relief Services, accessed 20 November 2010, http://crs.org/haiti/recovery-transition.

31. Brian Oakes, "Assessing Mercy Corp's Cash-for-Work Program in Haiti," accessed 20 November 2010, www.mercycorps.org/countries/haiti/22856.

32. Buss, *Why Foreign Aid to Haiti Failed*.

Critical Thinking

1. What can the international community do to improve the implementation of foreign aid in Haiti?

2. What conditions existed in Haiti before the earthquake that made it difficult to rebuild?

3. What can be done to prepare for natural disasters like the Haitian earthquake?

CAROL ADELMAN is the Director of the Center for Global Prosperity (CGP) at Hudson Institute where she lectures, writes, and advises media on economic growth, foreign aid, global philanthropy, and international healthcare issues. She served as Vice Chairman of the Advisory Committee on Voluntary Foreign Aid for USAID from 2007–2009. Over the past 30 years, Adelman has served as director, consultant, and member in numerous nonprofit organizations, including the Center for International Private Enterprise of the US Chamber of Commerce, the Atlantic Council, the Council on Foreign Relations, and the American Red Cross.

UNIT 7
Global Environmental Issues

Unit Selections

Learning Outcomes

After reading this Unit, you will be able to:

- Discuss the dangers which climate change poses to human security.

- Explain why intergovernmental efforts to limit the greenhouse gases that cause climate change have failed.

- Discuss how a coalition of willing actors can make climate changes without a multilateral treaty.

- Determine what steps can be taken to persuade China to participate in a climate coalition of the willing.

- Explain why it is a challenge to involve pro-climate actors from the developing world in a climate coalition of the willing.

- Discuss the effects of Japan's nuclear disaster on nuclear agendas and policies in countries around the world.

- Explain why the global food system is breaking down.

- Discuss the relationship between food security and revolution and turmoil in developing countries.

Student Website

www.mhhe.com/cls

Internet References

Arctic Map
    http:geology.com/world/arctic-ocean-map.shtml
Food and Agricultural Organization
    www.fao.org
The International Atomic Energy Agency (IAEA)
    www.iaea.org
RealClimate
    www.realclimate.org
World Food Program
    www.wfp.org

Climate change is certainly the most important global environmental problem the international community faces, and one that the global environmental governance mechanisms have not yet been able to resolve. The scientific community has developed different models that attempt to predict the effects of the warming climate, which is caused by the release of greenhouse gases into the atmosphere. This has the effect of melting glaciers and ice sheets in Greenland and Antarctica, which can cause a rise in sea level affecting thousands of kilometers of coastlines around the world. The melting of the Arctic sea has geopolitical implications and will have effects on the exploitation of oil in the Arctic. The melting of the ice in Canada's fabled Northwest passage will allow goods to be shipped from Europe to Asia and Asia to Europe, subtracting thousands of miles from the traditional sea routes. Arctic states, such as Russia, are staking out their claims to adjacent continental shelves and seabeds in order to exploit the large amounts of energy that are available there.

Other effects of warming can result in droughts and famines in some regions of the world. For example, in July 2011, the Food and Agriculture Organization declared the existence of a famine in the southern part of Somalia. The food security system in Somalia has been compounded by the conflicts raging there over the past few decades, making it difficult for international aid workers to deal with the problem. International aid workers and organizations, which have been targeted by the various factions fighting each other in the ongoing conflicts is Somalia, have been reluctant to work in the country. The drought taking place throughout East Africa in 2011 will affect the lives of at least 11 million people, according to UN agencies. While famine stalks East Africa, Lester Brown, in his article on the geopolitics of food, points out that states like China and South Korea are renting large tracts of land in Africa to produce food for their own populations, while Africans starve. Brown also raises alarms about the rise in the price of food such as wheat and about the diminishing amount of food on reserve, despite the green revolution. The harmful effects of climate warming can result in desertification, killer storms such as hurricanes and typhoons, and devastating floods.

Nonetheless, the international community still has not been able to negotiate a binding treaty that will control the amount of greenhouse gases emitted by countries into the atmosphere, as a follow-up to the Kyoto Protocol, elements of which expire in 2012. Most importantly, the Obama administration has taken the position that it does not support the negotiation of a binding treaty dealing with climate warming. Thomas Hale writes in

© NRC File Photo

"A Climate Coalition of the Willing," that given the failure of intergovernmental efforts to come up with a treaty, a coalition of a wide assortment of actors from the international, national and sub-national levels of states, can come up with a second best effort to mitigate the effects of climate change without a multilateral treaty.

The earthquake, which occurred in Japan measured a magnitude of 9.0, was the worst that had occurred in the history of the country. The earthquake was also followed by a Tsunami, which wreaked havoc on a Japanese nuclear facility, located at Fukushima, resulting in the release of radioactive debris into the surrounding environment. The tragedy was compounded by the reluctance of Japanese officials to be open about what had really happened at the nuclear facility and especially about the dangers that stemmed from the damage of the facility. The nuclear disaster in Japan, also had implications for a number of other countries that rely on nuclear power. Germany for example, announced it would phase out the use of nuclear power. The European Union engaged in a review of its standards and guidelines that regulated the use of nuclear powerplants. Obviously, Japan's nuclear disaster has widespread international implications. As Caroline Jorant points out, "Fukushima will reshape nuclear agendas and policies in countries around the world."

A Climate Coalition of the Willing

Thomas Hale

Intergovernmental efforts to limit the gases that cause climate change have all but failed. After the unsuccessful 2010 Copenhagen summit, and with little progress at the 2010 Cancun meeting, it is hard to see how major emitters will agree any time soon on mutual emissions reductions that are sufficiently ambitious to prevent a substantial (greater than two degree Celsius) increase in average global temperatures.

It is not hard to see why. No deal excluding the United States and China, which together emit more than 40 percent of the world's greenhouse gases (GHGs), is worth the paper it is written on. But domestic politics in both countries effectively block "G-2" leadership on climate. In the United States, the Obama administration has basically given up on national cap-and-trade legislation. Even the relatively modest Kerry-Lieberman-Graham energy bill remains dead in the Senate. The Chinese government, in turn, faces an even harsher constraint. Although the nation has adopted important energy efficiency goals, the Chinese Communist Party has staked its legitimacy and political survival on raising the living standard of average Chinese. Accepting international commitments that stand even a small chance of reducing the country's GDP growth rate below a crucial threshold poses an unacceptable risk to the stability of the regime. Although the G-2 present the largest and most obvious barrier to a global treaty, they also provide a convenient excuse for other governments to avoid aggressive action. Therefore, the international community should not expect to negotiate a worthwhile successor to the Kyoto Protocol, at least not in the near future.

This, however, does not mean the world must resign itself to the dangerous ramifications of climate change, nor accept the limitations imposed by domestic politics in Beijing and Washington. By constructing a coalition of willing actors, the international community can make second-best, but still worthwhile, progress toward mitigating climate change without a multilateral treaty. Such a coalition would include all the countries, regions, provinces, states, cities, and towns who want to make progress toward limiting greenhouse gases. It should also include various governmental agencies e.g. environmental regulators, energy policy-makers, and transportation officials as well as private actors ranging from corporations to civil-society groups. Finally, it should allow individuals to do their part too. Many of these actors, ranging from the

European Union to New York City, from the U.S. Environmental Protection Agency to the Chinese Ministry of Environmental Protection, from Walmart to perhaps the reader of this article, already have done their part, in hundreds if not thousands of GHG mitigation programs and projects. Together, these initiatives constitute what political scientists might call the "regime complex" for the climate that is, the totality of governance initiatives, public and private, big and small, that seek to limit GHGs.[1]

With the multilateral approach deadlocked, policymakers and civil-society advocates need to turn to this larger range of governance tools and work to increase their ambition, scope, and effectiveness. A critical mass is necessary. By summoning a coalition of the willing for the climate, political leaders can take non-multilateral approaches to a scale where they can both make a substantive difference in the fight against climate change and lay the groundwork for a possible rebirth of the multilateral approach.

The Breakdown of Climate Multilateralism

It is important to understand why the intergovernmental approach is no longer sufficient. First, consider its record. Since the Rio Earth Summit of 1992, almost every country in the world has met regularly to coordinate a global response to climate change. Two decades of this multilateralism, under the United Nations Framework Convention on Climate Change (UNFCCC), have resulted in exactly one treaty requiring GHG reductions the 1997 Kyoto Protocol that committed rich nations to a miniscule five percent average reduction in emissions relative to 1990 levels. Even this proved too much for the United States, which refused to adopt the protocol, and indeed for many signatories such as Canada that are failing to meet their commitments. Developing countries faced no requirements at all.

Kyoto, which expires in 2012, was meant to pave the way for more significant cuts, but that goal remains distant as the breakdown in Copenhagen and continuing inaction in Cancun demonstrate. This is not to say that the UNFCCC process has not been useful indeed, it is absolutely essential, coordinating scientific knowledge about the issue, establishing a global carbon-trading mechanism, placing the issue at the top of the international agenda, etc. but the principal goal, preventing catastrophic climate change, is the only one that ultimately matters.

To be fair, no one expected the problem to be solved easily. Collective action problems tend to be more difficult when the number of actors is high, costs are proximate and clear while the benefits are distant and diffuse, and individuals have strong incentives to free ride on the sacrifices of others. By these measures, climate change is perhaps the toughest collective action problem society has ever faced. But even these issues could be overcome with strong leadership from the major powers. Unfortunately, domestic politics prevent the two countries that contribute more to climate change than any others, the United States and China, from adopting the international obligations required by the multilateral approach. Consider each in turn.

One might think that, with the Democrats in control of both Congress and the White House for the last two years, political conditions in the United States have been optimal for climate legislation. But that is wishful thinking, for two reasons. First, climate is not just a partisan issue. Although Republicans are almost unanimous in their opposition to firm caps on carbon reductions, Democrats face dissent within their ranks from members representing conservative, energy-intensive, or agricultural states. This imbalance is rooted in the Constitution of the United States. Although Senate action is required to ratify any international treaty, Senate votes are awarded equally to the 50 states, not weighted by population, meaning that less populated, carbon-dependent rural interests tend to disproportionately dominate.[2] And even in the House, climate legislation passed by only seven votes, with 43 Democrats joining the Republican opposition.

Second, on top of this structural bias, the U.S. political system has recently showed little capacity for far-reaching change. A culture of partisan obstructionism has brought public business to a standstill. Because the Obama administration needs to spend vast amounts of political capital to get anything through Congress, it has prioritized health care and job creation over climate change. The locus of this dysfunction is, again, the Senate, where a de facto super-majoritarian rule and a 59–41 partisan divide have made it impossible to pass ambitious legislation. With Republicans taking control of the House, climate legislation is unlikely to surface for at least two years.

The domestic politics of climate in China are less transparent than in the United States, but the outcome is equally clear. It is common to portray the Chinese Communist Party as an all-powerful ruler that could dictate changes in emissions policy tomorrow, if it decided to. In some sense, though, the party is even more constrained than the Obama administration. According to the Institute of Environmental Economics at Renmin University, the cost of strict emissions reductions would amount to about seven percent of GDP in 2050.[3] In the eyes of Party leaders, these costs are incompatible with maintaining the rising standard of living to which urban Chinese have become accustomed. Worse, they are incompatible with the rapid job creation needed to employ the millions of Chinese moving from the countryside to the cities. For a party judged largely

on economic performance, policies that threaten to reduce annual GDP growth below some minimal threshold commonly believed to be about eight percent would put the very stability of the regime into question.

It is also important to note the regional and sectoral dynamics at play within China. China's dynamic export sector requires cheap energy and is agnostic about its source. This is not true of China's enormous state-owned coal industry, concentrated in the central northern regions of the country. In poor provinces such as Shanxi and Inner Mongolia, coal is one of the most important industries. This concentration ensures that China's coal industry which provides more than half the country's energy needs has a strong voice at the national level, including among top leaders. The Party is no doubt reluctant to induce economic disaster in poor, politically important areas of the country. In addition, provincial governments retain enormous power over policy implementation, and are adept at resisting national policies through half-hearted implementation and misreporting. Such tactics have done much to undermine environmental regulation in China generally. For Beijing to overcome these habits, it would have to invest significant political capital in badgering regional governments to reduce emissions.

At the same time, it is true that Chinese leaders increasingly fear the costs climate change will impose on China and their hold on power in the future. As the government's own National Climate Change Assessment Report makes clear, many of China's largest and most productive cities sit in low-laying coastal areas vulnerable to sea-level rise and typhoons. The north and center of the country face the opposite problem: already struggling to find enough water for agriculture, industry, and personal use, they would become even drier.[4] For these reasons, China has taken ambitious measures to reduce the carbon intensity of its growth, and hopes to turn the climate-change threat into an opportunity by becoming the world leader in green technology and manufacturing.[5]

Unfortunately, none of this changes the fundamental political calculus in Beijing. Climate change will hurt China and the Communist Party a good deal in the future, and there are benefits to developing green technology now, but the costs of taking serious action in the near term remain unacceptably high. Given a choice between paying now or paying later, China's autocrats seem to make the same choice as elected officials in the United States.

Not only are both the United States and China blocked internally from taking action on climate change, these domestic blockages also reinforce each other. At a time of stress in Sino-U.S. relations, proponents of cutting greenhouse gases in both countries cannot be seen as capitulating to the other side. The U.S. Senate has firmly signaled its opposition to any deal that does not include countries such as China. And China committed to a rhetoric of fairness, developing country solidarity, and nationalism will not move unless the United States (which has a GDP per capita seven times that of China, emits four times as much carbon per person, and historically has emitted four times as much overall) does as well.[6]

Beyond Intergovernmental Approaches

A global treaty of the kind sought at Copenhagen and Cancun would be the best way to combat climate change. It would ensure participation at the scale needed to solve the problem and limit free riding. Such an approach has worked before; just before embarking on the UNFCCC process, the world created a multilateral regime to reduce ozone depletion. In the landmark 1987 Montreal Protocol, rich countries agreed to phase out ozone-damaging pollutants, poor countries were offered the funding and technology needed to comply, and today the ozone hole over Antarctica is closing while the world is less concerned about life-threatening radiation from the sun.[7]

But the best way is not always available. Multilateral efforts to regulate other environmental concerns such as forests and fisheries have also been stalled since the 1992 Rio Summit. In both these areas, however, rather than simply despairing at the lack of intergovernmental progress, concerned civil-society groups and corporations have created transnational regulations of their own. They have developed voluntary standards for sustainability and monitoring mechanisms to make sure the corporations that adopt the standards follow them. Corporations whose adherence to these standards, is confirmed by independent auditing agencies, may attach labels to their products to attract green-minded consumers and investors. The largest initiatives in these areas, the Forest Stewardship Council and the Marine Stewardship Council, each now covers about five percent of the world market in forests and fisheries, respectively.

Tools such as these are part of a rise in new forms of transnational governance. Private regulation, market mechanisms, networks of ostensibly domestic government agencies, multi-stakeholder partnerships, and other governance tools are joining traditional state-to-state international organizations. In the health field, partnerships such as the Global Fund and the Global Alliance for Vaccines and Immunizations, in which public and private actors cooperate to provide medicines to the poor, are now among the most important global institutions. In fields as diverse as economic regulation and counterterrorism, informal networks of government officials, not treaty-based international organizations, are the key actors.

Transnational governance has also exploded in the climate realm. A forthcoming report sponsored by the Leverhulme Trust identifies some 60 examples of "transnational climate governance," though the actual number is likely much higher. The C-40 network, for instance, brings together 40 of the world's largest cities to tackle climate change through specific reductions commitments.[8] The E-8 is a similar network among the world's largest electricity companies. The Worldwide Fund for Nature runs a Climate Savers program in which some of the world's largest companies including IBM, Coca-Cola, Nokia, and others commit to reducing their emissions. The Investor Network on Climate Risk is a group of investors with some $9 trillion in assets looking to invest in companies that monitor climate-related risk.[9] There are also hundreds, if not thousands, of "unilateral" actions by municipal and sub-national governments that seek to "think globally, act locally."[10]

Of course, not all of these programs are effective. Some amount to little, while others simply reinforce good behavior that would have happened anyway. And even if they were all perfect, they remain too ad hoc and limited in scope to dent the massive problem of climate change. Existing programs need to be strengthened and expanded, and more actors need to get involved. The challenge for policymakers, then, is to assemble a large enough coalition to bring these initiatives and others like them to scale.

Toward a Coalition of the Willing

Who would a coalition of the willing for the climate include? If we look only at nation-states, the balance of power between climate leaders (e.g. Europe, small islands) and laggards (e.g. the United States, China) seems tilted to the latter. But a closer look reveals that, even in these states, sub-national governments, states, provinces, cities, towns often have substantial discretion over policy choices which bear heavily on climate change. California, for example, can set its own vehicle emissions standards, which other states can choose to adopt. Although not all countries give their sub-units such powers, even more centralized countries grant localities significant discretion over transportation policy, power generation, and other climate priorities.

At this level of analysis, the United States as a whole has been much more proactive than Washington. The West Coast, Midwestern, and Northeastern states have each developed regional climate action plans which call on states to take concrete steps to limit GHGs. Some states have committed to specific reductions. The Northeastern states jointly aim to reduce carbon emissions by 10 percent by 2019, California by 25 percent by 2020. They are joined by the more than 1,000 mayors, representing some 86 million Americans, who have signed the U.S. Conference of Mayors' Climate Protection Agreement, pledging their cities to uphold the Kyoto Protocol voluntarily. A 2008 study estimated that existing sub-national initiatives in the United States, if fully complied with, could stabilize U.S. emissions at 2010 levels by 2020.[11]

National governments are not unitary monoliths either. In the United States, the Senate has blocked climate legislation, but the Environmental Protection Agency (EPA) has significant authority to regulate GHG emissions without congressional approval. And under President Obama, the federal government, the nation's single largest emitter, has itself become a climate leader. The President has ordered the government, including the military, to reduce its carbon footprint by 28 percent by 2020.[12]

There is similar support from important governmental actors in China. The national Ministry of Environmental Protection lacks the authority of the EPA, but has considerable scope to develop voluntary programs or other pro-climate initiatives. As long as it and other agencies and sub-national units do not cross the interests of powerful economic actors, they have considerable scope to reduce Chinese emissions for example, by embracing carbon-trading and technology-transfer schemes.

Indeed, municipal governments including Beijing and Tianjin have created voluntary carbon exchanges.

When one looks at private actors, there are even more possibilities. Some of the largest firms, including energy giants such as BP, have taken concrete steps to reduce their impact on the climate. Exelon, the largest U.S. utility company, has taken the drastic step of breaking with the International Chamber of Commerce on this issue, so as to disassociate itself from climate laggards. And Walmart, which, if it were a country, would be China's fifth or sixth largest export market, has told its suppliers it will be looking at their emissions. Market incentives from green consumers and investors can combine with enlightened corporate leadership and the threat of future regulation to push industry toward sustainability. Civil-society groups and not just the usual environmental ones are also taking the lead. For example, the Catholic Climate Covenant asks individuals to take the "St. Francis Pledge" to reflect on their impact on the climate and take actions to reduce their personal emissions.

Last, we should not forget the individuals all over the world who want to do their part for the climate they will leave their children. A December 2009 poll commissioned by the World Bank found that most individuals in the 15 countries surveyed were willing to do more and pay more to reduce climate change, including 55 percent of Indians, 62 percent of Americans, and 82 percent of Chinese.[13]

How Would It Work?

To make a difference, existing transnational and sub-national climate governance programs are going to have to get much bigger. As mentioned earlier, non-multilateral initiatives in areas such as forests and fisheries have made a difference for the firms and regions which participate, but not across the entire world. Fortunately, a clear majority of the world wants to do something about climate change. But how can the various climate leaders which together represent enormous slices of the global population and economy, wielding substantial political power coordinate outside a multilateral process that, because they are not necessarily sovereign states, disenfranchises them?

First, top political leaders should use their convening power to summon all willing parties into a global coalition for the climate. Only top political leaders for example, the heads of state of the G-20 have the standing to convene a coalition vast enough to make an appreciable difference. This recruitment must go beyond simply calling for participation; top political leaders should wield their prestige and influence to press key actors to join. Hosting a business roundtable on climate at the White House, Zhongnanhai, and other executive seats would be a good first step.

Involving pro-climate actors in the developing world will be a particular challenge. Existing programs, such as those cited earlier, are concentrated in wealthy countries because these societies tend to have stronger civil-society groups, a longer experience with voluntary regulation or other innovative governance mechanisms, and more stringent environmental regulations. Because future emissions will come mostly from the developing world (which will surpass the industrialized countries by 2018), this chasm must be broken if the coalition is to succeed.[14]

One way to engage the developing world is, perhaps ironically, to link the "bottom-up" approach with the UNFCCC itself. Although the coalition will not be a treaty organization, because it will include many non-sovereign actors without formal standing under international law, it should nevertheless be recognized and endorsed by the world body. This "nested" institutional design would enhance the legitimacy of the coalition and inject some needed dynamism into the multilateral process.

Second, members of the coalition will be expected to reduce emissions by choosing from a range of instruments some legally binding, some enforceable through "soft" measures such as transparency and market tools, and some merely aspirational. Different tools are appropriate for different kinds of actors, such as:

- "Mini-lateral" treaties: Ambitious countries could reach a separate climate deal without laggards. A limited treaty among, say, the European Union and leading developing countries such as Brazil and India could help a number of countries commit to substantial reductions. Such a club would be particularly effective if wealthy nations were willing to offer substantial adaptation aid and technology transfers through this mechanism.

- Unilateral regulation: A number of governments such as the European Union and its member states, the Northeastern U.S. states, and California have already agreed to reduce carbon emissions even without an international legal obligation. Together, these jurisdictions represent a substantial percentage of the world economy and population. The voluntary commitments submitted in the wake of the Copenhagen conference will build on these gains, but more should be done.

- Voluntary private regulation: Self-imposed emissions reductions and other pro-climate measures by firms have been minimal so far, thus representing a ripe area for growth. Numerous schemes exist, ranging from totally voluntary programs, such as the EPA's Energy Star program or the Worldwide Fund for Nature's Climate Savers, to agreements negotiated between firms and regulators such as the ambitious plans of the United Kingdom and Denmark. Governments can do more to fund and support these programs, either running them themselves or bringing together firms and civil-society groups to create their own programs.

- Individual commitments: Countries and firms are not the only ones who hold the key to solving climate change. Individuals' emissions represent an enormous amount of global emissions, especially in rich countries where per capita consumption of fossil-fuel energy sources is high. Numerous tools exist allowing concerned individuals to calculate their carbon footprints and suggest practical ways to reduce them.[15] Civil-society groups should take the lead in developing and publicizing these tools, potentially with government support.

These commitments could be registered and publicized in a central online clearinghouse. This registry, managed by a competent organization selected by the UNFCCC, could be modeled after a similar database relating to corporate social responsibility commitments run by the UN Global Compact Office. This registry would provide a public record of commitments, thus allowing coalition members to be held accountable.

Just as there are various commitments members of the coalition could adopt, these commitments come with various enforcement tools to make the commitments credible. Those actors adopting legally binding reductions would of course enforce them through standard law enforcement practices. For softer commitments, a range of enforcement mechanisms would be available and desirable. Companies could use credible reduction commitments as a powerful tool to attract climate-conscience consumers and investors. Doing so, however, raises the possibility that they would lose these customers and investors if they were found to be cheating on their commitments. Beyond market incentives, institutions found to be in violation of their commitments could be "named and shamed" by civil-society groups, imposing potentially costly reputational sanctions. Civil-society groups should devote more energy to this crucial watchdog role, and governments should provide resources to help independent groups play it.

Third, effective enforcement extends beyond merely punishing violators; carrots are needed as well as sticks. One crucial step would be to make sure that carbon markets around the globe continue to integrate once Kyoto expires. These markets allow governments and companies to outsource reductions to places where they can be done more cheaply, and so are vital to making GHG reductions widespread. Though not without difficulties, carbon markets are increasingly efficient. As the coalition's actions increase demand for carbon credits, it will be important for actors to be able to buy abatements from a range of markets.

As a further incentive, the climate coalition should also build a range of learning and capacity-building networks for different types of actors. Peer-to-peer networks of firms, regulators, civil-society groups, and individuals could develop and disseminate best practices for reducing emissions, thus making reductions more efficient. A model for such networks already exists in the UN's Global Compact.[16] Along the same lines, the coalition could organize technology transfer groups similar to the Montreal Protocol's technical committees, which were instrumental for diffusing ozone-safe technology around the world. These networks would make the coalition a club for innovation in learning, giving coalition members important advantages over climate laggards.

Fourth, coalition members could adopt various methods to pressure climate laggards to reduce emissions and to punish coalition members who break their commitments. Many of these pressures would be indirect. For example, the coalition's learning networks and technology committees would give laggards incentives to join the coalition. Moreover, by increasing demand for clean energy, climate leaders would drive the development of technologies and adoption methodologies, making it significantly easier for climate laggards to reduce their future emissions. High standards would also encourage companies benefiting from economies of scale to increase the environmental performance of their products globally, spreading climate-safe technology to laggards automatically. For example, California's high automotive emission standards have induced car manufacturers to sell cleaner cars throughout the United States.[17]

Beyond these indirect pressures, the coalition could coordinate its considerable influence to coerce climate laggards into better performance. Many consumers and investors, like the Investor Network on Climate Risk mentioned above, already direct their money to companies with proactive climate policies. These programs should be strengthened and expanded through explicit governmental support. Governments should also exercise their market power directly. Some already do so through the investment of public pension funds and through government procurement policies. For example, the Institutional Investors Group on Climate Change, a consortium of European pension funds and other large institutions representing some 4 trillion, has committed itself to climate-friendly investments. These efforts should be increased.

Targeted sanctions against climate laggards would be an even more forceful action. The European Union is considering a series of special tariffs on goods from laggard economies, and similar rules have been proposed by U.S. legislators. Although it remains uncertain how such rules would interact with global trade laws, it seems likely such "carbon tariffs" would be allowed as long as they were applied in a non-discriminatory fashion.[18] Other countries should follow suit, and make these sanctions as effective as possible by discriminating on a subnational basis, e.g. on a regional or even firm level to reward leaders and punish laggards. Targeting sanctions as specifically as possible would also make these pressure tactics more fair and minimize trade distortions.

Thinking Beyond the State

It is now clear that the multilateral approach, for all its strengths, can be held hostage by a few influential actors in just a few powerful countries. At least for now, the domestic politics of the United States and China to say nothing of the rest of the world form an insurmountable barrier to a global treaty on emissions reductions.

Given this stalemate, policymakers and civil-society advocates must recognize that there is more to climate governance than the UNFCCC. Across the world including in the G-2 counties, regions, cities, firms, government agencies, civil-society groups, and individuals are taking concrete steps toward a safer climate. Political leaders concerned with the climate should create a global coalition of the willing to direct their prestige and resources to these initiatives, expand their scope, and create others like them. In particular, the European Union, which has been unable to shift the G-2 through diplomatic pressure, will need to take the lead in bringing non-multilateral approaches to a global scale if it is to realize its aspiration to become the world's "environmental superpower."

To be sure, a global coalition of the willing is a second-best alternative to a multilateral treaty. It allows laggards to free ride on the sacrifices of leaders, and there is no guarantee it would attain the scale of reductions necessary to keep climate change within safe levels. It has never even been tried before. But we must not make the best the enemy of the good.

In the end, the greatest effect of a coalition of the willing for the climate might even be its potential to rekindle the multilateral process itself. By spurring the development of green technology and mitigation techniques, leaders would change the cost-benefit analysis that laggards face today. By targeting carrots and sticks at leaders and laggards, respectively, the coalition would strengthen existing constituencies for climate regulation, while also building new ones. By demonstrating that saving the climate and enhancing prosperity are not incompatible, the coalition would offer vivid evidence of the feasibility of change. In these ways, the coalition might unclog the very stalemate that makes it necessary.

Notes

1. See, for example, Robert Keohane and David Victor, "The Regime Complex for Climate Change," Discussion Paper 10–33, The Harvard Project on International Climate Agreements, Belfer Center for Science and International Affairs, Harvard Kennedy School, January 2010, http://belfercenter.ksg.harvard.edu/publication/19880/regime_complex_for_climate_change.html. Note, however, that their definition of the regime complex excludes private and sub-state actors.

2. See, for example, J. Lawrence Broz and Daniel Maliniak, "Malapportionment, Gasoline Taxes, and the United Nations Framework Convention on Climate Change," presented at the Third Annual Conference on The Political Economy of International Organizations, Georgetown University, Washington, D.C., January 28–30, 2010, http://dss.ucsd.edu/jlbroz/pdf_folder/wip/broz_maliniak_PEIO.pdf.

3. Antoaneta Bezlova, "China's Climate Change Plan: The Debate Goes On," Inter Press Service News Agency, November 6, 2009, http://ipsnews.net/news.asp?idnews 49166.

4. National Development and Reform Commission, "China's National Climate Change Programme," June 2007, www.ccchina.gov.cn/WebSite/CCChina/UpFile/File188.pdf.

5. For further information on Chinese climate-change policy, see the government's online informational portal, www.ccchina.gov.cn/en/; also see ChinaFAQs, an informational website sponsored by the Washington-based World Resources Institute, www.chinafaqs.org.

6. U.S. Energy Information Administration, "International Energy Statistics," http://tonto.eia.doe.gov/cfapps/ipdbproject/IEDIndex3.cfm?tid90&pid44&aid8.

7. For an overview of the negotiations of the ozone regime from the perspective of the chief U.S. negotiator, see Richard Benedick, Ozone Diplomacy: New Directions in Safeguarding the Planet (Cambridge, MA: Harvard University Press, 1998).

8. For more information, see the organization's website, www.c40cities.org; for a detailed study of "urban climate governance," see Heike Schroeder and Harriet Bulkeley, "Global Cities and the Governance of Climate Change: What is the Role of Law in Cities?," Fordham Urban Law Journal

36 (2009): p. 313, http://law2.fordham.edu/publications/articles/400flspub17715.pdf.

9. For more information, see the network's website, www.incr.com; for an analysis, see Michael MacLeod, "Private Governance and Climate Change: Institutional Investors and Emerging Investor-Driven Governance Mechanisms," St. Antony's International Review 5, no. 2 (February 2010): pp. 46–65.

10. For a partial list, see Mathew Hoffmann, "Climate Governance Experiments," http://matthewhoffmann.wordpress.com/climate-governance-experiments.

11. Nicholas Lutsey and Daniel Sperling, "America's Bottom-up Climate Change Mitigation Policy," Energy Policy 36, no. 2 (February 2008): pp. 673–685.

12. President Barack Obama, "Executive Order 13514 Federal Leadership in Environmental, Energy, and Economic Performance," October 8, 2009, http://edocket.access.gpo.gov/2009/pdf/E9-24518.pdf.

13. The countries surveyed were Bangladesh, China, Egypt, France, India, Indonesia, Iran, Japan, Kenya, Mexico, Russia, Senegal, Turkey, the United States, and Vietnam; see The World Bank, "Public attitudes toward climate change: findings from a multi-country poll," December 3, 2009, http://siteresources.worldbank.org/INTWDR2010/Resources/Background-report.pdf.

14. U.S. Energy Information Agency, "Greenhouse Gases, Climate Change, and Energy," www.eia.doe.gov/oiaf/1605/ggccebro/chapter1.html.

15. See, for example, the EPA's Household Emissions Calculator, www.epa.gov/climatechange/emissions/ind_calculator.html; the Nature Conservancy's Carbon Footprint Calculator, www.nature.org/initiatives/climatechange/calculator/?gclid CNyfr4DB4aQCFctL5QodVihNGg; or Carbon Footprint Ltd, www.carbonfootprint.com.

16. The UN Global Compact's registry can be found at www.unglobalcompact.org/ParticipantsAndStakeholders/index.html.

17. David Vogel, Trading Up: Consumer and Environmental Regulation in a Global Economy (Cambridge, MA: Harvard University Press, 1997).

18. Paul-Erik Veel, "Carbon Tariffs and the WTO: An Evaluation of Feasible Policies," Journal of International Economic Law 12, no. 3 (2009): pp. 749–800.

Critical Thinking

1. Why isn't the United States willing to support the Kyoto Protocol?
2. What are the effects of climate warming?
3. What is causing climate warming?
4. What is the position of most developing countries in signing a climate warming treaty?

THOMAS HALE is a PhD Candidate in the Department of Politics at Princeton University and a Visiting Fellow at LSE Global Governance, London School of Economics.

The Implications of Fukushima
The European Perspective

Caroline Jorant

On March 11, 2011, a magnitude 9 earthquake, followed by a very powerful tsunami, devastated the northeastern coast of Japan. With more than 25,000 deaths, in addition to the apocalyptic destruction of buildings, homes, and industries, the toll to the country and its environment has yet to be estimated. In the quake's aftermath, the specter of a meltdown at the country's Fukushima nuclear plant—with long-lasting repercussions not only in the region, but across the globe—gripped the world.

As the tragedy continues to unfold in Japan, it is premature to attempt to gauge from the immediate political reactions in Europe the mid- and long-term impact of the Fukushima accident on the development or dismantling of the continent's nuclear facilities. But it is not too soon to explore the differences of opinion on nuclear energy among the European Union member states—and to determine what common ground has been found as a result of the tragedy in Japan. From this we may be able to glean where Europe is heading.

There are currently 152 nuclear facilities located in 15 of the EU's states, supplying about one-third of its electricity. Since the onset of the nuclear crisis in Japan, the reactions of EU governments have differed greatly. Traditionally, countries without nuclear facilities—for example, Austria, Denmark, Ireland, and Luxembourg—have strongly opposed nuclear development. After Fukushima, such countries were only reinforced in their positions. At the same time, the countries that were already staunch supporters of nuclear energy—France, Finland, the United Kingdom, and Slovakia, among others—reiterated their support of nuclear energy.

Countries that were new to nuclear energy had a mixed reaction to the crisis. The Italian government, for example, immediately imposed a one-year moratorium and envisaged postponing a referendum on the decision to construct its first nuclear power plant. However, the referendum did take place as formerly planned on June 13, only three months after the Fukushima accident. Out of a rough 40 percent participation, an overwhelming majority voted negatively, certainly closing the perspectives for a nuclear programme in Italy for another long period of time.[1] Poland, on the other hand, confirmed its decision to build its first nuclear power plants by 2020.

Meanwhile, countries that had once envisioned phasing out their nuclear facilities did not simply revert to old form: The Netherlands announced that it would honor its one-month-old decision to begin constructing a new reactor in 2015, while Sweden confirmed its plans to replace its power plants at the end of their lifespans.

But the resounding shift in Germany, where nuclear energy has long been a hot-button political issue, will have the greatest impact on Europe's nuclear supply. Within days of the Fukushima tragedy, Chancellor Angela Merkel imposed a three-month moratorium on previously announced extensions for Germanys existing nuclear power plants, while temporarily shuttering seven of the 17 reactors that had been operating since 1981. Weeks later, on May 29, Merkel's government announced that it would close all of its nuclear power plants, which currently supply 27 percent of the country's electricity, by 2022.

A similar current has taken hold in non-EU Switzerland, where the government has proposed not to replace the five nuclear power plants currently in operation. Adopted by the National Council, this measure means a progressive phase-out of nuclear energy between 2019 and 2034.

The EU and the Nuclear Safety Issue

Nuclear energy in Europe benefits from a rather comprehensive and legally binding framework known as the Euratom Treaty. Adopted in 1957, this treaty was one of the three pillars in the founding of what is today the EU. It was understood from the start that in terms of economic and political development, the European community had a major stake in nuclear energy.

The treaty covers almost all aspects of nuclear power, from research and development to the supply of nuclear material, safeguards on materials, international cooperation agreements, and radiological protection. After Chernobyl, for example, the EU made several key decisions on protocol for future emergencies. Guidelines were set on contamination levels in foods, the early exchange of information, and mutual assistance in case of a future accident.

In the late 1990s, anticipating the need to find common ground for safety assessment in light of the EU's eastward expansion, the Western Nuclear Regulator Association (WENRA) was established. WENRA promotes safety based on the non-binding standards and recommendations of the International Atomic Energy Agency. It now operates as a network of chief regulators from EU member states and Switzerland, offering consensus on nuclear safety issues in the absence of a specific legal framework.

Even after the creation of the association, however, the EU nuclear community lacked a formal political and institutional body. In 2007, the European Commission created the European Nuclear Safety Regulators Group, which advises the commission on political and institutional matters related to nuclear safety.[2] But a debate remained over the EU's legal capacity to address nuclear issues, so in May 2009 a legally binding safety directive was adopted. Now, for the first time, there is a legal text that defines the nuclear principles that every EU country must respect and empowers the commission to hold member states accountable. This is the basis for the EU's common response to a nuclear disaster—and this was put into practice with the announcement of "stress tests" in response to Fukushima.

The Stress Test Approach

Within days of the tragedy in Japan, the European Commission organized an extraordinary meeting to discuss the repercussions. Energy ministers and nuclear regulators, along with some experts and industry representatives, agreed on principle to perform a series of stress tests to assess the safety and risk at 143 nuclear power plants across Europe. The goal was to draw early lessons from Japan's nuclear crisis and ensure that similar troubles would not befall Europe's nuclear reactor sites.

A stress test is defined as a targeted reassessment of safety aspects of nuclear power plants. Separately and independently performed by both operators and regulators, the assessments will ensure that adequate preventive measures are in place and evaluate how each nuclear plant would respond when faced with extreme situations. The idea is to test the facility's "defense-in-depth" logic—its layers of safeguards covering everything from the initial event (earthquake, flood) and the consequential loss of key functions (control of reactivity, fuel cooling, confinement of radioactivity) to the most desperate accident management situations (loss of electrical power and loss of heat absorption). Each system will be analyzed independent of the others.

Despite some controversy over what kind of security breaches—such as sabotage and terrorist acts—would be included in the tests, an agreement was ultimately reached to consider all types of accidents, whether caused naturally or by human error, though not to address security issues as such. The tests began on June 1 and will be completed and analyzed before the results are made public in April 2012.

What's Next?

The Fukushima accident promises to have an adverse impact on the development of nuclear energy in the EU, at the very least slowing its expected pace and magnitude. While no lives were lost in the crisis, its environmental consequence should not be underestimated and will take many years of hard work to mitigate. The crisis has also made clear the need to improve international cooperation and preparedness.

The EU initiative for a systematic safety review, however, should help to rebuild confidence in the capacity of the nuclear industry and its regulators to cope with the unexpected. The EU's desire to address the potential weaknesses of its reactors and to improve their capacity for crisis response shows that, in the aftermath of Fukushima, the right lessons are being learned.

This response is consistent with the EU's long-standing drive to strengthen nuclear safety. Given the diversity of positions on nuclear energy within the EU's ranks, the reaction has been bold and quick. Other countries should seek to emulate this mindset and contribute to a proactive and positive debate that puts international focus on how best to keep nuclear power safe. Nuclear energy in Europe should continue to contribute to a safe, secure, and low-carbon emission energy supply in the future. Although the German decision may steer a renewed debate in the next election campaigns in European countries about the nuclear and energy mix, it remains to be seen whether, in the long term, these sudden phase-out decisions will be reversed, as has been the case in the Netherlands and Sweden.

Notes

1. This decision was to be interpreted as a tactical government move to avoid jeopardizing the expected positive result of the referendum that was planned for spring 2011.

2. It is composed of representatives of all the nuclear authorities of the EU and of the radioprotection authorities, where no safety authority as such exists, as well as members of the European Commission.

References

Chang SH (2011) The implications of Fukushima: The South Korean perspective. Global forum. *Bulletin of the Atomic Scientists* 67(4): 18–22.

Cooper M (2011) The implications of Fukushima: The US perspective. Global forum. *Bulletin of the Atomic Scientists* 67(4): 8–13.

Critical Thinking

1. What can be done to prevent nuclear power plant disasters in the future?
2. Why does the Japanese nuclear disaster have international implications?
3. What has been the role of the International Atomic Energy Agency in dealing with the Japanese nuclear disaster?

CAROLINE JORANT currently works as a consultant in international relations in the energy sector, with a special emphasis on nuclear energy. Until June 2010, she was director of Non-proliferation and International Institutions at AREVA. She spent 13 years in the French nuclear industry, first with COGEMA and then with AREVA, overseeing international institutional affairs and intergovernmental agreements. From 1992 to 1997, she was the French representative to the Atomic Questions Group in the EU Council and worked at the French permanent representation to the EU. From 1981 to 1992 she worked with the Commissariat a l'Energie Atomique.

The New Geopolitics of Food

From the Middle East to Madagascar, high prices are spawning land grabs and ousting dictators. Welcome to the 21st-century food wars.

LESTER R. BROWN

In the United States, when world wheat prices rise by 75 percent, as they have over the last year, it means the difference between a $2 loaf of bread and a loaf costing maybe $2.10. If, however, you live in New Delhi, those sky-rocketing costs really matter: A doubling in the world price of wheat actually means that the wheat you carry home from the market to hand-grind into flour for chapatis costs twice as much. And the same is true with rice. If the world price of rice doubles, so does the price of rice in your neighborhood market in Jakarta. And so does the cost of the bowl of boiled rice on an Indonesian family's dinner table.

Welcome to the new food economics of 2011: Prices are climbing, but the impact is not at all being felt equally. For Americans, who spend less than one-tenth of their income in the supermarket, the soaring food prices we've seen so far this year are an annoyance, not a calamity. But for the planet's poorest 2 billion people, who spend 50 to 70 percent of their income on food, these soaring prices may mean going from two meals a day to one. Those who are barely hanging on to the lower rungs of the global economic ladder risk losing their grip entirely. This can contribute—and it has—to revolutions and upheaval.

Already in 2011, the U.N. Food Price Index has eclipsed its previous all-time global high; as of March it had climbed for eight consecutive months. With this year's harvest predicted to fall short, with governments in the Middle East and Africa teetering as a result of the price spikes, and with anxious markets sustaining one shock after another, food has quickly become the hidden driver of world politics. And crises like these are going to become increasingly common. The new geopolitics of food looks a whole lot more volatile—and a whole lot more contentious—than it used to. Scarcity is the new norm.

Until recently, sudden price surges just didn't matter as much, as they were quickly followed by a return to the relatively low food prices that helped shape the political stability of the late 20th century across much of the globe. But now both the causes and consequences are ominously different.

In many ways, this is a resumption of the 2007–2008 food crisis, which subsided not because the world somehow came together to solve its grain crunch once and for all, but because the Great Recession tempered growth in demand even as favorable weather helped farmers produce the largest grain harvest on record. Historically, price spikes tended to be almost exclusively driven by unusual weather—a monsoon failure in India, a drought in the former Soviet Union, a heat wave in the U.S. Midwest. Such events were always disruptive, but thankfully infrequent. Unfortunately, today's price hikes are driven by trends that are both elevating demand and making it more difficult to increase production: among them, a rapidly expanding population, crop-withering temperature increases, and irrigation wells running dry. Each night, there are 219,000 additional people to feed at the global dinner table.

More alarming still, the world is losing its ability to soften the effect of shortages. In response to previous price surges, the United States, the world's largest grain producer, was effectively able to steer the world away from potential catastrophe. From the mid-20th century until 1995, the United States had either grain surpluses or idle cropland that could be planted to rescue countries in trouble. When the Indian monsoon failed in 1965, for example, President Lyndon Johnson's administration shipped one-fifth of the U.S. wheat crop to India, successfully staving off famine. We can't do that anymore; the safety cushion is gone.

That's why the food crisis of 2011 is for real, and why it may bring with it yet more bread riots cum political revolutions. What if the upheavals that greeted dictators Zine el-Abidine Ben Ali in Tunisia, Hosni Mubarak in Egypt, and Muammar al-Qaddafi in Libya (a country that imports 90 percent of its grain) are not the end of the story, but the beginning of it? Get ready, farmers and foreign ministers alike, for a new era in which world food scarcity increasingly shapes global politics.

The doubling of world grain prices since early 2007 has been driven primarily by two factors: accelerating growth in demand and the increasing difficulty of rapidly expanding production. The result is a world that looks strikingly different from the bountiful global grain economy of the last century. What will the geopolitics of food look like in a new era dominated by scarcity? Even at this early stage, we can see at least the broad outlines of the emerging food economy.

On the demand side, farmers now face clear sources of increasing pressure. The first is population growth. Each year the world's farmers must feed 80 million additional people, nearly all of them in developing countries. The world's population has nearly doubled since 1970 and is headed toward 9 billion by midcentury. Some 3 billion people, meanwhile, are also trying to move up the food chain, consuming more meat, milk, and eggs. As more families in China and elsewhere enter the middle class, they expect to eat better. But as global consumption of grain-intensive livestock products climbs, so does the demand for the extra corn and soybeans needed to feed all that livestock. (Grain consumption per person in the United States, for example, is four times that in India, where little grain is converted into animal protein. For now.)

At the same time, the United States, which once was able to act as a global buffer of sorts against poor harvests elsewhere, is now converting massive quantities of grain into fuel for cars, even as world grain consumption, which is already up to roughly 2.2 billion metric tons per year, is growing at an accelerating rate. A decade ago, the growth in consumption was 20 million tons per year. More recently it has risen by 40 million tons every year. But the rate at which the United States is converting grain into ethanol has grown even faster. In 2010, the United States harvested nearly 400 million tons of grain, of which 126 million tons went to ethanol fuel distilleries (up from 16 million tons in 2000). This massive capacity to convert grain into fuel means that the price of grain is now tied to the price of oil. So if oil goes to $150 per barrel or more, the price of grain will follow it upward as it becomes ever more profitable to convert grain into oil substitutes. And it's not just a U.S. phenomenon: Brazil, which distills ethanol from sugar cane, ranks second in production after the United States, while the European Union's goal of getting 10 percent of its transport energy from renewables, mostly biofuels, by 2020 is also diverting land from food crops.

This is not merely a story about the booming demand for food. Everything from falling water tables to eroding soils and the consequences of global warming means that the world's food supply is unlikely to keep up with our collectively growing appetites. Take climate change: The rule of thumb among crop ecologists is that for every 1 degree Celsius rise in temperature above the growing season optimum, farmers can expect a 10 percent decline in grain yields. This relationship was borne out all too dramatically during the 2010 heat wave in Russia, which reduced the country's grain harvest by nearly 40 percent.

While temperatures are rising, water tables are falling as farmers overpump for irrigation. This artificially inflates food production in the short run, creating a food bubble that bursts when aquifers are depleted and pumping is necessarily reduced to the rate of recharge. In arid Saudi Arabia, irrigation had surprisingly enabled the country to be self-sufficient in wheat for more than 20 years; now, wheat production is collapsing because the non-replenishable aquifer the country uses for irrigation is largely depleted. The Saudis soon will be importing all their grain.

Saudi Arabia is only one of some 18 countries with water-based food bubbles. All together, more than half the world's people live in countries where water tables are falling. The politically troubled Arab Middle East is the first geographic region where grain production has peaked and begun to decline because of water shortages, even as populations continue to grow. Grain production is already going down in Syria and Iraq and may soon decline in Yemen. But the largest food bubbles are in India and China. In India, where farmers have drilled some 20 million irrigation wells, water tables are falling and the wells are starting to go dry. The World Bank reports that 175 million Indians are being fed with grain produced by overpumping. In China, overpumping is concentrated in the North China Plain, which produces half of China's wheat and a third of its corn. An estimated 130 million Chinese are currently fed by overpumping. How will these countries make up for the inevitable shortfalls when the aquifers are depleted?

Even as we are running our wells dry, we are also mismanaging our soils, creating new deserts. Soil erosion as a result of overplowing and land mismanagement is undermining the productivity of one-third of the world's cropland. How severe is it? Look at satellite images showing two huge new dust bowls: one stretching across northern and western China and western Mongolia; the other across central Africa. Wang Tao, a leading Chinese desert scholar, reports that each year some 1,400 square miles of land in northern China turn to desert. In Mongolia and Lesotho, grain harvests have shrunk by half or more over the last few decades. North Korea and Haiti are also suffering from heavy soil losses; both countries face famine if they lose international food aid. Civilization can survive the loss of its oil reserves, but it cannot survive the loss of its soil reserves.

Beyond the changes in the environment that make it ever harder to meet human demand, there's an important intangible factor to consider: Over the last half-century or so, we have come to take agricultural progress for granted. Decade after decade, advancing technology underpinned steady gains in raising land productivity. Indeed, world grain yield per acre has tripled since 1950. But now that era is coming to an end in some of the more agriculturally advanced countries, where farmers are already using all available technologies to raise yields. In effect, the farmers have caught up with the scientists. After climbing for a century, rice yield per acre in Japan has not risen at all for 16 years. In China, yields may level off soon. Just those two countries alone account for one-third of the world's rice harvest. Meanwhile, wheat yields have plateaued in Britain, France, and Germany—Western Europe's three largest wheat producers.

In this era of tightening world food supplies, the ability to grow food is fast becoming a new form of geopolitical leverage, and countries are scrambling to secure their own parochial interests at the expense of the common good.

The first signs of trouble came in 2007, when farmers began having difficulty keeping up with the growth in global demand for grain. Grain and soybean prices started to climb, tripling by mid-2008. In response, many exporting countries tried to control the rise of domestic food prices by restricting exports. Among them were Russia and Argentina, two leading wheat exporters. Vietnam, the No. 2 rice exporter, banned exports entirely for several months in early 2008. So did several other smaller exporters of grain.

With exporting countries restricting exports in 2007 and 2008, importing countries panicked. No longer able to rely on the market to supply the grain they needed, several countries took the novel step of trying to negotiate long-term grain-supply agreements with exporting countries. The Philippines, for instance, negotiated a three-year agreement with Vietnam for 1.5 million tons of rice per year. A delegation of Yemenis traveled to Australia with a similar goal in mind, but had no luck. In a seller's market, exporters were reluctant to make long-term commitments.

Fearing they might not be able to buy needed grain from the market, some of the more affluent countries, led by Saudi Arabia, South Korea, and China, took the unusual step in 2008 of buying or leasing land in other countries on which to grow grain for themselves. Most of these land acquisitions are in Africa, where some governments lease cropland for less than $1 per acre per year. Among the principal destinations were Ethiopia and Sudan, countries where millions of people are being sustained with food from the U.N. World Food Program. That the governments of these two countries are willing to sell land to foreign interests when their own people are hungry is a sad commentary on their leadership.

By the end of 2009, hundreds of land acquisition deals had been negotiated, some of them exceeding a million acres. A 2010 World Bank analysis of these "land grabs" reported that a total of nearly 140 million acres were involved—an area that exceeds the cropland devoted to corn and wheat combined in the United States. Such acquisitions also typically involve water rights, meaning that land grabs potentially affect all downstream countries as well. Any water extracted from the upper Nile River basin to irrigate crops in Ethiopia or Sudan, for instance, will now not reach Egypt, upending the delicate water politics of the Nile by adding new countries with which Egypt must negotiate.

The potential for conflict—and not just over water—is high. Many of the land deals have been made in secret, and in most cases, the land involved was already in use by villagers when it was sold or leased. Often those already farming the land were neither consulted about nor even informed of the new arrangements. And because there typically are no formal land titles in many developing-country villages, the farmers who lost their land have had little backing to bring their cases to court. Reporter John Vidal, writing in Britain's *Observer*, quotes Nyikaw Ochalla from Ethiopia's Gambella region: "The foreign companies are arriving in large numbers, depriving people of land they have used for centuries. There is no consultation with the indigenous population. The deals are done secretly. The only thing the local people see is people coming with lots of tractors to invade their lands."

Local hostility toward such land grabs is the rule, not the exception. In 2007, as food prices were starting to rise, China signed an agreement with the Philippines to lease 2.5 million acres of land slated for food crops that would be shipped home. Once word leaked, the public outcry—much of it from Filipino farmers—forced Manila to suspend the agreement. A similar uproar rocked Madagascar, where a South Korean firm, Daewoo Logistics, had pursued rights to more than 3 million acres of land. Word of the deal helped stoke a political furor that toppled the government and forced cancellation of the agreement. Indeed, few things are more likely to fuel insurgencies than taking land from people. Agricultural equipment is easily sabotaged. If ripe fields of grain are torched, they burn quickly.

Not only are these deals risky, but foreign investors producing food in a country full of hungry people face another political question of how to get the grain out. Will villagers permit trucks laden with grain headed for port cities to proceed when they themselves may be on the verge of starvation? The potential for political instability in countries where villagers have lost their land and their livelihoods is high. Conflicts could easily develop between investor and host countries.

These acquisitions represent a potential investment in agriculture in developing countries of an estimated $50 billion. But it could take many years to realize any substantial production gains. The public infrastructure for modern market-oriented agriculture does not yet exist in most of Africa. In some countries it will take years just to build the roads and ports needed to bring in agricultural inputs such as fertilizer and to export farm products. Beyond that, modern agriculture requires its own infrastructure: machine sheds, grain-drying equipment, silos, fertilizer storage sheds, fuel storage facilities, equipment repair and maintenance services, well-drilling equipment, irrigation pumps, and energy to power the pumps. Overall, development of the land acquired to date appears to be moving very slowly.

So how much will all this expand world food output? We don't know, but the World Bank analysis indicates that only 37 percent of the projects will be devoted to food crops. Most of the land bought up so far will be used to produce biofuels and other industrial crops.

Even if some of these projects do eventually boost land productivity, who will benefit? If virtually all the inputs—the farm equipment, the fertilizer, the pesticides, the seeds—are brought in from abroad and if all the output is shipped out of the country, it will contribute little to the host country's economy. At best, locals may find work as farm laborers, but in highly mechanized operations, the jobs will be few. At worst, impoverished countries like Mozambique and Sudan will be left with less land and water with which to feed their already hungry populations. Thus far the land grabs have contributed more to stirring unrest than to expanding food production.

And this rich country-poor country divide could grow even more pronounced—and soon. This January, a new stage in the scramble among importing countries to secure food began to unfold when South Korea, which imports 70 percent of its grain, announced that it was creating a new public-private entity that will be responsible for acquiring part of this grain. With an initial office in Chicago, the plan is to bypass the large international trading firms by buying grain directly from U.S. farmers. As the Koreans acquire their own grain elevators, they may well sign multiyear delivery contracts with farmers, agreeing to buy specified quantities of wheat, corn, or soybeans at a fixed price.

Other importers will not stand idly by as South Korea tries to tie up a portion of the U.S. grain harvest even before it gets to market. The enterprising Koreans may soon be joined by China, Japan, Saudi Arabia, and other leading importers. Although South Korea's initial focus is the United States, far and away the world's largest grain exporter, it may later consider brokering deals with Canada, Australia, Argentina, and other major exporters. This is happening just as China may be on the verge of entering the U.S. market as a potentially massive importer of grain. With China's 1.4 billion increasingly affluent consumers starting to compete with U.S. consumers for the U.S. grain harvest, cheap food, seen by many as an American birthright, may be coming to an end.

No one knows where this intensifying competition for food supplies will go, but the world seems to be moving away from the international cooperation that evolved over several decades following World War II to an every-country-for-itself philosophy. Food nationalism may help secure food supplies for individual affluent countries, but it does little to enhance world food security. Indeed, the low-income countries that host land grabs or import grain will likely see their food situation deteriorate.

After the carnage of two world wars and the economic missteps that led to the Great Depression, countries joined together in 1945 to create the United Nations, finally realizing that in the modern world we cannot live in isolation, tempting though that might be. The International Monetary Fund was created to help manage the monetary system and promote economic stability and progress. Within the U.N. system, specialized agencies from the World Health Organization to the Food and Agriculture Organization (FAO) play major roles in the world today. All this has fostered international cooperation.

But while the FAO collects and analyzes global agricultural data and provides technical assistance, there is no organized effort to ensure the adequacy of world food supplies. Indeed, most international negotiations on agricultural trade until recently focused on access to markets, with the United States, Canada, Australia, and Argentina persistently pressing Europe and Japan to open their highly protected agricultural markets. But in the first decade of this century, access to supplies has emerged as the overriding issue as the world transitions from an era of food surpluses to a new politics of food scarcity. At the same time, the U.S. food aid program that once worked to fend off famine wherever it threatened has largely been replaced by the U.N. World Food Program (WFP), where the United States is the leading donor. The WFP now has food-assistance operations in some 70 countries and an annual budget of $4 billion. There is little international coordination otherwise. French President Nicolas Sarkozy—the reigning president of the G-20—is proposing to deal with rising food prices by curbing speculation in commodity markets. Useful though this may be, it treats the symptoms of growing food insecurity, not the causes, such as population growth and climate change. The world now needs to focus not only on agricultural policy, but on a structure that integrates it with energy, population, and water policies, each of which directly affects food security.

But that is not happening. Instead, as land and water become scarcer, as the Earth's temperature rises, and as world food security deteriorates, a dangerous geopolitics of food scarcity is emerging. Land grabbing, water grabbing, and buying grain directly from farmers in exporting countries are now integral parts of a global power struggle for food security.

With grain stocks low and climate volatility increasing, the risks are also increasing. We are now so close to the edge that a breakdown in the food system could come at any time. Consider, for example, what would have happened if the 2010 heat wave that was centered in Moscow had instead been centered in Chicago. In round numbers, the 40 percent drop in Russia's hoped-for harvest of roughly 100 million tons cost the world 40 million tons of grain, but a 40 percent drop in the far larger U.S. grain harvest of 400 million tons would have cost 160 million tons. The world's carryover stocks of grain (the amount in the bin when the new harvest begins) would have dropped to just 52 days of consumption. This level would have been not only the lowest on record, but also well below the 62-day carryover that set the stage for the 2007–2008 tripling of world grain prices.

Then what? There would have been chaos in world grain markets. Grain prices would have climbed off the charts. Some grain-exporting countries, trying to hold down domestic food prices, would have restricted or even banned exports, as they did in 2007 and 2008. The TV news would have been dominated not by the hundreds of fires in the Russian countryside, but by footage of food riots in low-income grain-importing countries and reports of governments falling as hunger spread out of control. Oil-exporting countries that import grain would have been trying to barter oil for grain, and low-income grain importers would have lost out. With governments toppling and confidence in the world grain market shattered, the global economy could have started to unravel.

We may not always be so lucky. At issue now is whether the world can go beyond focusing on the symptoms of the deteriorating food situation and instead attack the underlying causes. If we cannot produce higher crop yields with less water and conserve fertile soils, many agricultural areas will cease to be viable. And this goes far beyond farmers. If we cannot move at wartime speed to stabilize the climate, we may not be able to avoid runaway food prices. If we cannot

accelerate the shift to smaller families and stabilize the world population sooner rather than later, the ranks of the hungry will almost certainly continue to expand. The time to act is now—before the food crisis of 2011 becomes the new normal.

Critical Thinking

1. What can the international community do to ensure global food security?

2. What are the factors that cause the price of food, such as wheat, to go up?

3. What are the causes of growing food scarcity?

LESTER R. BROWN, president of the Earth Policy Institute, is author of *World on the Edge: How to Prevent Environmental and Economic Collapse.*

Reprinted in entirety by McGraw-Hill with permission from *Foreign Policy*, May/June 2011, pp. 56–58, 61–62. www.foreignpolicy.com. © 2011 Washingtonpost.Newsweek Interactive, LLC.

Test-Your-Knowledge Form

We encourage you to photocopy and use this page as a tool to assess how the articles in *Annual Editions* expand on the information in your textbook. By reflecting on the articles you will gain enhanced text information. You can also access this useful form on a product's book support website at www.mhhe.com/cls.

NAME: _____ DATE: _____

TITLE AND NUMBER OF ARTICLE:
_____

BRIEFLY STATE THE MAIN IDEA OF THIS ARTICLE:

_____

LIST THREE IMPORTANT FACTS THAT THE AUTHOR USES TO SUPPORT THE MAIN IDEA:

_____

WHAT INFORMATION OR IDEAS DISCUSSED IN THIS ARTICLE ARE ALSO DISCUSSED IN YOUR TEXTBOOK OR OTHER READINGS THAT YOU HAVE DONE? LIST THE TEXTBOOK CHAPTERS AND PAGE NUMBERS:

_____

LIST ANY EXAMPLES OF BIAS OR FAULTY REASONING THAT YOU FOUND IN THE ARTICLE:

_____

LIST ANY NEW TERMS/CONCEPTS THAT WERE DISCUSSED IN THE ARTICLE, AND WRITE A SHORT DEFINITION:

NOTES

NOTES

NOTES

NOTES

NOTES

NOTES

NOTES

NOTES